George Finlay, Henry Fanshawe Tozer

A Smaller History of Greece

Vol. VI.: From its Conquest by the Romans to the Present Time

George Finlay, Henry Fanshawe Tozer

A Smaller History of Greece
Vol. VI.: From its Conquest by the Romans to the Present Time

ISBN/EAN: 9783744773799

Printed in Europe, USA, Canada, Australia, Japan

Cover: Foto ©ninafisch / pixelio.de

More available books at **www.hansebooks.com**

A
HISTORY OF GREECE

FROM ITS

CONQUEST BY THE ROMANS TO THE PRESENT TIME

B.C. 146 TO A.D. 1864

BY

GEORGE FINLAY, LL.D.

A NEW EDITION, REVISED THROUGHOUT, AND IN PART RE-WRITTEN,
WITH CONSIDERABLE ADDITIONS, BY THE AUTHOR,

AND EDITED BY THE

REV. H. F. TOZER, M.A.

TUTOR AND LATE FELLOW OF EXETER COLLEGE, OXFORD

IN SEVEN VOLUMES

VOL. VI

THE GREEK REVOLUTION. PART I

A.D. 1821 — 1827

Oxford

AT THE CLARENDON PRESS

M DCCC LXXVII

[*All rights reserved*]

CONTENTS.

BOOK FIRST.

EVENTS PRECEDING THE REVOLUTION.

CHAPTER I.

The Condition of the Modern Greeks.

	PAGE
Numbers of the Greek and Turkish races in Europe	1
Pashaliks into which the country inhabited by the Greeks was divided	3
Effect of the treaty of Kainardji on the Greek population	5
Distinction of Greek orthodoxy and Greek nationality	7
Social divisions of the Greek race	8
Greeks in Moldavia and Vallachia	9
Four general divisions of the Greek nation	10
Clergy	10
Primates	11
Urban population	12
Rural population	12
Municipal institutions	13
State of education	15
General condition of the people	17
Land-tax or tenths	17
Haratch or capitation-tax	18
Romeliots	18
Armatoli	19
Privileges of the province of Agrapha	22
Klephts	23
Moreots	24
Moreot klephts	26
Mainates	26
Islanders	27

CHAPTER II.

The Albanians.

Extent of country occupied by the Albanian race in Greece	28
Albanian Mussulmans of Lalla and Bardunia	29
Christian Albanians of the Dervenokhoria, Hydra, and Spetzas	30
Character and institutions of the Hydriots	31
The Albanians a distinct branch of the Indo-Germanic race	34
Two divisions, Gueghs and Tosks	35
Character, manners, and social condition of the Albanians	36
Administrative divisions of Albania	38
Military influence of the Albanians in the eighteenth century	38

	PAGE
And in Greece after the year 1770	40
Policy of Ali Pasha of Joannina	41
The Suliots the most remarkable tribe of orthodox Albanians	42
Their rise and social condition	43
Repeatedly attacked by Ali Pasha	45
Last war	47
The priest Samuel	49
Treachery of Suliots, and capitulation of Suli	50
Fate of the Suliots	51

CHAPTER III.

Sultan Mahmud and Ali Pasha of Joannina.

Character of Sultan Mahmud	53
State of the Othoman empire	55
Ali Pasha of Joannina	57
Ali's cruelty. Anecdote of Euphrosyne	60
Anecdotes of the Bishop of Grevena, and of Ignatius, metropolitan of Arta	63
Destruction of Khormovo	65
And of Gardhiki	67
Sultan Mahmud alarmed at Ali's power	69
Ali's attempt to assassinate Ismael Pasho Bey	70
Ali declared a rebel	70
His plans and forces	71
Sultan's means of attack	74
Ali convokes a divan	75
Both belligerents appeal to the Greeks	76
Operations in Albania	77
Ali is deserted by his sons	78
Recall of the Suliots	79
They join Ali	81
Khurshid Pasha of the Morea named Seraskier	82
Condition of the Suliots on their return	83
Their military system	84
Operations in 1821	87
Conduct of Khurshid before Joannina	88
Compared with that of Philip V. of Macedon	88
Suliots join the cause of the Greeks	91
Mission of Tahir Abbas to the Greeks	91
Death of Ali	94

BOOK SECOND.

THE COMMENCEMENT OF THE REVOLUTION.

CHAPTER I.

The Causes.

General progress of society	96
Secret societies	97

CONTENTS. vii

	PAGE
Philike Hetairia	98
Difficult position in which the Turks were placed	100
Plots of the Hetairists betrayed	101
Progress of education and moral improvement in Greece	103
Turks nationally more depressed than the Greeks	103
Influence of Roman law on modern Greek civilization	105
Improvement in the condition of the Greeks after the peace of Kainardji in 1774	106
Greeks live in Turkey under foreign protection	107

CHAPTER II.

The Operations of the Greek Hetairists beyond the Danube.

Character of Prince Alexander Hypsilantes	109
Relations between Russia and Turkey	112
State of the government and of the Rouman population in Moldavia and Vallachia	113
Invasion of Moldavia	116
Massacre of the Turks at Galatz	119
And at Yassi	120
Fury of the Mussulmans in Turkey	121
Revolution in Vallachia	122
Georgaki, Savas, and Vladimiresko	122
Hypsilantes at Bucharest	123
Sacred Battalion	124
Proceedings in Vallachia	125
Anathema of Hetairists by the patriarch	126
Russia disclaims the Revolution	126
Deceitful conduct of Hypsilantes	127
The murder of Vladimiresko	130
Battle of Dragashan	132
Flight of Hypsilantes	133
Operations in Moldavia	135
Affair of Skuleni	135
Death of Georgaki	137
Termination of the Revolution in Moldavia and Vallachia	138

CHAPTER III.

The Outbreak of the Revolution in Greece.

Extermination of the Turkish population	139
Preparations of the Othoman government	140
Operations of the Hetairists in the Morea	141
The archimandrite Gregorios Dikaios	142
Attempt of primates to defer the insurrection	143
Hostages summoned to Tripolitza by the Turks	144
Warning letter forged by the Greeks	145
First insurrectional movements in the Peloponnesus	146
Turks at Kalavryta surrender, and are murdered	147
Character of Petrobey	148
Taking of Kalamata, and first *Te Deum* for victory	149

b 2

CONTENTS.

	PAGE
Outbreak at Patras	151
Extermination of the Mohammedan population in Greece	152
Character and biography of Theodore Kolokotrones	153
His prayer at Chrysovitzi	158
Revolution at Salona, and character of Panourias	159
Salona and Livadea taken	160
Character of Diakos	161
Murder of Mohammedans	161
Acropolis of Athens besieged	162
Revolution at Mesolonghi	163
Vrachori taken, and Turks and Jews massacred	164
Revolution in the islands	166
Oligarchy and system of trade at Hydra	168
Spetzas first joins the Revolution	169
Psara follows	170
Insurrection at Hydra headed by Oeconomos	171
First cruise of the Greek fleet	173
Murder of the Sheik-ul-Islam	174
Fall of Oeconomos	176
Othoman fleet quits the Dardanelles	176
Greeks prepare fire-ships	177
Turkish line-of-battle ship burned off Mytilene	178
Kydonies sacked by the Turks	179
Squadron under Miaoulis on western coast	182

CHAPTER IV.

The Policy and Conduct of Sultan Mahmud II.

Policy of Sultan Mahmud	183
Suppressive measures and first executions of Greeks	185
Execution of the patriarch Gregorios	186
His character	188
Massacres of Greeks	189
Sultan restores order	191
Cruelties of Turks and Greeks	192
Rupture with Russia	194
Difficulties of SultanMahmud in 1821	196
Measures adopted to suppress the Greek Revolution	197
Order re-established in Agrapha	198
Among Vallachian population of Mount Pindus	199
Rapacity of the Greek troops	200
Insurrection on Mount Pelion suppressed	200
Revolution in the free villages of the Chalcidice	202
Among the monks on Mount Athos	203
Suppressed by Aboulabad Pasha of Saloniki	206
Insurrection on the Macedonian mountains	207
Sack of Niausta	208
Success of Sultan Mahmud in maintaining order	209

CONTENTS. ix

BOOK THIRD.

THE SUCCESSES OF THE GREEKS.

CHAPTER I.

The Establishment of Greece as an Independent State.

	PAGE
Victory of the Greeks at Valtetzi	212
Capitulation of Monemvasia	213
Capitulation of Navarin, and massacre of the Turks	214
Fraudulent division of the booty	215
Taking of Tripolitza, and capitulation of the Albanians	217
The heroine Bobolina	218
Sack of Tripolitza	218
Anarchy it produced	221
Cruise of the Othoman fleet in 1821	222
Violation of neutrality at Zante	223
Return of the Othoman fleet to Constantinople	225
Kolokotrones prevented from besieging Patras	226
Surrender of Corinth	226
Resources of the Greeks for carrying on the war	227
Administrative organisation which arose with the Revolution	228
Advantages and disadvantages of the communal system	230
A Peloponnesian senate formed	232
Arrival, character, and conduct of Prince Demetrius Hypsilantes	233
He claims absolute power	234
Arrival of Alexander Mavrocordatos	236
Organization of continental Greece	237
The Greeks demand a central government	239
Hypsilantes convokes a national assembly	239
The antagonistic positions of the national assembly and the Peloponnesian senate	240
Prince Demetrius Hypsilantes deserts the popular cause	240
The Peloponnesians make their senate independent	241
Constitution of Epidaurus	243

CHAPTER II.

The Presidency of Mavrocordatos.

Character and political position of Alexander Mavrocordatos	245
Affairs of Euboea, and death of Elias Mavromichales	246
Conduct of Odysseus at Karystos	249
Affairs of Chios	250
Invasion of the island by the Samiots	251
Prompt measures of Sultan Mahmud	253
Massacres of the Chiots	255
Greek fleet puts to sea	257
Constantine Kanares burns the capitan-pasha's ship	258

	PAGE
Operations of Greek fleet	259
Devastation of Chios	260
Mavrocordatos assumes the chief command in Western Greece	262
Treachery of Gogos	265
Defeat at Petta	266
Effects of this defeat	270
Death of Kyriakules Mavromichales	272
Capitulation of the Suliots	272
Affairs of Acarnania	273
Siege of Mesolonghi	274
Defeat of the Turks	276

CHAPTER III.

Fall of Athens—Defeat of Dramali—Fall of Nauplia.

Preparations of Sultan Mahmud for reconquering Greece	277
Defensive measures of the Greeks	278
Their quarrels and intrigues	279
Odysseus murders Noutzas and Palaskas	282
Capitulation of Athens	283
Massacre of men, women, and children	284
Expedition of Dramali	285
Corinth retaken—Turkish plans of campaign	286
First capitulation of Nauplia	288
Flight of Greeks from Argos	290
They defend the Larissa	291
Patriotic conduct of Prince Demetrius Hypsilantes	291
Number of Greek troops in the field	292
Defeat of Dramali	294
Greeks retain possession of the Burdjé	296
Operations of the hostile fleets	297
Second capitulation of Nauplia	299
Turkish inhabitants saved by Captain Hamilton of H.M.S. Cambrian	300
Kanares again destroys a Turkish line-of-battle ship	301
State of the naval warfare between the Greeks and Turks	302
State of affairs at Athens	303
Odysseus gains possession of Athens	304
Concludes an armistice with the Turks	306

CHAPTER IV.

The Condition of Greece as an Independent State.

Firmness of Sultan Mahmud	309
He adopts a conciliatory policy	310
Great fire destroys the Turkish armaments in 1823	311
Plan of campaign for 1823	312
Negligence of the Greek government	312
Olympian armatoli plunder Skiathos and Skopelos	313
Operations of the Turks	314
Death of Marco Botzaris	315
Advance of the Othoman army	316

CONTENTS.

	PAGE
Siege of Anatolikon	317
Operations of the Greek and Turkish fleets	318
Escape of eight Psarian sailors	320
Violation of Ionian neutrality	322
Misconduct of the sailors in the Greek fleet	323
Surrender of the Turks in the Acrocorinth	324
Lord Byron in Greece	324
First Greek loan contracted in England	328
First civil war	329
Mohammed Ali engages to assist the sultan	329
The political state of Greece in 1824	330
Position of Kolettes	332
Position of Mavrocordatos	333
Second civil war	334
Characters of Zaimes, Londos, and Sessini	334
Evil effects of the two civil wars	337
Wasteful expenditure of the two loans	338
Anecdotes	339
Military expenditure	340
Naval expenditure	341

BOOK FOURTH.

THE SUCCESSES OF THE TURKS.

CHAPTER I.

Naval Success.—Ibrahim in the Morea.

Destruction of Kasos	345
Destruction of Psara	347
Expedition of Mohammed Ali	349
The Baïram at Makri	350
Naval battles off Budrun	351
Failure of the Turks at Samos	355
Ibrahim driven back when off Crete	355
He lands in Greece	357
Greeks unprepared for defence	357
Greek army defeated	359
Egyptians take Sphakteria	361
Escape of the brig Mars	363
Capitulation of Pylos and Navarin	363
Success of Miaoulis at Modon	365
Kolokotrones appointed commander-in-chief	366
Death of the archimandrite Dikaios	367
Defeat of Kolokotrones at Makryplagi	368
Ibrahim repulsed at Lerna	369
Defeat of Kolokotrones at Trikorpha	370
Ibrahim ravages the Morea	371
Receives orders to aid in the siege of Mesolonghi	372

CHAPTER II.

The Siege of Mesolonghi.

	PAGE
Operations of Reshid Pasha	374
State of Mesolonghi.	374
Number of the garrison and of the besiegers	375
Arrival of the Othoman fleet	376
Arrival of the Greek fleet	377
Difficult position of Reshid	378
The mound	379
Treason of Odysseus	380
Military operations in continental Greece	382
Reshid withdraws to a fortified camp	384
Operations of the Turkish and Greek fleets	385
Ibrahim arrives before Mesolonghi	385
Lethargy of the Greeks and of their government	386
Turks take Vasiladi and Anatolikon	388
Offers of capitulation rejected	388
Turkish attack on Klissova repulsed	389
Defeat of the Greek fleet under Miaoulis	391
Final sortie	392
Fall of Mesolonghi	395

CHAPTER III.

The Siege of Athens.

Ibrahim's operations in the Morea during 1826	398
Reshid's operations in continental Greece	400
Athens invested, and battle of Khaïdari	401
Death of Goura	403
Grigiottes throws himself into the Acropolis	403
Karaïskaki's operations to raise the siege	405
Fabvier throws himself into the Acropolis	408
State of Greece during the winter of 1826–27	409
Expeditions under Gordon, Burbaki, and Heideck	413
General Sir Richard Church	418
Lord Cochrane (Earl of Dundonald)	420
Election of Capodistrias as president of Greece	421
Naval expedition under Captain Hastings	421
Greek traders supply Reshid's army with provisions	424
Operations of Church and Cochrane to relieve Athens	425
Massacre of the garrison of the monastery of St. Spiridion	427
Karaïskaki's death	429
Defeat of Sir Richard Church at the Phalerum	430
Evacuation of the Acropolis	432
Conduct of Philhellenes in Greece, England, and America	433
Lord Cochrane's naval review at Poros	436
Sufferings of the agricultural population	437
Assistance sent from the United States	437

HISTORY

OF THE

GREEK REVOLUTION.

BOOK FIRST.

EVENTS PRECEDING THE REVOLUTION.

CHAPTER I.

THE CONDITION OF THE MODERN GREEKS.

Numbers of the Greek and Turkish races in Europe.—Pashaliks into which the country inhabited by the Greeks was divided.—Effect of the Treaty of Kainardji on the condition of the Greeks.—Distinction between Greek orthodoxy and Greek nationality.—Social divisions of the Greek race.—Greeks in Moldavia and Vallachia.—Clergy.—Primates.—Urban population.—Rural.—Municipal institutions.—State of education.—Condition of the Greeks.—Land-tax.—Haratch. —Romeliots.—Armatoli.—Privileges of the province of Agrapha.—Klephts.—Moreots.—Moreot klephts.—Mainates.—Islanders.

THIS History records the events which established the independence of Greece.

As long as the literature and taste of the ancient Greeks continue to nurture scholars and inspire artists, Greece must be an object of interest to cultivated minds. Nor is the political history of the modern Greeks unworthy of attention. The importance of the Greek race to the progress of European civilization is not to be measured by its numerical strength, but by its social and religious influence in the East.

Yet, even geographically, the Greeks occupy so wide an extent of sea-coast, and the countries in which they dwell are so thinly peopled, that they have ample room to multiply and form a populous nation. At present their influence extends far beyond the territories occupied by their race; for Greek priests and Greek teachers have transfused their language and their ideas into the greater part of the educated classes among the Christian population of European Turkey. They have thus constituted themselves the representatives of Eastern Christianity, and placed themselves in prominent opposition to their conquerors, the Othoman Turks, who invaded Europe as apostles of the religion of Mohammed. The Greeks, during their subjection to the yoke of a foreign nation and a hostile religion, never forgot that the land which they inhabited was the land of their fathers; and their antagonism to their alien and infidel masters, in the hour of their most abject servitude, presaged that their opposition must end in their destruction or deliverance.

The Greek Revolution came at last. It delivered a Christian nation from subjection to Mohammedanism, founded a new state in Europe, and extended the advantages of civil liberty to regions where despotism had for ages been indigenous. In order to unfold its causes, it is necessary to describe the condition of the Greek people and of the Othoman government during the early part of this century.

When the Greeks took up arms, the numbers of the Greek and Turkish races in Europe were in all probability nearly equal, and neither is supposed to have greatly exceeded two millions. The population of continental Greece, from Cape Taenaron to the northernmost limit of the Greek language, was supposed to be not much greater than a million.[1] Another million may be added for the population of Crete, the Cyclades, the Ionian Islands, Constantinople, and the Greek maritime towns. If we add to this the Greek population of Asia Minor, the islands on the Asiatic coast, Cyprus, the trans-Danubian provinces, Russia, and other countries, the whole number of the Greek race cannot be estimated at more than three millions and a half.

---

[1] This is the estimate of Colonel Leake, the most accurate and observant traveller in Greece. *An Historical Outline of the Greek Revolution*, London, 1826, p. 20.

OTHOMAN DIVISIONS OF GREECE.

Two Christian races in the sultan's European dominions were more numerous: the Vallachian or Romanian race was not less than four millions; the Sclavonian, including the Bulgarian, which speaks the Sclavonic language, exceeded five millions [1].

The provinces in which the Greeks formed a majority of the inhabitants were divided into six pashaliks of high rank, and many smaller districts, governed immediately by inferior pashas.

1. The most important of the great pashas who ruled the Greeks was the capitan-pasha. Besides being the minister of the marine, and the commander-in-chief of all the naval forces of the empire, he was governor-general of the islands, and of part of the coast of Greece. Inferior pashas administered the affairs of Cyprus, Rhodes, and Mytilene under his superintendence.

2. The pashalik of the Morea was regarded as one of the most valuable governments in European Turkey, for it remitted a large surplus revenue annually to the sultan. It included the whole Peloponnesus, with the exception of Maina, which was under the jurisdiction of the capitan-pasha, and it extended beyond the Isthmus of Corinth, over the Dervenokhoria, embracing the whole of Megaris and a corner of Attica. The pasha of Naupaktos, or Lepanto, was also subordinate to the vizier of the Morea.

3. The pashalik of Egriboz included the whole island of Euboea and the adjoining provinces of Boeotia, Locris, and Attica. Thebes, Athens, Livadea, Salona, and Talanta, formed kazas, whose revenues were administered by voivodes appointed annually by the Sublime Porte. Athens was a provincial town belonging to the fief or arpalik of the kislaraga, who named its voivode, and this officer had an interest in protecting the inhabitants against the exactions of the pasha of Egriboz. In consequence of the great authority of the kislar-aga (the chief of the black eunuchs), the Christians

---

[1] Little dependence can be placed on the statistical accounts of the Othoman empire. Ubicini, one of the best authorities, in *Lettres sur la Turquie* (1853, p. 49), gives 60,000 as the population of Bassora. In the same year, the official registers at Constantinople were said to give only 5000; and English officers who visited it shortly after, during the Persian war, did not suppose that it could contain a greater number. In 1820 the population was estimated at 12,000, and it has been declining ever since.

of Athens enjoyed a considerable degree of local liberty. Tradition says that Athens owed this happiness to the beauty of one of her daughters, who proved as great a benefactress as the empresses Eudocia and Irene[1]. An Athenian slave named Vasilike became the favourite of Sultan Achmet I., and in order to relieve her fellow-countrymen from the tyranny of the Mussulmans of Negrepont, she obtained as a boon from her imperial lover that the revenues of Athens should be administered by the kislar-aga. But before the Greek Revolution broke out the reforms of Selim III. had placed Athens under the jurisdiction of the tchelebi-effendi.

4. Southern Albania formed a pashalik, which took its name from its capital, the city of Joannina. It had been long governed by Ali Pasha, who had annexed the greater part of Thessaly and all Western Greece, except Naupaktos, to his pashalik.

5. The pashalik of Selanik, or Thessalonica, extended over the greater part of Macedonia; but in its northern part there were many semi-independent beys, who farmed the taxes and land revenues. Even in the vicinity of Thessalonica, the descendants of Evrenos, whom the Turks call Ghazi Gavrinos, retained the appanage which Murad II. had conferred on their ancestor. They still held in fief the istira, or monopoly of the corn annually remitted to Constantinople[2].

6. The island of Crete formed a great pashalik, divided into three inferior military governments, under subordinate pashas, who resided in the fortresses of Candia, Khania, and Retymo. The district of Sphakia, which was inhabited by Christians alone, was governed by its own primates.

The wrongs of the subject Christians in Turkey have been loudly proclaimed, and the tyranny of the Othoman government has been justly condemned; yet for two centuries after the conquest of Greece, Christian subjects were as well treated by Turkish sultans as heretical subjects were by Christian kings. Indeed, the central government of the sultan, or the Sublime Porte, as it was termed, has generally treated its Mussulman subjects with as much cruelty and injustice as the conquered Christians. The sufferings of the Greeks were

---

[1] *See* vol. i. p. 174; vol. ii. p. 69.
[2] Ducas calls Evrenos, Abranezes; Chalcocondylas, Brenezes; p. 115, edit. Paris.

caused by the insolence and oppression of the ruling class and the corruption that reigned in the Othoman administration, rather than by the direct exercise of the sultan's power. In his private affairs, a Greek had a better chance of obtaining justice from his bishop and the elders of his district than a Turk from the cadi or the voivode.

The government of the sultan was the administration of a despot whose cabinet was composed of household slaves. The feudal system, which for two centuries lightened the weight of Othoman power to the Turkish population, was an inheritance of the Seljouk empire. The inherent defect of the Othoman government was the absence of a regular administration bound by fixed rules of law and a settled form of judicial procedure.

The treaty of Kainardji, in the year 1774, made a great change in the condition of the Greeks[1]. It afforded Russia a pretext for interfering in their favour whenever they were treated with gross injustice; and the interference of Russia soon led to like interference on the part of the other European powers; so that, before the end of the eighteenth century, the Christians in many parts of the sultan's dominions were beginning to acquire a recognized species of foreign protection. At the same time, the advantages which were conceded to the Greeks in the southern ports of Russia, added to the protection granted to them in Turkey, enabled them to extend their commerce and to acquire considerable wealth. The pashas in large commercial cities often found it less dangerous to enrich themselves at the expense of the Turks than to venture on open exactions from the Greeks. A provincial Mussulman could rarely find an advocate at the Porte; an oppressed Greek could either bribe a dragoman or interest a consul to awaken the meddling spirit that rarely sleeps in the breast of a diplomatist, and thereby secure the protection of some ambassador at Constantinople. But as it was evident that the whole fabric of society among the

---

[1] Russia founded her pretension to interfere in the affairs of the Greek subjects of the sultan on the 7th art., which consisted of two clauses having no direct connection with one another. By one the sultan promised to protect the Christian religion. By the other, he engaged to attend to the representations of the court of Russia relating to a particular Church mentioned in art. 14. This latter clause was made a pretext for arrogating a right of protecting all the orthodox Christians in Turkey.

Mussulman population of the Othoman empire presented an insurmountable barrier to the introduction of just laws and an equitable dispensation of justice, so experience at last proved that no foreign protection could secure the lives and properties of the subject Christians from the tyranny of a government which paid no respect even to the lives of its Turkish and Mussulman subjects. The sultan's government, like the government of the Roman emperors, was a monarch's household transformed into an imperial administration, and both destroyed the resources of their subjects and depopulated the regions they governed, without making any distinction between the conquerors and the conquered. A conviction that the Othoman empire was hastening to dissolution became prevalent both among the Christian and Mussulman inhabitants of European Turkey at the commencement of the present century.

In the year 1820 no Christian government, except that of Russia, considered itself entitled to interfere with the manner in which the sultan treated his subjects of the Greek Church. Any interference on the part of Great Britain, under the pretext that the king exercised a protectorate over the Ionian Islands, would have been treated as an unjustifiable assumption. The sultan would have considered himself as much entitled to suggest measures for governing the Mohammedans in India, as the King of England to advise any changes in the treatment of the Christians in Turkey. All questions relating to the East were then beyond the domain of public opinion, and very little was known in England concerning the condition of the modern Greeks.

The testimony of travellers was singularly discordant: some represented the Greeks as suffering intolerable oppression, as living in hourly fear of their lives or of the confiscation of their property; others declared that no people in Europe was so lightly taxed, and subject to so few personal burdens. They were said to enjoy a degree of religious liberty which the Catholics of Ireland might envy; and that they had a more direct authority over their municipal affairs than was possessed by the citizens in French communes. The Greek Church was known to possess considerable wealth and great political influence over all Turkey; Greeks exercised sovereign power in Vallachia and Moldavia, and derived great profits from the corruption that existed in every branch of the Othoman administration at Constantinople. The primates of Greece collected the greater part of the sultan's revenues in Europe; and the Greek municipalities were, in many districts, allowed to exercise an almost unlimited authority. It was evident that the condition of the Greeks presented many anomalies. At Constantinople, the Greek was a crouching slave; at Bucharest and Yassi, a despotic tyrant; at Chios, a happy subject; and at Psara, and in the villages of Mount Pelion, a free citizen.

A confusion of ideas has been produced by not distinguishing clearly between Greek orthodoxy and Greek nationality. The ancient Greeks paid great attention to purity of race; the modern Greeks have transferred their care to purity of doctrine. The Messenians preserved their manners and their dialect unchanged during centuries of exile; the Moreots have kept their orthodoxy untainted during ages of foreign domination. At present the Greeks are willing to intermarry with Vallachians, Russians, and Albanians of the Eastern Church; but to render a marriage lawful with a Catholic of the purest Hellenic descent, it would be necessary to rebaptize the spouse.

The tendency to forget everything but orthodoxy was cherished by the political privileges which the sultans conferred on the Greek Church. Its adherents formed a great community in the Othoman empire, known to the Turks by the national designation of Roum. The immense orthodox population of European Turkey and Asia Minor, embracing many nationalities, was confounded with the small number of the Greek race. Yet these two bodies were composed of heterogeneous elements, influenced by divergent interests and feelings, and to whose political union geography, language, and manners presented almost insurmountable obstacles. The people confounded orthodoxy and nationality, and the priests and the learned class looked forward to a restoration of the Byzantine empire, and to the establishment of the Greeks as a dominant race, by rendering political power a consequence of ecclesiastical authority. They deluded themselves with the dream that the Albanians, the Servians, the Bulgarians, and the Vallachians would submit to be ruled by Greek sovereigns and prefects, because they prayed under the guidance of Greek patriarchs and bishops.

The sultan recognized the patriarch of Constantinople as the ecclesiastical chief of all the orthodox Christians in European Turkey, and supported him in the exercise of an extensive civil jurisdiction over several nations. Among these, the Greeks really occupied the position of a dominant race. To the Vallachian and the Bulgarian, the Greek was in some degree what the Turk was to the Greek. The Greek language was the language of the church and the law which ruled the assemblage of nations called by the Othoman administration *Roum meleti*, or Roman nation. Indeed, the power and jurisdiction of the patriarch and synod of Constantinople, as it existed under the Othoman sultans, was an institution remodelled by Mohammed II.; and had the Othoman government found either Vallachians or Bulgarians fitter instruments to govern the orthodox community in accordance with Othoman interests, the patriarchs and the members of the synod of Constantinople would in all probability have ceased to be Greeks.

The great influence of the Greek race in the East is not, however, entirely derived from its priestly and literary superiority. It rests on a wide social basis, for the majority of the middle class consists of Greeks in many districts, where the cultivators of the soil and the mass of the people are of another race. A considerable part of the trade of Turkey was in their hands, and their communications were more frequent between the distant parts of the country than those of the other divisions of the population. All news was generally transmitted through a Greek medium, coloured with Greek hopes and prejudices, or perverted by Greek interests.

Yet, great as the ecclesiastical, literary, and commercial influence of the Greek race really was in European Turkey, the events of the Greek Revolution showed that the influence of Greek nationality had been greatly overrated by the Greeks themselves. Even in the Greek Church, ecclesiastical interest was more powerful than national feeling. A large part of the Greek nation made but feeble efforts to aid their countrymen when struggling for independence. The literary powers of the learned created a loud echo of patriotism; but thousands of wealthy Greeks continued to pursue their own schemes of interest and profit, under the protection of the sultan's government, during the whole period of the Greek Revolution.

The Greeks were divided into many classes, separated by social trammels as well as dispersed in distant provinces. It is not uncommon to find Constantinople spoken of as the capital of the Greek nation because it is the seat of the head of the orthodox church. This is a great error. The Greeks do not form one quarter of the population, and the agricultural population of the surrounding country consists chiefly of Bulgarians. The Turkish and Bulgarian languages are more extensively spoken than the Greek. The ancient Byzantium was a Greek colony, but the Constantinople founded by the great Constantine was a Roman city, in which Latin long continued to be the language of the government and the principal families. Since the conquest of the city by Mohammed II., the Greek population has formed a foreign colony in a Mussulman city. Its numbers have been recruited by emigrants from every part of the Othoman empire. The Phanariot families in the service of the sultan emigrated from different provinces. The merchants were generally Chiots, the shopkeepers Moreots, and the domestic servants natives of the islands of the Archipelago. The lower orders of the Christian population were recruited more extensively from the Sclavonians and Bulgarians in the northern provinces than from the Greeks. There was no permanent nucleus of a native Greek population in Constantinople as there was of a Turkish.

In Vallachia and Moldavia the Greeks formed a dominant race. They held there a position very similar to what the Turks held in Greece. The most lucrative offices were in their possession; the greater part of the ecclesiastical and national property was occupied by them under various titles and pretexts. Like the Turks in Greece, too, they were detested by the natives as fiscal extortioners and cruel oppressors; and it was only by the support they derived from the sultan's authority that they were able to maintain their position. That position was lost by the Greek Revolution.

The strength of the Greek race lay in the ancient seats of Greek liberty. In the Peloponnesus, in continental Greece, and in the Greek Islands, they not only formed the majority of the population, but they still possessed some municipal authority, and a considerable part of the landed property under cultivation. Even in Southern Epirus and in the Chalcidice of Macedonia they formed the majority of the agricultural population.

The Greeks were divided into four classes—the clergy, the primates, the urban population or townsmen, and the rural population or peasants. The marked separation of these classes deserves particular attention, as forming a characteristic feature of modern Greek civilization at the outbreak of the Revolution. This division exerted a powerful influence on society, and modified the effects of every political event. Each of these classes was connected with the sultan's government by different ties. Their religion, their language, and their hatred of Othoman domination were their bonds of union.

From the time Sultan Mohammed II. reorganized the Greek Church under the Patriarch Gennadios, Greek bishops had acted in their dioceses as a kind of Othoman prefects over the orthodox population. Ecclesiastical rank in the orthodox church was oftener obtained by bribing a vizier than by theological learning or Christian piety. Every diocese was loaded with debt in consequence of the simony which prevailed. The most observant traveller who visited Greece before the Revolution declares, that it is a common sentiment among the laity, that the bishops have been a great cause of the present degraded condition of the Greek nation; nor have the Greeks in general any esteem for their higher clergy, or for the monastic order from which the prelates are promoted. But Colonel Leake thinks that this is in some degree an injustice; for although the clergy were often instruments of oppression, and a bishop could hardly avoid acting like a Turk in office, the regular clergy kept the Greek language alive, and perhaps prevented the dissolution of all national union[1]. Yet this opinion may be questioned, for, by inducing the educated classes to study an imperfect and pedantic imitation of the classic language they prevented the improvement of the modern dialect; and, on

---

[1] Leake's *Travels in Northern Greece*, iv. 281. See an anecdote in *note* D to the second canto of *Childe Harold* concerning the Christian Basili.

the whole, the Greek nation seems to have done more to support the patriarchal and synodal church of the Othoman empire than that ecclesiastical establishment did to protect and improve the Greek nation.

At the commencement of the present century, the Greek clergy, sharing the general opinion that the Othoman empire was on the eve of its dissolution, began to expect a speedy deliverance by the advance of the armies of Russia. The priests contemplated being called upon, before the lapse of many years, to transfer their allegiance to the Czar of Muscovy; but by them the independence of Greece was never supposed either to be possible or desirable. An orthodox emperor seated on the throne of Constantinople would of course confirm and extend all the privileges of the Greek clergy.

The primates in Greece formed a substitute for an aristocracy. The real aristocracy of the Greek nation was exterminated by the Othoman conquest. Its members were either slain by the Turks, driven into exile, or induced to embrace Mohammedanism. Several apostates of distinguished Greek families obtained high rank in the sultan's service. Mohammed II. deliberately put to death every Greek who exercised any political influence, as the simplest mode of establishing tranquillity in Greece; and the torpid condition of Greek society for several generations attests the wisdom of his satanic policy.

The patronage of the Othoman government gradually created a Greek aristocracy of administrative agents and tax-gatherers. This aristocracy consisted of the Phanariots at Constantinople and the Kodja-bashis, or primates, in Greece. The moral and political position of this class has been well described by calling them 'a kind of Christian Turks.' A voivode or a bey purchased the taxes of a district as farmer-general. He then sublet the different branches of revenue to Greek primates, who again usually relet their portions in smaller shares to the local magistrates of the communities within the district. In this way the public revenues of Greece maintained three distinct classes of fiscal officers at the expense of the people.

Among the Greeks, as among every other people in the East, a broad line of distinction exists between the urban and the rural population. The citizen and the peasant occupy different grades in the scale of civilization. Their condition in society is more strongly characterized by their place of dwelling and the nature of their occupation, than by their nationality. This distinction is an inheritance of the Roman empire which survived all the vicissitudes of the Byzantine administration, and resisted the endeavours of the crusaders to introduce feudality as an element of Greek society. The Mussulman conquest made no unfavourable change in the relative position of the citizen and the peasant; but it must be noted, that at the time of the Turkish conquest the citizen in Eastern towns generally occupied a higher social position than the citizen of Western Europe in a corresponding occupation, though they laboured under great moral disadvantages. The servile position of the Christian subjects of the sultan, and the corruption of the Othoman administration, rendered deceit the best defence against extortion. Truth and honesty were impediments to the acquisition of wealth; and consequently the prosperous Greek trader was very rarely a better man than his poorer countrymen. Falsehood and fraud became habitual, and were considered by strangers as national qualities rather than individual characteristics.

The Christian population in the towns of Turkey was divided into corporate bodies, according to the trades exercised by individuals, in the same way as the Mussulman population; but the Mussulman corporations generally contrived to throw the burden of all local expenditure on the Christians. It was, therefore, only by counterfeiting poverty, or by bribing some powerful protector, that the Greek rayah could escape ruinous extortion; and it was only by simulating some bodily infirmity or chronic disease that he could evade being condemned to forced labour at inadequate wages.

A nation's strength lies in its rural population. In Greece this class has for ages been poor and neglected, yet the Mohammedan conquest tended on the whole to better its condition, for it destroyed the predial serfdom inherited from the Byzantine empire and enforced by the feudal principles of the Frank conquerors. It raised the peasants to the rank of free men, and converted them into the staple of Greek nationality. From their ranks the waste of city life was everywhere repaired, and the rural recruits transferred into the urban population an unadulterated supply of Greek feelings and traditions, which prevented the Othoman domination from denationalizing the city traders and reducing them to any identity of character with the dispersed Jews.

The agricultural population of Greece, as, indeed, the agricultural population throughout the East, from the Adriatic to the Bay of Bengal, was fixed in a stationary condition by fiscal laws. It was compelled to labour the land, and gather in the harvest, according to regulations framed to protect the revenue of the sovereign, not to encourage or reward the labour of the cultivator. The sovereign was entitled to one-tenth of the fruits of the soil, and from the moment the crop began to ripen, he became a joint proprietor in the whole. The property of the cultivator in nine-tenths of the crop was from that moment treated as a matter subsidiary to the arrangement relative to the disposal of the remaining tenth, which belonged to the sovereign. An industrious peasant could rarely make any profit by raising an early crop, or by improving the quality of his produce, for the farmer of the tenths mixed all qualities together, and was generally the principal dealer in produce in the district. No superiority of skill or increase of labour could, under such circumstances, secure a higher price where markets were distant and where no roads existed. The effects of this system of taxation on the condition of Greek agriculture may still be studied in the dominions of Sultan Abdul-medjid, or of King Otho, for they rival one another in the disastrous effects of their fiscal administration (A.D. 1859).

The municipal institutions of the Greeks under the Othoman government have been much vaunted. In reality they amounted to little more than arrangements for facilitating the collection of the tenth and other taxes on the produce of the soil by the agency of the Greeks themselves, in order to prevent the extermination of the agricultural population. The Othoman sultans appear to have had a clearer insight into the effects of an intolerable land-tax than the Roman emperors before the time of Diocletian.

The communal system in Greece has been sometimes considered to be a tradition of Hellenic liberty. Human institutions are rarely so durable; and it could not be expected that, in a land where the names of Sparta, Plataea, Olympia, and Delphi had fallen into oblivion, any relics of civil liberty should have been preserved by tradition. History tells us that every trace of Hellenic institutions was swept away by the Roman empire and the Christian church. The Greek city was supplanted by the Roman municipality. The provincial administration and the civil laws of Rome effaced every vestige of Hellenic freedom. The Christian religion and the laws of Justinian are the oldest social traditions of the modern Greeks.

Even the Roman municipal system was swept away by the centralizing despotism of the Byzantine emperors, and in the ninth century it was formally abrogated by Leo the Philosopher[1].

Oriental fiscality was the essence of the municipal institutions of the modern Greeks. Each district was assessed to pay a certain amount of taxes, and the repartition of a part of the sum to be paid by the Christians was left to the clergy and the primates. In some places the persons intrusted with this power were named by the Porte; in others they were elected by the people. The authority thus created was greater in the rural districts than in the towns. And in those parts of Greece in which there were few resident Turks, a popular election gave the institution a national character. But this municipal system was too intimately connected with bad principles of taxation to become a means of training a nation to freedom and justice. Like everything in the Othoman empire, it was full of anomalies. Some communities had the privilege of maintaining armed guards or Christian troops, called armatoli; some enjoyed their freedom under the guarantee of written charters from the sultans; some enjoyed great local privileges; and some were relieved entirely from the land-tax[2].

---

[1] *See* above, vol. ii. p. 236.

[2] The Greeks have forged many written charters. Mr. Tricoupi publishes one as genuine in the second volume of his *History of Greece* which carries proofs of its forgery, even though the date is omitted in Tricoupi's copy. Mr. Argyropulos, in his work on the *Municipal Administration of Greece* (Δημοτικὴ Διοίκησις ἐν Ἑλλάδι, p. 25), gives a copy of the document, with the date, year of the Hegira 1036—*i.e.*, A.D. 1626. It purports to be a ratification by Sultan Ibrahim of privileges granted by Suleiman the Magnificent to Naxos and other islands. Sultan Ibrahim ascended the throne in 1640. The document is full of historical and chronological blunders, and the part which is genuine is transcribed from a charter of a more modern date, or the blunders could not have been committed.

Nothing partaking of real self-government could exist wherever the dominant class of Mohammedans dwelt, intermingled with the Greek population, in a despotism like that of the Othoman sultans, in which the power of life and death was intrusted to local governors. Municipal liberty can have no vitality, unless the local magistrates are directly elected by the people, and responsible to the law alone. If a Mohammedan sultan or a Christian emperor can revoke the mandate granted by the people when the local magistrate has violated no law and neglected no duty, and can replace that local magistrate by a person of his own nomination, municipal institutions are nothing more than a convenience for assisting the central administration in ruling the people.

The slight hold which the municipal institutions of the modern Greeks had acquired in the affections of the people is demonstrated by the ease with which they were perverted by Capodistrias, and changed for a new system by the Bavarian Regency. Yet these institutions, though they did not possess the energy required for producing a national revolution, aided the Greeks in maintaining their struggle with the Othoman government, by supplying a system of local organization, which enabled them to call the whole strength and resources of the agricultural population simultaneously into action.

It has been already stated that the position and character of the Greek clergy tended to weaken the power of the Greek church, though ecclesiastical influence still remained the highest national authority. The next in importance was literary education, and those who dispensed it enjoyed a moral influence in society second only to the clergy. More learning existed among the modern Greek laity under the Othoman rule than is generally supposed[1]. Since the Revolution it has been more generally disseminated, but it does not appear to be more profound in those branches not immediately connected with profitable employment. The

---

[1] [Those who desire more information on this subject will find it in the Νεοελληνικὴ Φιλολογία of A. Papadopulos Vretos, 2 vols. 8vo., Athens, 1854-7, which gives a list of the books published by Greeks from the fall of the Byzantine empire to the establishment of the monarchy in Greece, both in the Hellenic and the Romaic tongue. One of the most striking features in this list is the great number of places in different countries of Europe at which these works were published. ED.]

state of education explains the failure of the missionaries sent from Europe and America to improve the religious ideas of the Greeks. In theological learning these missionaries were always inferior to many of the Greek clergy; in classical knowledge they were as much inferior to many lay teachers. During the period of destitution which succeeded the cessation of hostilities with the Turks, they were welcomed as teachers of elementary schools, and they were popular for a time, because they gave both instruction and books gratis; but, in order to make their schools of any use, they were obliged to employ Greeks as teachers. Differences arose among the missionaries themselves, and between the missionaries and their schoolmasters. The clergy, taking advantage of these disputes to recover their authority, succeeded in closing the schools of all the missionaries who did not allow the Greek priesthood to control the religious instruction of the pupils. The principle that the religious instruction of the children of orthodox parents can only be directed by the orthodox, has been adopted by the government since the Revolution of 1843, and applied to missionary schools even more stringently than had been done previously. As might have been expected, religious bigotry has received a stronger impulse than religious education.

For more than three centuries after the Othoman conquest the literature of the modern Greeks was almost exclusively confined to ecclesiastical subjects; and its language was not the spoken dialect of the people, but a pedantic imitation of the language of the fathers of the Church. The popular language, as written by merchants and traders, was disfigured by ignorance of grammar and orthography, to such a degree as to give it the appearance of a new tongue; but the popular songs and epistolary correspondence of this period, if written with a corrected orthography, prove their close connection with ancient Greek. Degraded as the condition of the Greeks was politically, it is probable that a larger proportion could read and write than among any other Christian race in Europe. The Greeks of every class have always set a higher value on a knowledge of letters than any other people. They have a national tendency to pedantism.

At the commencement of this century the effects of the French Revolution were strongly felt in Greece. Classic history was studied; classic names were revived; Athenian liberty became a theme of conversation among men; Spartan virtue was spoken of by women; literature was cultivated with enthusiasm as a step to revolution.

On the eve of the Revolution the condition of the Greek race might be represented under two different aspects, and innumerable facts might be cited to prove that both were true; yet, under the one, the Greeks would appear as oppressed and degraded, and, under the other, as a happy and prosperous people, enjoying many valuable privileges. A comparison might be instituted between the condition of the Greek rayahs under the sultan and the Russian serfs under the czar. The Christians who cultivated the soil in Turkey enjoyed a larger share of the fruits of their labours than the Christian peasantry in Poland and Hungary. The Greek citizen enjoyed a greater degree of liberty of speech, and possessed as much influence on the local affairs of his township, as the citizen of the French empire under Napoleon I. Nor were the orthodox in the East more galled by the restrictions which their religion imposed on them than the Catholics of Ireland.

The Greeks were allowed a considerable share of authority in the executive administration of the Othoman government. The patriarch of Constantinople, as I have already mentioned, was a kind of under-secretary to the grand-vizier for the affairs of the orthodox Christians. The dragoman of the Porte and the dragoman of the fleet, who were Greeks, were also virtually members of the sultan's government. The Christians of the Morea had also a recognized agent at Constantinople, and other Greek communities had recognized official protectors, who controlled the fiscal oppression and the arbitrary injustice of the provincial pashas. This recognition, on the part of the Othoman government, that the Greeks required some defence against abuses of power on the part of their rulers, proves that the sultans not only perceived the evils inherent in the constitution of the Othoman empire, but were also desirous of redressing them.

In some degree, and in several provinces of the empire, the agricultural population was always in the same condition, whether it was composed of Mussulmans or Christians. Both were oppressed by the same fiscal regulations, and both were retained in the same stationary condition. In the richest plains the peasant who cultivated the lands of a Mussulman aga or of a Christian primate, usually paid a seventh of the gross produce of the land to the sultan, and divided the remainder with his landlord. When the destruction of stock or a decline in the fertility of the soil rendered it impossible for the peasantry to perpetuate the race of cultivators on the proportion of the produce which fell to their share, they emigrated, or the race died out; and the frequency of this event, both in Europe and Asia, was apparent to every traveller. Abandoned villages and ruined mosques were met with in the richest provinces of the empire.

In addition to the land-tax paid in kind, the Othoman government compelled the cultivators of the soil to furnish a determinate quantity of grain for the supply of Constantinople. The loss incurred by this right of pre-emption was thrown on the peasantry.

The Christians regarded the haratch, or capitation tax, as the most offensive badge of their subjection. It reduced them to the condition of rayahs or ransomed subjects. Yet it was in general more galling from the manner of its collection than from the amount which each individual was obliged to pay. Its collection was made a pretext for enforcing many vexatious police regulations, and it was doubly hated because Mohammedans of the lowest class were exempted from its burden.

The haratch was frequently farmed to the worst class of a pasha's retinue; and in Greece it was often sublet in districts to the petty officers of the Albanian mercenaries. An insulting term was applied to these unpopular tax-gatherers, who were called gypsy-haratchers. The origin of the nickname was a popular opinion that gypsies were bound to pay double haratch, and the reproach conveyed was that the Albanians attempted to treat every man liable to the haratch as a gypsy.

So anomalous was the condition of different portions of the Greek population, that the inhabitants of some mountain districts in Romelia lived like a free people. Those who dwelt in Agrapha and the mountain-ranges that extend from Pelion and Olympus northward as far as the Greek language was spoken in Macedonia, enjoyed the right of bearing arms as armatoli. They elected their own primates or elders, and their local authorities collected the taxes due by the district. Their character was that of freemen, and was marked by a degree of courage and independence not to be found in other parts of Greece. Considerable numbers were engaged in commercial pursuits, which carried them into various parts of the sultan's empire, and into many ports of the Mediterranean and the Black Sea. Many travelled far into Austria and Russia. These wanderings enlarged their minds, and when they settled in their native towns, they became local magistrates, and displayed some signs of that active spirit that usually pervades commercial republics.

In the rude condition of Greek society and trade, the muleteers engaged in the transport of produce formed a numerous class, for everything was transported by pack-horses or mules. The number of this class was much greater than the depopulated appearance of European Turkey would have led a stranger to suppose possible. Coarse woollen cloth of different kinds, and the cloaks which imitate sheep-skins, were manufactured in the interior of the continent, and these bulky goods employed thousands of horses to convey them to the sea-coast. The cheese and butter of the mountains were transported into the plains, and the grain of the plains was carried back into the mountains. Considerable quantities of money were also constantly in movement, partly for purposes of trade, and partly as remittances to provincial officers, or to the imperial treasury. Every class considered it good policy to conciliate the *agoyiates*, or muleteers. Powerful pashas patronized them, wealthy merchants treated them with respect and confidence; they were favoured by Mussulman beys and Greek primates, and they were esteemed and trusted by the peasantry; their friendship was sought by armatoli, and their enmity was feared by klephts.

The shepherds were also a numerous class in Romelia. They were as independent, though not so influential, as the muleteers.

The peasants of the mountain districts, the muleteers, and the shepherds formed the best representatives of the Greek nation; and it was from among them that the ranks of the armatoli were recruited.

The armatoli were a Christian local militia, which had

existed in the Byzantine empire, and which had in some degree protected the Greek population against the Franks, the Servians, and the Albanians, during the anarchy that reigned in Greece and Macedonia, while the worthless race of the Palaeologoi ruled at Constantinople. The Greeks in the mountain districts, fearing anarchy more than despotism, generally submitted to the sultans on the condition of being allowed to retain their local privileges. The institution of the armatoli was thus adopted into the scheme of the sultan's administration. The Greek communities of the mountains collected their own taxes, and the Greek troops guarded the great roads through the mountain passes; but, as the sultans gradually increased the power and extended the authority of the central administration, the importance of the armatoli declined. The Dervendji-pasha, who represented the Kleisourarchs of the Byzantine emperors, stationed Turkish troops to guard the principal dervends, or passes, and circumscribed the service of the armatoli as much as possible to that of rural guards. In some districts the military authority which had been vested in the Christians was entirely transferred to the Mussulmans before the end of the last century. The case of the town of Servia is an instance, which commands the great road between Larissa and Monastir or Bitolia. The service of the armatoli was first rendered so burdensome, that the communities sought to purchase exemption from the obligation of furnishing additional armatoli. The money was employed to pay Albanian mercenaries.

The history of the armatoli, from the time of the Turkish conquest until the peace of Belgrade in 1739, has not met with the attention it deserves from the modern Greeks. The number of armatoliks recognized by the Othoman government is said to have been originally fourteen; but no correct list appears to exist. After the peace of Belgrade, the policy of diminishing the numbers of the armatoli was steadily and successfully pursued. To destroy the power of this Christian militia, the sultans, in the year 1740, departed from the ancient practice of the Porte, not to name an Albanian bey to the rank of pasha in his native country. Suleiman of Arghyrokastron, a man of activity and daring, was appointed pasha of Joannina and dervendji-pasha, with strict orders to watch the intrigues of the Greeks, who were suspected of being under the influence of Russia, and to circumscribe the power of the armatoli.

Suleiman fulfilled his instructions with much ability. He worked on the mutual jealousies which are the bane of Greek society. By tolerating the feuds of the captains, and then aiding the people who suffered from their hostilities, he gradually weakened the organization of the ancient captainliks, and introduced Albanian Mussulmans into Christian districts. The venality of some captains enabled him to purchase the chief military power in their district.

Kurd Pasha, another Albanian bey, succeeded Suleiman, and held the office of dervendji-pasha for fifteen years; at first, in conjunction with the pashalik of Joannina, and afterwards with that of Berat. Kurd acted under instructions similar to those given to Suleiman. His administration commenced about the time the Russians invaded the Morea; and this circumstance afforded him a reasonable pretext for diminishing the numbers of the armed Christians and reducing their pay. The severity of his measures against the armatoli, instead of being relaxed, was increased after the peace of Kainardji in 1774.

Ali of Tepelen became dervendji-pasha in the year 1787, with strict orders to pursue the same policy as Suleiman and Kurd. He destroyed the old system so completely, that the proud armatoli of earlier days were reduced to be local policemen in their native districts. Into every armatolik he introduced a number of Albanian Mussulman mercenaries. With the perfidy, cruelty, and vigour that formed his policy, he circumscribed the legal authority, and nullified the traditional privileges of the Christian militia, without openly abrogating their ancient charters. The jealousies of rival captains were encouraged and their hostilities overlooked until it served Ali's purpose to interfere. The Greek clergy and primates were prompted to make complaints against the exactions of the soldiers and the feuds of the captains. Bands of robbers (klephts) were tolerated, and even encouraged, until a case was made out which served as a popular pretext for introducing Mussulman Albanians into a Christian armatolik. During the government of Ali most of the districts, which had from time immemorial enjoyed the right of electing their captains of armatoli, were forced to waive this privilege, and request Ali to appoint their captain.

The last blow was given to the ancient system of armatoli at Agrapha by Ali. Mohammed II. is said to have confirmed the municipal independence and the privileges of the armatoli of this district by a written charter. When the sultans became the lords and protectors of Agrapha, it had long been engaged in hostilities with the Frank dukes of Athens and with the despots of Epirus. Its relations with the Othoman government were friendly, and its armatoli guarded the passes of Mount Pindus between Thessaly and Epirus, as they had done for ages under the Byzantine emperors. The population of Agrapha is of the Greek race, without the admixture of Bulgarian, Albanian, and Vallachian blood which pervades the neighbouring districts. It appears, indeed, to have successfully resisted the great Sclavonian colonization of Greece during the transformation of the Roman into the Byzantine empire, which implanted new geographical names on the rest of Greece. But though it resisted the social influence of the Sclavonians, it could not evade the policy of Ali: he succeeded in sowing dissensions among the population of this favoured district, and then, under the pretext of an anxiety to prevent hostilities between the rival factions, he persuaded the municipal authorities to reduce the number of the armatoli to two hundred men. Shortly after he found an opportunity of sending a Mussulman derven-aga, with three hundred Albanians, to remain as a permanent garrison in Agrapha.

When the authority of the armatoli declined, the klephts, or brigands, acquired political and social importance as a permanent class in the Greek nation. As long as the institution of the armatoli preserved its pristine energy, the klephts were repressed with a vigorous hand; but when the Porte began to reduce the numbers and curtail the privileges of the Christian militia, many discontented armatoli fled to the mountains, and lived by levying contributions on the cultivators of the soil. Where the government shows no respect for justice, lawless men are often supported by the lower orders of the people, as a means of securing revenge or of redressing intolerable social evils. A life of independence, even when stained with crime, has always been found to throw a spell over the minds of oppressed nations. The Greeks make Robin Hoods, or demi-heroes, of their leading klephts; they magnify the exploits of the class, and antedate its existence. The patriotic brigands of modern Greek poetry are a creation of yesterday. Even at the commencement of the present century, several of the most numerous bands in Macedonia consisted of as many Mussulmans as Christians, and Albanians were always more numerous in their ranks than Greeks.

During the government of Ali Pasha, the districts of Verria and Niausta were infested by a celebrated Mussulman klepht, named Sulu Proshova, whose band amounted to several hundred men, the majority of which was said to consist of Christians. The popular songs of the Greeks have given fame to the klephts, and the language in which the songs are written has caused scholars to exaggerate their merit as poetical compositions. The habitual cruelty of the klephts would have rendered pathos satire. Their most glorious exploits were to murder Turkish agas in mountain passes, as Lord Byron describes the scene in his 'Giaour[1].'

The ordinary life of the klepht was as little distinguished by mercy to the poor as it was ennobled by national patriotism. There is very rarely anything to eulogize in the conduct of criminals. But the klephts, after the treaty of Belgrade, became gradually more and more confounded with the armatoli in the ideas of the urban population of Greece, from the frequency with which Ali enrolled distinguished klephts among his Christian guards, and conferred on them commands of armatoli; while at the same time a constant desertion of discontented armatoli was recruiting the ranks of the klephts. This interchange of the members of the two corps at last created a certain community of feelings and interests. The existence of the klephts was necessary to render the services of the armatoli indispensable. Ali was often accused of

---

[1] The Greeks suffered far more than the Turks from the klephts. Rich primates were more defenceless than wealthy agas; and robbers require a daily supply of food. Every traveller in the East could cite proofs of this from his own experience. Two examples will suffice. Colonel Leake says: 'The master of the house in which I lodge (at Kalabaka), among his other misfortunes, has left an eye with the klephts.' *Travels in Northern Greece*, iv. 262. Mr. Dodwell says: 'Our lodging at Livanatis was in the cottage of a poor Albanian woman, who was lamenting the loss of her husband, who had been killed by the klephts, while her infant son was taken prisoner, whom she had ransomed with the savings of several years.' *Classical Tour*, ii. 59. Livanatis is a village peopled by Christian Albanians, near Talanta.

neglecting to suppress the depredations of the klephts, in order to extend his power as dervendji-pasha. But when any individual klepht incurred his hatred, neither valour nor caution could elude his vengeance. The treachery with which he murdered Katziko-Janni, and the cruelty with which he inflicted the most horrible tortures on Katz-Antoni, are celebrated in Greek songs with feelings of mingled admiration and abhorrence[1].

The people furnished the true type of the Greek race in Romelia; but in the Morea, the nation was represented by the proësti and primates. The people were of little account, for the primates were rarely elected by popular suffrage. Almost every local authority derived its power from the central administration of the pasha, and acted as fiscal agents of the sultan. Their insolence to the poorer class of Christians, and their exactions from the Greek peasantry, were only exceeded by the Mussulman Albanians who collected the haratch. In manners and dress they imitated the Turks, and they were accused of leaguing with the higher clergy to keep the people in ignorance and subjection. Before the Revolution, it was observed that education flourished more at Joannina, under the eye of the tyrant Ali, than at Patras or Tripolitza, under the care of Greek primates. Education owed its chief obligations to traders and monks.

The Greeks of all classes in the Morea lived in comparative ease and abundance, in spite of the exactions of Turks and primates. The very circumstance which made taxation arrest the progress of society, rendered its burden light on individuals. It was paid in kind at harvest-time. A part was taken from a heap. The population was thin, and no produce was raised that was not raised in abundance. At the time of harvest, therefore, the price was always low. The farmers of taxes were usually primates and large landholders; and whether they were Turks or Greeks, they had a virtual monopoly of the market. Merchants found it more advantageous to make their price with those who could furnish a whole cargo than to collect small quantities in detail, even at a lower price, but with the risk of not finding adequate

---

[1] Fauriel, *Chants Populaires de la Grèce*, i. 170.

means of transport to the port of embarkation, and of not being able to complete a cargo within a fixed period.

The well-being of the Moreot peasantry in many districts arose from a cause which was easily overlooked. They enjoyed the benefit of a large amount of capital vested in improvements in former days. Buildings, mills, watercourses, and cisterns facilitated labour and increased profits. But every generation saw some portion of this vested capital disappear, and with it a portion of the population vanished. Plantations of olive, mulberry, fig, and other fruit-trees, and vineyards producing wine or currants, occasioned so great a demand for agricultural labour, that the condition of the day-labourer was not inferior to that of the small peasant-proprietor. Indeed, no condition of society could be more favourable to the individual labourer. The demand for labour was limited, but wages were high, and the price of provisions was low.

The municipal organization of the Morea was more complete than in the other parts of Greece, but it was not so free. Each village elected its own Demogeront; the demogeronts and the people of the towns elected Proësti, and the proësti elected the primate of the province. The primates resided at Tripolitza, to transact the business relating to the whole Christian population of the pashalik. The proësti and primates, with the assistance of the bishops and abbots of the principal monasteries, elected a vekil or primate, who resided at Constantinople, as the official organ of communication with the sultan's ministers, and whose duty it was to keep the dragoman of the Porte and the dragoman of the fleet accurately informed concerning the affairs of the Greeks, as far as related to their respective departments. This system invested the aristocracy of the Morea with a considerable share of political power, and rendered it a check on the authority of the pasha.

The character of the Moreots was not viewed with favour by the other Greeks. The primates were accused of retaining the intriguing, treacherous, and rancorous disposition which the imperial historian Cantacuzenos tells us characterized them in the fourteenth century[1]. Nor were either the citizens

---

[1] Cantacuzeni *Historia*, p. 751, edit. Paris.

or the peasants supposed to be more imbued with the spirit of truth and justice. Their industry and intelligence were recognized; but their deficiency in candour, courage, and honesty was almost proverbial. A Moreot was supposed, as a matter of course, to be more inconsistent, envious, and ungrateful than any other Greek.

The primates generally maintained a few armed guards, partly to enforce their authority and collect taxes, and partly to defend their property from the klephts. But no regular armatoli ever existed in the Morea. Even the klephts of the Morea, who were mere brigands, were not numerous until after the social disorganization caused by the Russian invasion and the insurrectionary movements of 1770. The exploits of Zacharias and of Kolokotroni, though celebrated in unpoetic verses and in bombastical prose, were only the deeds of highwaymen and sheep-stealers. They lived habitually at the expense of the poor Christian peasants, and rarely ventured to waylay a rich Greek primate, still more rarely to plunder a Turkish aga. The song of Zacharias celebrates the destruction of Greek villages, the plunder of Greek priests, the insult of Greek women, the murder of one Greek child, and the ransom of another[1]. Dodwell mentions the readiness with which the Greek peasantry joined in hunting down the band of Kolokotroni, and with which the Greek bishops excommunicated the klephts[2]. Kolokotroni's own account of the events witnessed by Dodwell has been published, and it proves that nothing can have been more brutal than the life of a Moreot klepht. They were crafty and cruel, and if the trade was ever nobler, it must have been long before the days of Kolokotroni[3].

The Mainates and the Tzakonians must be excepted from the general description of the Moreot character. The former were remarkable for their love of violence and plunder, but also for their frankness and independence. The latter were distinguished by their peaceful habits, their honesty, and their industry. Both were considered brave. The Tzakonians kept

---

[1] Fauriel, *Chants Populaires de la Grèce Moderne*, vol. i. p. 76.
[2] *Classical Tour*, i. 76; ii. 371. Captain George is confounded with Kolokotroni; ii. 356.
[3] Διήγησις Συμβάντων, pp. 20, 21. Kolokotroni speaks of burning Greek villages, when he was a klepht, as a matter of no importance—ἔκαια τὰ χωρία, p. 14.

provision-shops in almost every seaport on the Aegean. The Mainates carried on piracy in every gulf[1].

The Greek inhabitants of the islands exhibited a great variety of character, for they lived under a diversity of social influences. The maritime population of Psara, Kasos, Kalymnos, and Patmos, was active, intelligent, and brave; the Sciots were industrious and honest; the inhabitants of Tinos and Syra, whether orthodox or Catholic, were timid and well-behaved—formed by nature and art to make excellent cooks and nurses. The characteristic of the islanders of the Archipelago was supposed to be timidity. The Turks who visited them only to collect tribute, and who saw them scamper off to the mountains when the tax-gatherers arrived, nicknamed them *taoshan*, or hares. Little did the Turks think that these hares were about to turn on the greyhounds and drive them back into their kennel.

---

[1] See the account of the condition of the Mainates in vol. v. pp. 113 foll. Colonel Leake relates two characteristic anecdotes of Mainate manners. *Travels in the Morea*, i. 272, 282. Kolokotroni tells us, in his Memoirs, that the Mainates forget everything when there is a question of gaining money. Οἱ Μανιάται λησμονοῦν ὅλα διὰ τὰ γρόσια. Διήγησις Συμβάντων τῆς Ἑλληνικῆς Φυλῆς ἀπὸ τὰ 1770 ἕως τὰ 1836, ὑπαγόρευσε Θ. Κ. Κολοκοτρώνης. Ἀθήνησιν, 1846.

they are still more numerous. They occupy the whole of Corinthia and Argolis, extending themselves into the northern part of Arcadia and the eastern part of Achaia. In Laconia they inhabit the slopes of Taygetus, called Bardunia, which extend to the plain of Helos, and, crossing the Eurotas, they occupy a large district around Monemvasia to the south of the Tzakonians, and to the north of a small Greek population which dwells near Cape Malea, in the district called Vatika. In the western part of the peninsula they occupied a considerable part of the mountains which extend from Lalla to the north-eastern corner of Messenia, south of the Neda. Besides these large settlements, there are some smaller clusters of Albanian villages to the north of Karitena, and in the mountains between the Bay of Navarin and the Gulf of Coron. The islands of Hydra and Spetzas were entirely peopled by Albanians.

Marathon, Plataea, Leuctra, Salamis, Mantinea, Eira, and Olympia are now inhabited by Albanians, and not by Greeks. Even in the streets of Athens, though it has been for more than a quarter of a century the capital of a Greek kingdom, the Albanian language is still heard among the children playing in the streets near the temple of Theseus and the arch of Hadrian.

Not more than a tenth of the Albanian population settled in Greece professed the Mohammedan religion. The most warlike tribes were those of Lalla, Bardunia, and Carystos in Euboea.

The Albanian Mussulmans of Lalla occupied a healthy and agreeable situation in an elevated plain on Mount Pholoë. Their scattered habitations formed a great village rather than a town. The principal men dwelt in towers capable of defence. Lalla contained upwards of 3000 inhabitants, and about 400 were well armed and well mounted.

The district of Bardunia took its name from a Byzantine castle, high up on the slope of Taygetus, near the sources of the river of Passava. It comprised the south-eastern declivities of the mountain, which run out into a broad ridge overlooking the lower valley of the Eurotas, and extending almost to the sea-coast near Marathonisi. For three centuries this district was possessed by Albanians, who were without any tradition concerning the period at which their ancestors had colonized the country, or embraced Mohammedanism. It may, perhaps, be inferred from this ignorance, that the Barduniots expelled the Sclavonian population, which the Byzantine writers tell us occupied this district at the time of the Turkish conquest, and that they embraced Mohammedanism to become landlords instead of peasants.

The Barduniots dwelt in fortified towers dispersed over the country, and both their situation and their valour enabled them to restrain the forays of the Mainates in the rich plains of Laconia. The exactions of the Barduniot agas were nevertheless often found to be almost as intolerable as the depredations of the Greeks of Maina. The whole population was able to arm about 2500 men. Between forty and fifty families held a superior rank in consequence of their large landed possessions.

The armatoli were not the only Christians in the Othoman empire who were authorized to bear arms. Several Albanian communities in Greece, though entirely composed of Christians, received this privilege from the sultan. The inhabitants of Megaris, who occupied five large villages, called Dervenokhoria, were particularly favoured by the Porte. The care of guarding the passes over mounts Cithaeron and Geranea, which lead to the Isthmus of Corinth, was intrusted to them; and they were relieved from several taxes, on the condition that they should furnish a body of armed men constantly on duty. The number of armed men in the five villages amounted to about 2000.

The most influential, though not the most numerous, portion of the Albanian population in Greece, consisted of the shipowners and sailors of Hydra and Spetzas, and of the boatmen of Poros, Kastri, and Kranidi.

The island of Hydra contained nearly twenty thousand inhabitants of pure Albanian race before the Greek Revolution.

It is a long ridge of limestone rocks, with only a few acres of soil capable of cultivation. The town is situated near the middle of the island, on the channel which separates it from Argolis. Seen from the sea, it presents a noble aspect, forming an amphitheatre of white houses, rising one above the other round a small creek which can hardly be used as a port. The houses cling like swallows' nests to the sides of a barren mountain, which towers far above them, and whose summit is crowned by a monastery of St. Elias. The streets are narrow, crooked, unpaved lanes, but the smallest dwellings are built of stone, and near the sea some large and solidly-constructed houses give the place an imposing aspect. In these houses the wealthy primates of Hydra resided at the breaking out of the Revolution. They lived, like most Albanians, a frugal, and, it may even be said, a penurious life. In their dress, their education, and their character, indeed, there was very little difference between the primate, the captain, and the common sailor of Hydra. The rich Hydriot usually displayed his wealth in erecting a large building near the sea, which served as a dwelling for his family and a warehouse for his goods. In some of the rooms the sails and cordage of his ships were stored; in others he lived [1].

The Hydriots of every rank displayed the peculiar character of the Albanian race. They were proud, insolent, turbulent, and greedy of gain. The primates were jealous and exacting, the people rude and violent. But both possessed some sterling virtues; and they were distinguished from the Greeks by their love of truth, and by the honesty with which they fulfilled their engagements. There were no traders in the Levant who paid more punctually than the merchants, and no sailors who took better care of ship and cargo than the mariners, of Hydra.

The civil government, conceded by the sultan and protected by the capitan-pasha, was entirely in the hands of the shipowners and retired captains, who formed a class of capitalists. About the year 1730, when the Albanian colony established itself in the then deserted island in order to escape the exactions of the pasha of the Morea, the local administration of the small trading community was intrusted to three elders, called, in the Albanian dialect, plekjeria, who were chosen by the people. The annual tribute paid to the sultan amounted to 200 piastres, a sum at that time not equal to £30

---

[1] Both Gordon (*History of the Greek Revolution*, i. 164) and Waddington (*Visit to Greece*, 102) speak of the costly marbles and splendid furniture at Hydra. The marbles were only flags from Leghorn with which the courts were paved; and the richest furniture consisted of a few damask chairs from Marseilles. Generally, the best houses of the Hydriot primates were not so expensively furnished as those of the Moreots. The houses were built at considerable expense, but were solid, not splendid. They still stand to bear evidence of the rude social condition of the Hydriots at the period of their greatest wealth.

sterling. When the islanders grew richer and more numerous, the number of elders was gradually increased, until it reached twelve. But the new settlers never acquired the full rights of the original colonists, and the government became an oligarchy, which indeed appears to be the type to which political society tends among the Albanians. The twelve elders were chosen by the capitalists, and formed a municipal council, divided into three sections composed of four members. Each section acted for four months, and met daily to transact business with the governor or head of the police, who was a primate of the island, named by the capitan-pasha, and commonly called the Bey.

The celebrated capitan-pasha, Kutchuk Hussein, who was a steady protector of the Hydriots and Spetziots, was the first who appointed a governor to act as the sultan's representative at Hydra. He did so at the request of the Hydriots, who found their municipal authorities unable to restrain the turbulence of rival factions, or to bring murderers to justice.

The family of Konduriottis was one of the most ancient and most distinguished in the island. It was founded by the younger son of an Albanian peasant of the dervenokhorion of Kundura, who settled as a boatman shortly after the expulsion of the Venetians from the Morea, and before Hydra received the colony which formed a regular community. Lazaros Konduriottis was the head of the family during the Greek Revolution. At his marriage his father was assassinated by the bravo of a rival family. Old Konduriottis saw Kolodemo, whom he knew to be an assassin, approaching him covertly during the ceremony. Suspecting his design, he placed a stool before his body, holding it in his hand. The murderer, however, advanced so close that old Konduriottis was forced to hold him at bay with the stool, and endeavour to push him towards the door. Kolodemo was in danger of being baffled, but by stooping down he contrived to stab his enemy with a long knife in the belly, and to escape, leaving the weapon in the wound. This assassination caused the Hydriots to petition the sultan to send a governor with the power of life and death. Kutchuk Hussein named a Hydriot called Bulgaris as the first governor, in the year 1802. Bulgaris had served with the capitan-pasha in the

HYDRA AND SPETZAS.

Othoman fleet, as quartermaster of the Christian seamen. The authority of the Christian bey was not, however, sufficient to control the turbulence of his countrymen, and assassination was never completely suppressed [1].

Hydra paid no direct taxes to the sultan, but it was obliged to furnish a contingent of two hundred and fifty able-bodied seamen to the Othoman fleet, and to pay them from the local treasury. The expense of this contingent amounted to 16,000 dollars annually. Besides this sum, about 4000 dollars were annually expended in presents to the capitan-pasha, to the Greek dragoman of the fleet, and to several officials employed at the admiralty and dockyard at Constantinople. To raise these sums, a tax of five per cent. was imposed by the local administration on the gains of every Hydriot, and some custom-duties were levied at the port.

The condition of Spetzas was very similar to that of Hydra. The population was smaller, the proportion of small capitalists was greater, and the local administration was more democratic.

A considerable portion of the coasting trade in the Archipelago was in the hands of the Albanians of Poros, Kastri, and Kranidi, who possessed many decked boats. Over this maritime population the Hydriots and Spetziots exercised supremacy.

Such was the position of the Albanian race in Greece, where its settlements were comparatively modern. In its native regions its political importance and moral influence had been constantly increasing during the latter half of the last century, and it had attained the acme of its power at the commencement of the Greek Revolution. In Albania a considerable proportion of the population had embraced the Mohammedan religion; but the Albanian Mussulmans were detested by the Osmanlis and hated by the Greeks. Their religion was hardly a matter of conscience with the majority. They were less bigoted than the Turks, and less superstitious than the Greeks. Their avarice was, however, insatiable, and for gold an Albanian Mussulman would

---

[1] Waddington (*Visit to Greece*) mentions that a band of assassins existed at Hydra during the early years of the Revolution; and many of their crimes might be cited to prove the correctness of his assertion.

willingly serve a Christian master, or a Christian Albanian a Mussulman chief, even if the service was to be rendered in deeds of blood.

The Albanian forms a distinct race among the nations of Europe. They have been supposed by some to be the representatives of the Pelasgians. They call themselves *Shkipetar*. Some suppose them to have occupied the regions they now inhabit before the days of Homer, and that they are the lineal descendants of the race to which the ancient Epirots and Macedonians belonged as cognate tribes. Alexander the Great must, according to these archaeologists, have spoken an ancient Albanian dialect at his riotous banquets with his Macedonian officers.

The researches of modern philology have established beyond question that the Albanian language is an early offset from the Sanscrit, and that its grammar was complete at as old a date as the oldest Greek dialect[1]. Nearly the same boundary separates the Hellenic from the non-Hellenic population at the present day as in ancient times. Thucydides calls the Amphilochians who dwelt at the head of the Gulf of Arta barbarians. Strabo says that one race inhabited the whole country, from the Acroceraunian Mountains to the borders of Thessaly and to the plain of Pelagonia, under

---

[1] The best works on Albania and its population are—Leake's *Travels in Northern Greece*, 4 vols., 1835; and *Albanesische Studien*, by Dr. J. G. von Hahn, 1853. For the language—1. *Researches in Greece*, by Col. Leake, 1814; 2. *Die Sprache der Albanesen oder Schkipetaren*, by Ritter von Xylander, 1835; 3. There is an excellent grammar and dictionary in the philological portion of the *Albanesische Studien* of Dr. von Hahn; 4. *Pelasgica*, by Dr. Reinhold of the Greek Navy, published at Athens, 1856. The most important philological dissertations are—1. An essay entitled *Ist die Albanesische Sprache eine Indo-Germanische?* by Th. Stier, published in the *Allgemeine Monatsschrift für Wissenschaft und Literatur*, Brunswick, November 1854; 2. *Ueber das Albanesische in seinen Verwandtschaftlichen Beziehungen*, by Franz Bopp, Berlin, 1855; 3. Περὶ τῆς Αὐτοχθονίας τῶν Ἀλβανῶν ἤτοι Σκιπιτάρ, by N. Γ. Νικοκλῆς, Göttingen, 1855; 4. *Das Albanesische Element in Griechenland*, by Dr. J. Ph. Fallmerayer, Munich, 1857. Several poems in the Albanian language have been printed at Naples, and one by Dr. Stier at Brunswick, in 1856. [The Albanian language is not, as stated in the text, an offset from the Sanscrit, but from the primitive Aryan language, from which Sanscrit also was derived. This conclusion, with regard to the independent position of the Albanian, was established by Bopp, in the dissertation mentioned above, the data for which were supplied by Von Hahn's *Albanesische Studien*. Bopp remarks that much of the system of inflections and many of the words are strikingly similar to Latin and Greek, yet not in such a way as to render it supposable that they have been borrowed from either; indeed, in most points it can be explained more readily by Sanscrit than by those languages. ED.]

the name of Epirots or Macedonians, for both spoke the same language[1].

Ancient Epirus was filled with Greek colonies, and the Greek race is now more numerous than the Albanian in the region immediately to the north of the Gulf of Arta. But, on the other hand, one-fifth of modern Greece is at present inhabited by Albanian colonists. The inhabitants of Albania, of the Shkipetar race, consist of two distinct branches, the Gueghs and the Tosks. The Gueghs dwell to the north of the valley of the Skumbi and the line of the Via Egnatia. That great artery of Roman life now forms a desolate line of separation between the two tribes. The dialects of these two branches are said not to differ more in their grammar than the Scotch of Ayrshire and the English of Somersetshire, yet a Guegh and a Tosk are unintelligible to one another at their first meeting. Both branches are subdivided into several tribes. Among the Gueghs several Catholic tribes retain their semi-independence, and uphold the Papal supremacy alike against the Mohammedan Gueghs and their northern neighbours, the fierce orthodox freemen of Montenegro. The Mirdites are considered the most warlike of the Christians. They are all Catholics, and boast that they are the descendants of the companions and soldiers of Skanderbeg.

The Tosks who dwell to the south of the Skumbi are the neighbours of the Greeks. The Albanian colonies in Greece are all composed of Tosks. This branch is divided into three great tribes, which are again subdivided into many septs—the Toskides proper, the Lyapides, and the Tchamides. The Toskides are generally Mussulmans, but among the Lyapides and the Tchamides several septs of orthodox Christians retained the privilege of bearing arms, even to the time of Ali of Joannina.

The Albanian aristocracy embraced Mohammedanism in the fifteenth century, but a considerable portion of the people did not apostatize until the end of the seventeenth century. Their conversion was caused by their desire to escape the tribute of Christian children, which compelled them to furnish recruits to the corps of janissaries and to the slaves of the

---

[1] Thucydides, ii. 68; Strabo, vii. p. 326.

sultan's household. As among the Greeks, apostasy was common among the higher classes at the time of the first irruptions of the Othomans, and a large proportion of the Albanian chiefs retained their property by changing their religion. Some of the Albanian beys, however, claim descent from the Othoman Turks who accompanied Sultan Bayezid I. and Murad II. in their expeditions, and there can be no doubt that Mohammed II. made some grants of lands and conceded high offices in Albania to several Turks. But, in most cases, the claim to Turkish descent rests only on a tradition that the ancestor of the present bey received a sandjak or some military fief from one of the sultans already mentioned; and, in nine cases out of ten, these grants were the rewards of apostasy, not of previous service. Like the Byzantine nobles at the time of conquest, the morality of the Albanian chiefs was such that they were not likely to become more wicked by becoming Mussulmans. Their change of religion was little more than a change of name and their marriage with three additional wives. The ties of family and tribe existed without modification, and they attest that the chieftains and the people of Albania have a common origin.

The whole of Albania, from the Gulf of Arta to the Lake of Skodra, is divided into innumerable lateral valleys by rugged mountains, which render the communications so difficult as to confine trade to a few lines of transport. The agricultural population is thinly scattered in these valleys, and, as in most parts of Turkey, those who cultivate the soil, even when they are Mussulmans, are considered as forming an inferior grade of society. But there is nothing to prevent the peasant, since he is free, from adopting a military life, and rising to wealth and power. In general, however, the soil is cultivated from generation to generation by the same families, and for centuries it has been cultivated with the same routine. From each yoke of land (zevgari) the landlord receives a rent paid in produce. The peculiarities of Albanian society are most marked in the manner of life among those who are the proprietors of the soil. All of this class consider that they are born to carry arms. The great landlords are captains and leaders. The peasant-proprietors are soldiers or brigands. Landlords, whether large or small, possess flocks, which supply them with milk, cheese, and wool, olive-trees which furnish them with olives and oil, and fruit-trees which enable them to vary their diet. Every landlord who was rich enough to lay up considerable supplies in his storehouses expended them in maintaining as many armed followers as possible, and if his relations were numerous, and his phara or clan warlike, he became a chieftain of some political importance. Every Albanian who can avoid working for his livelihood goes constantly armed, so that whenever the central authority was weak bloody feuds were prevalent. And at the commencement of the present century anarchy appeared to be the normal condition of Albanian society; Gueghs, Tosks, tribes, septs, pharas, towns, and villages were engaged in unceasing hostilities; open wars were waged, and extensive alliances were formed, in defiance of the power of the pashas and of the authority of the sultan.

Most of the towns were divided into clusters of houses called makhalas, generally separated from one another by ravines. Each makhala was inhabited by a phara, which was a social division resembling a clan, but usually smaller. The warlike habits of the Albanians were displayed even in their town life. Large houses stood apart, surrounded by walled enclosures flanked by small towers. Within these feeble imitations of feudal castles there was always a well-stocked magazine of provisions. Richly caparisoned steeds occupied the court during the day; lean, muscular, and greedy-eyed soldiers, covered with embroidered dresses and ornamented arms, lounged at the gate; and from an open gallery the proprietor watched the movements of his neighbours, smoking his long tchibouk amidst his select friends. The wealthy chieftain lived like his warlike followers. His only luxuries were more splendid arms, finer horses, and a longer pipe His pride was in a numerous band of well-armed attendants.

The Christian population of Albania diminished from age to age. The anarchy that prevailed during the latter half of the eighteenth century drove many to apostasy and many into exile. Colonies of Albanian Christians emigrated to the kingdom of Naples in the fifteenth century, and these emigrants were recruited in the sixteenth by numbers who fled from the burden of severe taxation, the exaction of unpaid labour, and the terrible tribute of Christian children. So many Christians sold their property, that the sultans were alarmed at the diminution of the capitation tax, and the difficulty of finding the necessary recruits for the janissaries and the bostanjis. This commenced so early, that Suleiman the Magnificent enacted that no Christian proprietor should be allowed to sell his land, if the sale tended to diminish these sources of the Othoman power. If a rayah disposed of his land or ceased to cultivate it, the spahi or timariot of the village was authorized to grant it to another family for cultivation. But no laws can arrest the progress of depopulation, as the history of the Roman empire testifies. Emigration continued, and when emigration was impossible, apostasy increased. At the commencement of the present century even the Greek clergy admitted that Mohammedanism was rapidly extending in parts of Albania which had previously adhered steadfastly to the Christian faith.

The administrative divisions of Albania have varied at different periods of Othoman history, but the positions of Skodra, Berat, and Joannina have rendered these cities the residence of pashas, to whom the rulers of the districts of Elbassan, Dukadjin, Delvino, and Tchamuria have generally been subordinate. These three pashaliks have been held by viziers or pashas of the highest rank. Many districts, Mohammedan, Catholic, and orthodox, enjoyed a recognized local semi-independence, protected by the sultan. Any common interest united pharas, makhalas, towns, communities, and beys in hostile array against a pasha, and even against the authority of the sultan. But when no danger existed of any external attack on their privileges, local feuds and intestine wars revived as fiercely as ever.

The power and influence of the Albanians steadily increased in the Othoman empire. In the East, the sword alone commands popular respect and political influence. During the last century, as the turbulence of the janissaries increased and their military value declined, the Albanians rose in consideration and power. In every province of European Turkey the Othoman race seemed to decline in courage as well as in wealth and number. The Albanians everywhere seized the military power when it escaped from the hands of the Turks. Every pasha enrolled a guard of Albanian mercenaries, in order to intimidate the ayans and Turkish landlords in his pashalik. The tendency of the Othoman government towards centralization had already commenced, though it still remained almost imperceptible amidst the existing anarchy. The Albanian mercenaries were used as instruments to advance this centralization; and the power they attained being more apparent than the end for which they were employed, even the Turks, who have always affected military tastes and habits, became imitators of the Albanians. At the commencement of this century, the Greeks from day to day feared the Turks less and the Albanians more.

The history of the Greek Revolution would often be obscure unless the importance of the Albanian element, which pervaded military society in the Othoman empire, be fully appreciated. A trifling but striking mark of the high position which the Albanians had gained was exhibited by the general adoption of their dress. Though a strong antipathy to the Mussulman Albanians had been always felt by the Othoman Turks, towards the end of the last century they began to pay an involuntary homage to the warlike reputation of the Albanian mercenaries. It became then not uncommon, in Greece and Macedonia, to see the children of the proudest Osmanlis dressed in the fustanella, or white kilt of the Tosks. Subsequently, when Veli Pasha, the second son of Ali of Joannina, governed the Morea[1], even young Greeks of rank ventured to assume this dress, particularly when travelling, as it afforded them an opportunity of wearing arms. The Greek armatoli and the Christians employed as police-guards, even in the Morea, also wore this dress; but it was the fame of the Albanians—for the military reputation of the armatoli was then on the decline and that of the Suliots on the ascendant—which induced the modern Greeks to adopt the Albanian kilt as their national costume. It is in consequence of this admiration of Albanianism that the court of King Otho assumes its melo-dramatic aspect, and glitters in tawdry tinsel mimicry of the rich and splendid garb which arrested

---

[1] Veli was pasha of the Morea from 1807 to 1812.

the attention of Childe Harold in the galleries of the palace of Tepelen; but the calico fustanella hangs round the legs of the Greeks like a paper petticoat, while the white kilt of the Tosk, formed of a strong product of native looms, fell in the graceful folds of antique drapery.

The relations of Mussulman and Christian Albanians were much more friendly than the relations of Albanians and Turks. The Albanian, unlike the Greek, felt the bonds of nationality stronger than those of religion. The hostile feelings with which he regarded the Othomans originated in the tyranny of Turkish pashas and the avarice of Turkish voivodes, cadis, and mollahs. Against the oppression of these aliens the natives, whether Mussulmans or Christians, had for many generations acted in common.

On the other hand, where orthodox Albanians and Greeks dwelt together, as in a considerable portion of southern Epirus, their common lot as Christians exposed them to the same exactions, and effaced the distinction of race. The obstinacy of the Albanian and the cunning of the Greek were employed for the same object, and exhibited themselves more as individual peculiarities than as national characteristics.

The power of the Albanians in Greece was greatly increased by the employment of a large force to suppress the insurrection excited by the Russians in 1770. Numbers of Albanian mercenaries maintained themselves for nine years in a state of merely nominal dependence on the pasha of the province, levying contributions from Turks and Greeks alike, and setting the authority of the sultan at defiance. They were at last defeated near Tripolitza by Hassan Ghazi, the great capitan-pasha, and almost exterminated; but fresh bands of Albanians were again poured into the Morea by the sultan during the Russian war in 1787, for it was well known that the Greeks regarded these rapacious mountaineers with far greater terror than Turkish troops.

It was at this time that Ali Pasha became dervendji, and about the same period all the pashas in European Turkey greatly augmented the number of Albanian mercenaries in their service. This demand for Albanian soldiers, which had gone on increasing for at least two generations, gave a considerable impulse to population; and so many of these mercenaries returned to their native villages enriched by foreign service, that a visible improvement took place in the well-being of the people about the time Ali was appointed to the pashalik of Joannina.

The policy of Ali Pasha was to centralize all power in his own hands. He followed the plans of his predecessors, Suleiman and Kurd, in depressing the armatoli; and he commenced a series of measures tending to weaken the influence of the Othoman Turks holding property in those parts of Greece and Macedonia subjected to his authority. His immediate object was to weaken the power of the sultan; the direct result of his conduct was to improve the position of the Greek race; for much of the authority previously exercised by the Othomans in civil and fiscal business passed into the hands of the Greeks, and not into those of the Mussulman Albanians, whose military authority Ali was constantly extending.

The Turks in Greece and Macedonia were a haughty, ignorant, and lazy race; but as spahis, timariots, or janissaries, they were affiliated with the most influential classes in the Othoman empire, and Ali did not venture to attack them openly. Their pride of race, as well as their personal interests, rendered them the irreconcilable enemies of the independent authority which he desired to establish. He therefore carried on an incessant war against them; but he conducted this warfare as a series of personal affairs. He strove to conceal his general policy, but he spared no secret intrigue to gain his ends, and often resorted to assassination as the speediest and most effectual means. He usually commenced his operations against his enemies by what Bentham calls vituperative personalities; and by imputing bad designs as a proof of bad character, he generally succeeded in fomenting family quarrels, for Turks are childishly credulous. He also encouraged the Greeks to complain of acts of injustice, and then, as the representative of the sultan's despotism, he judged the accused. If no other means could be found, he accused powerful beys of treasonable conduct, pretending that they held secret communications with the rebel pashas, then proscribed by the Porte; or with bands of klephts, who were as much a domestic institution in his pashalik as they have since been in King Otho's kingdom. In this way he rarely failed to obtain a warrant from the sultan sanctioning the execution of his enemy. By pursuing this policy steadily for more than a quarter of a century, most of the Osmanlis in Thessaly were impoverished, and several of the principal families ruined. The towns everywhere showed signs of decay; the best houses in the Turkish quarters were often tenanted by Greek or Vallach traders, or occupied by Albanian officers.

While the wealth and numbers of the Turkish race diminished, Ali took care to invest his own Albanian followers with the military authority he wrung from the hands of the Osmanlis; but the increasing influence of the Albanian race during the early part of the present century was not confined to the increase in the numbers and power of the Mussulman soldiery, nor to the augmentation of the commercial enterprise of the maritime population of Hydra and Spetzas. Several warlike Christian tribes still retained the privilege of bearing arms in Albania. In northern Albania these tribes were Catholic, but in southern Albania they were orthodox; and among the orthodox the Suliots were pre-eminent for their warlike qualities, even among the warlike population by which they were surrounded.

The Suliots were a branch of the Tchamides, one of the three great divisions of the Tosks. The constitution of their community deserves notice. The Suliots inhabited a district consisting of steep ranges of bare and precipitous mountains, overlooking the course of the Acheron; that river, uniting with the Cocytus in its lower course, forms a marshy lake, and renders the country at its mouth so unhealthy that it was considered the shortest road to the realms beyond the grave. In the immediate vicinity of Suli the mountains afford only a scanty pasture for goats; but when they ascend, broad ridges spread out covered with oaks; and when they rise still higher, their loftier summits protrude in rocky peaks above forests of pine.

The strength of Suli lay in the difficulty of approaching it with a large body of men, and of attacking well-trained riflemen in stone buildings without artillery. The deep and dark ravine of the Acheron renders Suli inaccessible in front. The lair of the Suliots lies imbedded in a lateral valley covered by two rocky hills, where a confluent joins the black waters of the Acheron[1]. The approach is by a gorge lower down, called Kleisura, which separates the mountain fastnesses from the fertile plains. Under the Byzantine emperors it appears that the rich and well-watered soil of the lower valleys maintained a numerous population. The district was once a bishop's see, whose cathedral church stood near the entrance of the Kleisura. At present the former population is represented by the Mussulman proprietors of Paramythia and Margariti.

When Sultan Murad II. conquered Joannina, the whole country, to the shores of the Ionian Sea, submitted to Mussulman domination. The territory afterwards occupied by the Suliots was granted as a military fief to a timariot, who resided at Joannina. Christian liberty and Suliot independence were in this district the growth of later years. For centuries the Christians paid haratch and the tribute of their children. The anarchy that prevailed during the victorious campaigns of the Venetians under Morosini, and the cession of the Morea by the treaty of Carlovitz in 1699, compelled many Christians to form armed companies for their protection against lawless bands of brigands. As the orthodox Greeks were at that time generally as little disposed to oppose the sultan's government as they were to unite with the Catholic Venetians, the pashas of Albania and northern Greece favoured the military ardour of the orthodox communities. Some of the companies of armed Christians, which have been confounded with the ancient armatoli, date only from this period, and the community of the Suliots cannot be traced to an earlier origin.

In the year 1730 the number of Suliot families which enjoyed the privilege of bearing arms was estimated at one hundred. The precise year when the right was officially recognized by the pasha of Joannina is not known. The armed Suliots were the guards of a small Christian district over which they exercised the authority of feudal superiors. Their own property was small, but they formed a military caste, and despised all labour as much as the proudest Mussulman. The soil in the richest portion of their territory was cultivated by peasants, who were of the Greek race. The

---

[1] [The ravine of the Acheron is dark, but its waters are singularly white. ED.]

name of Suliots was reserved for the Albanian warriors, who ruled and protected the agricultural population like the ancient Spartans. The peasants were distinguished by the name of the village in which they dwelt.

Anarchy prevailed in the greater part of southern Albania during the early part of the eighteenth century, and many Christians of the tribe of the Tchamides took refuge with the Suliot community. Its protection prevented the Mussulman communities in the neighbourhood from encroaching on the rights of any Christians who acknowledged themselves its vassals. But about the middle of the century they extended this protection so far as to become involved in feuds with their Mussulman neighbours. The hostilities which ensued induced the Suliots to recruit their force by admitting every daring and active young Christian of the tribe of the Tchamides to serve in their ranks. If any of these volunteers distinguished himself by his courage, and was fortunate enough to gain booty as well as honour, he was admitted a member of the Suliot community, and allowed to marry a maiden of Suli. In this way the community increased in numbers and in power. It was favoured by the sultan's government, as a check on the lawless independence of the Mussulman communities of Paramythia and Margariti; and it was supplied with arms and ammunition, and encouraged to defend its independence, by the Venetian governors of Parga and Prevesa.

Many attacks were made on Suli by the Mussulman agas of the vicinity, but they were always repulsed with such success that the Suliots gradually acquired the reputation of being the best warriors among the warlike Tosks.

The state of Suli now became an epitome of the state of Albania. The community was divided into pharas. The chiefs of the pharas formed alliances abroad in order to increase their influence at home, and the pharas were sometimes involved in civil broils. The assistance of the principal pharas was often solicited and richly remunerated by the neighbouring Mussulmans in their private feuds. The Suliot leaders, like the other Albanian chiefs of pharas, collected as many armed followers as possible; but their revenues were scanty, and the constitution of the Suliot community was democratic, so that the only way to reward followers was to make successful forays on the lands of those neighbours who

ALI PASHA AND THE SULIOTS.

refused to purchase immunity from depredation. Like most highlanders who dwell on barren mountains overlooking fertile plains, they levied contributions with unsparing rapacity whenever they could do so with impunity. Depredation they honoured with the name of war, and war they considered to be the only honourable occupation for a true Suliot. The poverty of the territory which the Suliots held in property, and their numbers, compared with the revenues of the district over which their protection extended, rendered it impossible for them to subsist in idleness without plundering their neighbours.

When Ali Pasha assumed the government of Joannina, in the year 1788, many complaints were made of the lawless conduct of the Suliots. Shortly before his nomination, they had pushed their forays into the plain of Joannina, and rendered themselves so unpopular that Ali deemed they were not likely to find any allies. In pursuance of his policy of centralizing all power in his own hands, he resolved to destroy the independent communities in his pashalik, whether Mussulman or Christian. Prudence required him to commence with the Christians, and circumstances appeared to favour his operations against the Suliots. But when he attacked them, all their neighbours were alarmed, recent injuries were forgiven, and new alliances were formed. Mussulman beys and the Venetian governors of Parga and Prevesa supplied them secretly with aid, and the first attacks of Ali on their territory were repulsed without much difficulty.

The intrigues of Russian agents drew the attention of the sultan to the affairs of Suli in 1792, and Selim III. ordered Ali to renew his attacks on a spot which was now looked on at the Porte as a nest of treason, as well as a nursery of brigandage. Russia having abandoned her orthodox partizans at the peace of Yassi, Ali again attacked the Suliots. Their power was now so great that Suli formed a little republic. Upwards of sixty villages and hamlets, inhabited by Christian peasants, paid tribute to the Suliots. That tribute, it is true, consisted only of a small portion of the produce of the soil. The Suliot territory at this time extended over all the mountain district on both sides of the Acheron, as far as the western bank of the Charadra. But the community of Suliots consisted of only 450 families, divided into nineteen pharas, or unions of families. The military force did not exceed 1500 men. Local disputes were violent among the chiefs of the pharas, and the inextinguishable jealousies of Albanian society had caused the Suliots to divide their habitations into four distinct villages or makhalas, called Kako Suli, Kiapha, Avariko, and Samoneva. The name of Kako Suli recalls that of Kakoilion, in the *Odyssey*[1]. It was a name of terror in Albania, as well as of hate and evil omen.

The attack of Ali on Suli, in the year 1792, failed completely. His numbers enabled him to force the Kleisura from the south, and to gain temporary possession of Kako Suli by assault. But the troops of the pasha were unable to keep the position they had won, and their loss in the vain attempt was so severe that, in retreating from the village, they abandoned all their advanced positions in the valley. Many beys were deserted by their followers, others quitted Ali's camp, and the desertion became so general that he himself returned hastily to Joannina. His hostilities lasted only three weeks; but the activity and daring displayed by the Suliots in the incessant skirmishing which they carried on, added greatly to their military reputation. Unfortunately, their confidence in their own powers became from this time so overweening that they pursued a more selfish policy than before. They began to fancy that their alliance was a matter of importance to the Emperor of Russia and the Republic of Venice, and they exercised their authority over the Christians in their territory with increased severity, and plundered their Mussulman neighbours with greater rapacity.

In the mean time, the power of Ali increased steadily. He seized the wealth of many rich agas, he murdered many powerful beys, and he reduced several independent communities to subjection. In the spring of 1798 he gained possession of the territory of one of the Christian communities from which the Albanian regiments in the Neapolitan service had drawn their recruits. Ali surprised Nivitza, on the coast of Chimara, with the assistance of the French general who

---

[1] [This comparison is hardly suitable. Kakoilios, the appellation of Troy in the Odyssey, signifies 'ill-fated Ilium,' and was applied to the city after its destruction; whereas Kako Suli, or 'Suli the terrible,' was so called from the terror its inhabitants inspired into the neighbouring Mohammedan tribes. ED.]

commanded at Corfu, in the most treacherous manner; and when he gained possession of the place, he put all the inhabitants to the sword with his usual cruelty. In the autumn of the same year he repaid the French for the criminal concessions they had made to win his favour, by obeying the sultan's orders, and driving them from their possessions in the south of Epirus. After defeating their forces at Nicopolis, he compelled them to surrender the fortresses of Prevesa and Vonitza.

Ali once more turned his arms against the Suliots, whose intrigues with Russia and France had excited the indignation of the sultan and the alarm of the Mussulman population of southern Albania. He now employed secret treachery as a more effectual means of victory than open hostility. The rivalries and dissensions of the pharas enabled him to gain over several chiefs, who entered his service as mercenary soldiers. He also contrived to seize and retain several members of the Suliot families who opposed his schemes, as hostages, at Joannina. Photo Djavella, the most powerful Suliot, became his partizan; and George Botzaris, with all his phara, entered his service, and was employed to guard the lands of the Mussulman and Christian cultivators of the soil, lying between the Suliot territory and the plain of Joannina, from the forays of their countrymen. By this defection the community lost the services of seventy families, and of about a hundred good soldiers.

Hostilities were commenced in 1799. George Botzaris commenced operations by attacking the advanced post of his countrymen at Redovuni with a body of two hundred Christian troops in Ali's service, but he was completely defeated, and died shortly after. As usual in similar cases of treachery and sudden death, report said that he was poisoned. Report, however, said that most of the deaths in the dominions of Ali Pasha at this time were caused by poison, so that if these reports deserve credit, the trade in deleterious drugs must have formed a flourishing branch of commerce in the pashalik of Joannina.

Treason is contagious, and Ali did everything in his power to propagate the contagion. He made high offers to most of the Suliot chiefs, but his faithlessness was too notorious for him to gain many partizans. At last he addressed himself to the whole community. He declared that he was resolved to repress all depredations; and as it was difficult for the Suliots to obtain the means of subsistence in their mountains, he invited them to emigrate to fertile lands which he offered to cede to them. If they refused his offer, he threatened them with implacable hatred, incessant hostilities, and inevitable extermination. To the chiefs of the pharas he made secret offers of money and pensions to those who would quit Suli. His offers were rejected, for it was evident that his object was only to sow dissension among the people, and prevent the chiefs from acting cordially together.

The experience Ali had gained by his defeat in 1792, prevented his making any attempt to storm the stronghold of the Suliots a second time. During 1799 and 1800 he confined his operations to circumscribing the forays of the Suliots, by occupying a number of strong positions, which he fortified with care. In this way he succeeded in shutting them up within narrow limits. The Suliots at this time were unpopular, and neither the Christian cultivators of the soil, nor the Greeks in general, showed much sympathy with their cause. Indeed, many Greek captains of armatoli served against them in the army of Ali.

In the summer of 1801, hunger began to be severely felt at Suli, and numbers of women and children were removed to Parga, from whence they were conveyed to Corfu, which was then occupied by the Russians, by whom they were well received. To prevent further communications with Parga, which was now the only friendly spot in Epirus, the pasha strengthened his posts to the westward; and to deprive the Suliots of all hope of assistance from the orthodox, he induced the Greek clergy to declare against them. Ignatius, the metropolitan of Arta, wrote a circular to his clergy forbidding the Christians in his diocese affording the Suliots any assistance, under pain of excommunication. Ali himself dictated a letter to the bishop of Paramythia, in the name of his superior the metropolitan of Joannina, ordering him to employ all his spiritual influence against the Suliots as a predatory and rebellious tribe [1].

The final struggle took place in 1803. The sultan supposed, not without some reason, that Ali connived at the

---

[1] Col. Leake has published this letter: *Travels in Northern Greece*, i. 513.

THE FINAL STRUGGLE.

prolongation of the war; for it seemed impossible that the Suliots could have resisted the power of the pasha of Joannina for more than four years, if that power had been vigorously employed. Information having been transmitted to Constantinople that the Suliots had procured considerable supplies of ammunition from French ships, the Porte sent peremptory orders to Ali to press the siege of Suli with greater activity. Hitherto the Suliots, attended by their wives, had often passed through the lines of the besieging force during the night, and plundered distant villages. The booty and provisions obtained in these expeditions were carried back by the women, who were accustomed to transport heavy burdens on their shoulders over paths impracticable to mules. New posts and additional vigilance cut off this resource.

The hero of Suli was a priest named Samuel, who had assumed the strange cognomen of 'The Last Judgment.' It was said that he was an Albanian from the northern part of the island of Andros; but he appears to have concealed his origin, for a hero in the East must be surrounded with a halo of mystery, though Samuel may have wished to erase from his memory everything connected with the past, in order to devote his soul to the contest with the Mussulmans, which he considered to be his chief duty on earth. He was an enthusiast in his mission; and as he was doing the work of Christ, he cared little for the excommunication of servile Greek bishops. The Suliots, who generally regarded every stranger with suspicion, received Samuel, when he first came among them as a mysterious guest, with respect and awe. At last, in the hour of peril, they elected him, though a priest and a stranger, to be their military chief. Religious fervour was the pervading impulse of his soul. His virtue as a man, his valour as a soldier, his prudence when the interest of the community was concerned, and his utter abnegation of every selfish object, caused him to be generally recognized by the soldiers of all the pharas as the common chief, without any formal election. His personal conduct remained unchanged by the rank accorded to him, and, except in the council and the field, he was still the simple priest. As he never assumed any superiority over the chiefs of the pharas, his influence excited no jealousy.

On the 3rd of September 1803, the troops of Ali gained

possession of the village of Kako Suli, in consequence of the treachery of Pylio Gousi, who admitted two hundred Mussulman Albanians into his house and barn during the night. Gousi sold his country for the paltry sum of twelve purses, then equal to about £300 sterling, which was paid to him by Veli Pasha, Ali's second son, who conducted the siege. The traitor pretended that his object was to obtain the release of his son-in-law, who was retained by Ali as a prisoner at Joannina. He considered affection to his own family an apology for treason to his country, but he took care to receive its price in money. About the same time, another Suliot, named Koutzonika, also deserted the cause of his countrymen. The defence of the Suliot territory was now hopeless.

One of the two hills which cover the approach to the ravine of Suli, called Bira, had been abandoned by the phara of Zervas two months before the treason of Gousi. Treachery placed the besiegers in possession of Kako Suli and Avariko. The second hill, called Kughni, and the village of Kiapha, were the only strongholds left to the Suliots.

Samuel had charge of the magazines on Kughni, and the position was defended by three hundred families. The men guarded the accessible paths, posted behind low parapets of stone called meteris, and the women carried water and provisions to these intrenchments under the fire of the besiegers, who treated them as combatants. The number of women slain and wounded during the defence of Kughni was consequently proportionably great. The little garrison dug holes in the ground under the shelter of rocks, and these holes when roofed with pine-trees, thick layers of branches, and well-beaten earth, formed a tolerable protection from the feeble artillery of the pasha's army.

Ali was extremely anxious to secure the persons of several Suliot chiefs. The indulgence of his revenge was one of his greatest pleasures. He therefore ordered Veli to treat with Photo Djavella, determined, if he could find an opportunity of seizing any of the Suliot chiefs, to violate the treaty which his son might have concluded. A capitulation was signed on the 12th of December 1803, by which the Suliots surrendered Kughni and Kiapha to Veli Pasha; and Djavella, Drako and Zerva, with their pharas, were allowed to retire to Parga. Ali in the mean time sent orders to place an ambuscade on the road to Parga, and seize the Suliot chiefs; but the agas of Paramythia, and some of the armatoli in Veli's army, hearing of the movement, sent secret warning to the Suliots, who, by a rapid march and a sudden change of route at the point of danger, baffled the treacherous designs of the pasha.

Samuel refused to trust to any capitulation with Ali or his sons, whom he knew no oath could bind. The fall of Suli seemed to terminate his mission. When the Suliots quitted the hill of Kughni, he retired into the powder-magazine with a lighted match, declaring that no infidel should ever employ ammunition intrusted to his care against Christians, and he perished in the explosion.

The selfish Suliots who had concluded separate treaties with Ali Pasha—Botzaris, Koutzonika[1], and Palaska—obtained nothing but disgrace by abandoning their countrymen. They had taken up their residence at Zalongo under a promise of protection, but Ali, as soon as he gained possession of Kiapha, sent a body of troops to attack them by surprise. About one hundred and fifty persons were seized and reduced to the condition of slaves. Twenty-five men were killed defending themselves, and six men and twenty-two women threw themselves over a precipice behind the village, to avoid falling into the hands of their inhuman persecutor. Albanian soldiers, on returning to Joannina, declared that they saw several young women throw their children from the rock, and then spring down themselves. The bodies of four children were found below. Botzaris succeeded in collecting together about two hundred persons, and the resistance he and his companions offered to their assailants enabled this body to escape. The soldiers of Ali were not so bloody-minded as the pasha. After some skirmishing, Botzaris was allowed to retire with the women and

---

[1] The treachery of Botzaris and Koutzonika is mentioned in a popular song on the fall of Suli:—

Μπρὲ ν' ἀνάθεμά σε Μπότζαρη,
Καὶ 'σένα Κουτζονίκα·
Μὲ τὴν δουλιὰν ποῦ κάμεταν
Τοῦτο τὸ καλοκαίρι.

Heaven's curse on you, O Botzaris!
And you too, Koutzonika!
Sad was the work you did
This summer.

The song is printed in Leake's *Researches in Greece*, p. 159.

children to Parga. But the cruelty of Ali was insatiable. He ordered Suliot families, who were living dispersed in different places, to be murdered; and he sent seventy families, who had surrendered at the commencement of hostilities, and whom he had treated with kindness until Suli capitulated, to inhabit the most unhealthy spots in his pashalik.

The Suliots who escaped to Parga passed over into the Ionian Islands, where they were hospitably received by the Russians. Many entered the Russian service; but when the treaty of Tilsit transferred the possession of the Ionian Islands to France, most of the Suliots passed from the Russian into the French service. Only a few who, like Palaska, were unpopular for their conduct during the fall of Suli, quitted Corfu with the Russians.

Ali Pasha constructed a strong fort at Kiapha, and converted the church of St. Donatos, the patron saint of Suli, into a mosque. A few Mussulman Albanians, from the pasha's native town of Tepelen, were established as guards of the district instead of the Suliots. The Christian peasants returned to cultivate the soil, and for several years they found the agents of the pasha less exacting and rapacious masters than the proud and needy Suliots.

The only Christian communities in southern Albania which now preserved the right of bearing arms, were the inhabitants of some mountain villages amidst the barren rocks of Chimara.

Such was the position of the orthodox Christians of the Albanian race, in the pashalik of Joannina, when Ali Pasha was declared a rebel by Sultan Mahmud.

CHAPTER III.

SULTAN MAHMUD AND ALI PASHA OF JOANNINA.

Character of Sultan Mahmud.—State of the Othoman Empire.—Ali Pasha of Joannina.—Ali's cruelty.—Anecdote of Euphrosyne.—Anecdotes of the Bishop of Grevena, and of Ignatius, metropolitan of Arta.—Destruction of Khormovo and of Gardhiki.—Sultan Mahmud alarmed at Ali's power.—Ali's attempt to assassinate Ismael Pasha Bey.—Ali declared a rebel.—Plans and forces of Ali.—Sultan's means of attack.—Ali convokes a divan.—Both belligerents appeal to the Greeks.—Operations against Ali.—He is deserted by his sons.—Recall of the Suliots to Albania.—They join Ali.—Khurshid named Seraskier.—Condition of the Suliots on their return.—Their military system.—Operations in 1821.—Conduct of Khurshid before Joannina.—Compared with that of Philip V. of Macedon.—Suliots join the cause of the Greeks.—Mission of Tahir Abbas to the Greeks.—Death of Ali.

IN the year 1820, the Othoman empire seemed to be on the eve of dissolution. Ali Pasha was in open rebellion at the head of a warlike nation, and with reasonable hope of establishing an independent throne in Albania. An insurrection of the Greeks was also awaited with some anxiety by almost every Christian in the Levant, excepting the English consuls.

Sultan Mahmud II. then ruled Turkey. He ascended the throne in the year 1808, in his twenty-fifth year, after a series of revolutions at Constantinople, caused by the attempts of his cousin, Sultan Selim III., to reform the public administration, and introduce military discipline in the corps of janissaries. Selim, who was dethroned in 1807, had neither energy nor talent. His successor, Mustapha IV., lost his crown and life, after murdering his cousin Selim in order to retain them, by a revolution that seated his younger brother Mahmud on the throne.

Mahmud II. had reigned twelve years; yet few of his subjects were acquainted with his personal character. The fate of his cousin and brother warned him that it would be dangerous to attempt reforming the abuses which, if they remained unreformed, would inevitably cause the dissolution of the Othoman empire at no very distant day. Mahmud revolved the condition of his empire, and the difficulties of his own position, constantly in his mind, and he persuaded himself that, in order to restore vigour to his empire, it was necessary to begin by centralizing all power in his own hands. His own prudence, and the seclusion of the serai, enabled him to conceal his ambitious projects, while the iron firmness of his character enabled him to perfect the design which for years he was compelled to keep in abeyance.

The personal appearance of Mahmud may be known to many from the numerous portraits, which represent it with tolerable accuracy. His face was sallow, and his beard, naturally dark, was artificially stained of a shining black. His expression was that of sombre melancholy rather than of stern severity; it was repellent, though not offensive. There was, however, something so artificial in his whole appearance in public, that a physiognomist might have been baffled by the unvarying mask with which Othoman etiquette clothes a sultan's countenance. He was of middle stature; but as, like most Turks, he had short legs, he appeared tall when on horseback or when seated.

Sultan Mahmud was long deemed a cruel and bloodthirsty tyrant, and death was for many years the lightest punishment he ever inflicted. It was said that he ordered all the females of his brother's harem to be thrown into the Bosphorus, and few travellers entered the court of the serai without seeing a head or a pile of ears and noses exposed in the niches at the gate. Dead bodies hanging from shop-fronts, or stretched across the pathway of a narrow street, were sights of daily occurrence, and proved that the sultan was indifferent to human suffering and regardless of human life. Yet he was really neither cruel nor bloodthirsty. The terrible punishments he inflicted were the result of habit and policy, not of passion. When his absolute power was firmly established, he ceased to inflict the cruel punishments which he had employed as a means of intimidation. The administration of his latter years was comparatively mild. Now, certainly, innate cruelty could not, after long indulgence, have assumed the mask of humanity; but policy may render a prince either cruel or merciful as he deems it expedient for his purpose. The fact is, that Mahmud, though he possessed little sympathy with humanity, restrained and ultimately subdued the Oriental ferocity which had from time immemorial formed a characteristic of the government of the Sublime Porte. When we count the number of lives sacrificed by public executions in the early years of his reign, it must not be forgotten that the power of life and death was then vested not only in the grand-vizier and the provincial pashas, but was also intrusted to the governors of petty fortresses, and to the captains of single frigates. Sultan Mahmud was a thoughtful, stern, and obstinate man, whose strongest characteristic was an inflexible will, not violent passions. The restraint with which he long suppressed his feelings, and the patience with which he waited for opportunities of carrying his plans into execution, misled many acute observers into the belief that he was a weak prince. Ali Pasha of Joannina was one of those who mistook the character of his master.

Few European statesmen in 1820 believed that it was possible to arrest the decline of the Othoman empire; many expected its immediate dissolution. Yet some competent authorities asserted that the reorganization of the sultan's administration was not an impracticable enterprise in the hands of an able and energetic sultan, and that its success would restore strength to the Othoman empire[1]. Both foreign relations and internal affairs, however, presented great difficulties to a reformer. Turkey was not comprehended in the general system of territorial guarantees established by the treaty of Vienna. This circumstance favoured the Russians in their schemes of aggrandizement, and the Greeks in their projects of revolution.

The Mussulman population of European Turkey was visibly declining both in wealth and number. This decline commenced when the Othomans ceased to recruit their ranks with tribute-children, slaves captured in war, and apostates. By some inexplicable social law, a dominant race almost invariably consumes life and riches more rapidly than it supplies them. In the wide extended empire of the sultan

---

[1] See some observations on this subject in the *Discours Préliminaire* of D'Ohsson's *Tableau Général de l'Empire Othoman*, p. ix. fol. edit.

the whole military service was performed by the Mussulmans, and in all foreign wars and domestic hostilities the loss always fell heaviest on the Turkish race. The prejudices of a warlike people prevented the Othomans from engaging in those occupations in which wealth is most securely accumulated; and if they were not entirely an aristocratic class, they were invariably a privileged caste of the population.

The long duration of the Othoman empire in Europe is a historical marvel. No other government ever combined so much political wisdom with so great a mass of social corruption. Taxation was always oppressive to the agricultural population, justice was corrupt, so that in these two departments the Mussulmans suffered as much from the vices of the administration as the Christians. Yet, with all its defects, the sultan's government retained hostile races and rival religions in daily intercourse without dangerous collisions, and ruled subject nations for generations without goading them to rebellion. Its peculiar feature was, that it always remained disconnected from every nation and race in its dominions. The sway of the sultan was not politically more closely identified with the supremacy of the Turkish than of the Arabic race. The theory of the government, even as late as the year 1820, was, that Sultan Mahmud was the despotic master of the empire, and that viziers and pashas exercised their authority in his name as his household slaves.

The empire seemed to be perishing from tyranny and weakness. Its tyranny had produced universal discontent, and among the Christians an eager desire to throw off its yoke. Its weakness invited ambitious pashas and lawless tribes to live in open rebellion. In some provinces the sultan's authority was lost. Algiers, Tunis, and Tripoli were virtually independent. Egypt had been so under the Mamelukes; and under Mohammed Ali its allegiance was still doubtful. Syria, Servia, Bosnia, and a part of Bulgaria, had been recently in a state of revolt. The Kurds of Armenia and the Arabs of Mesopotamia paid the sultan only a nominal allegiance. Ali Pasha of Joannina had long acted as an independent vassal, and had been treated as a sovereign both by France and England. Many Derébeys, whose castles commanded only a single valley, claimed a kind of feudal independence, on the ground that they held their lands from the time of the Seljouk empire, in Asia Minor, on the tenure of military service alone. The janissaries and the ulema, in Constantinople, were not more loyal than the feudal chieftains in the distant provinces. Anarchy and rebellion prognosticated to statesmen the inevitable and near fall of the empire. Omens and prophecies were cited as evidence that the fall was near by the people. The Greeks revived the prophecies which their ancestors had repeated when the Belgian Baldwin became master of Constantinople and was proclaimed Emperor of the East. Alexander I. of Russia was the *flavus Rex*, and the Turks represented the corrupted Greeks of the Byzantine empire.

The voice of nations attributed to Ali Pasha of Joannina the energy and talent which sultan Mahmud was supposed to want. His policy had increased the power of the Albanian race, and to the careless observer it appeared to rest on the firm adherence of a warlike nation. The Greeks were thriving in his dominions, and appeared satisfied with his government. Political speculators proclaimed that his independence would soon be established by a successful rebellion.

Ali was a type of the Albanian character. With all his energy and activity he was a mere savage. He was borne forward to power by circumstances whose current he followed, but which he was unable to control or guide. As a ruler he exhibited the qualities of an astute Albanian chieftain corrupted by exercising the despotic authority of a Turkish pasha.

The ancestors of Ali were Christians, who embraced Mohammedanism in the fifteenth century; though to Osmanlis and strangers he sometimes pretended that he was descended from a Turk of Brusa who had received a ziamet from Sultan Bayazid I. To his native clansmen he made no such boast. His family dwelt at Tepelen, a small town composed of a cluster of fortified houses inhabited by wealthy Mussulman landed proprietors. The agas of Tepelen enjoyed a degree of local independence which was maintained by something like a regular municipal organization. But the intense selfishness of the Albanian race broke out in frequent quarrels, and kept the place always on the verge of anarchy.

The great-grandfather of Ali, Mutza Yussuf[1], raised himself to considerable power by his personal valour. From him the phara of which he was the chieftain assumed the name of Mutzochusats. It is worthy of remark that in Albania, as in Greece in the time of Homer, no genealogy is carried by name beyond the great-grandfather of the most distinguished man. Mukhtar Bey, the son and successor of Mutza, was slain at the siege of Corfu, fighting against Schulenburg. Veli, the third son of Mukhtar, was accused of poisoning his two elder brothers to secure the chieftainship. Perhaps he poisoned himself, for, like his brothers, he died young.

Ali, the infant son of Veli, was left to the care of his mother, whose relationship to Kurd Pasha of Berat, a powerful Albanian chieftain, secured protection to the infant. The young Ali grew up in lawless habits. Sheep-stealing involved him in local feuds, and, falling into the hands of an injured neighbour, he was only saved from death by the interference of Kurd Pasha. He then entered the sultan's service, and was employed by Kurd as a guard of the dervens. He was brave and active, restless in mind and body, and utterly destitute of all moral and religious feeling; but his good-humour made him popular among his companions, and he displayed affection to the members of his family and gratitude to his friends. As he grew older and rose in power, he became, like most Albanians, habitually false; and, regarding cunning as a proof of capacity, his conversation with strangers was usually intended to mislead the listeners. During his long and brilliant career his personal interests or passions were the sole guides of his conduct. Within the circle of Albanian life his experience was complete, for he rose gradually from the position of a petty chieftain to the rank of a powerful prince; yet his moral and political vision seems never to have been enlarged, for at his greatest elevation selfishness obscured his intellect, and avarice neutralized his political sagacity. His ambition in some cases was the result of his physical activity.

Ali, like every Albanian or Greek who has risen to great power by his own exertions, ascribed his success solely to his own ability, and his self-conceit persuaded him that his own talents were an infallible resource in every emergency. He

---

[1] That is, Moses Joseph.

POLICY OF ALI PASHA. 59

thought that he could deceive all men, and that nobody could deceive him; and as usually happens with men of this frame of mind, he overlooked those impediments which did not lie directly in his path. As an Albanian, a pasha and a Mohammedan, he was often swayed by different interests: hence his conduct was full of contradictions. At times he acted with excessive audacity; at times with extreme timidity. By turns he was mild and cruel, tolerant and tyrannical; but his avarice never slept, and to gratify it there was no crime which he was not constantly ready to perpetrate.

The boasted ability of Ali was displayed in subduing the Albanians, cheating the Othoman government, and ruling the Greeks. His skill as the head of the police in his dominions gave strangers a favourable opinion of his talents as a sovereign. He found knowledge useful in his servants, he therefore favoured education. His household at Joannina had all the pomp and circumstance of an Eastern court; but it had no feature more remarkable than a number of young pages engaged in study. The children of Albanian Mussulmans might be seen in one antechamber reading the Koran with a learned Osmanli, while in another room an equal number of young Christians might be seen studying Hellenic grammar with a Greek priest.

Under Ali's government Joannina became the literary capital of the Greek nation, for he protected laymen who rebelled against the patriarch and synod of Constantinople, as well as priests who intrigued against the sultan. Colleges, libraries, and schools flourished and enjoyed independent endowments. He ostentatiously recommended all teachers to pay great attention to the morals of their pupils, and in his conversation with Greek bishops he dwelt with a cynic simplicity on the importance of religious principles, showing that he valued them as a kind of insurance against dishonesty, and a means of diminishing financial peculation. Greek, being the literary language of southern Albania, was studied by Mussulmans as well as Christians. Poems and songs, as well as letters and accounts, were written by Mohammedans in Greek, and many were circulated in manuscript. Unfortunately no collection of Mohammedan songs and poems has been published[1].

---

[1] Colonel Leake has published an abstract of a curious Greek poem by a

The cruelty of Ali excited horror in civilized Europe, but it extorted admiration from his barbarous subjects. The greatest compliment they could pay him was to praise his cruelty to his face. Persons still living have seen him listen with complacency to flattery embodied in an enumeration of his acts of direst cruelty, and shuddered at his low demoniacal laugh when his Greek secretaries reminded him how he had hung one man, impaled another, and tortured a third. Lord Byron might well say, that

'With a bloody hand
He ruled a nation turbulent and bold.'

One of his most wanton acts of cruelty has been much celebrated, and the circumstances which attended it deserve to be recorded, as affording a characteristic trait of Ali and of his government.

A Greek lady of Joannina excited the jealousy of Ali's daughter-in-law, the wife of his eldest son Mukhtar. Euphrosyne was the niece of Gabriel, the archbishop of Joannina, but she had neglected to study the lives of the saints, and turned her attention to naughty reading in the Greek classics. She possessed great beauty and singularly attractive manners. In an evil hour her classic tastes led her to revive the elegance and wickedness of the ancient *hetairai*, and for a time her graceful manners concealed her graceless conduct. Her husband visited Venice, fearing Ali's designs on his purse, and disliking the attentions of Mukhtar to his wife. During his prolonged absence the house of the fair Euphrosyne became the resort of the educated and wealthy young men of Joannina, and she received private visits and rich presents from Mukhtar Pasha without much effort to conceal the disgraceful connection. This conduct caused much scandal, and it was said that married ladies, whose husbands were not so far distant as Euphrosyne's, imitated her behaviour. A storm of indignation arose among Christian husbands and Mussulman

---

Mussulman Albanian, which is one of the most authentic sources of information for the early career of Ali. There is a copy of this poem in the library of the University of Athens, but the text is not so pure as in the copy from which Leake took his extracts. The copy at Athens has been transcribed by one logiotatos and corrected by another. The cruelty of Ali is thus vaunted :—

"Ὅσοι καὶ ἂν ἦταν στὰ χωριὰ τοὺς ἔφαγαν τὰ φίδια,
Τοὺς τζάκισε τὰ γόνατα καὶ πλάταις καὶ παγίδια.

—Leake's *Travels in Northern Greece*, i. 463-497.

wives. The complaints of Mukhtar's wife were at last made a pretext for punishment, but report said that Ali sought revenge because he had been an unsuccessful lover. His vices were notorious. Childe Harold remarked,—

> 'Yon hoary lengthening beard
> Ill suits the passions that belong to youth.'

Men said that the hoary beard attempted to conceal its evil passions under a veil of public duty. It was resolved to eradicate the great social evil of Joannina by some effectual measure of reform. Ali decided on a general massacre of the culprits, and never was cruelty perpetrated with more ruthless deliberation or greater barbarity.

Ali was in the habit of dining with his subjects at their own houses when he wished to confer on them an extraordinary mark of favour. He signified to Nicholas Yanko, whose wife was one of the proscribed, his intention to honour him with a visit. The men dine alone in Eastern lands. After dinner the great pasha requested that the lady of the house might present his coffee, in order to receive his thanks for the entertainment. When she approached, he addressed her in his usual style of conversation with Greek females, mixing kindness with playful sarcasm. Rising after his coffee, he ordered the attendants in waiting to invite several ladies, whose conduct, if not virtuous, had certainly not been scandalous, to visit Yanko's wife at her house.

Ali proceeded to the house of Euphrosyne, attended by a few guards, and, walking suddenly into her presence, made a motion with his hand, which served as a signal for carrying off the victim, who was conveyed to Yanko's house much more astonished than alarmed. Ali rode on to his palace and engaged in his usual employments. The ladies of the party assembled at Yanko's were soon discomposed by having an equal number of females of the very lowest order in Joannina thrust into the room by policemen. In a few minutes the whole party was hurried off to the church of St. Nicholas, Yanko's patron saint, at the northern extremity of the lake. There the unfortunate culprits were informed that they were condemned to death by the pasha. The wealthier were at first not much frightened, for Ali's avarice was so notorious that they believed their relations would either voluntarily ransom their lives, or be compelled to do so by the pasha. The worst punishment they feared was imprisonment in the convents on the islands of the lake.

Morning dawned before the party reached the church of St. Nicholas, and Mohammedan customs require that the execution of a sentence of death on females by drowning must be carried into effect while the sun is below the horizon. For twenty hours, ladies of rank and women of the lowest class remained huddled together, trembling at times with the fear of death, and at others confident with delusive hopes of life. At sunset a violent storm swept the surface of the lake, and it was midnight before they were embarked in small boats and carried to the middle of the lake. There they were thrown overboard, without being tied up in sacks according to the Mussulman formality in executing a similar sentence. Most of the victims submitted to their fate with calm resignation, sinking without an audible word, or with a short prayer; but some resisted to the utmost with piercing shrieks, and one whose hands got loose clung to the side of the boat, and could only be plunged under water by horrid violence. When all was finished, the police guards watched silently in the boats until morning dawned; they then hastened to inform the pasha that his orders had been faithfully executed. One of the policemen present, who had witnessed many a horrid deed of torture, declared long after that the scene almost deprived him of his senses at the time, and that for years the voices of the dying women were constantly echoing in his ears, and their faces rising before his eyes at midnight.

Several days elapsed before all the bodies were found and buried. In this instance Ali's cruelty excited extreme loathing among the Christian population. Seventeen females perished, and public feeling was so strong that their funerals were attended by crowds. Yet none of their relations had made an effort to save them, and the husbands of more than one were accused of being privy to the pasha's design. Ali, when he saw the violence of public indignation, thought it prudent to apologize for his severity by declaring that he would have pardoned all those who could have found an intercessor, and that he deemed his victims deserved death since no one spoke a word in their favour. This was mere hypocrisy; he knew the selfishness of his subjects.

ALI'S CRUELTY AND CUNNING. 63

The beautiful Euphrosyne was twenty-eight years of age. Being the niece of an archbishop, the orthodox cherished her memory with affection, as if she had been a martyr, instead of viewing her conduct with reprobation and her fate with pity. But public feeling expresses itself before public opinion is formed. The cruel fate of the elegant Euphrosyne awakened sympathy, but her sixteen fellow-sufferers died almost unpitied, though many of them were less blamable. Several songs were composed on the subject of her death, which were repeated over all Greece[1].

Ali's habitual exhibition of cunning and sagacity was considered as a display of political wisdom. His artifice allured the intellects of the subtile Greeks and the fancy of the enthusiastic Albanians. Colonel Leake, who was several years the diplomatic agent of the British government at his court, recounts an anecdote which proves that he was unable to lay aside his habits of deceit even when his good-nature prompted him to do an act of kindness. 'Not long ago he almost frightened to death the Bishop of Grevena, a mild and timid man, by a proceeding meant to increase the bishop's authority. Being about to visit Grevena, he ordered the bishop to prepare the episcopal palace for his reception, but instead of proceeding there, went to another lodging, pretending to believe that the bishop had so ordered it. Having sent for the unfortunate holy man of Grevena, he assumed an air of extreme anger, ordered the bishop to prison, and issued a proclamation that all persons having complaints against him should make a statement of their grievances. Nobody having appeared, the vizier sent for the bishop next day, and congratulated him on the proof

---

[1] According to the popular story, Mukhtar Pasha gave Euphrosyne an emerald ring which he had refused to his wife. She saw it on the hand of the lady at the bath, and hasteued to her father-in-law, who listened to her prayer for vengeance. A Greek song says,—

Δὲν σ'τ'ἔλεγα, Εὐφροσύνη μου,
Μὴ βάλης δακτυλίδι;
'Τι τὸ μανθάνει ὁ 'Αλῆ-πασᾶς,
Σὲ ῥίπτει μὲς στὴ λίμνη.

I told you, Euphrosyne, dear,
The ring, oh! do not take.
Ali the news will quickly hear—
He'll drown you in the lake.

[The account of this massacre given by Colonel Leake (*Travels in Northern Greece*, i. 401-4), who derived it from Yanko himself, adds some further details of the tragedy. Ed.]

that he had no enemies, and that he governed his flock with kindness[1].'

Another anecdote deserves notice because it illustrates the manner in which the Greek bishops in his dominions served as instruments of his avarice. Having observed that the bishops possessed more authority than his tax-gatherers, he resolved to employ them in collecting his revenues. He began the experiment by obliging the celebrated Ignatius, metropolitan of Arta, who afterwards escaped to Italy and resided at Pisa, to become the tax-gatherer of his diocese. The orders given to the bishop were severe, and he used little forbearance in his eagerness to win the pasha's favour. This severity caused many quarrels, without bringing an increase of revenue. Disturbances occurred, and Ali was compelled to listen to the complaints of the sufferers. As soon as the bishop had paid all the money he had collected into the pasha's treasury, Ali decided that a remission of taxation ought to be made, to the amount of £2000 sterling. The claimants compelled the bishop to refund the money, but Ali retained the fruits of his extortion.

It has been already mentioned that Ali was elevated to the rank of dervendji-pasha in the year 1787. The pashalik of Thessaly was united with that office. His activity obtained for him the pashalik of Joannina, in addition to his other commands, in the following year. His instructions required him to destroy the authority still possessed by the Christian armatoli, whose sympathies with Russia disquieted the Porte, and Ali carried out the views of the Othoman government with zeal and vigour.

At this period, a strong feeling in favour of increasing the direct authority of the sultan in the provinces far distant from the capital, had arisen both among Mussulmans and Christians. It was thought that the central government would restrain the exactions of the local pashas, and repress the feudal anarchy of the hereditary beys. Ali took advantage of this feeling to curtail the privileges of armatoli, ayans, and Mussulman and Christian communities alike. His firmness of purpose soon consolidated his authority both in Epirus and Thessaly; for at this early period of his career, justice

---

[1] *Travels in Northern Greece*, i. 407.

and equity were words constantly on his lips, and they appeared to direct his conduct. The armatoli had latterly become grievous oppressors of the peasantry. The ayans had always been the tyrants of the Christian population. The communities were powerless, except to increase the general anarchy. Ali constituted himself the redresser of wrongs, and he succeeded in establishing a degree of order which had not previously prevailed. Under the pretext of securing equal justice to all, he compelled every district which enjoyed the right of maintaining Greek armatoli to receive a garrison of Mussulman Albanians; while in those districts where the Turkish landlords were all-powerful, he placed detachments of armatoli to protect the cultivators of the soil. His energy secured to the people a larger share of the fruits of their industry than they had previously enjoyed, so that they willingly submitted to the contributions he compelled them to pay for his protection. His exactions were chiefly directed against the rich; and as he seldom allowed his agents to plunder with impunity, he was spoken of as a hard man but a just pasha.

The sultan supported Ali's plan of centralizing all power in his own hands, as long as it was evident that he was only the sultan's viceroy. The boldest beys were drawn into hostilities, and then overwhelmed with forces prepared in secret for their destruction. The wary were assassinated or poisoned. These murders generally removed men as cruel and treacherous as Ali, who, as the destroyer of a legion of tyrants, was considered a benefactor by a suffering people.

In the year 1796 he began to exhibit the ferocity of his character in its darkest colours. Khormovo was a Christian township, situated high up in the mountains, between the rivers Viosa and Dryno, and not far from their junction. The inhabitants were dangerous brigands; and it was said that for several generations they waylaid travellers under the guidance of their priest. A hollow tree, in the pass near the bridge of Tepelen, was long shown to travellers as the place of concealment of this orthodox priphti[1], from whence he uttered his oracular decisions concerning the fate of those

---

[1] The Albanian word for priest.

who were plundered. If the unfortunate prisoner was a Turk, he was hung on the tree; if a Greek in the service of the pasha or the sultan, he was drowned in the river; but if an Albanian, he was generally allowed to escape on payment of a ransom.

The Christians of Khormovo maintained their lawless independence by means of a close alliance with the Mussulmans of Gardhiki, a powerful community in the mountains to the south of the Dryno. Nearly thirty years had elapsed since the mother and sister of Ali had been seized in a civil war between the people of Khormovo and Gardhiki and the phara of the Mutzachusats. The ladies were treated with the grossest indignity, and they instilled into the breast of Ali their own rancorous longing for revenge. An occasion at last occurred of punishing the children for their fathers' crime. The territory of Khormovo was laid waste, the inhabitants shot down, the son of the priest was roasted alive, and a Greek poem, by a Mussulman, recounts with Oriental ferocity all the details of the tortures inflicted by Ali's soldiers on their unhappy prisoners [1].

The cruelty with which a Christian community was treated made very little impression, and was soon forgotten.

After a further interval of sixteen years, a new catastrophe struck all men with amazement and horror. The Mussulmans of Gardhiki were a powerful body, and their alliance with the inhabitants of Arghyrokastro enabled them to escape Ali's vengeance for forty-five years. The cause of his anger was generally forgotten and never mentioned.

Demir Dost, the principal aga of Gardhiki, was a brave and honourable man, who had aided Ali in subduing Khormovo. Ali, having determined to deprive the communities of Arghyrokastro and Gardhiki of the local privileges which their alliance had hitherto enabled them to maintain, marched against them in person. The peasantry declared in his favour; Demir Dost and sixty agas of Gardhiki were admitted to conclude a capitulation which permitted them to retain their

---

[1] 'Εμβῆκε ἀπὸ τὴν μία μεριὰ καὶ ἀπὸ τὴν ἄλλη βγαίνει,
Ποδοπατάει τὰ κορμιὰ καὶ ἀκόμι δὲν χορταίνει.
'Αλῆ Βελῆς βουλήθηκε ψυχὴ νὰ μὴν ἀφήσῃ,
Καὶ χύθηκαν τ' ἀσκέρι του σὰ μανιωμένοι λύκοι.
Τὸ σκοτεινὸ τὸ Χύρμοβο ἐγίνηκε βιράνι,
Καὶ Τζαοὺς Πρίφτης ἐγίνηκε κεμπάμπι εἰς τὸ τηγάνι.

MASSACRE OF GARDHIKIOTS. 67

property and territorial rights, on condition that they should reside at Joannina until the new civil and fiscal officers of the pasha were established in the district.

After the departure of the agas, the pasha summoned the people of Gardhiki to meet him at the Khan of Valiare, below Arghyrokastro, and on the other side of the Dryno. The pasha's agents declared that he wished to enrol a strong body of Gardhikiots in his service, and no better lure could be held out to attract the Albanian Mussulmans, who scorn to cultivate their lands if they can gain their living by military service. Gardhiki also, like most Albanian communities, had been long in the habit of sending mercenaries to every pashalik in the Othoman empire. The hope of becoming the instruments of Ali's power rendered the common people careless of the loss of a troubled independence, from which only the chieftains of the pharas derived any profit.

On the 27th of March 1812, about 670 Gardhikiots sat down to eat their mid-day meal in the Khan of Valiare, and in the large quadrangular court adjoining. Athanasios Vaïas, a Christian high in Ali's favour, was ready with a band of soldiers, who mounted on the walls of the enclosure, occupied the towers at its angles, and closed the gates. They opened a sudden fire of musketry on their unsuspecting victims, and it is said that two hundred fell at the first volley. The soldiers then raised diabolical shouts, in order to overpower the shrieks of the wounded and the dying, and kept up a continual fire, without intermission, for an hour and a half, until not a limb moved in the quadrangle, and the khan was enveloped in flames. The survivors, after the first volley, had vainly attempted to climb the wall and force the gates. The murderer had prepared the means of baffling every effort of despair.

Ali had not ventured to intrust many of his officers with the secret of the premeditated massacre, and the firing created some confusion among his troops; but he diverted the attention of the Mussulmans, who might have been inclined to favour the escape of the Gardhikiots, by a proclamation that the plunder of Gardhiki was granted to the soldiers. When plunder is to be gained, neither Albanians nor armatoli feel any sentiments of patriotism or humanity. All the troops whom Ali distrusted and wished to withdraw from the scene of the massacre were soon on their march up the mountain. The town of Gardhiki was sacked; the houses were plundered in regular succession, in order to insure to all a fair share of the booty; the women and children were carried off and reduced to slavery, in direct violation of the Mohammedan law; and all the fortified houses of the agas were burned to the ground. Demir Dost and the sixty agas who had retired to Joannina were murdered at the same time by Ali's order.

As soon as he had perpetrated this act of treachery and blood, Ali returned to Joannina, from whence he issued orders for the murder of every Gardhikiot who had escaped the massacre at the khan and the sack of the town. But this cruelty exceeded the limits of human wickedness, and his orders were disobeyed even by his own sons, who concealed many of his intended victims.

The deliberate extermination of a Mussulman community of eight hundred families was an act of atrocity that roused the indignation of every Mohammedan; and from that day Ali was accursed in the opinion of all true believers. The deserted habitations, blackened with fire, the desecrated mosques with their ruined minarets, the Mohammedan women and children weeping in slavery, cried loudly for vengeance. Yet Ali, in his intense selfishness, thought so much of the wrongs of his mother and his sister, and so little of the sufferings of thousands of innocent individuals, that he boasted of his wickedness, and commemorated his infamy in an inscription over the gateway of the Khan of Valiare. The entrance was walled up. The bones were left unburied in the court, and a marble tablet informed the passer-by, in both Turkish and Greek, that Ali was proud of the vengeance which he had inflicted on the enemies of his house. A curious poem in Greek, consisting of sixty-four verses, was circulated in manuscript, which was said to be an exact copy of the inscription, and to have been read over repeatedly to the pasha. It is a strange production, in the form of a conversation between the khan and the dead bodies. The building asks for information concerning the cause of their death. The dead bodies reply, that fifty years ago they had burned Ali's house and destroyed his clan, and they add, 'For this he slew us here, he razed our town, and ordered it to remain for ever desolate, for he is a just man.' In conclusion, Ali speaks a few warning words in his own person: 'I do not wish to do another similar act of severity, so let no man molest my house [1].'

Ali's power at last alarmed Sultan Mahmud, who was labouring night and day to circumscribe the authority of his pashas and great vassals. He had hitherto made but slow progress in establishing his system of centralization, but he had prepared the Porte for pursuing his policy with success. He availed himself of the universal indignation manifested at the murder of the Gardhikiots to diminish the power of Ali. The first step was to deprive Veli, Ali's second son, of the pashalik of the Morea, in August 1812, and send him to rule the insignificant pashalik of Larissa. Public opinion, which had favoured Ali in his plans of centralization at the expense of beys and communes, now favoured the projects of Sultan Mahmud at the expense of Ali. The Porte could alone afford protection against local tyranny: the sultan seemed to be the only authority in the Othoman empire who had a direct interest in enforcing an equitable administration of justice; every other authority seemed to derive a profit from injustice. Ali remained insensible to the change which had taken place in public opinion since he first attained the rank of pasha. This is not wonderful, for the ambassadors of the European powers at Constantinople, and their consuls in the provinces, were as blind to the increasing power of centralization as the Albanian pasha. The prudence of Sultan Mahmud was generally mistaken for weakness, and at the court of Joannina it was the fashion to speak of the anarchy and corruption that prevailed in the empire with great freedom, and of the dismemberment of Turkey as a probable event. The adroit flattery of Greek sycophants, the impolitic intrigues of European diplomatic agents, and the general improvement in the condition of the people under his government, induced Ali to believe that the hour had arrived when he might act as independent sovereign of Epirus with perfect security. Yet he had reached the edge of a precipice, and the vicissitudes of a long and eventful life, rich in social and political

---

[1] Leake's *Travels in Northern Greece*, i. 498.

changes, had exhibited its lessons of experience in vain. He fell pursuing the course of selfish criminal gratification, which he had often combined with the measures which raised him to power.

In the year 1819 Sultan Mahmud took advantage of the numerous complaints against the lavish expenditure and illegal extortions of Veli, to remove him from the government of Larissa to the still more insignificant pashalik of Lepanto. Ali saw clearly that the object was to circumscribe his power; but he attributed the measure to the influence of Ismael Pasho Bey, his active personal enemy, and not to the deep policy of Sultan Mahmud. All his malicious passions were roused, and he resolved to strike a blow that would destroy his enemy and intimidate his sovereign.

Ismael Pasho Bey was an Albanian of family and wealth, allied to Ali's house by blood. He had served the pasha of Joannina in youth with much devotion; but some cause of mutual distrust arose, and Ismael contrived to have his services transferred to Veli, when Ali's unworthy son was named pasha of the Morea in 1807. The hatred of Ali increased; but Ismael, warned in time, fled to save his life. For some years he escaped notice, but, finding that Ali's agents had discovered his place of residence, he removed to Constantinople, where he believed no assassin would venture to attack him openly. By attaching himself to the Ulema, frequenting the mosques with assiduity, and transacting the business of every Albanian who had any affair before the divan, he acquired some influence, and was named capidji-pasha.

In the month of February 1820 three Albanians made an attempt to assassinate Ismael Pasho Bey at noon in the streets of Constantinople. They were arrested; and, finding that their victim was only slightly wounded, they expected to save their lives by confession. They declared that they had been sent by Ali, pasha of Joannina, who had assured them that, in case of success, several members of the divan were prepared to protect them from punishment. This insinuation, that Ali possessed an overwhelming influence in the divan, offended Sultan Mahmud deeply. The assassins were immediately executed, and Ali was pronounced guilty of high treason. The traitor was summoned to present himself as a suppliant before the Sublime Porte within forty days. The pashalik of Joannina was conferred on Ismael Pasho. The period granted for repentance elapsed, and the new pasha was ordered to march against the rebel.

While Ali was pursuing his course of wickedness, he was acting as an instrument in the hands of Providence to advance the social progress of the Greeks. Indeed, the career of this celebrated man, with all his power and wickedness, would hardly have merited a place in history had circumstances not rendered him the herald of the Greek Revolution. The scenes of his eventful life produced very little direct change either in the political condition of the Othoman empire or of the Albanian nation.

When Ali received the news of his condemnation he was fully prepared to resist the sultan's authority, and his military arrangements for the defence of his pashalik were well planned. He had long revolved projects of rebellion in his mind, and the time appeared favourable for asserting his independence. The power of national feelings in upholding thrones and overthrowing dynasties was the theme of general discussion. A national revolution had just broken out in Spain, which was expected to produce great political changes in Europe. Ali was told by his political advisers that an appeal to the nationality of the Albanians and Greeks would induce them to unite in emancipating themselves from the Othoman domination and expose their lives and fortunes for his cause. He was liberal, therefore, of promises. He talked of constitutions and representative assemblies with as much fluency and as little sincerity as the kings of Spain, Naples, and Sardinia. He promised rewards to his troops, who believed in nothing but payments in coined money, and he invited the Greeks to co-operate with him in resisting the sultan, little foreseeing the consequences of his encouragement.

The soldiers of Ali were habituated to mountain warfare, and were intimately acquainted with every ravine and pass in the range of Mount Pindus. Every path that afforded ingress into Southern Albania from Macedonia and Thessaly was fortified sufficiently to resist Othoman infantry. A camp was formed to support every point which could be assailed, and easy communications were insured with the central magazines at Joannina by means of the lake. In everything the army of Ali appeared far superior to any force the sultan could bring against him.

The dispositions adopted for the defence of Southern Albania were the result of a long-meditated plan of resistance. From the north, Ali's dominions were exposed to an attack by Mustaï, pasha of Skodra, at the head of the Mussulman Gueghs and Catholic Mirdites, who were as good soldiers in mountain warfare as the Tosks and the armatoli. But Mustaï was, like Ali, an Albanian, and his career had been so similar, that he was not likely to view the ruin of his fellow pasha with favour, particularly as they had never been involved in any personal contests of importance. Ali had also secured several friends among the chieftains in the north, and he apprehended little danger from that quarter. The task of opposing the Skodra pasha was intrusted to Ali's eldest son, Mukhtar, pasha of Berat; but the right of Mukhtar's line of defence was exposed to be turned by a Turkish army assembled at Monastir, under the command of the Romeli-Valessi, which could penetrate into Albania by the pass of Devol, and thus unite with the Gueghs. Mustaï was the first of Ali's assailants who took the field. He advanced as far as Durazzo without meeting any opposition; but, after he had occupied Elbassan, he was recalled to the north by some movements among his unquiet neighbours, the Montenegrins, or he made their movements a pretext for retreating, in order to paralyze the advance of the Romeli-Valessi, whom he had no desire to see established in the valley of the river of Berat.

The direct line of approach for an army advancing to attack Joannina from the east is by the pass of Metzovo. Two great roads—one from Macedonia by the valley of the Indji-kara-sou, and the other from Thessaly by the valley of the Salamvria [1]—converge at this pass, and two powerful armies may be simultaneously prepared to force the passage, and maintained in its immediate vicinity by supplies from the fertile districts of Anaselitza, Grevena, and Trikkala.

---

[1] [The mountains above Metzovo, the Lacmon of ancient geography, are the great watershed of the part of Turkey that lies between the Adriatic and the Aegean. In them rise the five great rivers which the Author mentions in this place. Of the two that flow into the Aegean, the Salamvria was the Peneius of antiquity, the Indji-kara-sou, which is better known as the Vistritza, the Haliacmon. Of the other three, the Viosa was the Aous, the river of Arta the Arachthus, and the Aspropotamos the Achelous. ED.]

To protect this pass, an army of 15,000 men was encamped on the eastern slopes of Palaeovuni, between the sources of the Viosa and the river of Arta. It was commanded by Omer Vrioni, an Albanian chieftain, who had acquired considerable reputation as a soldier, and great wealth by his military service in Egypt, during the troubled times which preceded the consolidation of Mohammed Ali's authority [1]. The Albanian camp was established near the position occupied by Philip V. of Macedon after his defeat by Flamininus at the Fauces Antigonenses, or Kleisura of the Viosa, and where he lingered a few days, doubting whether he ought to march into Thessaly or fall back on Macedonia [2].

To the south of the pass of Metzovo there is another pass leading from Thessaly into the valley of the Aspropotamos, called Portais, or the gates of Trikkala; and there are several mountain paths farther south, by which light troops may march from the upper valley of the Spercheus and the head waters of the Megdova, by the valley of the Aspropotamos, into the valley of the river of Arta, and thus gain an entrance into the plain of Joannina. But the country through which these roads pass is intersected by successive ranges of high mountains and deep valleys, besides being occupied by Christian armatoli and by the indigenous robbers of Mount Kotziaka.

Ali committed the defence of the passes to the south of Metzovo to many local chieftains, Albanians and Greeks, Mussulmans and Christians.

The greatest danger to which he was exposed lay in the facility of landing troops on the southern coast of Epirus. Prevesa was the key of his maritime defences, and he intrusted its command to Veli, his second son, who fled from Lepanto on the first approach of a Turkish force.

When the sultan proclaimed Ali a traitor, and named Ismael Pasho his successor, the imperial authority was almost nominal in many provinces of the Othoman empire, and Mahmud had no army ready to enforce his authority. The janissaries at Constantinople were as little under his control as

---

[1] The Greeks erroneously assert that Omer Vrioni derived his name from the Byzantine family of Briennios, but it is notorious that he received it from the village of Vrionti, near Berat, of which he was a native.
[2] Livy, xxxii. 13; Leake's *Travels in Northern Greece*, i. 399.

the mercenaries of distant pashas. But no man then living had studied the condition of the Othoman empire with so much attention, or knew so well the strength and weakness of his own authority, as Sultan Mahmud. He alone understood how far he could make use of the instrumentality of rival pashas to destroy the rebel without allowing them to increase their own power. His systematic measures for strengthening the authority of the central administration, for reforming the Othoman government, and arresting the decline of the empire on the brink of destruction, were then as little suspected as the firm and daring character of the man who planned them.

The sultan intrusted the chief command of the army destined to attack Ali from the east to Ismael, the new pasha of Joannina. No person appeared likely to rally the discontented Albanians to his standard with so much certainty, and no one could be selected with whom it was more difficult for Ali to treat. Several pashas were ordered to assemble all their timariots and holders of military fiefs, and take the field with Ismael. The Othoman army was slowly collected, and it formed a motley assembly, without order and without artillery. Each pasha moved forward as he mustered his followers, with a separate commissariat and a separate military chest. The daily rations and daily pay of the soldier differed in different divisions of the army. Ismael was really only the nominal commander-in-chief. He was not a soldier, and had he been an experienced officer, he could have done little to enforce order in the forces he commanded.

Ali knew that his government was unpopular, but he acted under the usual delusion of princes who consider that they are necessary to the order of society. He considered himself the natural chief of the Tosks, and he believed that he could easily become the political head of the Greeks. He had heard so much lately of constitutions and political assemblies, that he expected to create a strong national feeling in his favour by promising the Greeks a constitution, and convoking the Albanian chieftains in a national assembly, though he had formed no very clear idea of what was meant by a constitution, or what a national assembly could really effect. His Greek secretaries, however, assured him that it would be easy to raise the Greeks in arms against the sultan, and his

ALI'S ASSEMBLY.

Mussulman councillors declared that every Albanian was ready to support him as their sovereign. To make himself a national monarch, in opposition to the Oriental despotism of the sultan, he convoked a divan to consider the question of raising supplies, that being the only means of assembling Albanian agas and Greek bishops in one assembly, without violating Mussulman usages and offending Mohammedan pride.

The divan met, and Ali addressed the assembly in Greek. He condescended to explain the motives which induced him to resist the sultan's authority. He pretended that he was persecuted by the viziers of the Porte, because he supported the interests of the Albanians against the Osmanlis, and protected the Christians against ruinous exactions. He invited all present to urge their countrymen to support him and his officers in the approaching hostilities, and assured them that their interests would suffer as much as his own if the Othoman army penetrated beyond the passes.

The assembled Mussulmans were either his partizans or his creatures. They testified their approbation of his discourse with the humility of Eastern ceremony. Each bey repeated gravely in succession, with emphatic solemnity, some trite compliment, or pronounced, with the air of having made a great discovery, 'Our lord, the vizier, speaks well; we are the slaves of his highness.' Even Ali felt that the scene was ridiculous, for he knew that the same words would be uttered, in the same tone, to his enemy Ismael, should he ever succeed in entering Joannina.

The Greeks remained silent. They felt no inclination to support the tyranny of Ali. It is certain that at this time the existence of an organized plan for proclaiming the Greeks an independent nation was not known to the clergy and primates of Northern Greece and Epirus. Though a secret society called the *Philike Hetairia* had made great progress in enrolling proselytes in Constantinople, the Morea, and the Ionian Islands, it had not succeeded in Joannina and among the armatoli. Greek historians tell us that the terror inspired by Ali Pasha's government prevented the apostles of the Hetairia from visiting his dominions[1]. But that is certainly

---

[1] Perrhaevos, 'Απομνημονεύματα πολεμικά, I. Tricoupi is of the same opinion, 'Ιστορία τῆς 'Ελληνικῆς 'Επαναστάσεως, i. 26.

not the whole truth. Many agents of the Hetairia travelled through Epirus, but they were deterred from attempting to make proselytes, from fear of treachery on the part of their countrymen. They found that both the bishops and the primates were too closely identified with Ali's administration, and derived too great profits from acting as his political and financial agents, to feel disposed to plot against his authority. The fear of betraying the schemes of the Hetairia to false friends was stronger than the fear of Ali's cruelty. The Hetairists were partizans of Russia, and the Romeliot Greeks did not generally connect their patriotic aspirations with Russian projects. They, moreover, generally despised the class of men who travelled as apostles of the Hetairia.

Suleiman Pasha, who succeeded Veli in the government of Larissa, was invested by the sultan with the office of dervendji when Ali was proclaimed a rebel. On assuming the official direction of the armatoli, and publishing the firman proscribing Ali, he invited all the sultan's faithful subjects to take up arms against the traitor. A circular was addressed to all Mussulmans, to those Christian communities which retained the privilege of keeping armed guards, and particularly to the captains of armatoli, inviting them to expel the adherents of Ali Pasha from their districts. The Greek text of this circular assumed the form of a proclamation, calling on the Christians to take up arms for their own protection. It is said to have differed materially from the Turkish copy, and the pasha's Greek secretary, Anagnostes, was supposed to have availed himself of the opportunity, in order to assist the designs of the Hetairists. Circumstances favoured the Greeks. The number of armed Christians in the mountains of Thessaly and Epirus was great, and both the belligerents felt the importance of gaining their assistance.

Several bands of Christian troops remained attached to Ali's cause. Odysseus, whom he particularly favoured, and who had been a page in his household, was intrusted with the chief command at Livadea. Stournari was stationed at Valtos, Varnakioti in Xeromero, Andreas Hyskos in Agrapha, and Zongas was sent to harass the communications of the Othoman army. But, as early as the month of June 1820, several bodies of armatoli joined the sultan's forces, while at the same time some captains took military possession of their capitanliks, and expelled the Albanian Mussulmans who remained faithful to Ali. For some time the Othoman authorities encouraged these enterprises. The armed Christians, however, knowing that they had nothing to gain by a decided victory either of the Turks or the Albanians, showed a disposition to remain neutral as soon as they had expelled the Mussulmans, and their attitude awakened the suspicion of the Porte.

The sultan was alarmed, and fearing some collusion with the rebel, he degraded Suleiman, and soon after put him to death. Mohammed Dramali was named his successor, and ordered to occupy all the passes leading from Thessaly into Epirus. In the mean time the main body of the Othoman army, under Ismael, advanced to Kalabak. The left wing, under Pehlevan Baba of Rutshuk, who was named pasha of Lepanto in place of Veli, descended into Greece. Pehlevan had distinguished himself as a leader of light cavalry on the banks of the Danube in the last war with Russia. He now marched at the head of the same active and disorderly troops through Thermopylae to Livadea, from which he drove Odysseus. Veli fled from Lepanto, and Pehlevan occupied all Aetolia and Acarnania without opposition, penetrated through the pass of Makronoro, which is a western Thermopylae, and fixed his head-quarters at Arta. Ali's defences were thus turned, and the road into the plain of Joannina was open to the Othoman army.

The summer was far advanced before the grand army commenced its operations, but its first movements were crowned with great success. Instead of attempting to force the pass of Metzovo, which Omer Vrioni was prepared to defend, Ismael sent a body of Albanians to seize the Portais or gates of Trikkala. This corps occupied the bridge of Koraki, took possession of the pass of Pentepegadhia, and opened communications with Pehlevan. Other detachments occupied the upper valley of the Aspropotamos and the valley of the river of Arta, where their arrival was welcomed by the native population, which consists of Zinzar Vallachs [1].

---

[1] This branch of the Vallachian race makes its appearance in the history of the Byzantine empire, under its present name, in the eleventh century, and in the twelfth it was so powerful as to be independent. See vol. iii. p. 224. [On the meaning of the name Zinzar see vol. iii. p. 227, *note* 4. ED.]

Omer Vrioni, finding that his position was turned, instead of falling back on Joannina and concentrating Ali's army in order to give battle to Ismael in the plain, treated with the Othoman commander-in-chief to obtain advancement for himself by deserting the rebel. He was promised the pashalik of Berat, then held by Ali's eldest son, Mukhtar. The army under his orders, which was encamped on Palaeovuni, dispersed. Many of the soldiers returned to their native villages to watch the progress of hostilities before choosing their side. Others immediately took service with Ismael.

Joannina was now besieged. Ali had barely time to burn the city in order to prevent his enemy finding cover in the houses. The citadel, which is separated from the city by a wet ditch, was well furnished with artillery, military stores, and provisions. The garrison amounted to six thousand men. Ali possessed an armed flotilla on the lake, which secured his communications with the mountains to the north. He expected to be able to cut off the supplies of the Othoman army, and compel Ismael to raise the siege before the arrival of his heavy artillery. The cowardice and treachery of his sons frustrated his plans.

A division of the Othoman fleet arrived off the Albanian coast during the summer, and as soon as Pehlevan occupied Arta, the capitan-bey besieged Prevesa. Veli possessed ample means of defending the place, but he was a coward. Ismael had been his friend in youth. Veli received promises of pardon, and was ordered to treat with the capitan-bey. He opened negotiations by pleading his filial obedience as an apology for his rebellion, and offered to surrender Prevesa with all its stores on being allowed to carry off his own wealth, and on receiving the promise of a pashalik, to which he might retire without degradation. Ismael ratified these terms, and Veli removed with his harem on board the Othoman fleet. The capitulation was respected, but both Ismael and Veli were subsequently put to death by the sultan's orders.

Mukhtar, who had abandoned Berat to fortify himself in Arghyrokastro, soon followed his brother's example. He was not destitute of courage, but he was brutally selfish, and he was bribed to desert his father by a promise of the pashalik of

Kutaieh. In quitting Albania, he persuaded his youngest brother Salik to accompany him.

The surrender of Prevesa, Berat, and Arghyrokastro enabled Ismael to obtain supplies of every kind, but the communications between his camp and the fleet were so difficult and so ill-managed, that heavy guns and ammunition were brought up very slowly. His rear was often attacked by the partizans of Ali, and, being compelled to look out for allies among the Albanians, he remembered the glorious exploits of the Suliots, and their implacable hatred to Ali. Sultan Mahmud authorized him to put them again in possession of Suli, and the capitan-bey was instructed to treat with them. The Suliots had now lived as exiles at Corfu for seventeen years, eating the bread of charity bestowed on them in turns by the Russians, the French, and the English, as each became the masters of the Ionian Islands. The proposals of the capitan-bey were soon accepted; the Suliots crossed over into Albania, and received Ismael's authority to invest the fort of Kiapha, which Ali had constructed to command Suli. The fort was garrisoned by Mussulman Albanians faithful to Ali. The numbers of the Suliots were not sufficient to blockade it closely, and the Othoman commander-in-chief neglected to furnish them with rations. In a short time they were in a starving state, and, to obtain the means of subsistence, began to levy contributions on the Christian peasantry in the pashalik of Joannina who had submitted to the sultan. Ismael, forgetting his own neglect, was offended at their depredations in his pashalik. Personally he was a bigot, and not inclined to favour the establishment of an independent tribe of Christians in the vicinity of his capital. The Mussulmans of Margariti and Paramythia, who had submitted to his authority, warned him against the danger of allowing the Suliots to gain possession of the strong fort of Kiapha. He felt the force of their reasoning as much as he wished to secure the assistance of the Suliots; and, hoping to gain time, he ordered them to join his army before Joannina, promising them both pay and rations, with which he could not easily supply them in Suli.

The starving Suliots were compelled to obey; but as their only object in returning to Albania had been to regain possession of their native mountains, they considered themselves cheated by the pasha, and henceforward they regarded all Ismael's conduct with distrust. They found that they were stationed in the most exposed situation, and when Ali's forces sallied out to attack them in overwhelming numbers the Othoman troops in the nearest quarters came slowly to their assistance. In this difficult position they owed their safety to their own vigilance and valour. They adopted every precaution to guard against a surprise either from friend or foe, and their military precautions justified the reputation they had long enjoyed of being the best soldiers in Albania.

In the month of October 1820, Ismael opened his fire on the fortress of Litharitza, which forms an acropolis to Joannina; but the heavy guns and mortars which he had transported from Prevesa were so ill-managed that the casemated batteries of the besieged suffered little; while the guns of the fortress enfiladed the whole site of the ruined city, and impeded the approaches of the Turks against the citadel of the lake, which was the centre of Ali's strength, and from which he frequently made desperate sallies on his enemy.

The military incapacity of Ismael, and his unfitness for the office of seraskier, became daily more apparent. He had dispersed the fine army of Omer Vrioni, and gained possession of Prevesa without difficulty; he expected to conquer Joannina as easily. Instead, therefore, of pushing the siege with vigour, he devoted his whole attention to the measures which he considered most likely to render his pashalik profitable to himself. His care was confined to his own territory, and his general negligence enabled the partizans of Ali to attack his convoys, and permitted the cavalry of Pehlevan, and the Gueghs of Dramali, to plunder the country in every direction. The villages on the great roads in Epirus, Thessaly, and Northern Greece were deserted by their inhabitants. Ali, well informed of all that was passing, watched the progress of the siege without alarm. He was still ignorant of the character of Sultan Mahmud, and did not suspect that he was the real antagonist who was playing the game against him.

The Suliots felt that they were treated with scorn. Their rations were bad, and they received no pay. Ismael, and many Mussulmans in Albania and Greece, entertained a suspicion that the Greeks were plotting an insurrection in concert with Russia to assist Ali, and he was so imprudent as to display his ill-will to all classes of Christians.

Ali took advantage of his rival's imprudence with his usual sagacity. Long conversations were carried on during the night between the Suliots and his Albanians. The Suliots told their grievances, the Albanians expressed sympathy, and boasted of their advantages. A formal negotiation was opened, and it terminated in the Suliots forming an alliance with Ali, whom they had long regarded as their bitterest enemy. The critical position in which both parties were placed forced them to cast a veil over the past. The Suliots regained possession of their native rocks. Ali resigned the proudest conquest of his long career. He abandoned the policy of his government to save his life. He promised to put the Suliots in possession of his fort at Kiapha; they engaged to join his partizans, and fall on the rear of the sultan's army. Hostages were given, for both sides were suspicious, and looked with some anxiety to the result of their strange alliance.

About midnight on the 12th of December 1820, the Suliots suddenly quitted the seraskier's camp before Joannina, and marched rapidly towards Suli by the road to Variadhes. A week after, Murto Tshiali, Ali's faithful adherent, put them in possession of Kiapha, with all its military stores and provisions. He also paid a sum of money to each of the chiefs of pharas, in order to enable them to take the field. In January 1821 the Suliots formed a junction with a corps of fifteen hundred Mussulman Albanians under the command of three chieftains devoted to Ali, of high military reputation—Seliktar Poda (the sword-bearer), Muhurdar Besiari (the seal-bearer), and Tahir Abbas, a bey of great personal influence.

It was necessary for the Suliots to re-establish their authority over the Christian villages which had formerly paid them tribute or black-mail; otherwise they must have remained always dependent on Ali Pasha for their subsistence. The Othoman authorities already occupied several posts in the Suliot territory. The Suliot chiefs and their Mussulman allies resolved to make these positions their first object of attack. Two months were consumed in this operation. After some severe skirmishing, Devitzana and Variadhes, which command the two roads leading from Suli to Joannina, and Lelova and

Kanza, which open an issue into the plains of Arta and Prevesa, were conquered.

But in the mean time Ali's position had grown much worse. The severity of the winter had not, as he expected, forced Ismael to raise the siege, and he had himself fallen into a trap he had prepared for his enemy. Letters which he had written to the Seliktar Poda and the Suliots, concerting measures for a combined attack on the Othoman camp, fell into the hands of Omer Vrioni. They were answered as if they had arrived safely at their destination, and the garrisons both of Litharitza and the citadel were induced to make a sortie, which led them so far into the Othoman camp that it was with great difficulty they effected their retreat, leaving half their number dead on the field. This defeat took place on the 7th of February 1821, and from that day Ali was compelled to act cautiously on the defensive.

Sultan Mahmud saw that the conduct of the pashas before Joannina was compromising the success of the campaign. He punished the incapacity of Ismael and the insubordination of Pehlevan by removing them from their commands. Pehlevan was immediately condemned to death; Ismael was sent to defend Arta in a subordinate position, and Khurshid Pasha of the Morea, a sagacious veteran, replaced him as seraskier before Joannina[1]. Ismael's misconduct, when Arta was attacked by the Suliots, the Albanians, and the Greek armatoli, in the month of November 1821, caused him to be exiled to Demotika, where he was decapitated. Khurshid assumed the command of the Othoman army at the beginning of the month of March 1821. The Greek Revolution broke out in the Morea shortly after, and both the fate of Ali Pasha and the fortunes of the Suliots became subordinate episodes in the military operations of Sultan Mahmud's reign.

The Suliots henceforth derive their historical importance from their connection with the great national struggle of the Greeks. Their characteristics as an Albanian tribe were gradually lost after they were finally expelled from Suli by

---

[1] Khurshid was pasha of Egypt before Mohammed Ali, and was the first Turk who attempted to form a regular corps consisting of Negro soldiers. He failed in the attempt, which his successor resumed at a later period more successfully. Burckhardt's *Travels in Arabia*, i. 147.

Sultan Mahmud's officers, and became dependent for their existence on their pay as Greek soldiers. But their condition when they returned from Corfu to regain possession of their native mountains deserves to be recorded, since it marks the great transition of society in Southern Albania during the first quarter of the present century.

During sixteen years of exile the Suliots were thrown into close connection with the modern Greeks. Their communal organization remained in abeyance; but their absence changed the condition of the Christian peasantry who had lived under their protection. Many of the cultivators of the soil found themselves better off as the tenants of Ali Pasha than they had been as the vassals of the Suliots; and when that tribe returned, they found the inhabitants of the villages in their former territory unwilling to become again the agricultural serfs of the Suliot confederacy. The Suliot warriors also were so reduced in number that they were compelled to seek recruits from among the Christian peasants, in order to counterbalance the strength of the Albanian Mussulmans with whom they were forced to act. It was therefore absolutely necessary to give the Suliot community a new constitution.

This was done. The subject villages sent deputies to a general council, and every soldier enrolled under a Suliot chief was admitted to the privileges of a native warrior. This circumstance was considered an event of great social importance in Albanian society. It separated the Suliots from the great family of the Tchamides, and overthrew the organization of the pharas. It is not easy for strangers to understand the change which this revolution produced. They cannot estimate the violence of the pride of class among the Albanians, nor the strength of local patriotism or prejudice among the Suliots. In the month of March 1821, when the Revolution broke out in the Morea, the Suliots knew nothing of the Philike Hetairia, and cared nothing for the independence of the Greeks[1], yet Greek ideas had already produced a change in the political civilization of this rude tribe of

---

[1] [These statements are contested by Mendelssohn Bartholdy in his *Geschichte Griechenlands* (vol. i. p. 125), who maintains that Botzaris and the leaders of the Suliotes were acquainted with the Hetairia, that the Suliote movement was immediately connected with the Greek Revolution, and that that Revolution broke out, not in March, 1821, but in December, 1820. ED.]

Albanians. The principles of civil equality and of the brotherhood of all the orthodox had been imprinted on their minds. They were made to feel that they were citizens and Christians as well as Suliots. They were drawn into the vortex of the Greek Revolution without their forming any preconceived design to aid the Greeks, just as they had been led by circumstances to aid their enemy Ali Pasha. But, once engaged in the cause, they embarked in it with their usual vehemence, and formed the van of its warriors, sacrificing their beloved Suli, and abandoning all the traditions of their race, to join the modern Greeks and assume the name of Hellenes.

The intellectual progress of the Suliots in civil affairs, under the influence of Greek ideas, contrasts strangely with their obstinate rejection of the military lessons taught them by the Russians, the French, and the English, who placed the power of discipline and science in war constantly before their eyes. The legions of Napoleon and the regiments of England showed them the secret of rendering small bodies of well-trained soldiers a match for hosts of undisciplined troops, but they refused to learn the lesson. They deliberately rejected the advantages they might have derived from discipline and tactics, because no Suliot would sacrifice the smallest portion of his self-importance. The spirit of personal independence which made every individual Suliot pay only a limited obedience to the chief of his phara, rendered the chiefs of the pharas unwilling to obey a commander-in-chief, so that a Suliot army of 700 men was a kind of Polish diet. Unfortunately for the Greeks, the brilliant courage of the Suliots induced the unwarlike leaders of the Revolution to overrate the value of the Albanian system of warfare. The Greeks had taught the Suliots some valuable social lessons; the Suliots in return taught the Greeks to adopt the military barbarism of the Albanians, to despise the restraints of discipline, and to depreciate the value of the tactics and science of civilized nations. Their lessons entailed many calamities on Greece during the revolutionary war.

The Suliots had some reasons for adopting their system in defending their own mountains against the pashas of Joannina, which were inapplicable to the defence of Greece

SULIOT MILITARY SYSTEM.

against the Turks. The nature of the Suliot territory, serrated with deep ravines converging at acute angles, forced the Suliots to guard several passes. Their numbers were small, so that their enemies were enabled to attack many points with overwhelming numbers. To meet this danger, it was necessary to adopt some system of defensive warfare, by which a few men could effectually check the advance of a large body. They obtained this result by selecting positions commanding those passes which their assailants could not avoid. In these passes a few men were posted in such a manner as to be concealed from the approaching enemy, but so disposed that each Suliot occupied a station overlooking the same portion of the road. A concentrated fire was thus brought to bear on the gorge of the pass. Every shot was expected to prove mortal.

The military science of the Suliot captains was displayed in the selection of these positions, and in disposing the men who occupied them. The great art was by a sudden fire to encumber the narrowest part of the pass with the dead and wounded. It was also necessary for every man to have a second rifle ready, in order to prevent the enemy from availing himself of numbers, and rushing forward to storm the Suliot position. A perfect knowledge of the ground, the eye of an eagle, the activity of a goat, and the heart of a hero, were required to make a perfect Suliot warrior. It has often happened that a band of twenty-five Suliots has arrested several hundred men, until their countrymen could arrive in numbers sufficient to throw themselves in the rear of the enemy and capture his baggage.

When circumstances rendered retreat unavoidable, it was an important part of the tactics of the Suliots to abandon their position simultaneously, and remove unperceived into some new position equally suited for defence. In these operations each warrior watched the movements of his companions as carefully as those of the enemy; for it was as great a fault to remain too long in a position as to abandon it too soon. A wound received by unnecessary exposure was, at Suli, as disgraceful as an act of military disobedience. No soldier was entitled to compromise the public safety to win personal glory. This species of defensive warfare required great powers of endurance, and a facility of moving unperceived among stones and stunted brushwood, which could only be acquired by long habit. An active youth becomes a good regular soldier in six months, but as many years were spent in exercising a Suliot warrior, before he was admitted to take his place in a chosen band appointed to defend an important pass. Every man was there called upon to perform the part of a cautious general as well as of a daring soldier.

The system of attack practised by the Mussulman Albanians bore great similarity to these defensive tactics. The assailants dispersed in an extended semicircle round the point of attack, and crept forward, covering themselves with every irregularity in the ground. The first object was to ascertain the exact position and the numbers of the enemy; the second to outflank him. The first approach was usually made during the night; and before the grey mist of the morning rendered objects visible to any eyes but those of Albanian marksmen, a volley was often poured on the sentinels, who looked up cautiously to examine the ground; or the two parties were already mingled together, and forced to engage hand to hand.

It has been mentioned that when the Suliots were joined by the Mussulman Albanians in Ali's interest, they were compelled to attack the Othoman posts in order to expel them from the Suliot territory. Many of their allies had fought against them in 1803, but this circumstance only increased the mutual emulation. Tahir Abbas and the Muhurdar were not men to yield the palm of valour to Botzaris and Djavellas. Though the posts of Bogonitza, Lelova, Variadhes, and Toskesi were defended by strong bodies of Gueghs, they were stormed one after the other.

A curious story is told of the manner in which the Suliots gained possession of Variadhes[1]. That position was occupied by about a thousand Gueghs and Sclavonian Mussulmans from Macedonia. The only well was without the Turkish lines, though completely under cover of their fire. Five Suliots crept to this well during a dark night, and let down into it a dead body and a pig cut up in quarters. In spite of the silence they maintained, the Turks suspected that

---

[1] Perrhaevos, 'Απομνημονεύματα πολεμικά, i. 41.

somebody was attempting to draw water, and wounded two Suliots with their fire. In the morning the Mussulmans discovered what their enemies had done. They reproached the Christians with carrying on war dishonourably, and of using unlawful weapons. The Suliots replied, 'The well is in our country, and if you don't like the water, you can find many good springs in the territories of Ismael the seraskier.' After some disputing, the Turks were compelled to accept the terms offered by the Suliots, and retreat to the camp before Joannina.

Khurshid Pasha, who replaced Ismael as seraskier, assumed the government of the Morea in the month of November 1820. The state of Greece already caused some alarm at Constantinople, but the rebellion of Ali was considered the real source of danger, and the conquest of Joannina was therefore the first object of the sultan's care. As soon as Khurshid reported that there was no immediate cause of alarm in his pashalik, he was ordered to leave a kehaya at Tripolitza, and take the command of the army before Joannina. On his arrival he found the Othoman army thoroughly disorganized, and he set to work with energy to remedy the evils created by his predecessor's misconduct. Nothing astonished him so much as the military position which the armatoli had assumed in the confusion. He perceived, that though the armed Christians had generally ranged themselves under the banner of the sultan's seraskier, they were employed in strengthening themselves, not in weakening Ali Pasha. His first business was to reorganize his troops, increase their numbers, and collect supplies of ammunition and provisions, preparatory to attacking Joannina with vigour. While thus engaged, he was astounded by the news that all the Morea, the islands, and a great part of continental Greece had suddenly taken up arms, and that his communications with his pashalik were cut off both by land and sea. During the whole of the summer of 1821, his operations were completely paralyzed; but he wisely determined to keep Ali closely besieged, and to redouble his exertions to destroy the great rebel. There can be no doubt that this was the most prudent resolution he could adopt in the choice of difficulties which was offered him.

The conduct of Khurshid has been severely blamed by some military critics. They consider his torpidity while the

Greeks gained possession of Acarnania and Aetolia, a proof of his incapacity. But it must be remembered, that when the Greek Revolution broke out, his army did not exceed twenty thousand, and a part of his force consisted of Christian armatoli, on whom he could no longer depend. He was compelled to maintain the blockade of Joannina, to oppose the progress of Ali's partizans and of the Suliots in Epirus, to keep open his communications with Arta and Prevesa, and to garrison the pass of Metzovo; while he could not summon a single man to his assistance from Thessaly or Macedon, lest he should be cut off from his magazines at Larissa and Thessalonica, and from direct communication with Constantinople.

Those who depreciate Khurshid's military talents observe that his camp before Joannina was only eighteen hours' march from the pass of Makronoros; that Arta and Prevesa were occupied by Othoman garrisons; and that Bekir Djokador (the gambler), who was governor of Prevesa, commanded the Gulf of Arta, with the flotilla under his orders. It is argued that by landing a body of troops at Karavaserai, the pass of Makronoros might be turned, and a body of troops marched to Vrachori in nine hours. The fertile plains of Acarnania would have enabled the Othoman cavalry to render good service by confining the Greek armatoli to the hills, and thus communications might always have been kept open with Lepanto and Patras.

The classic student is reminded of the rapid marches of Philip V. of Macedon, and his brilliant operation in destroying Thermus, the capital of the Aetolians. The ruins of Thermus are still seen towering over the central plain of Aetolia, on a rocky hill about six miles east of Vrachori. Like many other classic spots, they have now a Sclavonian name. Both the ruins and the district in which they lie are called Vlokho[1]. The operations of Philip V. afford a signal proof of the wonders that may be effected by rapid movements, strict discipline, and able tactics. The Macedonian troops were landed at Limnaea (Karavaserai) in the afternoon. They marched all night, and reached the Achelous (Aspropotamos) at daybreak. The distance is twenty-five miles. Crossing the river,

---

[1] Leake's *Travels in Northern Greece*, i. 129 foll.

they pushed forward, and reached Thermus, situated about fifteen miles from the river, late in the afternoon. The city was surprised and systematically sacked. The public buildings were burned, and, as far as time permitted, the statues were broken to pieces. Next day Philip commenced his retreat. The great fatigue which his troops had undergone during the two preceding days and nights compelled him to move leisurely, and his men were encumbered with booty. He spent three days in his retreat, before he crossed the Achelous and regained Limnaea[1].

Khurshid had perhaps more than once an opportunity of imitating the Macedonian king; but those who have written the history of the Greek Revolution have estimated the obstacles to his making the attempt too lightly. It was even difficult for him to calculate how far defection might spread among the Mussulman Albanians, if he absented himself from the Othoman camp for a single day. The Sclavonian beys and the Gueghs often behaved with great insubordination while he was present. There could be no hope of success unless he headed the expedition in person. His absence from the camp might enable Ali to raise the siege of Joannina; the defeat of the expedition might afford him an opportunity of rousing all Southern Albania against the sultan, and of forming an alliance with the insurgent Greeks. It must not also be overlooked that, during the month of May 1821, Khurshid detached nearly ten thousand men from his army, partly to reinforce the garrisons of Patras and Tripolitza, and partly to watch the vale of Tempe and the passes over the Cambunian mountains, and to keep in check the armatoli of Olympus and Ossa. By his prudence, chiefly, the Greek Revolution was prevented from spreading northward, after the execution of the patriarch Gregorios on Easter Sunday (22nd April).

The personal position of Khurshid was one of great delicacy. The interests of the Othoman empire, and his duty to the sultan, commanded him to prosecute the siege of Joannina, and keep Ali at bay in his last stronghold. But his own honour, and the safety of his family, called on him to march to Tripolitza, protect his harem, and save the Mohammedan population of his pashalik. The fate of the Othoman empire

---

[1] Polybius, v. 5 *seq.*

probably depended on his decision, and he chose like a patriot. It is the duty of the historian to give the just meed of praise to able and honourable conduct, whether the actor be an enemy or a friend, a Mohammedan or a Christian, a Turk or a Greek.

The Suliots did everything in their power to profit by the weakness of Khurshid's army: they attacked Prevesa, and attempted to interrupt the seraskier's communications with Arta. Their endeavours to gain possession of Prevesa depended for success on secret negotiations, not open assaults. They were frustrated by the conduct of their Mussulman allies, who feared lest they might become independent of Ali's assistance, and abandon his cause to secure a separate arrangement with the sultan. Their operations on the Arta road also met with only temporary success.

On the 6th of August 1821, the united forces of the Mussulman Albanians and the Suliots attacked a convoy of provisions and ammunition on its way from Arta to the seraskier's camp. The Suliots had not yet united their cause with that of the Greeks, so that no common measures were concerted with the Christians who had taken up arms in Acarnania and Aetolia. The Suliots still confined their views to securing the independent possession of Suli. The allied force, after plundering the Turkish convoy, attacked the troops of Khurshid stationed to guard the pass of Pentepegadhia, and stormed their position in a brilliant manner. In this exploit the Mussulman Albanians were more numerous than the Suliots. The Muhurdar had 500 men under his command, while Drakos, who led the Suliots, had only 200 [1]. Had they been able to retain possession of the pass, which might probably have been done with the assistance of the Greek armatoli, Khurshid would have been compelled to raise the siege of Joannina. The seraskier saw the danger, and sent an overwhelming force to recover the lost position and keep open his communications. This force compelled the allies to retire, and from that time the Suliots began to lose ground. Ali could no longer supply them with either rations or pay, and they began again to plunder the Christian cultivators of the soil, who sought protection from Khurshid, and with the

---

[1] Perrhaevos, i. 45.

assistance of these pillaged Christians the seraskier gradually succeeded in extending the sultan's authority over the whole of the Suliot territory. The agas of Margariti and Paramythia also regarded the Suliots with increased animosity since the outbreak of the Greek Revolution. The Suliots now turned to the Greeks for assistance, who had already established themselves firmly in Aetolia and Acarnania, and were preparing to attack Arta.

Mavrocordatos then acted as dictator in Western Greece. The captains of armatoli had already sent the Suliots several warnings of the danger of delivering Ali. The power of Khurshid was not feared. Indeed, the authority of Sultan Mahmud in Greece and Epirus was considered at an end. The agents of the Greek government, the friends of Mavrocordatos, and the captains of armatoli, all urged the Suliots to quit the cause of Ali and join that of Greece. They justly observed, that the cause at issue was that of Greece and Turkey, and that, whether Ali or Khurshid proved victorious, the victor would immediately turn all his forces against the Christians, and in the first place against the Suliots. The Suliots did not deny the truth of these observations, but they resolved not to break their plighted faith with the Mussulman Albanians, who had assisted them in their greatest difficulties. These Mussulman allies were at last persuaded that Ali's interest required the support of the Greeks.

In the month of October 1821, Khurshid gained possession of Litharitza, and Ali found himself hard pressed in the fortress on the lake. The batteries of the besiegers destroyed several magazines, and incessant showers of shells rendered the place almost untenable. The Greeks began to be alarmed lest Khurshid should immediately get possession of the immense treasures which they believed were heaped up in Joannina, and became consequently of a sudden eager to form an alliance with the Albanian Mussulmans who still adhered to Ali's cause. Several communications took place, and at last Tahir Abbas and Ago Besiari resolved to visit Mesolonghi, in order to confer with Mavrocordatos in person, and concert measures for assailing the rear of Khurshid's army, and opening an entrance into Ali's fortress.

Tahir Abbas was a man of experience and sagacity, whose long intercourse with the Greeks rendered him perfectly acquainted with their character, and prevented his being deceived by their wiles. On the other hand, the Greeks laid themselves open to his observation by underrating his talents. They considered him ignorant and stupid, because he spoke Greek with the rude accent and simple phraseology of the Epirot peasantry. Mavrocordatos and the Greek captains, with that overweening confidence in their intellectual superiority which makes the Greeks so often 'the fools of their own thoughts,' trusted to their powers of deception for using Ali's partizans as blind instruments. By feigning to see things as they wished him to see them, Tahir Abbas heard everything they ought to have concealed. He saw that many Greeks considered the Revolution a movement excited by Russia to destroy the Othoman empire, and that it would soon be openly supported by the Emperor Alexander. He perceived that the Greeks were fighting for their independence and for their religion; and, as a Mohammedan, he would have considered the contest a war of extermination, even had he not seen evidence of the fact at every step he took in his journey to Mesolonghi. Though familiarly acquainted with the captains of armatoli, he was astonished at the numbers of veteran soldiers he saw under their command. He was even more astonished at the spirit of independence already displayed by the rayahs or Christian peasantry. The Greeks committed a great error in allowing him to pass through Vrachori, where the blackened walls of Turkish palaces, the desecrated mosques and ruined minarets, could not escape his attention, and where their pride induced them to point out also the unburied bones of murdered Mussulmans, and the unveiled faces of women who had dwelt in the harems of beys, serving as menials in Greek families. The scrutinizing mind of Tahir Abbas seized the fact that a new phase had commenced in Turkish history; that henceforward the Mussulmans in Europe would have to sustain a long war with all the Christians who had been hitherto their obsequious serfs. When he reached Mesolonghi, he observed to an Italian whom he had known at Joannina, that the Revolution was the mortal combat of two religions. Of course he felt an internal satisfaction at making this declaration. As a sincere Mohammedan, he felt assured that though God might punish for a while the vices of the Othomans, eventually the victory would rest with Islam.

It did not require the sagacity of Tahir Abbas to perceive that it was impossible to conclude a treaty of any value either with Mavrocordatos or the Greek government. The intrigues and tergiversations of those with whom he negotiated revealed the anarchy that prevailed in the public administration, and the dissensions that existed among the leading men. Finding that he could obtain no money in Greece to enrol a body of Mussulman Albanians, and being convinced that it would be an act of folly to co-operate with Greek troops without a force sufficient to insure respect and good faith, he returned to his countrymen, who were still acting with the Suliots, determined not to serve as an instrument of Greek policy. He found that a part of the Suliots had already joined the armatoli.

In the mean time the conquest of Litharitza had convinced the Albanians that it was neither prudent nor possible any longer to resist the sultan's authority. Elmas Bey, who had commanded the Albanians, arrived from Tripolitza, and gave a horrible picture of the cruelty of the Greeks. Khurshid availed himself of this favourable opportunity to open negotiations with the partizans of Ali, and Tahir Abbas having informed them that it was impossible to come to any terms with the Greeks, the negotiations were soon terminated. The Albanians separated from the Suliots, but informed them that they would not act against them in the Suliot territory. The Suliots retired to their mountains, and the Greeks were compelled to abandon their operations against Arta.

Ali was now living in a bomb-proof cellar, clothed in a bundle of dirty embroidered garments, defending the castle of the lake with a diminished and intimidated garrison. Khurshid was watching his prey with the vigilance of a lynx. The Albanian beys, who had hitherto done everything in their power to thwart the operations of the seraskier, were now so much alarmed at the progress of the Greek Revolution, that they became eager for the triumph of the sultan. At last, in the month of January 1822, partly by treachery and partly by surprise, Khurshid's troops gained an entrance into the citadel of the lake, and Ali had barely time to shut himself up in the tower which contained his treasures and his powder-magazine. From this spot he entered into negotiations with Khurshid, who readily agreed to all his demands. Khurshid promised to spare Ali's life; and the aged tyrant, who had never respected a promise or spared an enemy, flattered himself that he could escape the vengeance of Sultan Mahmud. As he was destitute of any feeling of honour or of that pride which makes life insupportable after defeat, and as he had no personal vengeance to gratify by dying in defence of his treasury, he probably considered that at the worst it was more dignified for a pasha, and an unwieldy old man of eighty-two, to die by the bow-string than to be mangled in an explosion or slaughtered in an assault. Khurshid, on the other hand, had received the express orders of the sultan to send Ali's head to the Sublime Porte, and his difficulties rendered it absolutely necessary for him to get possession of Ali's treasury. Both he and Ali knew that a pasha's promise is valueless against a sultan's order. Khurshid gained possession of the tower, and removed Ali's treasures, which he found by no means equal to his expectations. Ali retired to a kiosk in one of the islands of the lake.

On the 5th of February 1822 a meeting took place between Ali and Mohammed Pasha, who was appointed Khurshid's successor in the pashalik of the Morea. When Mohammed rose to depart, the two viziers, being of equal rank, moved together towards the door with all the ceremonious politeness of Othoman etiquette. As they parted, Ali bowed low to his visitor, and Mohammed, seizing the moment when the watchful eye of the old man was turned away, drew his hanjar, and plunged it in Ali's heart. He walked on calmly to the gallery, and said to the attendants, 'Ali of Tepelen is dead.' The capidji of the Porte entered the hall of conference, severed the head from the body, and carried it to the citadel, where it was exhibited to the troops before being sent off to Constantinople[1]. A tumult arose between the Albanians and the

---

[1] [The scene of Ali's death was a small monastery of St. Panteleemon, situated close to the shore of the island, in a sheltered nook beneath a rock. The place of meeting of the viziers was a small balcony, upon which open two or three chambers. When I visited the spot in the summer of 1853, the occurrence was described to me according to the local tradition, which differs somewhat from the account given in the text. According to this, Ali was not mortally wounded, but managed to retire into one of the adjoining rooms. The sultan's troops, however, entered the place, and the Albanians, who commanded the court from the cliffs above, being prevented from firing on them by the presence of one of their comrades who was within, the hostile soldiery made their way into the chamber below that in which Ali was, and, firing through the thin wooden floor, succeeded in

Turks, in which several persons were killed ; but order was quickly re-established by the seliktar of Khurshid, who rode among the soldiers, announcing that the seraskier had given orders for the immediate payment of all the arrears due to the army, and that he would soon march into the warmer and more fertile region of Thessaly, and prepare to invade Greece, where booty and slaves would be obtained in abundance. Everywhere he was received with acclamation, and the Albanians as well as the Turks shouted, 'The dog Kara Ali is dead. Long life to Sultan Mahmud and his valiant seraskier, Khurshid Pasha.'

The head of Ali was exposed at the gate of the serai. A few weeks after, four heads of pashas occupied the same niche, placed side by side. They were the heads of Ali's sons, Mukhtar, Veli, and Salik, and of his grandson Mahmud, the son of Veli. They had been allowed to live quietly in Asia Minor until the old lion of Joannina was hunted down. The heads were buried at the cemetery before the gate of Selivria, where five marble tombs, ranged in a line, still arrest the attention of the traveller. The wicked father and his worthless sons are united in death. Filial ingratitude and Othoman treachery are recorded in pompous inscriptions teaching piety.

---

killing him. The holes in the floor where the bullets passed through are still to be seen. His favourite wife, Vasilike, was in the neighbouring room at the time of his death, and if the monster's orders had been carried into execution, she would have been put to death immediately after; happily, however, her life was saved. ED.]

BOOK SECOND.

THE COMMENCEMENT OF THE REVOLUTION.

CHAPTER I.

THE CAUSES OF THE GREEK REVOLUTION.

The causes produced by the improvement of society.—Secret societies.—Philike Hetairia.—Difficult position in which the Turks were placed.—Plots of the Hetairists betrayed.—Progress of education and moral improvement among the Greeks.—Turks nationally more depressed by the Othoman government than Greeks.—Influence of Roman law on modern Greek civilization.—Improvement which took place after the peace of Kainardji, in 1774.—Greeks living in Turkey under foreign protection.

THE Greek Revolution was the natural result of general causes: its success was the consequence of peculiar circumstances. Various events afforded the Greeks under the sultan's domination opportunities of acquiring knowledge and experience, and the development of their minds rendered the tyranny of the Turks insupportable. When a nation desires independence, a revolution is probable; but when it is spurred into action by an appetite for revenge as well as by a passion for liberty, a revolution becomes inevitable.

The most striking feature in the Othoman administration was the utter want of any judicial organization for the dispensation of justice. The judicial administration of Turkey only contemplated revenge for acts of injustice, not the distribution of justice to those who suffered wrong. A novelist has observed that when the Turks cut the wrong man's head off, they found a consolation in the fact that after it was over it could not be helped; the vengeance of the law was wreaked, though an additional act of injustice was perpetrated. Now, both the good and the bad qualities of the Greeks rendered them peculiarly liable to become the victims of the precipitancy of Turkish justice and of the injustice of Turkish judges. The Othoman government constantly pointed out to them the inestimable value of constitutional liberty by practical lessons, and educated them to prepare for a revolution as soon as they ceased to feel as slaves. It was not necessary for them to become acquainted with the writings of Voltaire or the theories of Rousseau. The same moral and political causes which produced the French Revolution produced the Revolution in Greece. English liberty and American independence had struck chords that vibrated wherever civilized men dwelt.

Education among the Greeks was the herald of liberty. Several individuals endowed schools, and sought to raise their countrymen from the degradation to which they had sunk towards the middle of the last century. The French Revolution certainly gave an unnatural degree of excitement to all political ideas. Its crimes and its grandeur fixed the attention of Europe on Paris. The Greeks were excited to proclaim their rights as members of the human race more loudly, and to urge their nationality as a reason for throwing off the Othoman yoke more openly, when they found similar doctrines supported by powerful armies and glorious victories in other lands. It was everywhere the fashion for the discontented subjects of established governments to imitate the French. The influence of the clubs of Paris was peculiarly calculated to produce a powerful impression on the minds of the Greeks; for it seemed to prove that great results might be effected by small assemblies, and that words, in which Greece has always been rich, might be employed as an effectual weapon to overthrow governments, and to do the work of swords. The Greeks began to form literary clubs and secret societies, with the vain hope that the Othoman empire might be destroyed by such inadequate instruments.

Two societies are supposed to have contributed directly to accelerating the epoch of the Greek Revolution, and to have aided in insuring its success. These were the Philomuse Society, founded at Athens in 1812, and the Philike Hetairia, established at Odessa in 1814. But these societies ought rather to be considered as accessories before the fact than as causes of the Revolution. The Philomuse Society was a kind of literary club, and it contributed the funds which enabled many men who took a distinguished part in the Revolution to acquire a European education. The Philike Hetairia was in its origin a political society, and it taught the Greeks, in every province of the Othoman empire, to expect immediate assistance from Russia as soon as they should take up arms, and thereby propagated the conviction that a contest with the Turks, far from being a desperate enterprise, was one which was sure of success.

As the Philike Hetairia was a political society expressly established to accelerate and direct a revolution in Greece, its composition and proceedings deserve to be noticed. The power of secret societies is very apt to be overrated, and in no case has the influence of a secret political society been more unduly magnified than in the case of the Philike Hetairia. Historians have recorded its exploits[1]: they have displayed its weakness, and revealed the ignorance and incapacity of its members. While its proceedings were veiled in mystery, they were easily magnified; when its acts were all fully known, it was evident that its conduct deserved contempt. It had, however, many paid agents, and many political adventurers gained both influence and profit by entering its precincts. It is not wonderful, therefore, that its historians have been its panegyrists. Many of the best Hetairists were more directly under the influence of Russian orthodoxy than of Hellenic independence, and many of the best men who distinguished themselves in the Greek Revolution were not Hetairists.

The first members of the Philike Hetairia were bankrupt merchants and intriguing adventurers, possessed of some cunning and great enthusiasm. Fanaticism was then one of the characteristics of every member of the Oriental or

---

[1] Gordon, *History of the Greek Revolution*, i., Introd. p. 41. Φιλήμων, Δοκίμιον Ἱστορικὸν περὶ τῆς Φιλικῆς Ἑταιρίας, Athens, 1834; Ξάνθος, Ἀπομνημονεύματα περὶ τῆς Φιλικῆς Ἑταιρίας, Athens, 1845; Φιλήμων, Δοκίμιον περὶ τῆς Ἑλληνικῆς Ἐπαναστάσεως, 2 vols., Athens, 1859.

Orthodox Church. The Russians felt it; the Greeks often affected it. Turkey was supposed to be on the eve of dissolution, and Russia to be on the point of gaining possession of Constantinople. The Philike Hetairia was formed when these opinions were predominant, and by men who entertained them. It prospered. Subscriptions were easily collected; and agents, called apostles, were sent among the orthodox population of Turkey to preach hatred of the Turks and devotion to the czar of Russia. The supreme direction of the society was, unfortunately, always in the hands of incapable men, and the apostles were often so ill selected that the members who resided in Greece refused to intrust them with large sums of money, and feared to confide their lives and fortunes to their prudence.

When this society was founded, orthodoxy and Greek nationality were so generally confounded, that the traders of Odessa who framed its organization called the popular class of initiated brethren by the barbarous appellation of Vlamides, from the Albanian word *vlameria*, signifying brotherhood. In all probability the Philike Hetairia would have soon expired of inanition had it not been kept alive by its members making use of the name of Alexander I., Emperor of Russia, who was generally supposed to grant it his secret protection. For several years it watched in vain for a field of action. The rebellion of Ali Pasha at last opened a chance of success. Had that rebellion not occurred, the Hetairists would have remained powerless until hostilities occurred between Russia and Turkey.

The influence of secret societies on national movements can only be powerful when these movements coincide with the general impulse to which the societies owe their own existence. But men are more disposed to attribute great events to anomalous causes than to trace patiently the gradual operation of natural impulses. The schemes of the Hetairists at Odessa were wild and visionary—the object of the inhabitants of Greece was definite and patriotic. The Hetairists proposed to set fire to Constantinople, to burn the arsenal, to destroy the fleet, to assassinate the sultan, to murder his ministers, and to efface the memory of the Sicilian vespers by a general massacre of the Mussulman population in the capital of the Othoman empire. And so infatuated were they, that the advantages and disadvantages of these diabolical projects are coolly discussed in a history of the Philike Hetairia published at Athens in the year 1834[1]. These counting-house Catilines of Odessa imagined that they could overthrow an empire by burning an arsenal and assassinating a prince. They overlooked the possibility of arousing the just indignation and bloody vengeance of millions of warlike Mohammedans, who would have rushed to Constantinople to defend the Turkish domination, and who, when the conspirators had destroyed the fountain-head of all the vices of the Othoman administration, might have laid the foundations of a new and more powerful Turkish empire.

The increased boldness of the Greeks in European Turkey after the commencement of hostilities with Ali Pasha did not escape the observation of the Mussulmans. The attention of the sultan and his ministers was repeatedly called to the conduct of Russian agents, and to the bold language held by many Greeks. Yet it is not surprising that the operations of the Philike Hetairia escaped the observation of the Othoman government, though its existence was discovered by the Russian police as early as 1818, for the Turks employ no spies. Russia also, by permitting her consuls and dragomans in the Levant to act as agents and couriers for the Hetairists, both concealed their intrigues and encouraged their activity. Apathetic as the Turks were, they could not overlook the great alteration which took place in the demeanour of the Greeks during the year 1820. The attitude assumed by the Christians was often seditious. Russian agents were always ready to protect them, and the evidence of a secret understanding seemed to be so strong that all foreign merchants, except the English consuls in the Levant, considered a rising of the Greeks and a war between Russia and the Porte to be inevitable.

The position of the Othoman authorities in the provinces where the Greeks were numerous was one of considerable difficulty. The conduct of the Russians rendered it dangerous for any pasha to venture on taking measures for restraining the insolence of the Greeks before receiving express instruc-

---

[1] Φιλήμων, Δοκίμιον Ἱστορικόν, p. 310.

tions from Constantinople. Any attempt to disarm the Greeks would have produced little effect in those provinces where it could have been carried into execution with ease, and any attempt to disarm the Christians in Romelia would have caused all the armatoli to join the cause of Ali Pasha. It would hardly have been prudent to disarm even the unwarlike Moreots without making a great addition to the Othoman forces then in the peninsula. When we reflect, therefore, on the delicate circumstances in which the Turkish officials were placed, it must be owned that they were not wanting in that combination of prudence and courage, toleration and cruelty, which has enabled three millions of Mussulmans to retain ten millions of Christians in subjection for four centuries. Yet every hour was bringing the antagonism of the Greeks and Turks nearer to a hostile collision, and it was by a general disarming of the Greeks that a revolution could alone be avoided. The fear that this measure would be considered by Russia as a declaration of war, prevented its adoption by Sultan Mahmud at a period when it was still practicable.

The existence of the Philike Hetairia was betrayed to Ali Pasha, and communicated by him to the Porte shortly before his proscription. Several Hetairists betrayed their companions to the Turks, and several apostles were assassinated by the Greeks[1]. An apostle named Aristides Popoff was executed at Adrianople; another, Demetrius Hypatros, was murdered by Zaphyros, the primate of Niaousta. The plan of a general insurrection of the orthodox was revealed to the Porte by a Greek named Asemaki: the papers of some of the apostles were seized in consequence of this revelation; and a number of letters were discovered which spoke of projects for murdering all the resident Turks in various towns on the Danube and on the shores of the Archipelago. Mr. Tricoupi, the Greek historian of the Greek Revolution, who was formerly employed in the English consulate at Patras, and has since been King Otho's minister in England, thinks that the existence of a secret police might have saved Turkey; and he reproaches the Othoman government with its deficiency in this branch of despotism[2]. He overlooks

---

[1] Φιλήμων, 313, 314, 316, 319.
[2] Τρικούπη, Ἱστορία τῆς Ἑλληνικῆς Ἐπαναστάσεως, i. 26. Οἱ συμμῦσται ἤρχισαν

the fact that the vices as well as the virtues of the Turks disqualify them from being efficient spies. The secret police of the Othoman empire must therefore have been intrusted to Greeks; and it is not probable that Greek spies would have revealed anything to the Turks sooner than Greek traitors. It was the absence of all systematic scheme of espionage that rendered the sultan's government, in the opinion of many Greeks, preferable to that of Venice, of Austria, and even of Russia. The best historian of the Greek Revolution, General Gordon, errs in saying that 'the stupid Moslems never entertained the least suspicion of a plot hatched in the midst of them;' but he adds, that 'the lynx-eyed police of the Russian empire (from a different cause, doubtless) was as blind as a mole to all matters connected with the society[1].' The fact, however, is, that neither Sultan Mahmud nor his ministers required to be informed by traitor Hetairists that the Greeks had long been intriguing against the Othoman domination, under the direction of and in concert with Russian agents. But it was fortunate that the treachery of the Hetairists did not enable the sultan to obtain any information concerning the grand project for his own murder, and for a general massacre, until after the outbreak had taken place. When that scheme became known the sultan could not be reproached with apathy. His anger, indeed, got the better of his policy, and he made the wickedness of the Hetairists a pretext for excessive cruelty to the Greek nation.

It must be observed that very few of the Greek officials in the Othoman service, a body of men usually called Phanariots, were admitted members of the Philike Hetairia. They were not trusted by their countrymen. Halet Effendi, Sultan Mahmud's nishandji and favourite minister, made use of the Phanariots as spies both on the orthodox clergy and on the Greek nation; and, trusting to their vigilance, he refused to believe the reports which reached the Porte that the Greeks were plotting a general insurrection. He considered it incredible that the sultan's rayahs could risk a rebellion

---

νὰ ἐργάζωνται ὑπὸ τὴν ἰδίαν Ὀθωμανικὴν ἐξουσίαν τυφλώττουσαν περὶ τὰ τοιαῦτα, ὡς μὴν ἐχουσαν ἀστυνομίαν πρὸς ἀνακάλυψίν των.

[1] Gordon, *History of the Greek Revolution*, vol. i., Introd. p. 48. Compare Φιλήμων, Δοκίμιον περὶ τῆς Ἑλληνικῆς Ἐπαναστάσεως, i. 121, 123.

as long as the Porte avoided a war with Russia. His influence with Sultan Mahmud rendered this opinion the guide of Othoman policy, and prevented the grand-vizier from taking some measures of precaution suggested by the provincial pashas in Greece.

It may now be asked by my readers, What was the real cause of the Greek Revolution, if they are to consider the rebellion of Ali Pasha and the machinations of the Philike Hetairia and Russian agency only as secondary causes? The Greek Revolution was the result of the multifarious moral as well as political causes which enlarge a nation's intelligence and awaken its feelings. The dispensations of Providence had turned many circumstances to the advantage of the Greek race. Individual virtues had been developed, and individual improvement accelerated and extended. The consequence was an increase of moral energy, a desire of action, and a longing for a national and political existence. The fulness of time had arrived: the corruption and servility of the Greek race, which had retained it in a degraded condition from the time of its conquest by the Romans, had been expiated by ages of suffering under the Othoman yoke; and the Greeks felt prepared to climb the rugged paths of virtue and self-sacrifice. The cause of the Greek Revolution embraces the history of the national character, and forms a section of the records of humanity not to be circumscribed by a survey of contemporary political events.

The Revolution was facilitated by the moral and physical decline of the Othoman race. That decline was in no small degree the result of the social circumstances which inevitably undermine the energy of every privileged dominant class; but it proceeded also from the constitution of society in Mohammedan countries, and particularly from the sultan's despotism, which consumed the riches and paralyzed the energy of the Osmanlis more effectually than that of the Christians. Nothing is more certain than that during a considerable period of Othoman history the Turkish population of the provinces was subjected to as much moral and political restraint as the Greek. This fact has been so generally overlooked, that it is difficult to state it plainly without having the air of advancing a paradox. The Mussulmans were a dominant class on account of their religion, but the Turkish population of Asia, whose feudal institutions were older than the Othoman empire, had always been an object of jealousy to the Othoman government at Constantinople. It is too much the habit to identify everything that is Turkish and Othoman in the sultan's empire. For ages the highest offices in the Othoman government were conferred on favourites of the sultan, and the cabinet was composed of men educated in his palace, or taken from domestic employments in the imperial household. In that household a slave was more honoured than a free man. The ordinance of the Mosaic law was in full vigour. 'The servant that is bought for money, when thou hast circumcised him, then shall he eat thereof' (of the passover). 'A foreigner and a hired servant shall not eat thereof.' A long period elapsed before the cabinet of the sultan contained many Turks who were born subjects of the sultan, and the counsels of the sultan were generally shared, and the conduct of the grand-vizier controlled, by purchased menials in the palace. With these men, the hereditary beys, agas, and timariots had no sympathy, and little political connection; nor could the slaves of the imperial household understand or support the feudal institutions of the Turkish race, of which they rarely heard, except as obstacles to their measures. A Turk might possess patriotism as well as religious zeal: an Othoman official might be a good Mohammedan and a devoted servant of the sultan, but in him palace prejudices occupied the place of national feelings.

We ought not to feel astonished, therefore, when we find that provincial Turks rose with greater difficulty to high rank in the Othoman service than Greeks, and possessed less influence in the administration of the empire. The Turkish aga was ill suited for an Othoman instrument. He was deficient both in knowledge and servility. The Greeks possessed both in a high degree. A wicked government requires unprincipled agents; and during the whole of the eighteenth century the Greeks held several important offices in the sultan's government because they were without principle.

Greek influence was both ecclesiastical and civil. The authority of the patriarch and synod of Constantinople, as an administrative agency in the Othoman government, was very great. It formed a more efficient protection for the orthodox Greeks than the Ulema did for the rights of the Mohammedan Turks. The dragoman of the Porte and the dragoman of the fleet formed a more direct representation of the Greek people in the Othoman government than the Turks of Asia Minor possessed. Roman law, which regulated the civil relations of the Greeks, was better preserved and more equitably administered than the feudal institutions of the Seljouk empire, or the ordinances of the Othoman sultans, which regulated the civil rights and protected the property of the Turks. This circumstance, that a Greek could speak of equity as something permanent, while a Turk could only regard it as arbitrary, gave the Greek population a moral superiority over the Turkish, in one of the most important elements of society.

The Romans, by imposing their jurisprudence on all the nations they conquered, conferred a great benefit on Greece. The Greeks have ever been self-willed and presumptuous. Every Greek has always been eager to enforce judgment on others, and ready to defy law whenever he could do so to his own personal advantage with a hope of impunity. The Romans forced the Greeks to acknowledge the principle that justice ought to be invariably administered according to fixed forms of judicial procedure. The attempt was made to render the law more powerful and more permanent than the government. A sense of the value of justice was transfused into the minds of the Greeks, and its basis being enlarged by the conversion to Christianity, it was never lost. This combination of law and religion, which is so interwoven into the national existence as to influence every individual mind, is the great element of the social superiority of the Greeks over the Turks.

The sense of equity appears to be as strong in the mind of the individual Turk, and he is not so ready to gratify his selfishness by acts of injustice as a Greek is. Yet there can be no doubt that both life and property were, on the whole, more insecure among the Turkish population of the Othoman empire than among the Greek. The want of laws, judicial institutions, and legal forms of procedure, rendered the administration of justice arbitrary, and retained Turkish society in a state of barbarism. If the solution of the Eastern question require the regeneration of the Turkish power, this end cannot be attained without the introduction of a fixed legislation and a systematic code of procedure. If the Turks persist in despising law and contemning justice, the Eastern question, instead of being solved, must be exploded. New combinations and new governments must arise, and many Eastern questions will soon become Western ones. The five great Powers of Europe cannot regulate the waters of the political inundation of which they appear neither to know the depth nor the level.

The condition of the Greek population in Turkey was, as has been already mentioned, greatly bettered by the treaty of Kainardji in 1774. A considerable increase of its numbers in the commercial cities and maritime provinces soon became apparent. The Turkish government began also at this period to be more dependent on the state of its finances, and this circumstance increased the political power of the Greeks, who were growing richer while the Turks were growing poorer. The sultan and his ministers persisted in relieving themselves from every financial difficulty by acts of bankruptcy. In this species of dishonesty the Othoman empire surpassed the Austrian. When a demand was made on the sultan's treasury, which it was deemed necessary to discharge without delay, and the sum in the hands of the treasurer did not amount to more than two-thirds of the sum due, the discrepancy was arranged by adding one-third more of alloy to the coinage. Two hundred thousand piastres' worth of bullion were thus converted into three hundred thousand piastres in money, and the debt was paid. By these depreciations of the coinage, which followed one another in rapid succession, Greek capitalists were very often gainers, Turkish landlords invariably losers.

While wealth was flowing into the hands of the Greeks, and ebbing from the coffers of the Turks, the ambition of the Greeks was directed to the sultan's service by a number of the highest official prizes in the Othoman administration. A slippered Greek, without stockings, a taoushan of the Archipelago, might become a sovereign prince beyond the Danube. Mavroyeni, a Greek secretary of the great capitan-pasha Hassan Ghazi, after serving as dragoman of the fleet, was appointed Prince of Vallachia.

A still more striking advantage which the provincial Greeks

enjoyed over the Turks was the facility of obtaining a complete exemption from the principal evils of the Othoman administration, by placing themselves under the protection of some foreign power. A practice had grown up in the Othoman empire of granting charters of denaturalization called berats, which placed the born subjects of the sultan in the situation of subjects of some friendly sovereign, to whom their allegiance was transferred. The number of Greeks who obtained this privilege was very large, and it often enabled them to transgress all the laws of the empire with impunity. The beratlis lived in the midst of the Turkish population, evading many of the heaviest financial burdens to which even Mohammedans were subjected, and carrying on commerce without paying the same duties or being amenable to the same laws in their transactions. They were even protected in their persons from the gripe of the Othoman police by the ambassador or consul to whom their allegiance was virtually transferred. This class of Christians was known to share largely in the profits of debasing the coinage, defrauding the custom-house, and cheating the people by local monopolies. An instance is recounted of a Greek beratli who realized a large fortune by forging a new coinage of more intrinsic value than the debased issue from the sultan's treasury. He had taken his measures to have his forged money ready for circulation at the same time as the government. It was not difficult, in the greater part of the empire, to persuade the people that the coinage which contained most pure metal was the lawful money, and the forger made his fortune by cheating less than the sovereign [1].

Individuals belonging to this privileged class were the most active agents of the Greek Revolution; and many who enjoyed the protection of Russia were members of the Philike Hetairia. The protection they enjoyed insured their escape from punishment, should their complicity be discovered. In this way a vast body of the orthodox, who retained as much of their connection with the patriarch and the ecclesiastical Greek nationality as suited their purpose, lived in the Othoman empire relieved not only from the yoke of the sultan, but almost from the restraint of every other govern-

---

[1] This story may not be true, but it is neither impossible nor improbable.

ment. It is needless to point out that such a position engendered the vices of avarice, falsehood, and dishonesty, or that these emancipated slaves, suddenly converted into privileged freemen, conducted themselves in general with extreme arrogance. The Turks were insulted whenever it was possible to insult them with impunity, and the Turks, in spite of their forming a dominant caste in the empire, had no revenge but the poor consolation that they could beat the lowest class of Christians whenever they thought fit. Under these circumstances, the hatred of the Turks and Greeks became every day more violent. Both were justly irritated by chronic and irremediable evils in the condition of the society in which they lived. They felt what Milton tells us, 'that justice is the only true sovereign and supreme majesty upon earth,' but how to place themselves under the authority of the empire of justice they knew not.

CHAPTER II.

The Operations of the Greek Hetairists beyond the Danube.

Character of Prince Alexander Hypsilantes. — Relations between Russia and Turkey.—State of the government and of the Rouman population in Moldavia and Vallachia.—Invasion of Moldavia.—Massacre of the Turks at Galatz and Yassi.—Fury of the Turks.—Revolution in Vallachia.—Georgaki, Savas, and Vladimiresko.—Hypsilantes at Bucharest.—Sacred battalion.— Proceedings in Vallachia.—Anathema of the patriarch.—Russia disclaims the revolution.—Deceitful conduct of Hypsilantes.—The murder of Vladimiresko. —Battle of Dragashan.—Flight of Hypsilantes.—Affair of Skuleni.—Death of Georgaki.—Termination of the revolution in the principalities.

IN the year 1820 the managers of the Philike Hetairia became sensible that they did not enjoy the confidence of the Greek nation. The ablest, the honestest, and the most influential men kept aloof from the society of the apostles, or, if they became members, expressed openly their distrust in the persons who represented the secret direction. To inspire general confidence, it was necessary that some person of character, experience, and talent should be known as the executive chief, though the names of his councillors might remain enveloped in mystery. The revolutionary projects of the Greeks were publicly discussed; the existence of a secret society was generally known, and the impossibility of delaying an insurrection was universally felt; yet the managers of the Hetairia were so destitute of practical capacity, that they had not prepared any depôts of arms and ammunition, and had not organized a single battalion. The revenues of the society had been spent by the apostles in travelling and in taverns, and the capacity of the managers exhausted in writing instructions and drawing plans remarkable only for vague patriotism and impracticable ambition. The storm was about to burst, and the magicians, who fancied they had raised it, felt themselves incapable of steering the vessel in which they were embarked with Greece and its fortunes. One man, by common consent, was deemed equal to the task of bringing Greece safe through the hurricane. That man was Count John Capodistrias. The supreme direction was offered to him, but he refused it without allowing the agents of the Hetairia to unfold their plans or explain the nature of their enterprise, and it remains still a question how much of their schemes was known to him. He was certainly not ignorant of the revolutionary projects of the society and of the Greeks generally; but he distrusted the capacity of the Hetairists, and he had no confidence in the energy and perseverance of the people: he was not without patriotism, but his patriotic feelings were not stronger than his personal ambition[1].

Capodistrias having refused the supreme direction, it was offered to Prince Alexander Hypsilantes, who, though he knew nothing about the society previously, accepted it without hesitation, and immediately assumed an absolute command over the Hetairists, their plans and resources. Hypsilantes was the eldest son of the hospodar of Vallachia, whose deposition in 1806 had served Russia as a pretext for commencing war with Turkey. Bred at a despotic court, where the will of the sovereign conferred all social, political and military rank, he had lived only with men servile to those in power, and insolent to those who were their inferiors. He had risen to the rank of major-general in the Russian service, distinguished himself as an officer, and lost his right arm at the battle of Culm. His experience of life was gained in courts and camps; he possessed considerable abilities and many superficial accomplishments, but he was extremely ambitious, and his inordinate vanity, joined to the high value he set on the princely title which his father had obtained from the Othoman sultan, became a subject of ridicule to some of his Greek followers in the trans-Danubian principalities. The Greek Revolution could hardly have fallen under the direction of a man less suited to be a nation's leader than Alexander Hypsilantes.

---

[1] Gervinus (*Geschichte des neunzehnten Jahrhunderts seit den Wiener Verträgen. Aufstand und Wiedergeburt von Griechenland*, i. 141) asserts that Capodistrias encouraged Hypsilantes to accept by assuring him that Russia would eventually aid his enterprise.

He was so ignorant of the feelings of the Greek mountaineers and seamen, that he believed the whole people ready to hail him as their monarch. Still, it may be doubted whether he would have embarked in a contest with Turkey, had he not been persuaded that the Emperor Alexander I. would support his enterprise. His education, moreover, taught him to overrate the power of Russia in the international system of Europe. He believed that it would find no serious difficulty in annexing Moldavia and Vallachia, and that to accomplish that annexation, and indemnify him for his services in creating the opportunity, a new state would be founded in Greece, of which he would be declared the sovereign.

The private character of Alexander Hypsilantes was respectable, his public conduct contemptible. He was a man of agreeable manners and a good disposition, possessing the instruction usually acquired in a well-conducted school-room, and the conversational eloquence familiar to courts. As a soldier he had displayed personal courage; he boasted of his patriotism as a Greek, but his visions of patriotism were blended with dreams of a principality or a throne. His personal good qualities were neutralized by great defects. Though active in words, he was sluggish in action. Though brave as a soldier, he was timid as a general; and when placed at the head of an enterprise which could only succeed by rapid and decisive movements, he was slow and irresolute. Deficient in the art of reading men's characters, he collected round him a crowd of would-be courtiers, and disgusted his military and democratic partizans by the ill-timed princely airs he assumed. He was also ignorant of military tactics, negligent of discipline, and deficient in that sense of order which enforces obedience and replaces the want of administrative experience. Unfortunately, his character was tainted with a worse vice. He had no reverence for truth himself, nor did he appreciate its value in others. He began and ended his great enterprise with acts of deceit and falsehood.

Secret societies are usually hot-beds of internal intrigue. Men who throw off the restraint of those moral obligations which command their obedience in one case, are not likely to respect any laws that restrain their desires. It has been already mentioned that traitors were found among the Hetairists. Acts of misconduct or of treachery induced the superior direction of the society to order its apostles to be assassinated, and Hypsilantes is accused of being privy to these assassinations[1].

The relations between the Russian and Turkish governments were almost hostile. The Greeks had some reason to expect assistance from the Emperor Alexander I., the Turks good grounds for distrusting him. The secret treaty which he had concluded with Napoleon I., after the conferences at Erfurt, for the incorporation of Moldavia and Vallachia in the Russian empire, was known to Sultan Mahmud, who saw little reason for placing any reliance in the assurances or the honour of Christian emperors after the treacherous conduct of Napoleon to the Porte on that occasion[2]. The treaty of Bucharest had indeed restored the trans-Danubian principalities to Turkey, but several circumstances gave the sultan reason to suspect that Russia would seek an early opportunity of reconquering them. In order to facilitate an invasion of Turkey at a future period, the Emperor Alexander, when he saw that he would be compelled to make peace, issued an inhuman order to his generals in Bulgaria to destroy the towns of Nicopolis, Sistova, Rutshuk, and Silistria, before evacuating them, and to lay waste all the country south of the Danube before retiring beyond the river[3]. These barbarous proceedings, and the falsehood and injustice of the Christian powers in many of their dealings with the Porte, made Sultan Mahmud extremely suspicious of the good faith of all Christian princes. The iniquitous invasion of Egypt by France in 1798; the unjust attempt to coerce the Porte by Great Britain in 1807; the violation of his engagements by Napoleon at Tilsit; the projected dismemberment of the Othoman empire at Erfurt, and the protection granted by Austria to fraudulent employés, who, like Karadja, the fugitive hospodar of Vallachia, decamped with large sums of public

---

[1] Gordon, i. 88; Tricoupi, i. 40; Philemon, Φιλική 'Εταιρία, 250 and 267. But in a recent work of the same author, the complicity of Hypsilantes in the assassination of Kamarenos at Galatz is denied, and it is ascribed to other Hetairists. 'Ελληνική 'Επανάστασις, i. Proleg. Several assassinations are enumerated by Speliades, 'Απομνημονεύματα, i. 4, 10, 21, 23.
[2] The contents of this treaty are given by Bignon, viii. 5.
[3] Rizos Neroulos (*Histoire de l'Insurrection Grecque*, 210, 213) mentions these wanton and inhuman ravages. In the war of 1828 and 1829, Russia pursued the same policy, and the whole Dobrudsha was depopulated before it was restored to the sultan. The villages were all burned, and hardly a house was left standing in many towns.

money, destroyed all confidence in the honesty of Christians and the honour of sovereigns.

On the other hand, it was impossible for Christian nations to view the treatment of their fellow-Christians in Turkey without indignation. The conduct of the officials in the Russian consulates was at variance with both justice and international law, but the conduct of the Othoman government was so unjust, that all means of protecting men from its abuses seemed equitable. Tyranny on one side and fraud on the other had, in the year 1820, produced a degree of mutual exasperation, which rendered an outbreak both inevitable and necessary. The sultan was forbidden by treaty to send Othoman troops into the Principalities without the consent of Russia, and Prince Hypsilantes believed with some ground that the Emperor Alexander would avail himself of his right to oppose their entry, or at least that he would insist on a joint occupation; and it is not improbable that, if the prince had acted with energy and capacity, and the Greek Hetairists with more courage and honesty, the one or the other must have happened. The ambition of Alexander was, however, counteracted by the principles of the Holy Alliance, and his policy was modified by the revolutionary movements of the Spaniards and Italians.

The government of the Greek hospodars in Vallachia and Moldavia was extremely oppressive, and the condition of the Rouman population under their government was more wretched than that of the Greeks under the Turkish pashas. The hospodars were men who had passed the best years of their lives in the dangerous but profitable offices of dragoman of the Porte or the fleet. From a position of servility they were suddenly invested with arbitrary power over a defenceless foreign population. They were aliens in the land they ruled, as the Turks were aliens in Greece. That, like Othoman pashas, they proved rapacious tyrants, was the natural consequence of their position and their education. Yet, while at Yassi and Bucharest they wasted the wealth of the provinces in the splendour of a court, and treated their Rouman subjects as a nation of slaves, they were regarded by their master and the divan only as tax-gatherers and policemen. The sole merit of a hospodar with the Othoman government consisted in the regularity with which he remitted his tribute, and the liberality with which he bribed the sultan's favourites and the ministers of the Porte. As the fiscal agent of the sultan he was terrible to his subjects, and as an extortioner, for his own profit, he was hateful. The hospodars themselves amassed large fortunes in a few years[1], and every new hospodar came attended by a crowd of hungry and rapacious Greeks, who usually arrived loaded with debts, but who expected, like their master, to enrich themselves during a short tenure of office. An army of Greek, Albanian, and Bulgarian policemen and soldiers alone enabled the hospodars to enforce their authority; and this force would not have sufficed without the support of the powerful suzerain at Constantinople, whose name was a shield to his vassal.

The trans-Danubian Principalities, like all the fertile provinces of the Othoman empire, were compelled to furnish the capital with supplies of provisions. The system of ancient Rome was revived by the Othoman sultans. A contribution of wheat, called istira, was exacted from the fertile plains of Macedonia, Thessaly, and Thrace. Originally the cultivator of the soil received a fair indemnification for his grain, but before the commencement of the Greek Revolution, the depreciation of the Othoman coinage rendered the price paid by the istiradji almost illusory. In Vallachia and Moldavia the export of almost every article of produce was monopolized by the administration for the benefit of the inhabitants of Constantinople and the profit of the hospodars[2]. To fulfil this duty with exactitude, the hospodars were allowed a right of pre-emption for a certain quantity of grain and a fixed number of cattle, in addition to the tenth of the gross produce of the soil, which they received as the land-tax of the Othoman empire. The right of pre-emption gave rise to abuses and exactions, which formed a severe burden on the people, and a sure means of enriching the hospodars and their Phanariot followers. A large extra supply was always collected under the pretext of paying the expense of transport, and covering the losses that might take place among the cattle.

---

[1] Zallony (*Essai sur les Fanariotes*, p. 64) says that hospodars have carried off ten millions of francs after enjoying office for only two years.

[2] Wilkinson (*Description of Moldavia and Vallachia*, French translation, p. 68) says that the only articles of export exempted from monopoly were wool, yellow berries (*Rhamnus Infectoria*), and hare-skins, which were exported in foreign ships. Gordon, *History of the Greek Revolution*, i. 93.

STATE OF THE PRINCIPALITIES.

The hospodars themselves often became grain-merchants and cattle-dealers, and made large sums of money by evading the monopolies they rigorously enforced on others. The Othoman government sent annually to the Danube vessels capable of conveying 1,500,000 kilos of wheat to Constantinople[1]; and when a greater quantity was required, the hospodars were allowed to provide for the purchase and transport of this extra quantity by a special tax on their provinces. After this notice of the principal burdens on the agricultural population of the Principalities, it is needless to attempt any description of their misery. They were the wretched slaves of a race of rapacious oppressors, who were also themselves slaves.

The native race in Vallachia and Moldavia claims a descent from the Roman colonies which settled in Dacia; but as the same language is spoken by a large part of the population in eastern Hungary, in Transylvania, in Bessarabia, on Mount Pindus, and in the valley of the Aspropotamos, it may be that this race represents a people which occupied the same countries before the coming of the Romans, but whose language had a considerable affinity with Latin, and who received the civilization of Rome, though they had resisted that of Greece[2]. In 1821, the Rouman race numbered six millions of souls, and its lot was most unhappy. The boyards and the native nobility had been demoralized by the government of the Greek princes—they were tyrants of the peasants who cultivated the soil. The greater part of the land belonged either to large proprietors, who were like feudal lords, or to monasteries and ecclesiastical establishments. Though the cultivator was in reality a free colon, his condition was as degraded and helpless as that of a serf attached to the glebe. He was bound to work a certain number of days on a piece of land of which the whole produce belonged to the landlord. He had no prospect of ever improving his condition by his own industry, for his landlord had the power of sending him to cultivate land of an inferior quality at any time; and the landlord's steward could exercise every power belonging to

---

[1] Nearly 200,000 quarters. A considerable number of cattle and sheep were also conveyed to Constantinople by sea, but many were driven there by land.
[2] [This is an unlikely supposition. On the origin of the Wallachians *see* above, vol. iii. p. 228. ED.]

the landlord. The result was, that the Roumans were a sluggish race, nor had they, like the Greeks, the consolation of meeting with any sympathy among the Christians of happier countries. During the occupation of the Principalities by the Russians from 1808 to 1812, they had suffered severer exactions than the Greeks of the Peloponnesus had suffered at the same time from Veli Pasha. The subsequent extortions of Karadja and Kallimaki had prevented them from recovering from the exactions of the Russians. It is not, therefore, wonderful that the Rouman population regarded the Greeks with a deep-rooted hatred, and that the idea of Greek princes and Phanariot officials coming to them as the heralds of liberty appeared to be a bitter mockery.

Alexander Hypsilantes crossed the Pruth, attended by a few followers, on the 6th of March 1821. He had concerted his measures with Michael Soutzos, the reigning hospodar, and the leading Phanariot officials in the province who had been admitted members of the Hetairia. Hypsilantes believed that he was entering on a smooth and brilliant career; that Moldavia and Vallachia would submit to his government at his mere requisition; that the machinery of administration would move smoothly on as under the suzerainty of the sultan, with the advantage that he should be able to retain in his own hands the sultan's tribute; that a European congress would relieve him from every difficulty, and the protection of the Emperor Alexander secure to him either a principality on the Danube or a throne in Greece.

The first acts of Hypsilantes betrayed his utter incapacity for the post into which he had thrust himself. Instead of endeavouring to gain possession of Ibrail, which alone could have enabled him to proceed in his enterprise with any prospect of success, he took up a position at Yassi, where his presence was unnecessary. The hospodar, Michael Soutzos, and the postelnik, Rizos Neroulos, were amiable, weak-minded, and ambitious men. They shared all Hypsilantes' foolish hopes of Russian intervention; and, like him, they forgot that neither Providence nor Russia was likely to assist men who neglected their own affairs. Had Hypsilantes rendered it difficult for the Turks to enter the Principalities, Russia might have refused to allow them to make the attempt. To gain the support of the people it would have been necessary to promise the Roumans liberty, and to insure them some guarantee against the oppression of the Greeks and Russians, rather than an imaginary relief from the Turkish yoke; for in the minds of the agricultural population in the Principalities, Turkish tyranny was regarded as a phrase for expressing Phanariot rapacity. But Hypsilantes as a Russian protégé, and Michael Soutzos as a Phanariot tax-gatherer, had no thought of increasing the liberties or lightening the burdens of the people. Hypsilantes therefore, as leader of the Greek Revolution, took his stand in Moldavia as the chief of a band of foreign mercenaries, striving to conquer the Rouman country in order to transfer the suzerainty from the Sultan of Constantinople to the Czar of Russia.

The invasion of the Hetairists overthrew the civil government, which derived its authority from the Porte; and Alexander Hypsilantes issued a proclamation as supreme head of a new order of things, in which, instead of marking his confidence in himself and his army, he boasted in enigmatic phrases that Russia protected his enterprise, and that her assistance would insure his triumph[1]. His fatuity looked like a satire on revolutions. In action he was as destitute of energy as he was deficient of prudence in counsel. Instead of marching to surprise the enemy and secure a strong military position, he trifled away his time in idle ceremonies or absolute inaction.

The treason of Michael Soutzos and several of the Moldavian ministers placed the whole financial and military resources of the province at Hypsilantes' disposal, and he was already in possession of a large sum of money[2]. A considerable body of troops, consisting of soldiers who had served in the Russian and Servian wars, might have been assembled

---

[1] See this document in Speliades, i. 36, and the observations on Hypsilantes' indecision in Rizos Neroulos, *Histoire de l'Insurrection Grecque*, 282. Tricoupi (i. 55), who writes in the spirit of equity and good faith, quotes the words as they are given in a short proclamation of Hypsilantes to the Moldo-Vallachians, dated 23rd February (7th March), 1821, published by Photeinos (p. 33). The passage is modified in the long proclamation, dated the 24th February (8th March), printed by Speliades, which corresponds very nearly with that published by Philemon in his recent work entitled Δοκίμιον περὶ τῆς Ἑλληνικῆς Ἐπαναστάσεως (ii. 79); but in this the passage is entirely omitted. A comparison with other sources, however, proves that more than one of the documents printed by Philemon have been subjected to unfair manipulation. Compare the allusion in the proclamation to the Greeks in the Principalities as that document is printed by Philemon, ii. 85.

[2] Rizos Neroulos, *Insurrection Grecque*, 295.

in a few days by an energetic leader with active lieutenants. The Hetairists had already secured the support of the ablest officers in the command of the troops under arms in both Principalities; and as Alexander Soutzos, the hospodar of Vallachia, died a few weeks before Hypsilantes crossed the Pruth[1], the whole military force in the two Principalities might have been concentrated on the banks of the Danube. The number of Greek sailors at Galatz would have enabled a man of promptitude to secure the command of the river by a fleet of gun-boats. The civil and military administration might have been more easily centred in the hands of the commander-in-chief of the army in a camp before Ibrail, than at Yassi or Bucharest. By repealing every monopoly and commercial restriction, the good-will of the landed proprietors, as well as of the merchants and seamen, would have been gained. By rapid movements and vigorous attacks, the few Turkish troops then in the Dobrudsha might have been dispersed, and all the fortresses below Galatz taken. The whole course of the Danube from Orsova to the sea would, in all probability, have been in the possession of a daring soldier who had known how to conduct a national revolution, before the Othoman government had moved a single soldier; but Alexander Hypsilantes had neither the hand, the head, nor the heart capable of conducting a daring enterprise. He neither centralized the administration, nor concentrated the army, nor collected military stores, nor formed magazines. In short, he did nothing but play the prince and leave every matter of importance to chance.

The Hetairists were ready for vigorous action, and were looking anxiously for orders while Hypsilantes was preparing to cross the Pruth. Anarchy was the natural consequence of a band of conspirators being left without precise instructions and without any recognized chief. It is not surprising, therefore, that the first deeds of the Revolution brought dishonour on the cause. Galatz is the principal port of Moldavia; several Turkish merchants resided in the town, and some Turkish vessels lay in the port. As in the

---

[1] Alexander Soutzos, the hospodar of Vallachia, was not of the same family as Michael Soutzos, the hospodar of Moldavia. He died suddenly on the 1st February, 1821. He was accused of having revealed as much as he had discovered of the plots of the Hetairists to the Turks, and it was thought that he had been poisoned by them; but these reports have been denied.

Othoman empire foreign sovereigns retain the sole civil and criminal jurisdiction over their subjects, it naturally followed that in the Principalities the sultan alone possessed any authority over the resident Mussulmans : a Turkish officer was therefore stationed at Galatz with a few guards, in order to enforce obedience to the police regulations and fiscal laws of Moldavia on the part of the Turks. A Greek named Karavia commanded the Christian troops in the service of the hospodar. Like Michael Soutzos and Rizos Neroulos, he was a member of the Hetairia, and being intrusted with the secrets of the conspirators, he availed himself of the vague communications and the negligence of Hypsilantes in omitting to issue precise orders, to make an infamous attempt to enrich himself by plundering the Turks. He was an Ionian by birth, and had acquired some military experience in the Russian service, and some property in the service of Karadja, the hospodar of Vallachia.

The night before Hypsilantes quitted the Russian territory, Karavia assembled the Hetairists and his band of mercenaries (called Arnaouts in the Principalities, though composed of Greeks, Servians, and Bulgarians, as well as Albanians), and after informing them that a revolution was about to take place under Russian auspices, he led them to attack the Turkish officer and his men. Some of the Turks were surprised and murdered, but others succeeded in shutting themselves up in a house, which they defended for a short time. Karavia then authorized his men to capture or murder the Turkish merchants in the town, and began to break open and plunder their warehouses and take possession of their ships. Turks of every rank, merchants, soldiers, and sailors, were surprised and murdered in cold blood. The native population of Galatz took no part in this infamous transaction ; they neither stained their hands with blood, nor disgraced themselves by robbing their guests. Indeed, the cruelty of Karavia and the licentiousness of his Arnaouts terrified the Moldavians, who saw little prospect of enjoying either order or security under the government of the Hetairists [1].

---

[1] The most accurate account of the revolution in the trans-Danubian provinces is in Gordon's *History of the Greek Revolution*. He obtained a large number of original documents from one of Hypsilantes' principal officers, and he was

The sanguinary and revengeful passions awakened by the assassination of the Mussulmans at Galatz spread rapidly over the whole province, in consequence of the misconduct of Hypsilantes and the timidity of Michael Soutzos. About fifty Othoman soldiers were stationed at Yassi as a guard of honour. They had no duty but to uphold the dignity of the suzerain by the mere fact of their presence at the court of the hospodar. Before Hypsilantes entered the city, Soutzos persuaded the bash-besli-aga to order his guards to lay down their arms, under a promise that their persons and property should be protected. The Turks were not inclined to resist the Hetairists, for they shared the general opinion that they formed the vanguard of a Russian army. The Othoman soldiers were then ordered to remain in their quarters and the Turkish merchants to be imprisoned, under the pretext that this measure was necessary to insure their safety. Yet as soon as the news of the murders at Galatz reached the capital, both the Othoman soldiers and the Turkish merchants were murdered in cold blood, under the eyes of Michael Soutzos and Alexander Hypsilantes, without these princes making an effort to save their lives, or uttering a word of reprobation at this disgraceful violation of a sacred promise. Hypsilantes had even the weakness and the wickedness to approve of the murders of Karavia at Galatz, and thus to ratify those which he had witnessed at Yassi.

The consequence of this misconduct was that similar assassinations were committed in other places, and the Albanian and Greek soldiers considered that they were authorized to rob and murder every Mussulman whose property excited their cupidity, or whose conduct afforded a pretext for revenge. Much disorder ensued, the difficulty of enforcing discipline was increased, and every captain of a company took the liberty of acting without orders.

The treasury of the Hetairia at Yassi contained a much smaller sum than Hypsilantes had expected to find in it. His own ignorance of financial administration rendered him

---

acquainted both with the country and the leading men. Compare the account of the affair at Galatz circulated at the time, as given in a curious work published in lithography at Bucharest, with the indication, Leipzig, 1846; Οἱ Ἄθλοι τῆς ἐν Βλαχίᾳ Ἑλληνικῆς Ἐπαναστάσεως τὸ 1821, συγγραφέντες παρὰ Ἠλία Φωτεινοῦ, p. 29, with that of Φιλήμων, περὶ τῆς Ἑλλ. Ἐπαν. i. 125, and Gordon, i. 100.

helpless, and his counsellors could suggest nothing better than following the example of Karavia's Arnaouts, and plundering the rich. Hypsilantes, therefore, commenced his administrative operations by seizing a wealthy banker, whom he accused of being hostile to the Revolution, and of concealing funds belonging to the Hetairia. The first accusation was not a crime, and the second was false; but Paul Andreas was glad to pay the prince several thousand pounds to escape out of his hands[1]. This act of extortion alarmed the native boyards and all the wealthy Roumans, who, afraid of being robbed by the Greeks, availed themselves of every opportunity of escaping into Russia and Austria.

The murders committed by Karavia, without securing any military advantage, inflicted a severe blow on the cause of the Hetairists. A panic terror seized the people in all the towns on the southern bank of the Danube, and the Turkish inhabitants and Othoman garrisons were roused from the apathy in which they were living and the state of neglect in which they had been left by the sultan's government. As the news of the murders at Galatz and Yassi flew from one city to another, embellished with a hundred horrid exaggerations, the Mussulmans everywhere flew to arms; and it may be truly said that the most efficient support of Othoman domination at this crisis was the cruelty of the Greeks, not the energy of Sultan Mahmud. The wickedness of the Hetairists proclaimed the Revolution at its commencement to be a war of extermination. The Mohammedans accepted the decision of their enemies with ferocious joy, for they deemed that it made their cause the cause of justice and of God. They took up arms to avenge the murder of their brethren, and to defend their race and their religion from bloodthirsty aggressors.

While the Turks were preparing with unusual promptitude for war, Hypsilantes was trifling away his time at Yassi in the silliest manner. He conferred high military titles on his followers: captains at the head of a hundred men were made generals, and in this way acquired an opportunity of proving

---

[1] Gordon says 160,000 ducats, erroneously for piastres (i. 100); but Tricoupi reduces the sum to 60,000, about 2000*l*. sterling at the then rate of exchange (i. 54).

that they were equally unfit for both offices. Karavia was rewarded for bringing indelible disgrace on the enterprise by being named a general. The extreme folly of Hypsilantes in promoting the members of his suite was rendered more offensive by his omitting to confer any military distinction on the three ablest officers in the Principalities, who were actually at the head of considerable bodies of efficient troops. These men were Theodore Vladimiresko, a Vallachian boyard; Savas, a Greek of Patmos; and Georgaki, of Olympus. They were all Hetairists, and the neglect with which they were treated inspired Vladimiresko and Savas with suspicions that Hypsilantes and his Phanariot advisers wished to supersede them in their commands. So rapidly did the prince reveal the weakness of his character, that during his stay at Yassi not a single Moldavian of any rank joined his standard [1].

After allowing two months to pass unemployed, when every day ought to have been commemorated by exploits, Hypsilantes reached Bucharest on the 9th of April 1821.

The three military chiefs neglected by the commander-in-chief were the real men of action in this unfortunate revolution.

Georgaki of Olympus had been commandant of the Arnaout guard in Vallachia at the death of the hospodar Alexander Soutzos. He was a man of courage and good sense, who had acquired some military experience in the Russian service, and who was enthusiastically devoted to the cause of Greece, without having formed any precise ideas concerning the means by which her liberty could be secured. Like most of his countrymen, his predominant idea was hatred of the Turks, and to secure a victory over his enemies he was ready to forge chains with which Russia might bind both Turks and Greeks. He was a sincere patriot, but no politician. His influence over the Greek and Albanian soldiers in the Principalities was great, for he was acknowledged to be their bravest leader; but he had no sympathy with the Rouman population, and he was not liked by the native boyards.

Savas of Patmos was a mere mercenary captain, but he was a man of cunning, courage, and ambition, who, under

---

[1] Rizos Neroulos, *Histoire de l'Insurrection Grecque*, 292.

an able and energetic chief, might have been rendered an active and daring officer. He had been appointed commandant of the garrison of Bucharest by the regency which administered the government of Vallachia after the death of Alexander Soutzos. Savas' confidence in the cause of the Hetairists had been greatly diminished by their proceedings from the time Hypsilantes crossed the Pruth until he arrived at Bucharest. He perceived that he was distrusted; and a new hospodar, Skarlatos Kallimakes, having been appointed by the Porte, he conceived hopes of advancing his interests better by allying himself with the Phanariot hospodar, who was sure of being supported by the sultan, than with the princely adventurer, who seemed by no means certain of receiving any effectual support from Russia.

Theodore Vladimiresko was a lesser boyard, who had risen to the rank of lieutenant-colonel in the Russian service, and obtained the cross of St. Vladimir, from which he took his surname. He had as deep-rooted and as patriotic an aversion to Othoman domination as any Greek; but he had also a strong aversion to the Greeks as the agents of Turkish oppression in his country. He had joined the Philike Hetairia because it was a society of the orthodox, which he hoped might be useful in delivering his countrymen from the state of bondage in which they were living; but he had no intention of becoming a passive instrument of Greek intriguers. He was ambitious, cruel, and suspicious, without either the dashing courage of Georgaki or the plausible manners of Savas. His deceitful conduct warranted the Greeks in regarding him as a traitor to their cause; but if Vallachian historians had alone written the history of the enterprise of the Hetairists with the fixed purpose of lauding nationality as the first of political virtues, Vladimiresko would have been represented as a patriot and a hero.

Hypsilantes reached Bucharest with only two thousand troops under his immediate orders. But he was already surrounded by a court and a crowd of adventurers, seeking to advance their fortunes by crowding his antechamber, and by treating him with Oriental servility. There was no military system in his army; and at Bucharest the conduct of his troops persuaded even the unwarlike Roumans that he was utterly unfit for the task he had undertaken. A few days after his arrival, everybody inquired with alarm how the enterprise was likely to terminate. The infatuation of Hypsilantes still led him to expect success from the interference of Russia, and not from his own exertions; but many of his followers began to perceive that Russia, like Hercules, would in all probability be in no hurry to assist a lazy waggoner through the muddy road into which he had voluntarily plunged. In the mean time, while Hypsilantes was waiting to receive the gift of a throne, he amused himself and his mimic court by taking into his service a company of comedians, and plundering the treasury of the monastery of Maryeni to fit up a theatre [1].

The greatest disorder already reigned among the troops in both Principalities. The soldiers were left without pay, and at times without rations, so that they lived at free quarters among the peasantry; and all discipline was relaxed. A numerous staff of officers, in rich and fantastic dresses, hastened to and fro in the streets of Bucharest from morning to night, apparently intent on business, but without producing any result. Secretaries transmitted arbitrary requisitions for money and provisions to every district from which anything could be extracted; and Hypsilantes had himself the impudence to issue orders to prepare quarters for a Russian army, which he declared the emperor had placed under his command.

The only corps formed by the Hetairists, whose discipline and good conduct merits praise, was a corps of volunteers called the Sacred Battalion, composed of about five hundred young men of the higher and middle ranks, full of enthusiasm for the cause of liberty. They adopted a black uniform, and placed the effigy of a death's-head on their caps as a sign of their oath that they would die or conquer. Theirs, however, was no vain boast.

'Rousing the vengeance blood alone can quell,
They rushed into the field, and, foremost fighting, fell.'

Unfortunately, many of these young men were ill fitted to encounter the hardships of a campaign, by their extreme youth and their previous habits. Yet, though they suffered severe privations on the march, they behaved with spirit and order, and were everywhere praised by the peasantry for their discipline.

---
[1] Gordon, i. 106.

Georgaki of Olympus had also an efficient body of cavalry under his orders, but its numbers did not exceed two hundred well-mounted troopers.

The garrison of Bucharest, under the command of Savas, amounted to a thousand men, and composed an efficient corps of veteran mercenaries.

Vladimiresko was encamped at the monastery of Kotratzani, in the immediate vicinity of the capital, with three thousand pandours, or Vallachian light cavalry. His force was in good order, and he had adopted prudent arrangements for securing ample supplies of provisions and military stores. A good deal of intrigue was going on among all who possessed any share of civil or military power in Vallachia. Savas, as commandant of the garrison of Bucharest, had been ordered by the regency to defend the capital against Vladimiresko, who, at the instigation of the Hetairists, had commenced an insurrection in Little Vallachia immediately after the death of Alexander Soutzos, in order to distract the attention of the Othoman government. But the conduct of Hypsilantes in Moldavia having convinced Vladimiresko that the prince was too incompetent to have been selected by the Russian cabinet as the leader of a revolution, he advanced towards Bucharest, in order to watch the progress of events, and preserve his own position as an independent Vallachian chief. On the 29th of March, while Hypsilantes was trifling away his time on the road between Yassi and Bucharest, Vladimiresko encamped before the Vallachian capital, and published a proclamation to the inhabitants, breathing a spirit of Rouman patriotism, declaring that he came to aid them as the champion of his native land, and inviting them to send deputies in order to discuss with him the measures to be adopted for laying before the Porte a detailed statement of the evils they suffered from the rapacity of the Phanariots. It was evident that Vladimiresko had abandoned the cause of the Hetairists.

When Hypsilantes reached Bucharest, neither Vladimiresko nor Savas would acknowledge him as commander-in-chief. Both distrusted him, and both were aware of his incapacity; but as they distrusted and hated one another, both opened communications with him, hoping to render his influence subservient to the furtherance of their own projects.

The sultan had now assembled a considerable number of Turkish troops on the southern bank of the Danube. Hypsilantes had only one chance of terminating his enterprise with honour. He might still beat up the quarters of the enemy before they could concentrate a force sufficient to overwhelm the Principalities like an avalanche. Instead of taking the field, he commenced a series of intrigues with the boyard and the Patmian, in which each of the three negotiators endeavoured to cheat the other two. This wretched scene of cunning was brought to a termination by an event that would alone have sufficed to ruin the enterprise. The news arrived at Bucharest that the patriarch of Constantinople had issued an anathema against the Hetairia, and cursed Hypsilantes and his adherents. The enterprise of Hypsilantes was no longer the cause of orthodoxy, and the Roumans were eager to express their detestation of a scheme which they attributed to Greek ambition. The scandalous behaviour of persons in the prince's suite, and the want of discipline among his troops, disgusted the Vallachians, who saw that the corps of Savas and Vladimiresko behaved in an orderly manner, and respected the property of the citizens[1].

While the feelings of the Rouman population were in this state, the news arrived that Russia disclaimed all complicity with the Hetairists, and that the Emperor Alexander reprobated the conduct of Hypsilantes. A congress of European sovereigns which met at Laybach declared that the members of the Holy Alliance were hostile to all revolutionary movements; and the Russian emperor gave the strongest proof of his reprobation of Hypsilantes' conduct by announcing his determination to preserve peace with the sultan, and consenting to the entry of Othoman troops into the transDanubian Principalities for the purpose of suppressing the troubles caused by the prince's insane project. At the same time he dismissed Hypsilantes from the Russian service.

The anathema of the patriarch and the policy of the Russian emperor awakened open opposition to the Hetairists on the part of the clergy and the natives, and encouraged Savas and Vladimiresko to treat the assumption of supreme

---

[1] Triccupi, i. 61.

OPPOSITION OF RUSSIAN EMPEROR. 127

power by Hypsilantes as an idle pretension, which they admitted only to advance their own private interests. They both opened secret communications with the sultan's officers, though neither of them appears to have attached any importance to the fact that the sultan was, by the constitution of the orthodox church of Constantinople, the legal supporter of the patriarch's authority. Many boyards, who had hitherto believed that the enterprise of Hypsilantes would eventually receive Russian support, now fled to Austria, and before quitting the Principalities, transmitted to the Porte strong declarations of devotion to the sultan's government, and gave strict orders to their stewards to throw every obstacle in the way of the Hetairists, and afford every facility to the advance of the Othoman troops.

The decision of the Emperor Alexander was announced to the boyards of Moldavia at Yassi on the day Hypsilantes entered Bucharest; and he received the news of his own dismissal from the Russian service, and of the consent of the Russian government to the advance of the Othoman troops, a day or two later, by letters from Nesselrode and Capodistrias, written by order of the emperor. These letters upbraided him for his folly in commencing the Revolution, and for his falsehood in making use of the emperor's name in a manner both unbecoming and untrue. He was ordered to lay down his arms immediately, as the only reparation he could make for the many evils he had created by his unreasonable ambition. From this moment it was evident that the Revolution was hopeless, and it was clearly the duty of Hypsilantes to terminate his military and political career as speedily, and with as little injury to the Principalities, as possible. Had he frankly communicated the contents of the documents transmitted to him by the Russian embassy at Constantinople to his principal officers, and concerted openly and honourably with Savas and Vladimiresko the measures necessary to be taken for preserving order and securing a general amnesty, he might still have saved thousands from ruin and death, and his own name from dishonour. But his vanity was so extravagant, his incapacity so deplorable, and his conscience so weak, that he persisted in his habit of deceit.

The policy of Russia was known to everybody in Bucharest

a few hours after the prince had read his letters. Georgaki of Olympus and the principal officers waited on him to know the precise nature of the communications he had received, in order to decide on their future operations. They were received with the ceremonial of a royal court. Hypsilantes listened to their request with an affected air of condescension and self-satisfaction, but he could not prevent an expression of pettishness revealing itself in his reply; and he had the baseness to assure the officers that, though the Emperor Alexander deemed it necessary to disapprove of his conduct openly, in order to preserve peace in Europe, his imperial majesty had privately ordered Capodistrias to assure him that the Hetairists were not to lay down their arms until they were informed of the issue of proposals in favour of the Greeks, which the Russian minister at Constantinople was instructed to lay before the Porte. He informed them also that, under the circumstances, he had no intention of attacking the Turks, and that he believed the Othoman troops at Rutshuk and Silistria would not invade the Principalities. When he made these statements, he knew that every word he uttered was false.

Hypsilantes was now at the head of a small and irregular army, almost entirely destitute of artillery, but with this force he took the field. Yet even then, instead of hastening to the Danube to cover Bucharest, and gain honour at least by some brilliant exploit, he crept away towards the Austrian frontier. His proceedings induced both Savas and Vladimiresko to suspect that he was playing some secret game for his own advantage, of which they were to be the dupes. They resolved to imitate the example, and turn the troubled aspect of public affairs to their own profit at his expense. Both of them carried on active negotiations with the Othoman commander at Rutshuk. Savas expected to obtain promotion by betraying the prince into the hands of the Turks. Vladimiresko is said to have believed that, by balancing between the different parties, he might at last succeed in inducing the Porte to name him hospodar of Vallachia. If this accusation be true, he must have been a worthy rival of Prince Alexander Hypsilantes in military diplomacy and political credulity.

The consent of Russia to the suppression of the Revolution by Othoman troops, made it necessary for Hypsilantes to fight immediately, or escape rapidly. He had so completely neglected military business while he was at the head of his army, that on entering on the campaign he was almost without ammunition, and to supply the want he commenced active operations by plundering the stores of Vladimiresko of six thousand pounds of powder. The troops behaved as ill as their leader: they plundered the baggage of the metropolitan bishop, and of several boyards, who were fleeing for safety to the Austrian territory.

The Turks, who had assembled considerable forces at Ibrail, Silistria, Giurgevo, and Widin, encountered no serious opposition in marching to Yassi and Bucharest. On the 27th of May they reached Bucharest, and the pasha of Silistria entered it on the 29th. Savas, though in negotiation with the Turkish authorities, followed the revolutionary army in hopes of finding an opportunity of making the prince prisoner, and delivering him into the hands of the pasha of Giurgevo. Vladimiresko also followed the movements of Hypsilantes; for by recognizing him as commander-in-chief, he had compromised his own position as an independent Vallachian leader. The movements of Hypsilantes indicate that his object in taking the field was to prevent the Othoman cavalry cutting off his retreat to the Austrian frontier. He formed a camp at Tergovisht, where he threw up intrenchments, and declared that he would await the attack of the Turks. But Vladimiresko, having resolved also to consult his own safety, and having made dispositions for marching into Little Vallachia, where he expected to maintain himself with advantage until he had brought his negotiations with the Othoman officers to a favourable termination, Hypsilantes became so alarmed lest his retreat should be cut off, that he ordered Vladimiresko to be arrested, or slain as a traitor. A conspiracy of Hetairists had been already formed among the officers in the Vallachian army, in consequence of the dissatisfaction felt at his communications with the Turks. A part of the correspondence of the Vallachian chief with the kehaya of the pasha of Giurgevo had been intercepted, and placed in Hypsilantes' hands. The prince showed this correspondence to Georgaki, and upbraided him with having initiated Vladimiresko into the secrets of the Hetairia, telling him that it was his duty to remedy the evils produced by his imprudence, which could only be done by arresting the traitor. Georgaki, who was brave and loyal, undertook the task without hesitation. While at Piteshti, he was invited by a party in the Vallachian camp at Goleshti to assist them in putting an end to the authority of Vladimiresko; and on receiving this invitation, he hastened forward with a body of cavalry. He found a council of officers assembled to receive a communication of the greatest importance; and at this assembly, Georgaki boldly accused Vladimiresko of treachery, and declared that he was sent to summon the Vallachian leader to answer for his conduct before the commander-in-chief of the army. Vladimiresko, who despised Hypsilantes, and regarded Georgaki as his friend, did not consider that he exposed himself to much danger by submitting to the arrest and returning to Hypsilantes' camp in company with Georgaki. He knew that many of his own officers were dissatisfied with his conduct, and he feared that, if he refused to justify himself voluntarily, they might have deserted his cause openly. He counted on the attachment of his soldiers and the inferior officers of the Vallachian army, as a sufficient guarantee for his personal safety. Though cruel and selfish, he was not an adept in treachery and falsehood, and his conscience reproached him for intriguing with the Turks, when he listened to the language of truth and honour, simply and frankly uttered by Georgaki, whom he had always admired and respected. He felt that he had violated his duty to his country, which probably affected him far more than any violation of his oath to the Hetairists.

Hypsilantes still lingered at Tergovisht when Vladimiresko was brought before him. Though himself meditating the treachery of abandoning his followers, he reproached the Vallachian chief for his treachery to the Hetairia in rude and opprobrious language. Vladimiresko retorted that he had served his country better than his accusers, and excused his correspondence with the Turks, by asserting that the intrigues of Savas had compelled him to countermine that officer. Instead of ordering Vladimiresko to be tried by court-martial, Hypsilantes pretended to pardon him; but two nights after he allowed some of his Greek partizans, who were the most determined enemies of Rouman nationality, to hurry the Vallachian chief out of the town, and to murder him with their swords and yataghans[1]. The incapacity of Hypsilantes prevented his deriving any advantage from this assassination, though it increased his little army by an addition of four thousand men, four pieces of artillery, a considerable supply of ammunition, and a well-filled military chest.

Savas, alarmed at finding that all his dealings with the Turks were known, quitted Hypsilantes with his whole force, and joined the Othoman troops.

The Hetairists were now in danger of being surrounded by three divisions of the Turkish army advancing from Bucharest, Giurgevo, and Widin. On the 8th of June the advanced guard from Bucharest engaged a body of Hetairists near Tergovisht, and both parties claimed the victory. Hypsilantes, however, moved off to Piteshti with such precipitation that he lost twelve waggons, laden with biscuit, and part of the baggage of his army, in the river Dimbovitza; and one corps abandoned the line of march, and retreated to Kimpolunghi. The Othoman troops occupied Tergovisht, and the prince pursued his march northward to Rimnik. His movements were so evidently without any military object, that his followers became persuaded that his own personal safety alone occupied his thoughts. After remaining three days at Rimnik, on the Olta, he resolved to attack a body of Turkish cavalry which had advanced from Kraïova and taken post at the village of Dragashan, about thirty miles from his camp. The force under his command amounted to four thousand infantry, twenty-five hundred cavalry, and four guns.

On the 19th of June 1821, Prince Nicolas Hypsilantes, at the head of the sacred battalion, supported by Karavia, with five hundred cavalry and four guns, took up a position before the Turkish post at Dragashan. Georgaki sent forward a strong body of Vallachian infantry to occupy the road to Kraïova, and thus cut off the retreat of the Turks. The revolutionists required rest, for they had made a long march over heavy ground wet with rain. Georgaki, who was the superior officer, resolved to attack the enemy next morning; and to prevent the Turks from escaping to Kraïova, he strengthened the Vallachian infantry with a body of horse. As soon as these arrangements were completed, he despatched

---

[1] Compare Gordon, i. 113; Tricoupi, i. 149; and Photeinos, 132.

an orderly to the head-quarters of Prince Alexander Hypsilantes, urging the commander-in-chief to hasten forward and secure the glory of the day. The envy of Karavia frustrated the prudence of Georgaki. He hated the Olympian, because in the hour of danger all men's eyes were turned on that gallant soldier, and he now resolved to rob him of what seemed to the less experienced Cephalonian an easy victory. Karavia succeeded in persuading Nicolas Hypsilantes, who was as weak as his brother, to disobey the precise orders of their superior officer, and to advance with the sacred battalion and the artillery to attack the Turks, assuring him that, with the support of the cavalry, of which Karavia had five hundred in advance, it would be easy to storm Dragashan.

The Turkish force amounted to eight hundred men. Its officers were fully aware of their dangerous position, and were anxiously watching for an opportunity to escape, when they perceived the sacred battalion advance to attack them. They immediately saw that, if they could destroy it before it could receive succour, they might still succeed in effecting their retreat. The sacred battalion was composed of brave and enthusiastic youths, but their bodies were not hardened by active life, and they had not yet acquired the steady discipline of veterans. Wearied with a fatiguing march, and stiff with a short rest, they were suddenly formed, and led hurriedly forward to attack the enemy. The Turkish cavalry was drawn up, waiting an attack; but it was carefully concealed behind the buildings of the village, which covered it from the fire of the artillery. While the weary Greeks were moving slowly forward, the Turks darted on them from their hiding-places. Galloping furiously, with loud shouts, into the intervals between the companies, before the sacred battalion could form squares, they broke its order in a dozen places by a heavy fire of pistols and carbines. But though broken, the men behaved with courage; and, true to their oath, they fell bravely fighting round their standard. Very different was the conduct of Karavia and the cavalry; they fled without crossing sabres with the Turks, and spread terror among the troops in the rear, by the exaggerated accounts they gave of the Othoman forces, as an excuse for their cowardly behaviour.

Georgaki, after terminating all his arrangements for the morrow, was preparing to take some rest when he heard the sound of guns. Assembling a few officers, and placing himself at the head of his own veteran troopers, he galloped to the field, and, by an impetuous charge on the dispersed Turks, recaptured the standard of the sacred battalion and two guns. The Othoman cavalry soon rallied, and, securing two of the guns they had taken, and about forty prisoners, they prepared to attack Georgaki, who was obliged to retire, after saving about one hundred men of the sacred battalion, and forming a guard to protect the Greek army, which was seized with a panic. The Vallachians, on the road to Kraïova, dispersed, each man seeking his own home. This trifling engagement terminated the military career of Prince Alexander Hypsilantes. He was about nine miles in the rear when he received the news of his defeat, and he fled without delay to Rimnik, where he was soon followed by his brother Nicolas and the other fugitives [1].

Hypsilantes now began to fear that the Hetairists, and some of those who had followed his fortunes without being allowed to enter his apartments by the 'sacred staircase,' which he reserved for his friends and the dignitaries of his court [2], would detain him in Vallachia by force, in order to negotiate for their common safety. He had, however, resolved to make his escape with his own suite into Austria; and to effect this object, he resorted to his usual system of deceit and falsehood. It is even said that he forged letters, announcing that the Emperor of Austria had declared war with the sultan, and that the general commanding in Transylvania desired to hold a conference with Prince Hypsilantes on the frontier. It is certain that he communicated this news to those about him, and ordered public rejoicings in his camp to celebrate the event. He even carried his hypocrisy so far as to order a solemn service of thanksgiving to God to be celebrated in the church of Kosia, amidst repeated volleys of musketry [3]. Under cover of this trick, he escaped with his

---

[1] An idea of the different accounts of the affair of Dragashan which were circulated among the Greeks, may be formed by comparing Gordon, i. 120, and Tricoupi, i. 153, with Photeinos, 153.
[2] Photeinos (137) mentions the dissatisfaction which this 'sacred staircase' caused among the Greek officers who were not Phanariots.
[3] Compare Gordon, i. 122, and Tricoupi, i. 157.

two brothers and a few of his personal friends to the Austrian territory, on the 27th of June. With his usual fatuity and presumption, he promised the troops whom he abandoned, that he would send an aide-de-camp to conduct them to the quarters assigned to them in Austria, in virtue of the arrangements he had concluded. But as soon as this wretched adventurer found himself in safety, he issued an order of the day, to which he affixed a false date, as if it had been written at Rimnik. In this document he heaps insulting accusations on the Greeks and Roumans, who had supported his cause, naming several as fools, traitors, and cowards, and speaking of his own exploits with bombastic self-gratulation [1].

The flight of Hypsilantes was the last scene of the drama enacted by the Philike Hetairia in the Principalities, where the rash ambition of its supreme head and the utter incapacity of its members brought great calamities on the people, and laid the foundations of an anti-Greek feeling, which has ended in depriving the Greeks of all political power in those provinces, but which has not been entirely without some good effect, for it contributed to develope projects of national independence.

The fate of Hypsilantes hardly deserves to be recorded. Austria treated him as a Russian deserter, and would readily have surrendered him to be tried and shot by a Russian court-martial, had the Emperor Alexander felt the slightest wish to make a military example. But the emperor, having no wish to increase the punishment of one whom he considered sufficiently punished by the disgraceful issue of his enterprise, conveyed an intimation to the Austrian government, that the prince would be left at its disposal. Austria, always hostile to revolutions, and irritated by the reports which Hypsilantes had spread of her having declared war with the sultan, retained him as a prisoner until the year 1827. He was then released, and died at Vienna in the following year. The public career of Prince Alexander Hypsilantes offers not one single virtuous or courageous deed

---

[1] Tricoupi (i. 158) and Philemon ('Ελληνικὴ 'Επανάστασις, ii. 184) give what is doubtless a correct version; but Photeinos (160) publishes another text, which appears to have circulated in Vallachia, where he wrote. The difference, though verbally great, does not alter the sense. Philemon conceals the fact that the date is false. The individuals named were probably deserving of blame, but surely their leader, who abandoned his own soldiers, was not entitled to reproach them.

on which the historian can dwell with satisfaction. He was a contemptible leader, and a worthless man.

The traitor Savas was disappointed of his reward. He was invited to Bucharest by the pasha of Silistria, and when he waited to receive wealth and honour for his devotion to the sultan, he was beheaded for having connived at the treason of the Hetairists.

In Moldavia, the sultan's authority was re-established without difficulty. As soon as the boyards heard that Russia disclaimed all connection with the Hetairists, they deposed Michael Soutzos, who fled to Russia, without making an effort to uphold the cause in which he had embarked. But a Greek named Pentedekas, who had been deputed by Hypsilantes to direct the administration and forward supplies to the army, arriving at Yassi shortly after the flight of the deposed hospodar, assembled a few troops, and took possession of the government in defiance of the boyards. Prince George Cantacuzenos, who came to Moldavia from Hypsilantes' army, because he pretended to have it in his power to draw supplies of money and provisions from his estates in Bessarabia, acted as lieutenant-general. He stationed himself near the Russian frontier, and when the Othoman forces entered Yassi on the 25th of June, he deserted his troops, and placed his own person in security by crossing the Pruth.

The only military exploits which reflected any honour on the Greeks in the Principalities, were those performed after the commander-in-chief had escaped into Austria, and his lieutenant-general into Russia. The officers, who had retired to Skuleni with Cantacuzenos, refused to follow him in his flight over the Pruth. They declared that they had sworn to defend the cause to the last, and that they could not abandon it without a battle, in which there was always a chance of victory for brave men. They said that it was no disgrace for civilians to retire from the dangerous position they occupied, but military honour commanded soldiers to remain. The lieutenant-general paid no attention to their observations.

About four hundred men, Greeks, Albanians, and Servians, intrenched themselves, as well as the time and their means allowed, at Skuleni, on the banks of the Pruth, where they were attacked on the 29th of June by a strong body of

Othoman troops, who brought up six guns to play on their camp. Nothing could surpass the valour with which the Christians defended their position. The Turks made several attempts to storm it under cover of the fire of their artillery, but were repulsed. Their grape-shot and rifles, however, gradually thinned the numbers of their enemies. Russian officers who viewed the engagement from the left bank of the Pruth, declared that the Greeks behaved like veteran troops. At last the number of the defenders became insufficient to man the intrenchments. The Othomans redoubled their assaults, the fire of their guns was concentrated on one point, and a body of cavalry, covered by a round of grape from the artillery and a heavy fire of musketry, charged over the earthworks into the midst of the camp. Those who were not killed on the spot plunged into the river, and many gained the Russian bank in safety. This gallant affair at Skuleni terminated the Revolution in Moldavia.

The Turks, after their victory at Dragashan, occupied all Little Vallachia, where order was easily established. Most of the Hetairists in the Principality escaped over the Austrian frontier, but a few bands of irregulars retreated eastward through Vallachia, attempting to reach Moldavia, from whence they expected to gain the Russian frontier. Georgaki was one of those who refused to follow the example of Hypsilantes. Collecting a number of determined men, who resolved neither to owe their lives to Austrian protection nor to Turkish mercy, he proposed to fight his way to the Russian frontier. Once in Russia, he had no doubt that he should soon be able to find means to transport himself and his companions to Greece, where he now learned that the battle of freedom could alone be fought. He was joined by a Macedonian captain, named Pharmaki, who was at the head of two hundred and fifty men.

The two chiefs were surrounded by the Turks long before they could gain the Moldavian frontier, for the indiscipline and misconduct of Hypsilantes' troops, and the exactions of the Hetairists in levying contributions, had created a feeling of animosity in the breasts of the Rouman population. The consequence of this was that the Turkish officers were accurately informed by the peasantry of every movement of

Georgaki and Pharmaki, while those leaders could obtain no information concerning the position and movements of the Turkish troops. After many almost incredible marches and hairbreadth escapes, the Greek chiefs were at last completely surrounded by their enemies, and blockaded in the monastery of Seko. All provisions were cut off; every road was barricaded, and no possibility of escape remained. The Turks offered terms of capitulation, which were rejected. Georgaki occupied a belfry, which stood at a short distance from the principal building. With a few soldiers he defended the approach to the monastery for some time; but the upper part of the belfry tower being of wood, was set on fire, and its garrison had no choice but to rush through a heavy fire of the enemy to gain the main building, to perish in the flames, or to surrender at discretion: what really occurred in the belfry is not known with certainty. Georgaki had repeatedly declared, as danger became more and more imminent, that he would never submit to the Turks, and it is certain that he threw open the door of the belfry, and invited all who wished to escape to run as quickly as possible to the monastery. Immediately after the powder-chest exploded. One man only escaped[1].

Pharmaki defended the monastery for a fortnight, until both his provisions and ammunition were exhausted. The Turks were extremely anxious to make a few prisoners, and after a long negotiation they persuaded Pharmaki to surrender with about twenty men on the 4th October. Thirty-three Greeks who refused to trust the promises of the Turkish officers, that their lives would be spared, escaped on the night previous to the surrender, and gained the Austrian frontier. Whatever promises were made by the Turkish officers, were as usual disclaimed by the sultan, when his enemies were in his power. The soldiers were put to death as soon as an order for their execution could arrive from Bucharest. Pharmaki was sent to Constantinople, where he was tortured and then beheaded.

Thus terminated this ill-judged attempt to make a Greek revolution in foreign provinces, without offering to the native population any guarantee for a better administration of

---

[1] Tricoupi, i. 166; Philemon, 'Ελληνικὴ 'Επανάστασις, ii. 208.

justice, or any prospect of increasing the liberties of the nation. The Roumans, long oppressed by their Phanariot princes, had strong reasons for detesting the enterprise, which, if successful, seemed likely to render the Greek domination in the Principalities perpetual, by placing them under the powerful protection of Russia. Fortunately both for the Roumans and the Greeks, their nationalities escaped that strangulation which would have been the inevitable effect of the rapid extension of Russian power in European Turkey at this period. Unfortunately the conduct of Hypsilantes and the Hetairists sullied the national character of the Greeks with a deep stain, which was only partially effaced by the noble conduct of the troops at Skuleni and the patriotic devotion of Georgaki. It was reserved for the native land of the Hellenic race to prove that Greece could still arm heroes in her cause.

CHAPTER III.

THE OUTBREAK OF THE REVOLUTION IN GREECE.

Extermination of the Turks in Greece.—Preparations of the Othoman government.
—Operations of the Hetairists in the Morea.—The Archimandrite, Gregorios
Dikaios.—Attempt of primates to defer the insurrection.—Hostages summoned to Tripolitza by the Turks.—Warning letter forged by the Greeks.—
First insurrectional movements in the Peloponnesus.—Turks at Kalavryta
surrender, and are murdered.—Character of Petrobey.—Taking of Kalamata,
and first Te Deum for victory.—Outbreak at Patras.—Extermination of the
Mohammedan population in Greece.—Character and biography of Theodore
Kolokotrones.—His prayer at Chrysovitzi.—Revolution at Salona, and character of Panourias.—Salona and Livadea taken.—Character of Diakos.—
Murder of Mohammedans.—Acropolis of Athens besieged.—Revolution at
Mesolonghi.—Vrachori taken, and Turks and Jews massacred.—Revolution in
the islands.—Oligarchy and system of trade at Hydra.—Spetzas first proclaims the Revolution.—Psara follows.—Insurrection at Hydra headed by
Oeconomos.—First cruise of the Greek fleet.—Murder of the Sheik-ul-islam.—
Fall of Oeconomos.—Othoman fleet quits the Dardanelles.—Greeks prepare
fire-ships.—Turkish line-of-battle ships burned off Mytilene.—Kydonies sacked
by the Greeks.—Squadron under Miaoulis on western coast of Greece.

IT would require Shakespeare's richness of language to give adequate expression to the intensity of passion with which the modern Greeks rose to destroy the power of their Othoman masters.

In the month of April 1821, a Mussulman population, generally of the Greek race, amounting to upwards of twenty thousand souls, was living, dispersed in Greece, employed in agriculture. Before two months had elapsed the greater part was slain—men, women, and children were murdered on their own hearths without mercy or remorse. Old men still point to heaps of stones, and tell the traveller, 'There stood the pyrgos (tower) of Ali Aga, and there we slew him, his harem, and his slaves;' and the old man walks calmly on to plough the fields which once belonged to Ali Aga, without a thought that any vengeful fury can attend his path. The crime was a nation's crime, and whatever perturbations it may produce must be in a nation's conscience, as the deeds by which it can be expiated must be the acts of a nation.

The feeling that a great social convulsion was at hand became general both among the Mussulman and Christian population of the Morea towards the end of 1820. The prolonged resistance of Ali Pasha persuaded every class that a revolution was inevitable, yet both Mussulmans and Christians carefully avoided every act tending to accelerate the outbreak. Each party seemed to be waiting for a signal from a distance, and the winter was passed in anxiety and hope.

The Greeks were unwarlike. The Turks were dispersed over the country in single families or in small towns, and without local leaders. Both parties habitually postponed adopting a decisive line of conduct. Procrastination is quite as characteristic of Greek bishops and primates as of Turkish pashas and agas. The Greeks expected aid from Russia— the Turks looked to the sultan for orders and for assistance. The Greeks, who were preparing for a revolution, formed no magazines of provisions, and collected no military stores. The Turks, who deemed an insurrection of the Christians inevitable, neglected to repair their fortresses, to lay up stores of provisions, and to fill the cisterns with water in the strong castles scattered over the face of the country, which were capable of being rendered impregnable to insurgents without discipline and without artillery.

During the summer of 1820, however, Sultan Mahmud was so much alarmed by the reports he received concerning the state of the Christian population in Greece, that he sent an officer to the Morea, to put the principal fortresses in a state of defence. With the exception of Tripolitza, all these fortresses were situated on the sea-coast, and in all there was a Mussulman population accustomed to bear arms. They might all have been repaired and provisioned simultaneously; but the Turks considered that their fleet could bring succour at any time, and the armed Mussulmans were confident that no Christian subject of the Porte would dare to meet them in the field. The sultan's order was not carried into execution, though it is possible that he believed the contrary.

In the month of November 1820, Khurshid Pasha arrived in the Morea, with strict orders to watch the machinations of the Greeks and the intrigues of the Russian consular agents. He reported that in his pashalik there was no immediate danger of any disturbance; and the sultan, finding that Ismael was conducting the operations against Ali Pasha with great incapacity, ordered Khurshid to take the command of the army before Joannina, and leave a deputy to govern the Morea during his absence. Khurshid quitted Tripolitza in January 1821, leaving Mehemet Salik as his kaimakam, a young man of an arrogant disposition and no military experience. The garrison of Tripolitza was soon after strengthened by a reinforcement of a thousand Albanians.

The Philike Hetairia had made more progress in the Morea than in the other parts of Greece. Many of the higher clergy, the primates, and the men possessing local influence, had been initiated during the years 1819 and 1820; but the misconduct of some of the travelling agents, or apostles (as they were called), and the imprudence with which they admitted crowds of members, in order to receive fees, frightened the primates. Their distrust in the direction of the society was increased by an order to remit all the pecuniary contributions collected in Greece to the treasury at Constantinople. The impolicy of this order, at a time when it was a matter of the greatest urgency to collect stores in the mountains of Greece, where the Turks could hardly watch, and would be unable to control, the movements of the people, was so apparent that the Moreot Hetairists determined to establish a local treasury, and to investigate the mystery in which the direction of the society was enveloped. An active correspondence was carried on between the Hetairists in Greece and those in Constantinople and Russia, through the agency of the Russian consulate at Patras, which insured both secrecy and safety. In the autumn of 1820 the Moreots were informed that Prince Alexander Hypsilantes had assumed the supreme direction of the Hetairia, and that seven local ephors were appointed to conduct the business of the society in Greece. A local treasury was also constituted under the control of the ephors. This appears to have been the wisest measure ever adopted by the supreme direction, and it was forced on it by the common sense of the Moreot Hetairists. The conspiracy in Greece was now fully organized. Germanos, the Metropolitan Bishop of Patras, who has left memoirs of the Greek Revolution, was the most distinguished member among the ephors [1].

The confidence of the Greek Hetairists in the judgment of Prince Alexander Hypsilantes was soon shaken by the conduct of one of his agents. The most active apostle in the Morea at this time was the Archimandrite, Gregorios Dikaios, commonly called Pappa Phlesas, a most unclerical priest, but a bold conspirator. The licentious conduct, the carelessness of truth, and the wasteful expenditure of this man, rendered him unfit for any secret business where prudence was required. The Archbishop of Patras accuses him of shameful dishonesty, declaring in his *Memoirs* that the archimandrite sold eighty barrels of gunpowder, which were sent from Smyrna to Poros shortly before the outbreak of the Revolution [2]. Pappa Phlesas spent the money in riotous living and travelling; and wherever he went he announced that Russia would soon declare war with Turkey, and send an army to deliver Greece from the Othoman yoke. To his intimate associates he revealed the plan of the 'Grand Project,' which included the assassination of the sultan and the conflagration of Constantinople as a part of its programme. In the state of affairs in Greece, neither the discourses nor the financial co-operation of such an agent could do any good. Yet this man, with all his vices, proved that he possessed both patriotism and courage by his honourable death. After inflicting many deep wounds on political morality by his shameless peculations, and on the orthodox Church by his barefaced profligacy, he fell on the field of battle, fighting gallantly to arrest the progress of Ibrahim Pasha, as will be recorded in a future page.

It is difficult for those who travel from London to Constantinople in a week, to form any idea of the difficulty of obtaining information which existed in the East during the first thirty years of the present century. Little could be learned with accuracy concerning the events that happened

---

[1] Ὑπομνήματα περὶ τῆς Ἐπαναστάσεως τῆς Ἑλλάδος, Athens, 1837.
[2] Pp. 9, 22.

in the nearest province, and the wildest reports were circulated, and obtained credence even among men of education. Newspapers were unknown, and private correspondents had rarely access to authentic sources of information. The Hetairists, therefore, found all men ready to believe their wildest assertions. We need not therefore be surprised to find that, in the Morea, the Greeks were universally persuaded that a Russian fleet would appear in the Mediterranean in the spring of 1821, and land an army to expel the Turks from Greece. The confidence inspired by this conviction was so great, that the primates deemed it necessary to adopt some precautions to allay the popular effervescence. They felt that they were exposed to become the victims of the precautionary measures which the Othoman government habitually adopted to prevent insurrections. They feared that they should be suddenly arrested, and carried off to Tripolitza as hostages for the tranquillity of their countrymen.

The Turks heard the reports which were current, and were quite as much alarmed as the primates. They called on the kaimakam at Tripolitza to take measures for preventing an insurrection of the Christians. At this crisis the leading Hetairists in the country round Patras held a meeting at Vostitza, the ancient Aegium, in the month of February 1821, to decide on the course they ought to pursue. The assembly was a revival of the Achaian League. Many bishops and primates were present. Pappa Phlesas attended the meeting, and when urged to be more cautious in his proceedings, he ridiculed the terror of the primates, persisted in his assertion that Russian aid was at hand, and pleaded the commands of Hypsilantes as his authority for urging on the people. The principal members of the assembly resolved to imprison him in a monastery, but no one ventured to arrest the impetuous priest. At last the meeting decided on sending two messengers to obtain accurate information concerning the projects of the supreme direction of the Hetairia, and the precise nature of the support it was to receive from the Russian government. One of these messengers was sent to Ignatius, the Archbishop of Arta, who was living at Pisa in Tuscany, and who was supposed to be well acquainted with the intentions of the Russian cabinet. The other was deputed to confer with Prince Alexander Hypsilantes, and ascertain the real extent of his military preparations. The agents of the supreme direction had already fixed the 6th of April as the day on which the Revolution was to break out simultaneously in every province and city of the Othoman empire in which the Greeks were numerous. The assembly of Vostitza now decided that in the Morea the outbreak should be adjourned until the ephors received answers to their communications from Ignatius and Hypsilantes.

Matters had already gone too far for the people to stop at the beck of the bishops and the primates. No fears for the personal safety of a few could damp the general enthusiasm. The Hetairists at Vostitza did not entirely neglect to prepare for the Revolution which they wished to delay. They raised among themselves the sum of £2000 sterling by a private subscription, and they deputed several monks of Megaspelaion to collect money to purchase arms and ammunition. But their counsels displayed more selfishness and timidity than was justified at a moment when even prudence dictated enthusiasm and boldness as the only safe policy. Indeed, it must be recorded here, as on many future occasions, that the Greek Revolution was emphatically the work of the people. The leaders generally proved unfit for the position they occupied, but the people never wavered in the contest, and from the day they took up arms they made every object in life subordinate to the victory of the orthodox church and the establishment of their national independence.

As soon as the kaimakam of Khurshid had received sufficient reinforcements, he summoned the principal members of the Greek clergy and the primates to a meeting at Tripolitza. He gave as a pretext for the assembly, that he wished to concert measures for counteracting the intrigues which Ali Pasha was carrying on among the Greek population, and which threatened to endanger public tranquillity. If the Greeks obeyed his summons, he resolved to detain them as hostages; if they disobeyed, he believed that he was strong enough to arrest and punish them.

The bishops and primates of the Morea usually met twice a year at Tripolitza, to receive the communications of the Othoman government from the pasha, and concert concerning measures of taxation and police. The meeting at Vostitza having decided that no movement was to take place until the return of the messengers sent to Pisa and St. Petersburg, several bishops and primates obeyed the orders of the kaimakam, hoping to deceive the Turks, for whose stupidity the Greeks have a great contempt, and expecting to obtain permission to return home before any general insurrection occurred. Others, however, did not consider it prudent to trust their persons in the hands of the Turks. Germanos, the Archbishop of Patras, the Bishop of Kernitza, and the primates of Patras, Vostitza, and Kalavryta, fearing lest the Turks had procured some evidence of their conspiracy, sought pretexts for delaying their journey. Germanos was at last compelled to set off, but he halted at Kalavryta, where he was joined by several primates, and a plan was devised to gain more time. The metropolitan and his friends forged a letter purporting to be a warning from a friendly Turk at Tripolitza; for though they were ready to consign every Mussulman in Greece and Constantinople to destruction, they thought it natural enough that a Mussulman should have some feeling of humanity towards them. This forged letter declared that the kaimakam had resolved to put several Greeks of influence to death, in order to prevent a general insurrection of the Christians, by depriving the people of their leaders. It was contrived that this letter should be delivered after the party had quitted Kalavryta. The letter was read in the presence of servants and muleteers. The clergy and the primates affected the greatest terror. A consultation was held by the roadside, and the whole party set off to the monastery of Laura.

The general opinion in Greece is, that on reaching the monastery of Laura they proclaimed the Revolution. But this is not correct [1]. They sought to allay the suspicions of the Turks of Kalavryta and Vostitza, by informing them of the receipt of the forged letter, and by asking them to guarantee their personal safety at Tripolitza. In the mean time, to avoid being arrested in a body, they dispersed, and

---

[1] The legends of the revolution suppose that the Archbishop Germanos gave the signal by raising the standard of the cross on the 25th of March (6 April). The event is assumed to be historical, and its memory is perpetuated by an annual solemnity and national festival. Poetry and painting have lent their aid to fix the popular imagination on the event and on the day.

each began to collect armed men for his defence. This was not difficult, as the apostles of the Hetairia had persisted in fixing the 6th of April as the day on which the Revolution was to commence. Various acts of brigandage were committed, in the confidence that impunity would soon be secured. The Turks discovered that several mills recently repaired by the Greeks near Dimitzana were not destined to grind corn, but were actively employed in manufacturing gunpowder.

The first insurrectional movements took place at the end of March 1821. Many Mussulmans were attacked and murdered in the mountains of Achaia on the 28th. Three Turkish couriers carrying letters from the kaimakam to Khurshid, which were supposed to contain a pressing demand for additional troops, were waylaid by the Hetairists, and slain at the village of Agridha, in the valley of the Krathis. Eight Albanian Mussulmans engaged in collecting the haratch, were murdered near the lake of Phonia, by Soliotes, a Hetairist of some local influence, so called from being a native of the village of Soli, in the valley of the Krathis. A party of Albanian Mussulmans who had landed at the khan of Akrata, and were on their way to join the ranks of their countrymen in garrison at Tripolitza, were attacked at Bersova, and defended themselves vigorously. Twenty were killed, and the rest were compelled to lay down their arms [1].

---

[1] Mr. Tricoupi's account of the commencement of the Revolution in Achaia is sometimes inaccurate. As he rarely cites his authorities, he often takes the liberty of transcribing them when they are Greek, and of translating them literally when foreign. The event mentioned in the text affords an example. The Archbishop Germanos in his *Memoirs* (p. 16) writes thus:—Συγχρόνως ἄλλοι Καλαβρυτινοὶ ἐφόνευσαν δύω σπαχίδες Τριπολιτζιώτας εἰς τὰ χωρία τοῦ Λιβαρτζιοῦ, καὶ πάλιν ἄλλοι εἰς τὸν Φενεὸν τοὺς Γυφτοχαρατζίδες. This Mr. Tricoupi transcribes (i. 77), Συγχρόνως ἐφονεύθησαν καὶ δύο Σπαΐδες Τριπολιτσώται κατὰ το Λιβάρτσι, χωρίον τῶν Καλαβρύτων. Ἐφονεύθησαν καί τινες Γυφτοχαρατσίδες ἐν τῷ χωρίῳ τῆς Κορινθίας Φονιᾷ. The word γυφτοχαρατσίδες proves the plagiarism. The archbishop uses the term, as the Greeks generally employed it, to mark contempt and hatred for the soldiers employed in collecting the haratch from the peasantry, as is mentioned above at p. 18. In a grave historian the word gipsy-haratchers becomes vituperative personality, imputing bad character to excuse murder. Mr. Tricoupi calls these affairs mere acts of brigandage (λῃστρικά), but brigands do not select detachments of well-armed Albanian mercenaries, on their way to seek service, with empty purses, as objects of attack. Phrantzes and Spcliades ('Απομνημονεύματα, i. 59) give a more correct account of these events. These accounts of the early ambushes of the Christians, and the slaughter of dispersed bands of Mussulmans, may be compared with that given by Philemon, Δοκίμιον ἱστορικὸν περὶ τῆς Ἑλληνικῆς Ἐπαναστάσεως, iii. 8-64.

Soliotes became an officer of some distinction, and his friends boasted that he was the first who shed Turkish blood during the Revolution in Greece.

The events connected with Germanos and the primates of Achaia have often been cited as the first revolutionary movements. But the truth is, that the people, at the instigation of the Hetairists, took up arms boldly while their superiors were temporizing. Asimaki Zaimes, the silent primate of Kalavryta, considering that his friends were carrying their evasions too far, endeavoured to force them to take a decided course by an act of brigandage[1]. He had several armed Christians in his service, and he sent two to waylay Seid Aga of Lalla, who was transporting a considerable sum of money. Kyr Asimaki thought that an act of highway robbery of this nature would put an end to the indecision of his countrymen. Seid Aga escaped from the ambuscade, and carried his treasure to Tripolitza, where his report confirmed the prevailing rumours that the Greeks had taken up arms. The Mussulman rabble rose in tumult, and would have put to death the bishops and primates who had already arrived, had not the kaimakam saved them by lodging them in the house of the Hasnadar aga.

Arnaout-oglou, the voivode of Kalavryta, was on his way to Tripolitza when some of his attendants were attacked by a band of Greeks lying in ambush at a mountain-pass near Kleitor. He immediately turned back, and gave the alarm to the Mussulman population of Kalavryta. The Turks hastily collected their families and their most valuable movables in several large houses which appeared capable of defence; for they were convinced that the long-talked-of insurrection of the Greeks had commenced. They were immediately besieged by 600 armed Christians. On the 2nd of April the outbreak became general over the whole of the Morea. On that day many Turks were murdered in different places, and all communication by the great roads was cut off.

On the 3rd of April 1821, the Mussulmans of Kalavryta surrendered, on receiving a promise of security. That promise was soon violated. About three hundred fell into the hands

---

[1] Kyr Asimaki, as his countrymen called him, carried his silence so far that a modern Greek historian tells us that he often remained in society smoking his pipe for hours without uttering a single word. He was a counterpart, in the Oriental style, of the Laird of Dumbiedykes, whom the Duke of Argyll had seen thrice tipsy, and only heard speak once. The attack on Seid Aga was made on the 29th or 30th of March. This is the Kyr Asimaki whose worse than Turkish oppression as a farmer of taxes drove the peasantry from their lands; he is mentioned by Leake, *Travels in the Morea*, ii. 225.

of the Greeks; and in the month of August, Colonel Raybaud found that the greater part of the men had then been murdered, and that the women and children were dispersed as slaves or domestic servants in the houses of the Greeks[1]. Arnaoutoglou, who was the representative of one of the wealthiest Mussulman families in the Morea, and who had lived on terms of intimacy and apparent friendship with several primates, was left in a state of abject destitution, while his former friends were members of the Greek government, and were wasting the revenues of their country in unseemly extravagance. He regained his liberty at an exchange of prisoners in 1825.

More decisive operations took place at the same time in Messenia. Petrobey of Maina, Theodore Kolokotrones, and Niketas, were the actors in these events. Theodore Kolokotrones and Anagnostaras, both celebrated chiefs of klephts, had returned secretly to the Morea, in order to prepare for the general insurrection. The Othoman authorities, hearing that they were lurking in Maina, sent a message to Petros Mavromichales, the bash-bog or bey, requesting him to arrest them. As Maina was under the jurisdiction of the capitan-pasha, the pasha of Morea could not do more than invite Petrobey's co-operation in the measures which it was resolved to adopt for the purpose of maintaining order among the Christians. The Turks entertained no doubt of Petrobey's fidelity. His rank was supposed to insure his attachment to the authority of the sultan, from which it was derived, and it was known that one of his brothers had embraced the Mohammedan religion, and risen to be a pasha.

Petrobey had been early initiated into the Hetairia. He was a restless, vain, bold, and ambitious man, lavish in expenditure, and urged to seek change by a constant want of money. He was deficient in ability, but more prompt to form courageous resolutions than most of his countrymen in high station. His frank, joyous disposition, and his numerous family of sons, brothers, and nephews, who were active and daring men, gave him great personal influence. He sent one of his sons to Tripolitza to allay any suspicions which the

---

[1] Raybaud, *Mémoires sur la Grèce pour servir à l'Histoire de la Guerre de l'Indépendance*, i. 365. This work is one of the best on the early events of the Revolution.

kaimakam might have adopted; but he continued to protect Kolokotrones and Anagnostaras, and to assist the machinations of the Hetairists. At this time another of Petrobey's sons was at Constantinople, where he resided as a hostage for his father's fidelity, according to the custom of the Turks. Both escaped to Maina, either through the negligence, the prudence, or the humanity of their guardians. Had Petrobey been a man of capacity, he might have placed himself at the head of the Greek Revolution, and rendered himself either the president of a Greek republic or the prince of a Greek state; but his habits of self-indulgence made him always sacrifice the future for the present. He neglected to make any political use of his great personal influence, and of the official authority he held among the warlike population of Maina.

The Hetairists had sent a supply of ammunition to be concealed in the recesses of Mount Taygetus. The voivode of Kalamata, hearing that bodies of armed Greeks had assembled on the flanks of the mountain towards Messenia, and that long trains of pack-horses returned with heavy loads from the shore of Maina to the villages in his neighbourhood, considered that the insurrection was on the eve of breaking out. He called together the resident Turks, and they resolved to retire with their families to Tripolitza. It was already too late.

Murad, a Mussulman on friendly terms with the Christians, was the first who departed with all his family. He was stopped on the road by Niketas and slain. His widow and children were driven back to Kalamata. This happened on the 2nd of April, and served as a signal for a general rising of the Christians in Messenia. Before many hours elapsed a number of Turkish families were surprised and murdered.

On the following day, Kalamata was besieged by two thousand Greeks, led by Petrobey and Murzinos, another Mainate chief, and accompanied by Anagnostaras, Kolokotrones, and Niketas. On the 4th the place capitulated. The Turks received solemn promises that their lives would be protected, but these promises were given as a lure to prevent desperate men offering an obstinate resistance. The prisoners were soon dispersed among their captors to serve as domestic slaves, and before many months elapsed the men had all been slain. Phrantzes, an ecclesiastic and a Hetairist, but one of the most candid historians of this early period of the Revolution, owns, in the proverbial expression of Greece, that 'the moon devoured them[1].'

On the 5th of April 1821, the Greeks sang their first thanks to God for victory. The ceremony was performed on the banks of the torrent that flows by Kalamata. Twenty-four priests officiated, and five thousand armed men stood round. Never was a solemn service of the Orthodox Church celebrated with greater fervour, never did hearts overflow with sincerer devotion to Heaven, nor with warmer gratitude to their church and their God. Patriotic tears poured down the cheeks of rude warriors, and ruthless brigands sobbed like children. All present felt that the event formed an era in the history of their nation; and when modern Greece produces historians, artists, and poets, this scene will doubtless find a niche in the temple of fame.

A few days after this memorable celebration, Petrobey, as commander-in-chief of the first Greek army in the field, published a proclamation, in conjunction with a few primates who assumed the title of the Senate of Messenia. This document was addressed to all Christian nations: it declares that the Greeks were determined to throw off the Othoman yoke, and solicits the aid of Christendom in giving liberty to suffering Christians[2].

The Albanian Mussulmans of Bardunia abandoned their towers as soon as they heard of the murder of Murad Aga by Niketas. About sixty families fled to Monemvasia; the others retired more leisurely to Tripolitza. They passed through Mistra on their way. The unwarlike Turks of that city were thrown into a state of frantic consternation by this retreat of the warlike Barduniots. The whole Mussulman population hastened away with their co-religionists; and as they had no time to carry off their property, they deposited their most valuable movables in the houses of their Christian friends. The night was passed by the Turks in anguish, but by the Albanians in refreshing sleep. At daybreak, the well-

---

[1] Τοὺς κατέφαγε τὸ φεγγάρι, Phrantzes, i. 335.
[2] Gordon (i. 183) gives a translation, with the date 9th April (28th March), 1821; Tricoupi (i. 368) gives the Greek text, with the date 25th March (6th April), which most copies bear.

mounted Albanians pursued their journey. They were followed by the Turks of Mistra who possessed horses, or had succeeded in purchasing or in hiring them during the night. But many families, old men, women and children, lingered behind, and were murdered on the road. The population of Laconia was estimated at 110,000 Christians and 15,000 Mussulmans. It is impossible to ascertain the exact number murdered in attempting to escape to Monemvasia and Tripolitza, or surprised before they could quit their dwellings; but it was at the time supposed to amount to two-thirds of the whole.

Some disorders occurred at Patras on the 2nd of April, but the outbreak of the Revolution took place on the 4th. Hostilities were commenced by the Turks in consequence of the arrival of some fugitives from Kalavryta, and a party of Albanians from the Castle of Lepanto. On the 6th, numerous bodies of armed Greeks arrived, under the direction of the Archbishop Germanos and several other leaders. One party carried before its leader the heads of five Turks who had been murdered at Vostitza. On the following morning, divine service was performed by the archbishop; and all the Greeks assembled took an oath to deliver their country from the Turks, or die in the attempt[1]. Enthusiasm was not wanting, but anarchy rendered it unavailing. The primates, the city population, and the Ionians, who hastened to take part in the contest, conducted their military operations with singular awkwardness and incapacity. They were unable to form an effectual blockade of the small citadel which overlooks the town, and the insurgents who attacked the Albanian Mussulmans of Lalla so mismanaged their movements that they allowed that small but warlike tribe to effect their retreat to Patras. This addition to the garrison of the citadel saved that fortress at the commencement of the Revolution, and the Turks found means to keep possession of it during the whole war.

The Greeks soon gathered in considerable numbers on the hills round all the fortresses held by the Turks, and endeavoured to cut off their communications with the surrounding

---

[1] The work of Mr. Green, who was then at Patras, is the best authority for the dates of these events. *Sketches of the war in Greece*, by P. I. Green, late British consul for the Morea, p. 10.

country. They were still unable to meet their enemies in the field. On the 11th of April they suffered a defeat near Karitena, and on the 15th a still more serious rout at Patras. But their determination to prosecute a mortal combat was in no way diminished by these checks.

In the mean time the Christian population had attacked and murdered the Mussulman population in every part of the peninsula. The towers and country houses of the Mussulmans were burned down, and their property was destroyed, in order to render the return of those who had escaped into fortresses hopeless. From the 26th of March until Easter Sunday, which fell, in the year 1821, on the 22nd of April, it is supposed that from ten to fifteen thousand Mussulmans perished in cold blood, and that about three thousand farm-houses were laid waste. Most of those who were then murdered were Greeks, whose forefathers had embraced the religion of Mahomet to escape the tribute of Christian children, and the majority consisted of women and children.

The fury of slaves who rend their bonds, and the fanaticism of religious hatred, have in all ages hurried men to the perpetration of execrable cruelties. Homer told his countrymen that slavery robs man of one-half of his humanity; and three thousand years have not made men much better, though they have made Greeks a good deal worse. The extermination of the Mussulmans in the rural districts was the result of a premeditated design. It proceeded more from the vindictive suggestions of Hetairists and men of letters, than from the revengeful feelings of the people, or the innate barbarity of the klephts. Most of the historians of the Greek Revolution have recoiled from recording the crimes which the people perpetrated, but a nation's cause is best served by writing its history in the spirit of Thucydides and Tacitus.

The Hetairists were generally civilians; of the apostles few became military leaders. They were men in a secondary social position; and, like men who believe that their merits have been overlooked, they were irritable and violent. Destitute of the generous courage and the warm feelings that would have enabled them to lead their countrymen to battle, they employed all their eloquence to fill every Greek breast with the fiercest desire of vengeance. It was their policy to render peace impossible by what they called baptizing the Revolution in blood. They awakened implacable hostilities, and left it to others to find the means of gaining victories. In a mortal struggle, they believed that the cause of the Christians was sure of ultimate success. They inculcated the necessity of exterminating every Mussulman, because the Turkish population in Greece was small, and could not be renewed. They knew that the Greeks were far too numerous to be exterminated by the Turks, even should Turkey produce a Mussulman Philike Hetairia. The slaughter of men, women, and children was therefore declared to be a necessary measure of wise policy, and popular songs spoke of the Turks as a race which ought to disappear from the face of the earth[1].

The military incapacity of the Hetairists and primates threw the conduct of the war into the hands of the chiefs of klephts. This was a sad misfortune for the nation, as it perpetuated a state of anarchy in the army of Greece during the whole of the Revolution. The military system that prevailed in the Morea will be best described by giving an account of the career of a distinguished leader. Theodore Kolokotrones offers the best type of the class. He became the head of a considerable political party; he has left memoirs that throw considerable light on his personal character and conduct; and general attention was so long fixed on his proceedings that he can already be tried before the great tribunal of public opinion[2].

Theodore Kolokotrones was fifty years old at the commencement of the Revolution. Age had somewhat tamed the violence of his passions without lessening his personal vigour, and both his physical and mental qualities fitted him to be a leader of irregular bands. A large head, a bold countenance, a steady eye, and a profusion of black hair,

---

[1] A song in everybody's mouth at this time said—
Τοῦρκος μὴ μείνῃ 's τὸν Μωρεά
Μηδὲ 's τὸν κόσμον ὅλον.
Phrantzes (ii. 377, *note*) mentioning that the Moreot Turks were useful to Ibrahim Pasha as guides when he invaded the Morea, remarks, ἐπ' αὐτῷ τούτῳ οἱ "Ελληνες εἶχον δίκαιον νὰ μὴ ἀφίσωσι ζῶντα ποδάρι ἐκ τῶν Πελοποννησίων Ὀθωμανῶν, ' the Greeks were in the right not to leave a living foot of the Peloponnesian Othomans,' a strong opinion for a Christian priest.
[2] Διήγησις Συμβάντων τῆς Ἑλληνικῆς Φυλῆς ἀπὸ 1770 ἕως 1836: *see* also Philemon, iii. 412.

gave some dignity to an aspect that did not conceal looks of cunning and ferocity. His powerful frame exceeded the middle size, and his voice had the volume of sound required in mountain warfare. He possessed constitutional good health, and that self-complacency which produces habitual good-nature. His manners had a degree of roughness well suited to conceal his natural cunning; and he had adopted an appearance of boisterous frankness as a veil for his watchful duplicity. He possessed a persuasive style of discourse, and by selecting common popular phrases he gave pointed expression to his sound sense, and rendered his speeches more effective by their contrast with the Hellenic affectation of his lettered rivals. He was orator enough to lead his audience to a desired conclusion by a well-told fable, and to misguide their passions by a cleverly-selected apophthegm. But with these good qualities he had many defects. Nurtured as a brigand, he could never distinguish very clearly right from wrong, justice from injustice; and he had an instinctive aversion to order and law. His patriotism was selfish, and his occasional acts of magnanimity cannot efface the memory of his egoistical ambition and sordid avarice during the period of his greatest power. He received from nature a clear intellect and a hard heart, and his education and experience in life corrupted without enlarging his feelings [1].

The family of Kolokotrones followed the profession of arms from the time the Othomans conquered the Morea in 1715, acting alternately as local police-guards and brigands. When the capitan-pasha Hassan Ghazi subdued the Albanians and re-established order in 1779, the father of Kolokotrones was compelled to seek refuge in Maina, where he was slain by a detachment of Turkish troops in the following year.

The young Kolokotrones was nurtured among the civil broils of the Mainates; but at the age of fifteen he settled in the district of Sambazika, on the northern slope of Mount Taygetus, and at twenty he married the daughter of the proëstos of Leondari. For seven years he lived on his wife's property, acting generally as one of the rural guards of the

---

[1] In his autobiography he draws his own character with the candour inspired by a strong feeling of self-sufficiency and an imperfect sense of honour and honesty. He narrates many instances of his own brutal insolence and arbitrary violence with repulsive simplicity. Διήγησις, 135.

district. But the peasants observed that he was a man of the musket, and not of the plough. He was frequently accused of poaching in the sheepfolds of the neighbouring villages, and at last some acts of brigandage against the Greek cultivators of Emblakika (the Stenyclerian plain) caused the pasha of the Morea to give orders for his arrest. This decided his fate. At the age of twenty-seven he became a brigand by profession.

For nine years he lived an irregular life, sometimes supporting himself by robbery, and sometimes sheltering himself from the vengeance of his enemies by taking service as a local guard with some primate or abbot. But the Greek peasantry of the Morea were at last so tormented by the rapacity and cruelty of the klephts that they invited the Turks to assist in hunting them down, and both primates and monasteries were obliged to abandon them to their fate. Dodwell, during his travels, witnessed some of the operations by which the klephts were destroyed[1]. Several members of Kolokotrones' family were slain. The bands were all broken up, and Theodore Kolokotrones, finding that there was no safety for him even in Maina, fled to the Ionian Islands in 1806. In his *Memoirs*, he complains of the suffering caused by the filth of long-worn garments as rivalling the pangs of hunger[2]. Those who have seen a Greek army at the end of a summer campaign with unwashed fustanellas must feel some surprise at this declaration on the part of a veteran brigand.

When Kolokotrones escaped to Zante, the Ionian Islands were under the joint protection of Russia and Turkey; but the Russians patronized the brigand, though the enemy of their ally. During the war which broke out between Russia and Turkey soon after, Kolokotrones cruised in what he called a privateer, and others a pirate boat; but falling in with two Othoman ships, he was in danger of terminating his career at the yard-arm, when an English frigate, heaving accidentally in sight, saved him. England was then at war with Turkey, and the frigate (the Sea Horse) immediately engaged the Turks, which enabled Kolokotrones to sheer off.

In the year 1808 he performed the exploit which added most to his reputation as a military chief. Ali Pharmaki,

---

[1] *Travels in Greece*, ii. 353, 372.   [2] Διήγησις, 29.

the most powerful aga of Lalla, was attacked by Veli Pasha of the Morea. The fathers of Ali Pharmaki and of Theodore Kolokotrones had formed an alliance of brotherhood during the troubled times which preceded and followed the victory of Hassan Ghazi[1]. Ali and Theodore had never met, but so many reciprocal services had been rendered by daring klephts and turbulent Lalliots, that the tie of brotherhood was the strongest obligation on the honour of a klepht. The power of Veli Pasha, and still more that of his father Ali Pasha, the old lion of Joannina, intimidated the Albanian Mussulmans, and Ali Pharmaki could not find a single ally. His tower at Lalla was on the point of being besieged, and his own followers and relations were insufficient to defend it. He remembered his family alliance with Kolokotrones; and as a last resource he sent to Zante to claim the assistance due by their fathers' ties of brotherhood. Kolokotrones recognized the obligation as a sacred duty, even though urged by a Mussulman, for the partizans of orthodox Russia had not then inflated the bigotry of the Greeks to the degree of rendering religion an apology for the violation of every principle of private morality and national honour. Kolokotrones collected sixteen good soldiers among his ancient companions, and hastened to shut himself up with Ali Pharmaki in his tower at Lalla. Veli attacked the place without artillery, and was repulsed. He then wasted several weeks in blockading it, but the local chieftains and his Albanian mercenaries were more anxious to prolong the contest than to capture Ali Pharmaki, so that the besieged found opportunities of renewing their supplies of provisions and ammunition. The discontent of a powerful party in his own camp at last compelled Veli to make peace with Ali Pharmaki, who, however, insisted as a condition of his submission that Kolokotrones and all his followers should be allowed to return to Zante in safety. The honourable conduct of Kolokotrones on this occasion gained him a high reputation among the Mussulmans, as well as among the Christians, in Greece.

After the Ionian Islands were ceded to France, Kolokotrones kept up his connection with the Morea, and became a dealer in cattle, which were imported in considerable

---

[1] [On the custom of forming 'fraternal friendships,' see vol. ii. p. 229, *note* 4. Ed.]

numbers for the use of the troops. When the English took possession of Zante in 1810, he entered their service. He was almost forty years of age, and as he had no sympathy with the English character nor with British policy, his conduct was entirely guided by his personal interests. He received high pay from England, and the improvement of his social position enabled him to carry on his intrigues in the Morea with more effect. His reason and his prejudices alike taught him to regard Russia as the only sincere ally of Greece and the only irreconcilable enemy of Turkey, which the Greeks generally are very apt to consider as one and the same thing. Kolokotrones entered the English service as a captain, and was present at the assault of Santa Maura, where the Greek regiment gained no laurels. He was subsequently promoted to the rank of major, but his military service gave him no tincture of military knowledge, and he remained ignorant of tactics and insensible of the value of discipline. After the peace, he remained two years on the staff, drawing pay and doing nothing. He was then reduced, and returned to his old profession of a cattle-dealer.

The Russians had not overlooked his talents, and he was connected with all the projects formed under Russian auspices to prepare for insurrections against the Turks. He was early initiated into the secrets of the Hetairia.

On the 15th of January 1821 he left Zante to join those who were preparing for the outbreak. Landing at Kardamyle, in Maina, he remained concealed in the house of Murzinos, one of the most powerful chieftains on the coast, waiting the signal for the general rising of the Christians. It has been mentioned that he was present at the taking of Kalamata. On the 6th of April he quitted the Mainates, in Messenia, to seek an independent sphere of action at Karitena. His band consisted of 300 men, but of these only thirty were under his own immediate command. He assumed, however, the chief direction; and, on his march through the plain of Leondari, he ordered all the peasants to take up arms, enforcing his orders with threats to burn the dwellings of the tardy. He passed the ruins of Megalopolis, repeating the name of Epaminondas. But he knew nothing of the personal virtues and profound tactics of that great man; nor, had he known them, would he probably have felt a wish to imitate them, though the peculiar circumstances in which Greece was placed rendered those virtues and that science the qualities best adapted to make their possessor the hero of the Revolution, and to insure its speedy success.

Karitena was soon invested by 6000 men, but on the 11th of April a corps of 500 Turkish cavalry from Tripolitza attacked and dispersed this force, which was destitute of order. Kolokotrones was compelled to escape with such precipitation that he lost his rifle, and reached Chrysovitzi alone. A small church of the Panaghia stands at the entrance of the village. He entered it, and prayed for the deliverance of Greece with a fervour that remained impressed on his mind to his dying day. In the enthusiasm of his devotion he imagined that he received a revelation announcing that his prayers were granted, and he rose reanimated, and with all his vigour restored. Kolokotrones was too brave to conceal the circumstances of his flight, and too much of a veteran to complain of a panic among young soldiers; but the facility with which he saw 6000 armed men dispersed by 500 cavalry inspired him with a great contempt for the courage of the peasantry. This contempt became very prevalent among the military classes during the Revolution, though it was as unjust as it was impolitic. But most of the captains and soldiers attributed the successes of the Christians, often very erroneously, to the stratagems of brigands and the valour of armatoli. Yet a careful study of the history of the Revolution has established the fact, that the perseverance and self-devotion of the peasantry really brought the contest to a successful termination. When the klephts shrank back, and the armatoli were defeated, the peasantry prolonged their resistance, and renewed the struggle after each successive defeat with indomitable obstinacy.

In the Morea, the Greeks were soon masters of all the open country, and the whole Christian population was in arms. But in continental Greece the armatoli whose warlike habits and military knowledge would have insured equal success though against more formidable Turkish forces, remained for some time luke-warm. Many of their captains were interested in upholding the sultan's authority, for they were drawing high pay in his service. Many Christian soldiers were unwilling to quit Khurshid's camp until the fall of

Joannina, for the seraskier had promised to pay all arrears due to his troops as soon as he gained possession of Ali's treasures. These circumstances, and the distrust felt in the leading Hetairists, rendered the armatoli slow to join the Revolution. But national feelings and religious antipathies could not be long repressed by personal interests.

The Albanian Christians of the Dervenokhoria took up arms on the 4th of April. Their primate, Hadji Meleti, who enjoyed great personal consideration, was a member of the Hetairia. The example of Megaris induced the Albanian peasantry of Attica and Boeotia to join the cause.

Salona (Amphissa) was the first town in continental Greece of which the insurgents gained possession. As soon as the news that the people were in arms at Kalavryta reached Galaxidhi, Panourias, who had served in Ali Pasha's troops, persuaded the primates of Salona to proclaim the independence of Greece, and summon all the Christians to throw off the Turkish yoke. The direction of a revolutionary movement could not have fallen into worse hands. Panourias had been a robber before he became a soldier, and he remained always a chief of brigands, not a leader of warriors. He had acquired some knowledge of the fiscal and military system by which Ali Pasha extorted money and maintained troops, and he employed this knowledge at Salona for his own profit. General Gordon has correctly described him as a type of the klephtic chiefs, whose influence proved exceedingly injurious to the success of the Greek arms and to the progress of Greek liberty. These extortioners retarded the progress of the Revolution northward by their rapacity, which terrified several of the Christian communities on Pindus, Olympus, and Ossa, where there were many armed men, into opposing the advance of the revolutionary forces. Gordon's words ought to be carefully weighed by those who desire to form a correct idea of the causes of the success and failure of the Greeks in their early military operations in continental Greece. He says, 'Panourias was the worst of these local despots, whom some writers have elevated into heroes; he was, in fact, an ignoble robber hardened in evil. He enriched himself with the spoils of the Mohammedans of Salona and Vostitza; yet he and his retinue of brigands compelled the people to maintain them at free quarters, in idleness and luxury, exacting not only bread, meat, wine, and forage, but also sugar and coffee. Hence springs the reflection that the Greeks had cause to repent their early predilection for the klephts, who were almost all (beginning with Kolokotrones) infamous for the sordid perversity of their dispositions[1].'

The Turks of Salona retired into the ruins of the castle built by the Counts of Soula on the remains of the impregnable citadel of Amphissa[2]. They were immediately blockaded by the Christians from the country round, including the sailors from the flourishing town of Galaxidhi. After some skirmishing, the Turks were cut off from the water, though an abundant stream gushes out just below the rock on which the castle stands; and on the 22nd of April they surrendered, receiving a promise that the Greeks would spare their lives. Yet before many days elapsed they were murdered, with other Mussulmans from Lidoriki and Malandrino. A few only were spared to serve as domestic slaves.

Livadea was the principal town in Eastern Greece, on account of the wealth and social position of its Christian population, though it contained only about ten thousand inhabitants, of whom eight hundred were Mohammedans. The town was a vacouf, and the civil government was administered by a voivode, who farmed the revenues from the imperial mosques. The military command was in the hands of the dervendji-pasha, who kept an officer with a small garrison to guard the defiles of Phocis. During the latter part of Ali Pasha's administration, the Greek primates possessed more influence than the Othoman authorities. The resident Mussulmans were poor.

When the news reached Livadea that the Greeks had blockaded Salona, the place was occupied by a detachment of Mussulman Albanians and by a small body of armatoli. The Mohammedans, being far inferior in numbers to the Christians, retired into the deserted castle above the town, which is said to have been built by the Catalans while they were masters of the duchy of Athens and Neopatras. They were immediately besieged by the Christian population, strengthened by the arrival of many armatoli, who remained in the villages on Parnassus and Helicon, unable to continue

---

[1] Gordon, *History of the Greek Revolution*, i. 400.
[2] Livy, xxxvii. 5.

in the service of Ali Pasha, and not having been admitted into that of the seraskier.

Diakos became the military leader of the Christians, a man justly celebrated for his courage and patriotism. He was a native of the village of Mussonitza, on the northern slope of Mount Vardhousi (Korax). His baptismal name was Athanasios, and though called 'the deacon,' he had never received orders, nor did he wear a beard. In early youth he was placed in the monastery of Aghios Joannes, at Artotina, where he grew up a strong, active lad, fonder of the mountain air than of his book, though he learned to write intelligibly, but with little attention to grammar and orthography. To avoid the infamous persecution of the voivode of Lidoriki, who saw him on a visit to the monastery, he quitted that sanctuary, and the hegumenos recommended him to the protection of a celebrated klepht, Skaltzodemos. Diakos soon gained the good-will of his new companions, and his reputation for courage became so celebrated, that a few years after, when he separated from Skaltzodemos, Ali Pasha admitted him into the ranks of the armatoli as an officer. When the sultan proclaimed Ali a rebel, Odysseus was intrusted with the command of the armatoli stationed at Livadea, and it was his duty to defend the Triodos and the roads leading to Salona by Delphi. Diakos was his lieutenant. Odysseus, without making any attempt to resist the advance of Pehlevan Pasha, fled to the Ionian Islands, and Diakos, seeing the forces of Ali dispersed, remained in privacy without seeking to enter the seraskier's service. He appears to have had some knowledge of the approaching Revolution. The moment he heard of the movement of his countrymen he joined those who were besieging the castle of Livadea.

The Mohammedans defended that place until the 25th of April, when want of provisions and water compelled them to surrender at discretion, and men, women, and children were all slain. The victors thought only of dividing the spoil; but Diakos exerted himself with some effect to save a part of the booty for the purchase of military stores.

About this time eight hundred Mohammedans were exterminated in the district of Talanti.

The whole Christian population of Eastern Greece, Albanian

and Greek, was now up in arms. The advanced spring had drawn many Turks into the country to inspect the state of the crops, to make their arrangements as spahis or farmers of the tenths, for sub-letting the pasture-lands, and for removing the flocks to their summer quarters. The majority were surprised and butchered. From Cape Sunium to the valley of the Spercheus, in hundreds of villages, Mussulman families were destroyed, and the bodies of men, women, and children were thrown into some outhouse, which was set on fire, because no orthodox Christian would demean himself so far as to dig a grave for the carcase of an infidel[1]. The Turkish inhabitants of Thebes and of several villages in Bocotia and Euboea escaped into the fortress of Negrepont.

Athens was a town of secondary importance in Greece, fallen as the other towns of Greece then were. In population it was equal to Livadea; but one-half was of the Albanian race, and both the Christian and Mussulman inhabitants were an impoverished community, consisting of torpid landed proprietors and lazy petty traders. Yet Athens enjoyed a milder local administration than most towns in Greece. It formed a fiscal appanage of the Serail. Its ancient fame, and the existing remains of its former splendour, rendered it the resort of travellers, and the residence of foreign consuls, who were men of higher attainments than the commercial consuls in most of the ports of the Othoman empire[2].

The Mussulmans of Athens formed about one-fifth of the population. They were an unwarlike and inoffensive race. The voivode's guard consisted of sixty Mussulman Albanians, who were the only soldiers in the place. The Greeks were not more enterprising or courageous than the Turks.

The first reports of a general insurrection of the Christians caused the Mohammedans to transport their families and their valuable movables into the Acropolis, and to fill the empty and long-neglected cisterns with water. On the 23rd of April the Turks seized eleven of the principal Christians, and carried them up to the Acropolis as hostages. This act irritated the

---

[1] Many ruined buildings have been pointed out to the Author in different parts of Greece as the scenes of these murders by the murderers themselves, and on one occasion he was present when the bones of several victims, well known in the district, were dug up in preparing to rebuild the house in which they had been slain.

[2] M. Fauvel, consul of France, and M. Gropius, consul of Austria.

Athenians, who sent messengers inviting the Albanian villagers of Mount Parnes to come to their assistance. On the night of the 6th of May, the people of Menidhi and Khasia, who represent the Acharnians of old, though they are Albanian colonists of a recent date, scaled the wall of the town near the site now occupied by the royal stables. About sixty Mussulmans were surprised in the town and slain. Next day the Acropolis was closely blockaded. Hunger and thirst committed great ravages among the besieged as summer advanced, but they held out obstinately, until on the 1st of August 1821 they were relieved by Omer Vrioni.

The real military strength of Greece lay in the population of Aetolia and of Pindus. But for some time the armatoli resisted the solicitations of the apostles of the Hetairia, and refused to take up arms against the sultan.

Mesolonghi was the first place in Western Greece that joined the Revolution. On the 1st of June a Greek squadron of twelve sail, manned by the Albanians of Hydra and Spetzas, made its appearance in the Aetolian waters, and the few Albanian soldiers in the place retired. On the 5th the inhabitants of Mesolonghi and of the neighbouring fishing-town of Anatolikon proclaimed themselves parts of independent Greece. The resident Mussulmans were arrested and confined as prisoners. As usual, most of them were murdered in a short time. Only the families of the higher ranks were spared. The men were crowded together in one room, the women and children in another. But even this lasted for a brief period. The men who had been spared during the first massacres were afterwards deliberately put to death, and the women and children were dispersed as slaves in the families of the wealthier Greeks. Colonel Raybaud saw a few of the men still alive in the month of August 1821, but these were all murdered shortly after[1]. Dr. Millingen describes the state in which Lord Byron found the women and children at the commencement of 1824: 'The wife of Hussein Aga, one of the Turkish inhabitants of Mesolonghi, imploring my pity, begged me to allow her to remain under my roof, in order to shelter her from the brutality and cruelty of the Greeks. They had murdered all her relations and two of her

---

[1] Compare Tricoupi, i. 298, who conceals the murder of the Mussulmans, with Raybaud, i. 294 and 365.

boys. A little girl, nine years old, remained to be the only companion of her misery[1].' This woman and a few more, with their children—in all, twenty-two females—then formed the sole remains of the Mussulman population of Mesolonghi. They were all sent by Lord Byron to Prevesa.

Vrachori, the capital of the province of Karlili, was the most important town in Western Greece. It contained five hundred Mussulman families, among whom were several great landed proprietors whose ancestors had received grants of the estates of the Frank nobles at the time of the conquest. The town is situated in a fertile district, on the high-road between Joannina and Lepanto, and at the commencement of the Revolution it was occupied by a garrison of three hundred Albanian Mussulmans. It contained about six hundred Christian inhabitants and two hundred Jewish.

On the 9th of June, Vrachori was attacked by two thousand armatoli, who entered the Greek quarter, and, by burning several Turkish houses, compelled the Mussulmans to intrench themselves in some large isolated dwellings, whose courtyards were surrounded by high walls. In a few days, the arrival of Varnakiotes, Tzonga, and some other captains of armatoli, increased the number of the Greek troops to four thousand. The besieged were soon without provisions.

The Albanians then separated themselves from the resident Turks. Nourka, their chief, the derven-aga of Karlili, was on terms of intimacy with many captains of armatoli. The Albanians were poor and warlike—the Turks rich and defenceless. Nourka offered to retreat with his band, if the Greeks would allow him to retire unmolested with his followers, carrying away their arms and all their property. The Greek leaders consented to these terms; but Nourka and his Albanians, not satisfied with their own property, determined to appropriate to themselves as much as they could carry away of the wealth of the Turks and Jews, in order that it might not fall into the hands of the Greeks. During the night, they plundered the Turks and tortured the Jews to collect money and jewels; and having secured the connivance of some of the Greek chiefs, they passed through

---

[1] Millingen, *Memoirs on the Affairs of Greece*, p. 99. The Author heard the widow of Hussein Aga tell her melancholy tale holding her little daughter Hatadjé by the hand.

the blockading force, and gained a long march before their escape was generally known in the Greek camp.

The Turks and Jews had expected to purchase the protection of the captains of armatoli with the riches which the Albanians had carried off. As soon as they could venture to do so, they informed the Greeks of Nourka's treachery, and laid down their arms on receiving a promise of personal safety. That promise was immediately violated. The massacre commenced with the Jews. Men, women, and children were slain in cold blood, with circumstances of atrocious cruelty. The poorer Mussulmans next shared the same fate, and only a few of the wealthiest of the five hundred families that inhabited Vrachori escaped, through the protection of Varnakiotes and Tzonga [1].

The inhabitants of Zapandu, a small Mussulman hamlet about two miles from Vrachori, seeing that no promise could bind the Greeks, refused to listen to any terms, and defended themselves valiantly until their chief was killed. Worn out with hunger and fatigue, they at last surrendered at discretion, and were put to the sword. Only a few Albanian soldiers in the place were allowed by the armatoli to retire to Arta.

During the summer, the troops of Khurshid Pasha made two attempts to penetrate into Acarnania by the passes of Makronoros, but both were defeated. The second was repulsed on the 30th of June.

Thus, in about three months, the Christians had rendered themselves masters of the whole of Greece to the south of Thermopylae and Actium, with the exception of the fortresses, which were all blockaded. Had they understood the value of military discipline, they would in all probability have succeeded in expelling the Turks from Greece before the end of the year, for the fortresses were inadequately supplied, both with ammunition and provisions [2].

It has been already mentioned that nationality was a

---

[1] The Author heard a distinguished Greek chief narrate the atrocities then committed, and boast of the part he took in instigating the soldiers to commit them; and this was in the presence of General Gordon, who was known to be writing a history of the Revolution.

[2] The following fortresses remained in the hands of the Turks: In the Morea—Tripolitza, Nauplia, Corinth, Patras, with the castle of the Morea, Navarin, Modon, Coron, and Monemvasia. In continental Greece—Athens, Zeituni, Lepanto, and the castle of Romelia, and Vonitza. In Euboea—Negrepont and Karystos.

secondary feature of the Greek Revolution at its commencement. The Greeks furnished the greater part of the soldiers who fought against the sultan, but Albanian ships and Albanian sailors formed two-thirds of the Greek navy.

Those who believe that revolutions are invariably produced by the material oppression of governments must be at a loss to point out the proofs of their theory at Hydra, Spetzas, Psara, and Kasos, or to trace the Revolution in those islands to its true causes. Under the sultan's government the four islands enumerated were lightly taxed, and allowed to regulate their internal affairs like independent republics. Fewer restrictions were placed on personal liberty and on commercial enterprise than in most Christian countries. The local magistrates were elective, the taxes were collected by Christians, and there were no resident Mussulmans. In few countries did the mass of the population live more at ease. Yet the inhabitants, whether Albanians or Greeks, were as discontented under the sultan's government in 1821, as the inhabitants of the Ionian Islands under the protection of Queen Victoria in 1858. Their advancing civilization inspired them with a longing for political independence. They believed that the possession of civil and religious liberty would render every private citizen virtuous, and every commercial speculation prosperous.

Early in the eighteenth century the sultans perceived that their treaties with the Christian powers had conceded privileges to foreigners which were ruinous to the commercial interests of their own subjects. Turkish and Greek traders were liable to pay higher duties, both of import and export, than strangers. When the sultans became desirous of reviving native commerce, they discovered that the first thing to be done was to protect the traders against the exactions of their own officials. They attempted to do this by exempting some barren islands from the fiscal administration of the empire. Under this protection colonies of Albanian seamen settled at Hydra and Spetzas, and colonies of Greek seamen at Psara and Kasos, who built ships and formed self-governing communities. In this way a considerable commercial navy grew up under the Othoman flag almost unobserved by Christian powers; and when the Revolution broke out, these four islands were populous and flourishing. The Albanians of the two first, who were much more numerous, differed considerably in manners and character from the Greeks of the other two. The Hydriots were the most sincere; the Psarians were the most courteous.

Two rocky promontories on the continent, Trikeri on Mount Pelion, and Galaxidhi on the Gulf of Corinth, were also commercial towns, enjoying self-government and many privileges under the sultan's protection.

In 1821 the commercial navy of Greece, Albanian and Greek, consisted of nearly 350 brigs and schooners of from 60 to 400 tons, besides many smaller vessels, the whole manned by upwards of 12,000 sailors[1].

Psara was inhabited by 6000 souls. Its geographical position enabled it to watch the ocean-paths to the greatest commercial cities of the sultan's dominions. The indefatigable activity of its seamen, and the illustrious deeds of one of its sons, Konstantine Kanares, have given it an honourable position in Greek history.

The government of Psara was democratic; all the citizens voted at the election of the magistrates, and among the lively and intelligent Greeks of the island the individual merits of each were recognized as titles to civic rank. Both the people and the government formed a strong contrast to those of Hydra, where wealth created a false kind of chieftainship, and the national traditions of the Albanian pharas were transmuted into feelings of party animosity. In Psara every man who possessed a house, who shared in the risks of a trading voyage, or who supported a family, though he might be only a private sailor, attended the annual assembly of the people, and gave his vote for the election of forty councillors. These councillors chose the demogeronts or magistrates, who held office for a year, and who consulted the councillors on all affairs of importance.

---

[1] The following appears to be an accurate account of the naval force of Greece in 1821:—

Hydra contained 4000 families, with 115 ships exceeding 100 tons.
Spetzas   „   1600   „   „   60   „   „
Psara   „   1200   „   „   40   „   „
Kasos   „   1500   „   „   15   „   „
Trikeri   „   400   „   „   30 vessels of various sizes.
Galaxidhi „   600   „   „   60   „   „

The number of vessels between 60 and 100 tons in all Greece was supposed to amount to 200, and there were many decked boats in every island and port.

The government of Hydra was very different, as has been already narrated, being in the hands of rich oligarchs, and administered by twelve primates[1].

The system of trade was the same in all the islands. The captains were as ignorant of the science of navigation as the sailors, but they were experienced pilots and good seamen. When such men were intrusted with valuable ships and rich cargoes, it was necessary that their interests should be deeply engaged in the success of the speculation, stimulated to constant watchfulness, and directly promoted by a quick voyage. But not only the captain—all on board also received a portion of the gain. The owner of the ship, the capitalist who purchased the cargo, the captain, and the sailors, were all partners in the success of each voyage, according to a settled rate. The division was made after deducting the capital invested in purchasing the cargo and the price of the ship's provisions. Then five per cent. was set apart for the municipal treasury at Hydra, and one per cent. for the church and monastery. The remainder was divided into a fixed number of shares; the ship received its proportion as freight, the capitalist his share as profit, and the captain and sailors their respective shares as wages. Even the cabin-boy received a half or quarter share, as the case might be. Thus everybody was interested in performing a quick and safe voyage, and reaching the port of destination with an undamaged cargo. The consequence was, that the Albanian and Greek ships performed the quickest passages and realized the largest gains of all those that navigated the Mediterranean.

This system had its inconveniences in war as well as its advantages in peace. While it encouraged the crews to extraordinary exertions, it introduced a degree of equality and a habit of consulting those on board, which proved an insurmountable obstacle to the introduction of naval discipline during the war with the Turks. No difficult or dangerous enterprise could be undertaken without assembling all the quartermasters and old seamen on the poop, and discussing the project. Sometimes a second council was held before the mast before the captain's orders were obeyed.

The general peace of 1815 caused a great reduction in the

---

[1] *See* above, p. 32.

price of grain on the continent of Europe, and a fall of freights in the Mediterranean. In the year 1820 the gains of the Albanian Islands, which had the principal share in the carrying trade between the Black Sea ports and those of Italy, France, and Spain, were still further reduced by an abundant harvest in Western Europe, and by the fear of a war between Russia and Turkey. Many ships remained unemployed at Hydra and Spetzas. The sailors were discontented; and all classes began to look for relief to the revolutionary projects which had been disseminated among the people by the apostles of the Hetairia and by the agents of Ali Pasha. Towards the commencement of 1821 the revolutionary spirit had made great progress in all the naval islands.

Spetzas was the first to proclaim its independence. Several of the primates were members of the Hetairia. Their ships were rotting in the port; the sailors were clamouring for pay. Every Christian had of late made it a part of his creed that the Othoman empire was on the eve of dissolution. Everybody declared that a Russian war was inevitable. Ali Pasha employed the whole disposable force of the sultan. The Turks were despised as much as they were hated. Enthusiasm for civil and religious liberty animated every rank of society, and a general insurrection of all the orthodox in European Turkey would, according to the assurance given by numbers of political adventurers, soon insure the success of a revolution in Greece.

A public meeting of the whole population was held at Spetzas, and the flag of independent Greece, bearing the cross rising above the crescent, was hoisted on the highest mast in the port[1]. Eight brigs were immediately fitted out to cruise off the coast of the Morea; and these vessels, knowing that an Othoman corvette of twenty-six guns and a brig of sixteen guns, greatly under-manned, were waiting at Milos to receive the annual contingent of sailors from the Albanian

---

[1] It is often difficult to fix the precise date of important events during the Greek Revolution, for inaccuracy is common both in the manuscript and the printed copies of official documents. Skylitzes Homerides, who was present, gives the 26th March (6th April) as the date of the declaration of independence at Spetzas. Συνοπτικὴ Ἱστορία τῶν τριῶν ναυτικῶν νήσων, printed at Nauplia in 1831. But Philemon gives ground for retarding it to the 3rd (15th) April; Δοκίμιον ἱστορικὸν τῆς Ἑλληνικῆς Ἐπαναστάσεως, iii. 100.

islands, sailed thither, and captured them by surprise. The Mussulmans on board were carried to Spetzas, where many were murdered in cold blood, and others were tortured with such horrid cruelty, that shame has induced the Greeks to throw a veil over this first victory of the Greek navy, in order to conceal the crimes which accompanied it.

Psara followed the example of Spetzas on the 23rd of April. The Psarians then commenced a series of depredations which made them a terror to all the Mussulman population on the sea-coast. The Turks were preparing an expedition in Asia Minor to relieve their countrymen in the Morea. Their preparations were rendered abortive by the destruction of a large transport laden with military stores, and by the capture of four small vessels carrying two hundred troops and a supply of provisions, destined for Nauplia. The Psarian schooners cruised up and down the coast from Tenedos to Rhodes, destroying or capturing every vessel that could not gain a secure port. By paralyzing the attempts of the Turks to send supplies to Greece, these operations facilitated the reduction of Monemvasia and Navarin.

While the Spetziots and Psarians were fighting the battles of liberty, the primates of Hydra were resisting the wish of the people to join the Revolution. At Hydra, as we have seen, wealth alone gave rank and power—the distinction of the different ranks of society was there strongly marked. The proportion of large ships was greater than in the other islands, and at this time the number of destitute was proportionably increased, so that the stagnation of commerce, which put an end to speculative voyages, caused much suffering among the families of the sailors. The people called loudly for revolutionary measures. The primates opposed a change, which would put them to the expense of fitting out their ships for an unprofitable and dangerous service. In vain the patriots of Spetzas and Psara urged them to hoist the Greek flag. A popular insurrection terminated their opposition by setting aside their authority. But it was not until the 28th of April that the people succeeded in proclaiming the independence of Hydra, and its union with the Greek state.

This insurrection affords an insight into the social condition of the Albanian islanders. The captains of ships, who were not themselves shipowners, formed a middle class, whose influence was not inconsiderable, particularly when want of employment rendered their interests identical with those of the people. Antonios Oeconomos, an unemployed captain, who was a member of the Hetairia, commenced enrolling a band of volunteers when the apostles transmitted the final signal for an outbreak. On the night of the 11th of April he assembled his followers, and at daybreak they rang the bell which was sounded to convoke public meetings. Oeconomos attended the assembly surrounded by a body of armed men, and invited the sailors to take possession of the ships in the port, and proclaim the Revolution in Hydra.

The demogeronts for the current four months were Lazaros Conduriottes, Ghika Ghiones, Demetrios Tsamados, and Vasili Budures. The governor or bey, named by the capitan-pasha, was George Bulgares the younger. These men, instead of holding their usual meeting at the monastery and communicating directly with the people, were so intimidated by the insurrection, which they knew well was directed against their treasure-chests, that they abandoned their posts and left Oeconomos master of the field. He immediately installed one of his own partizans, Nicolas Kokovila, as governor. The people were emboldened by this easy victory to declare, without any circumlocution, that their first business was to obtain money. Three days were spent in degrading negotiations, and all parties displayed the most revolting selfishness. The wealthy primates tried to diminish the demands of the demagogues by gaining over some of the unemployed captains to act as their advocates, while the popular leaders endeavoured to impose as large payments as possible on their personal enemies. In the end the people collected and divided among themselves the sum of 30,000 dollars. These affairs of personal interest having been arranged, the people felt less animosity towards the primates; and the popular leaders, in order to retain their ascendancy, found it necessary to direct public attention to the Revolution.

Two Spetziot vessels appeared off the port, bearing the flag of Greece, and Oeconomos seized the occasion to propose that the ships in the port of Hydra should be armed without delay, and a proclamation issued throwing off the sultan's authority, and announcing that Hydra formed a part of the Greek state. The oligarchs availed themselves with prudence of the opportunity which was thus presented of recovering their influence. They opened direct negotiations with the captains and sailors who had previously served in their ships. The pressing wants of the populace having been relieved by the distribution of the money extracted from the primates, individual interests and connections again operated, and private sympathies and party feelings came into play. Oeconomos, who observed the reaction, made a vain attempt to deprive the shipowners of the right of selecting the captains to command their ships. He desired to form a revolutionary committee, whose members should exercise the whole executive government; but the character of his associates was well known, and did not inspire sufficient confidence. Fear, interest, and patriotism now combined to make both parties anxious for a reconciliation. After some concessions it was effected; concord was restored, the proclamation of independence was viewed as the ratification of a general amnesty; and on the 28th of April a solemn service was performed in the church, and the Greek flag was hoisted on all the ships at Hydra.

Spetzas, Psara, and Hydra lost no time in concerting common operations, and a Greek fleet soon assembled under the command of Jakomaki Tombazes, a Hydriot primate of some nautical science. He was an amiable and judicious man, but he was deficient in decision, and habitually sought the advice of others, listening often to those who had less knowledge and courage than he possessed himself. He could not comprehend that an imprudent measure, executed with promptitude and vigour, is in war more effective than a wise measure feebly and slowly carried out. He was one of the few men of rank in Hydra, at the commencement of the Revolution, who treated strangers with kindness; and an English Philhellene of the highest character, whose praise was only given where it was due, said of him emphatically, that he was a worthy and honourable man[1].

The enterprise which promised the greatest success to the Greek fleet was an attack on the Othoman ships then cruising off the coast of Epirus. They were ill-manned, and so un-

---

[1] Note of Frank Abney Hastings, in the Author's possession. Strictly speaking Tombazes was only admiral of the Hydriot squadron. The Spetziots and Psarians had each their own admirals, but the superior power of Hydra gave a marked precedence to her admiral.

prepared to resist, that they would in all probability have fallen into the hands of the Greeks. A naval victory in the western seas would have weakened Khurshid's army to such a degree that he would have been unable to send succours to Patras and Tripolitza; it would have revived the courage of the partizans of Ali Pasha, roused the Christians to take up arms in many districts where they remained quiet, and perhaps enabled the Greeks, with the assistance of the Suliots, to gain possession of Prevesa and Arta.

Unfortunately, just as the fleet was about to sail for Epirus, Neophytos Vambas arrived at Hydra, and induced the primates to change its destination with the lure of the conquest of the rich island of Chios. Vambas was a Chiot; he was a scholar and a patriot, but he was a pedant and a visionary. During the early period of the Revolution he obtained considerable political influence by attaching himself to Prince Demetrius Hypsilantes. Nature intended him for a professor, not a politician. His ignorance of the business of active life; his incompetence to judge men's characters; his persuasion that all men could be directed by general maxims; and his own inability to appreciate the value of times and circumstances, and to seize the opportunities they afforded, rendered him an unsafe counsellor, and made his political career injurious to his country. On the other hand, after he was excluded from political life, his career as a teacher was honourable to himself and useful to his country, for he cultivated the moral and religious feelings as well as the intellects of his pupils, and formed some of the best, if not the ablest, men of his time.

The first cruise of the Greek navy was productive of no important result. Many prizes were made, and the sailors gained a good deal of booty; but no discipline was introduced into the service, and the little order that had previously existed in the ships while they were merchantmen was relaxed. Regulations for the equitable distribution of prize-money were adopted by universal suffrage before the fleet sailed, and it was decided that a proportion should be set apart for the public treasury, in order to meet the general expenditure of the war in which the nation was engaged [1]. These regulations

---

[1] The regulations relating to prizes and prize-money are printed by Skylitzes Homerides; App. 20.

were disregarded by the crews which succeeded in capturing prizes; they cheated their companions and defrauded the public. Their piratical conduct, and particularly the plunder of an Austrian vessel at Tinos, caused them to be regarded with fear by all the commercial states in the Mediterranean; and the cabinets of Europe watched suspiciously the proceedings of a powerful naval force, in which no discipline prevailed, and which set all public and private law at defiance.

The disorderly conduct of the Greek navy, and particularly of the Hydriot ships, during this cruise, must be attributed in part to the wilful neglect of the primates. They tolerated the criminal proceedings of the sailors that they might win them over from the party of Oeconomos. They winked at every licence for the purpose of gaining their own selfish ends. One particular capture deserves to be noticed, because it occurred under circumstances where a little firmness on the part of the officers would have saved Greece from a load of infamy, and prevented the Turks from excusing many of their subsequent cruelties with the name of vengeance.

Two Hydriot brigs, commanded by Sachturi and Pinotzi, captured a Turkish vessel with a valuable cargo, among which were some rich presents from Sultan Mahmud to Mehemet Ali, pasha of Egypt. A recently deposed Sheik-ul-Islam, or patriarch of the orthodox Mussulmans, was a passenger on board, accompanied by all his family. It was said that he was on the pilgrimage to Mecca. He was known to have belonged to the tolerant party in the Othoman government. There were other Turkish families in the ship. The Hydriots murdered all on board in cold blood; helpless old men, ladies of rank, beautiful slaves, and infant children, were butchered on the deck like cattle. An attempt was afterwards made to extenuate this unmerciful conduct, by asserting that it was an act of revenge. This assertion is false. Those who perpetrated these cruelties did not hear of the execution of their own orthodox patriarch until after they had murdered the orthodox patriarch of their enemies. The truth is, that both by land and sea the war commenced as a war of extermination. Fanatical pedants talked of reviving the glories and the cruelties of classic times as inseparable consequences of Greek liberty. They told how the Athenians had exterminated the inhabitants of Melos, and how the Spartans had put all their Athenian prisoners to death after their victory at Aegospotami.

The manner in which the immense booty taken by Sachturi and Pinotzi was divided, proved as injurious to the Greek cause as the barbarous ferocity displayed in acquiring it. The crews refused to conform to the national regulations which had been adopted before going to sea. Violent dissensions arose with the crews of other ships entitled to a share of the booty, and the quarrels that ensued became so violent that several ships quitted the fleet and went off cruising on their own account. All united action became impossible ; and thus the best opportunity of striking a decisive blow while the Turks were still unprepared for resistance was allowed to escape.

The wealth gained by the sailors diminished the influence of the popular faction under the leading of Oeconomos, and afforded the oligarchs an opportunity of re-establishing their power. The demagogue had made use of the selfishness of the sailors to win authority, by offering greater allurements to their selfishness; the oligarchs now deprived him of all power. Neither party addressed themselves to the better feelings of the people, who, if they had found worthy leaders, would not in all probability have been found wanting in patriotism and honour ; but, as it happened, the passions of a turbulent population were excited instead of being restrained. The ambition of the oligarchs and of the demagogue was equally unprincipled.

When the Hydriot ships returned from their first cruise, Oeconomos saw that his only hope of maintaining himself in the position he had assumed was by placing himself at the head of a patriotic party. He therefore proposed to enforce the wise and equitable regulations voted by common consent before the fleet put to sea, and demanded that a portion of every prize should be set apart for the national service. The primates opposed this just and prudent measure because it was advocated by Oeconomos, and supported the sailors in their unjust misappropriation of the whole booty. They paid dearly in after days for this desertion of their country's cause to gain their party objects. Oeconomos found himself without partizans, for no one trusted his patriotism, and he learned too late that honesty is the best policy, even in politics. The band of bravos who had joined him when he excited the people to plunder the rich, now adhered to the primates, who supported the sailors in plundering the national treasury. These bravos were an institution in the community of Hydra, and they knew that the oligarchs were always sure to want their services, while the demagogues could easily dispense with them[1].

The oligarchical party made an attempt to assassinate Oeconomos, instead of driving him from power by a public vote. The attempt failed, but a violent tumult ensued, in which the democratic party was defeated by a fire of musketry from the houses of the primates, and a few rounds of grape from the ships in the port. Oeconomos escaped in a boat, but was captured before he could reach the Morea. He was saved from the vengeance of the primates by the sailors, who allowed him to retire to Kranidi; but he was subsequently arrested, and imprisoned in a monastery near the lake of Phonia. From this confinement he escaped shortly after the taking of Tripolitza, and endeavoured to reach Hydra, where the people, informed of his escape, were anxiously waiting for his arrival, but he was assassinated at Kutzopodi, near Argos, by order of the primates.

The Samiots joined the Revolution as early as lay in their power. A Spetziot vessel anchored off Samos on the 30th of April. The people of Vathy immediately took up arms, and murdered all the Turkish families in the place. The primates of the island, however, succeeded in saving the lives of the Mussulmans who resided in Chora, with the aga and cadi. They were hurried into boats, and landed safely on the opposite shore of Asia Minor. Samos was then declared independent, and united with the Greek state. Its inhabitants lost no time in preparing to carry on the war vigorously, by making descents on the coast of Asia Minor.

The Othoman fleet quitted the Dardanelles on the 3rd of June. It consisted of only two line-of-battle ships, three frigates, and three sloops of war, and was very ill-manned, and altogether in bad condition. The Greek fleet had already put to sea on its second cruise. One division, under Andreas

---

[1] See an anecdote at p. 32.

Miaoulis, a name destined to become one of the most renowned in the annals of the Revolution, consisting of twelve brigs, sailed to blockade Patras and watch the Othoman squadron on the coast of Epirus. The principal division, consisting of thirty-seven sail, under Jakomaki Tombazes, cruised in the Archipelago, to wait for the Othoman fleet.

On the 5th of June the Greeks fell in with one of the Turkish line-of-battle ships off the north of Chios. It fled, and anchored in the roads of Erissos. The Greeks who pursued it passed in succession far astern, and fired their broadsides without producing any effect. It was necessary to devise some other mode of attack, and it was resolved to make use of fire-ships.

The exposed situation of Psara, the difficulty of sustaining a contest with the large ships in the sultan's navy, and the danger of an attack from the whole Othoman fleet, had been the subject of much deliberation among the Psarians. The destruction of the Turkish fleet at Tchesmé was naturally much spoken of, and the success obtained by the three fire-ships of the Russians inspired the Psarians with high hopes[1]. It was therefore resolved to fit out several fire-ships at Psara ; but with the usual dilatory habits of the Greeks in carrying even their wisest resolutions into execution, not one of these was ready to accompany the fleet when it sailed.

After the Turkish line-of-battle ship had been cannonaded ineffectually at her anchorage in the bay of Erissos, a council of captains was held on board Tombazes' ship. As there was some danger of the enemy putting to sea and escaping before a fire-ship arrived from Psara, various projects for his destruction were discussed. Some proposed cutting the cable during the sea-breeze, and letting the Turk drift ashore. Tombazes observed that an English naval officer, with whom he had spoken, told him that fire-ships would prove their best means of attacking the line-of-battle ships and heavy frigates of the Othoman navy. It has been erroneously supposed that Tombazes considered this as the first suggestion of the use of fire-ships by the Greeks[2]. The Psarian admiral, Apostoles,

---

[1] *See* vol. v., *Greece under Othoman Domination*, p. 260.
[2] Tricoupi's account of this council (i. 275) has caused a good deal of discussion in Greece, and it is corrected by Kotzias, 'Επανόρθωσις τῶν ἐν τῇ Σ. Τρικούπη ἱστορίᾳ περὶ τῶν Ψαριανῶν πραγμάτων ἱστορουμένων.

then said, that it was not necessary to wait for the arrival of the fire-ships from Psara, as there was more than one of his countrymen in the fleet who had served with the Russians at Tchesmé, and knew how to prepare a fire-ship. The word was passed for any person acquainted with the method of preparing fire-ships to come on board the Admiral. A teacher of navigation at Psara, who was serving as captain's secretary in one of the Psarian vessels, answered the summons, and undertook the task. His name was John of Parga, but he was generally known by the nickname of Patatuka, which is a term of contempt used by Greek seamen to designate northern merchantmen, with their heavy tops and small topsails, and to depreciate the nautical science of those who navigate with small crews. A Psarian, named John Theodosios, gave up his vessel to be converted into a fire-ship, on receiving a promise of forty thousand Turkish piastres, to be paid by the treasuries of the three naval islands; and volunteers came forward to man her for a bounty of one hundred dollars each. This *brulotto*, or fire-ship, was soon ready, but it was manoeuvred timidly, and burned uselessly.

On the 6th of June the cannonade was resumed, but at too great a distance to inflict any injury on the Turk, though the Greeks lost one man killed and two wounded. A second fire-ship was prepared, but a stiff breeze during the night prevented the Greeks from making use of it.

On the 7th one of the fire-ships fitted out at Psara joined the fleet, and on the morning of the 8th the Turk was again attacked. The second fire-ship, prepared in the fleet by John of Parga, was commanded by a Psarian named Pappanikolo, and manned by eighteen sailors. The fire-ship which arrived from Psara failed, in consequence of the timidity of those on board, who fired the train too soon. Pappanikolo displayed greater skill and courage in his bold enterprise, and he was well supported by his crew. He ran his ship under the bows of the Turk, and did not light the train until she was firmly fixed. He then jumped into his boat and rowed off to the Greek fleet. The flames mounted into the sails of the fire-ship in an instant, for both the canvass and the rigging were saturated with turpentine, and they were driven by the wind over the bows of the line-of-battle ship, whose hull they soon enveloped in a sheet of fire. The flames and the dense clouds of smoke which rushed along the deck and poured in at the ports, rendered it impossible to make any effort to save the ship, even had the crew been in a much better state of discipline than it was. The cable was cut, and two launches full of men left the ship. Many of the sailors jumped overboard and swam ashore; but it is supposed that between three and four hundred persons perished. About 11 A.M. the magazine exploded, and left her a complete wreck. This conflagration was the beacon of Greek liberty.

The remaining ships of the Othoman fleet were so terrified by the disaster of their consort, that they sought safety within the Dardanelles. The moment was favourable for a daring enterprise. The Turks were astounded and unprepared. But Tombazes was not a man of energy, and the Greek fleet was not disposed to obedience; so this opportunity of striking a great blow was allowed to pass unemployed, and no crisis of the war in future years occurred which was so favourable to the cause of Greece. Tombazes anchored at Moschonnesia, near Kydonies. He appears to have taken this injudicious step at the solicitation of those who wished to facilitate the escape of some wealthy Greek families. But it is possible that he shared the delusive hopes of those who believed that a million of orthodox Christians would take up arms in Asia Minor at the appearance of the Greek fleet.

Kydonies was a commercial town, which supported within itself, or in the adjoining villages, a prosperous Greek population of thirty thousand souls[1]. It had only existed for forty years, and owed its flourishing condition to the privileges conceded to it by the sultan. Its municipal authorities were elected by the people, and the local administration was controlled by the bishop and the primates. No maritime city on the coast of the Mediterranean enjoyed a higher degree of civil liberty. But after the massacre of the Turks at Galatz and Yassi was known to the Mussulmans, the zealots became eager to plunder the wealthy inhabitants of Kydonies as a profitable revenge. The pasha of Brusa, alarmed for the safety of a place which contributed largely to the revenues of

---

[1] The Turkish name of Kydonies was Haïvali, which, like the Greek, signifies a quince. Gordon (i. 297) says it contained 3000 stone houses, several handsome churches, an episcopal palace, 40 oil-mills, 30 soap-works, two magnificent hospitals, and a celebrated college, founded in 1813.

his pashalik, was desirous of protecting the Greeks, and to effect this he stationed a corps of his own guards in the vicinity, with strict orders to prevent any irregular troops from entering the town. His measures were effectual until the execution of the patriarch; but when it was known that the sultan had put many influential Greeks to death, their punishment was assumed by fanatical Mohammedans to be a licence to plunder and murder all orthodox Christians; and the bands of Turkish militia who were marching to suppress the insurrection on the Danube, sought eagerly for an opportunity to sack a wealthy Greek town like Kydonies. The news of the destruction of the Turkish line-of-battle ship on the coast of Mytilene gave them an additional incitement. To protect the place, the pasha of Brusa sent orders to his kehaya to take up his quarters, with a strong body of guards, in the town. The wealthy inhabitants, on hearing of the pasha's determination, felt that they were no longer safe. Their protectors would make many purchase life with the sacrifice of their property, and put some to death, according to the usual principles of Othoman policy, which regarded intimidation as the surest means of preserving tranquillity. At the same time they saw little prospect of the kehaya being able to prevent the irregular bands from entering the place, and rendering it a scene of pillage and slaughter. They naturally looked out for any chance of escape. On the 14th of June they sent a deputation to Tombazes, begging him to assist and protect their embarkation on board the Greek fleet. On the same day the guards of the kehaya took up their quarters in the town. On the following day the embarkation commenced.

The launches of the Greek ships arrived at daybreak, armed with swivels, and manned by select crews. A party of eighty Romeliot soldiers was landed on the beach to protect the families who embarked. The kehaya in the meantime made his own arrangements for preventing the escape of the wealthy citizens, whom he regarded as pledges for the tranquillity of the Christian population. He occupied some houses near the beach, and endeavoured to drive off the Romeliots and the boats of the fleet by opening on them a heavy fire. The Kydonians, fearing lest their escape should be prevented, occupied some houses in rear of the Turks, and began to skirmish with them. The swivels of the launches, the rifles of the Romeliots, and the fire of the Kydonians, soon cleared a safe line of retreat. But the firing served as a signal to the Turks to commence plundering the town. The shops in the bazaar were first emptied; private houses were then ransacked, and at last women and children were seized, to be sold as slaves. An unparalleled scene of confusion ensued, but the disorder enabled as many as the boats would hold to escape without difficulty. The Turks, however, in order to prevent those who lived at a distance from the sea from reaching the beach, set fire to several houses in the middle of the town. The Greeks, to stop the advance of the Turks, set fire to other houses, and fire being used as a species of intrenchment by both parties, before night arrived great part of Kydonies was in ashes.

On the day of this catastrophe, the Greek fleet saved about four thousand persons, and on the following day one thousand more were brought off to the ships. Tombazes behaved with great humanity. He received seven hundred persons on board his corvette, and did everything in his power to alleviate their sufferings. He had a kind heart, though he was a phlegmatic man. But his example was not followed by many of his countrymen. Wealthy families were compelled to purchase a passage to the nearest Greek island by giving up the greater part of the property they had saved. Not a few of those whose houses at Kydonies had been filled with servants, were henceforth obliged to gain their bread as menials in Greece. Those who were unable to escape, were either murdered or enslaved. The slave-markets of Brusa, Nicomedia, Smyrna, and Constantinople, were for some months crowded with young Greeks from Kydonies; and if mere physical well-being were the great object of man's existence, these slaves might be regarded as more fortunate than many of their countrymen who preserved their liberty.

On the 22nd of June, 1821, the Greek fleet returned home to secure its plunder and divide its gains. The sailors did not even wait until the month for which they had received payment in advance had expired. The honours of the cruise were won by the Psarians, in consequence of the bold exploit of Captain Pappanikolo. The booty gained was very great, but unfortunately no small portion of it was extorted from the fugitives who fled from their native homes in Asia Minor.

The squadron of twelve ships which sailed to the west coast of Greece performed no exploit of importance, though its appearance, as has been already mentioned, roused the inhabitants of Aetolia to take up arms[1]. At its approach a Turkish corvette and four brigs quitted Patras, and retired under the guns of Lepanto, where the Hydriots did not venture to attack them. Cutting-out was not an exploit practised in Greek naval warfare, and an attempt to destroy them with fire-ships failed. The Greek squadron passed through the Dardanelles of Lepanto into the Gulf of Corinth during the night, and returned again, without suffering any loss from the formidable castles which command the passage through these narrow straits.

---

[1] *See* p. 163.

CHAPTER IV.

THE POLICY AND CONDUCT OF SULTAN MAHMUD II.

Policy of Sultan Mahmud.—Suppressive measures and first executions of Greeks.—Execution of the Patriarch Gregorios.—His character.—Massacres of Greeks.—Sultan restores order.—Cruelties of Turks and Greeks.—Rupture with Russia.—Difficulties of Sultan Mahmud in 1821.—Measures adopted to suppress the Greek Revolution.—Order re-established in Agrapha, among the Vallachian population on Mount Pindus.—Rapacity of the Greek troops.—Insurrection on Mount Pelion suppressed.—Revolution in the free villages of the Chalcidice.—Among the monks of Mount Athos.—Suppressed by Aboulabad Pasha of Saloniki.—Insurrection in the Macedonian mountains.—Sack of Niausta.—Success of Sultan Mahmud in maintaining order.

DURING the Greek Revolution, Sultan Mahmud gradually revealed to the world the full extent of his abilities, and the unshaken firmness of his character. His conduct has been justly condemned as combining Mussulman bigotry with the immemorial ferocity of the Othoman race; but experience seemed to prove that cruelty was the most effectual instrument for governing Oriental nations, and Sultan Mahmud knew how to temper his cruelty with policy. The Greeks entertained the project of exterminating the Mussulmans in European Turkey; the sultan and the Turks believed that they could paralyze the movements of the Greeks by terrific cruelty. Both parties were partially successful.

Sultan Mahmud is represented by the historians of the Greek Revolution as an inhuman monster. They have even attributed to him the project of exterminating his Christian subjects, which is said to have been discussed and rejected by two of his predecessors, the ferocious Selim I. and the vicious Ibrahim. The Greeks have given him the epithet of 'the butcher.' Yet his conduct was guided by political principles, which in the year 1821 were considered prudent at

Constantinople, and which would not have been considered unmerciful by Louis the Great or our James II., if applied to rebellious heretics. The acts of Sultan Mahmud were not the result of personal fury, they were the deliberate acts of a sovereign, regulated by the laws and customs of the Othoman empire. He treated the rebellious janissaries with even greater severity than the insurgent Greeks. Some excuse also might be urged for his passion, if he allowed revenge to increase the number of his victims after he discovered 'the grand project' of the Hetairists to assassinate himself and his ministers, and to burn his arsenal and his capital. He then tolerated massacres of the Greek population at Constantinople and Smyrna, which he might have suppressed by a vigorous exercise of his authority. But even in these cases, it ought not to be overlooked that his position was extremely difficult. He was suspected by the janissaries of hostility to their corps, and he knew that his enemies were the persons most active in inciting the fanatics to attack the Christians. Sultan Mahmud was one of those despots (not unknown on the thrones of Christian monarchies) who believed that Heaven had invested him with a divine right to rule his subjects. He was lawgiver and sovereign, caliph and sultan. It was his duty to punish rebellion, and to avenge the blood of the innocent Mussulmans who had been slaughtered as martyrs at Galatz, at Yassi, and in Greece. As Britons, we must remember the cry for vengeance which arose in our hearts when we heard of similar atrocities committed on our countrymen and our kindred in India.

When the plots of the Hetairists were first discovered by the Turks, they were treated very lightly by Halet Effendi, the sultan's favourite counsellor. But when the news arrived that the prince of Moldavia, one of Halet's creatures, had joined the rebels, the Othoman government was awakened to a sense of the danger of a revolution among the Greeks, and the sultan's confidence in Halet Effendi was shaken. The first measures of precaution were not violent. All Greeks who were not engaged in business were ordered to quit Constantinople, and search was made for arms in the houses of suspected persons. But when the sultan obtained some information concerning the grand project of the Hetairists, he ordered all true believers to arm in defence of their religion, and summoned the patriarch and synod of Constantinople to excommunicate Alexander Hypsilantes, Michael Soutzos, and the rebels beyond the Danube, who were responsible for the murder of many helpless Mussulmans. This act of excommunication, signed with the usual formalities on the communion-table, was immediately issued as a proof of the loyalty of the orthodox church to its protector the sultan[1].

Any good effect which the promptitude of the clergy produced on the Othoman government was destroyed by the flight of Michael Soutzos' brother, and several other Phanariots, who were fortunate enough to learn the news of the invasion of Moldavia before it reached the Porte. During the time which elapsed between the 12th and the 20th of March, many wealthy Greeks escaped secretly to Odessa, and in ships bound to different places in the Mediterranean. These departures, and a general belief that an insurrection of the orthodox population of the empire would be supported by a declaration of war by Russia, caused great alarm among the Mussulmans in European Turkey. On the 21st of March the sultan was informed of the massacres at Galatz and Yassi, and on that day the grand-vizier ordered seven Greek bishops to be arrested, but at the same time to be treated with all the respect due to their high rank.

On the 26th of March the Turks in Constantinople mustered in arms, and a considerable number of irregular troops were brought over from Asia. On the 3rd of April, the very day on which the Christians in the Morea commenced the general massacre of the Mussulman population, the first execution of Greeks took place at Constantinople. Several Hetairists, whose complicity in the grand project was inferred on what the Othoman government considered satisfactory evidence, were executed. Some days after, sixteen Hetairists of inferior rank were also executed. But it was not until the sultan received reports of the murder of thousands of Mussulman families in Greece, that his vengeance fell heavy on the Christians. He then ordered the grand-vizier to select a number of Greeks invested with official rank, and regarding them as hostages for the good

[1] The acts of excommunication by the patriarch and synod are printed by Philemon, ii. 309, 317.

conduct of their countrymen, he commanded that they should be publicly executed in the manner best calculated to strike terror into the hearts of their co-religionaries. The recognizances of these men were held to be forfeited, and they were sacrificed as an expiation for the blood of the slain Mohammedans. On the 16th of April the dragoman of the Porte, Murusi, was beheaded in his official dress, and during the following week several Greeks of distinction were beheaded and others hung.

At last an execution took place which caused a thrill of horror from the centre of Constantinople to the mountains of Greece and the palaces of St. Petersburg. On Easter Sunday, the 22nd of April 1821, the Patriarch Gregorios was executed, or, as the orthodox say, suffered martyrdom, by order of the sultan, as an accessory to the rebellious scheme of the Hetairists.

Shortly after sunset on Saturday evening, the whole quarter of the Phanar was occupied by patrols of janissaries, who were stationed there to preserve order during the unseemly tumult with which the Greeks desecrate their ceremonies in commemoration of our Saviour's death and resurrection. At midnight, the Patriarch Gregorios performed the usual service in his cathedral church, surrounded by the clergy. At the earliest dawn, the new dragoman of the Porte, Aristarchos, attended by an Othoman secretary of the reis-effendi, entered the patriarchate, and invited the patriarch to a meeting in the hall of the synod, to which the leading members of the clergy, the archonts of the nation, and the heads of the Greek corporations, were already convoked. The patriarch appeared. A firman was read, declaring that Gregorios the Moreot, having acted an unworthy, an ungrateful, and a treacherous part, was degraded from his office. Orders were immediately given for electing a new patriarch, and after the rejection of one candidate, Eugenios, bishop of Pisidia, was chosen, and received his investiture at the Porte with the usual ceremonies.

While the new patriarch was assuming the insignia of his official rank, the deposed patriarch was led to execution. He was hung from the lintel of the gate of the patriarchate, with a fetva, or sentence of condemnation, pinned to his breast. The old man met death with dignified courage and pious resignation. His conscience was at ease, for he believed that he had fulfilled his duty as a Christian priest by concealing from an infidel sovereign the existence of an orthodox conspiracy, of which he may have obtained detailed information only in the confessional[1]. His only error may have been that of voluntarily placing himself at the head of the Greek Church by accepting the patriarchate after he knew of the existence of the schemes of the Hetairists, and when his official engagements to his sovereign were in direct opposition to his patriotic sentiments, and what he considered his Christian duties.

Three of the bishops, who had been previously arrested, were also executed on Easter Sunday.

In the evening, the grand-vizier, Benderli Ali, walked through the streets of the Phanar, attended by a single tchaous. On reaching the gate of the patriarchate, he called for a stool, and sat down for a few minutes, looking calmly at the body hanging before him. He then rose and walked away without uttering a word. Othoman justice is deeply imbued with the principle that men in high office are hostages to the sultan for order in his dominions, and that they ought to expiate crimes of the people which are attributed to their neglect. Several circumstances tended to make the Patriarch Gregorios peculiarly culpable in the eyes of Sultan Mahmud. He had allowed the family of Murusi to escape to the detested Muscovites; he had connived at the flight of Petrobey's son to join the rebellious Greeks; and a Hetairist had been arrested having in his possession letters of the patriarch mixed up with letters of Hypsilantes' agents[2].

The body of Gregorios remained publicly exposed for three days. It was then delivered to the Jews to be dragged through the streets and cast into the sea. This odious task is rendered a source of horrid gratification to the Jewish

---

[1] It is perhaps impossible to ascertain with certainty whether, as many assert, the patriarch was regularly informed of all the plans of the Hetairists, for those who make the assertion consider that they are honouring his memory.
[2] The Othoman government was doubtless perfectly aware that letters which Hypsilantes had transmitted to the Russian embassy had been forwarded by Baron Strogonoff to the patriarch, and that their delivery had enabled several conspirators to escape to Russia. The Turkish ministers subsequently declared that they possessed eleven letters addressed by the patriarch to conspirators in the Morea, but these letters would in all probability have been published had they contained direct proof of the complicity of Gregorios in the plots of the Hetairists. *See* Gervinus, i. 210, 215.

rabble at Constantinople, by the intense hatred which prevails between the Greeks and the Jews throughout the East. The orthodox, who regarded Gregorios as a martyr, watched the body, and at night it was taken out of the water and conveyed in an Ionian vessel to Odessa, where the Russian authorities welcomed it as a holy relic, which the waters had miraculously cast up to strengthen the faith, perhaps to animate the bigotry, of the sultan's enemies[1]. The body was interred with magnificent ecclesiastical ceremonies and much military pomp. In Christendom it was supposed that the Jews had been ordered to ill-treat the body of Gregorios, in order to inflict an additional insult on the Christian religion; but this was a mistake. This outrage on humanity was then a part of Othoman criminal justice, and it was inflicted alike on Mussulmans and Christians. About a year after the execution of the deposed patriarch, Hassan Bairaktar, of the 21st oda of janissaries, headed a mutinous band of Mussulmans, who plundered many Christian families. He was shot resisting a patrol appointed to protect the Greeks, and on the 22nd of June 1822 his body was dragged through the streets of Constantinople by the Jews, and cast into the sea.

Gregorios was a man of virtue, and his private character commanded the respect of his countrymen. His talents for conducting official business induced the Othoman government to place him three times on the patriarchal throne; and on the last occasion he was called to his high office expressly that he might employ his acknowledged influence to preserve tranquillity among an excited population animated by the rebellion of Ali Pasha of Joannina, and by the prospect of a Russian war. Gregorios was therefore fully aware of the responsibilities and dangers of the position he assumed. He was versed in the intrigues of the divan and of the Phanariots. He knew that a great conspiracy of the orthodox existed; and there is no doubt that, like most of his countrymen, he believed that Russia would throw her shield over the rebels. He took up a false position as patriarch, which ought to have shocked his moral feelings. In executing him Sultan Mahmud

---

[1] The funeral oration delivered at Odessa by the presbyter and oeconomos Konstantinos Oeconomos, was published at St. Petersburg in 1824 in Greek and German.

MASSACRES OF THE GREEKS.

acted in strict conformity with the laws of the Othoman empire. Every Mussulman regarded him as a perjured traitor. Every Greek still cherishes his memory as a holy martyr.

Various circumstances at this time made it a matter of policy with several influential classes among the Turks to encourage religious bigotry, and inflame the fury of the populace of Constantinople against the Christians. Sultan Mahmud was suspected, both by the ulema and the janissaries, of a design to curtail their wealth and diminish their privileges. They seized the opportunity now offered for embarrassing his government. They openly called on all true believers to revenge the Mussulmans whom the Christians had murdered, and they magnified the numbers of the slain. The sultan and his ministers were intimidated by the threatening aspect of the tumult which was created. A revolution seemed impending among the Turks, as an immediate result of the revolution among the Greeks. To calm the spirit of insurrection, and tranquillize the minds of the janissaries, Sultan Mahmud deemed it necessary to admit three members of the corps to permanent seats in the divan on the 5th May 1821.

Anarchy, or something very near anarchy, prevailed at Constantinople for three weeks. Bands of the lowest rabble, headed by agents of the ulema, and by insubordinate janissaries, paraded the quarters of the capital where the Christians resided, and visited the villages on the Bosphorus, robbing and murdering the rayahs. The patriarchate was broken open, and the monks escaped by the roof, and found the means of reaching some Turkish houses in the neighbourhood. To the honour of the Mussulmans it must be recorded that they concealed the Christian ecclesiastics from the fury of the mob.

Sultan Mahmud is said to have viewed the first outbreak of Mussulman bigotry with satisfaction. He interpreted it as a proof of enthusiastic attachment to his person and government, and as a testimony of patriotic zeal for the dynasty of Othman. He distrusted both Halet Effendi, hitherto his favourite minister, and Benderli Ali, his grand-vizier, whom he considered too favourable to the Greeks, and too fearful of Russia. He suspected them of advocating a policy of moderation, in order to serve their own selfish ends.

On the 15th of May, Salik Pasha succeeded Benderli Ali in the office of grand-vizier, and the executions of the Greek clergy and archonts immediately recommenced. Four bishops, previously arrested, and who had hitherto been spared, were now hanged in different villages on the European side of the Bosphorus, from Arnaout-keui to Therapia. As numbers of Christians escaped daily from Constantinople in foreign vessels, the Porte adopted measures to prevent the departure of its subjects without passports[1]. On the 20th of May the patriarch informed the orthodox subjects of the sultan, that every five families were to give mutual security for all the members of which they were composed, and that if any individual quitted the capital without a passport from the Othoman authorities, the heads of families were to be severely punished. This measure surpassed the severity even of the Russian police.

At Smyrna greater disorder prevailed than at Constantinople. Bands of brigands and fanatics, who had taken up arms in Asia Minor under the pretext of marching against the rebellious Christians on the banks of the Danube, entered Smyrna, where they knew there was a large Christian population, and where they consequently hoped to obtain both booty and slaves without any fighting. The Greeks in the city and in the surrounding villages were attacked and plundered as if they had been a hostile population. Fathers of families were murdered; women and children were carried off and sold as slaves. Many Turks of rank attempted in vain to put a stop to these atrocities. The mollah of Smyrna and several ayans were slain, for defending the Christians, by the Mussulman mob. The strongest representations on the part of the ambassadors of the European powers could only obtain the adoption of measures tending to protect foreigners. The Christian subjects of the sultan were left exposed to the attacks of lawless brigands, and some weeks were allowed to elapse before the military officers of the sultan made any effort to restore order.

At Smyrna the massacre of the Greeks was repeated when news arrived of the cruelties committed by the Christians after the taking of Tripolitza.

Similar scenes of pillage and murder were enacted in most

---

[1] Compare the measures adopted against the subjects of Venice, chiefly Zantiots, Cephalonians, and Sclavonians, May 16, 1797. Zinkeisen, *Geschichte des Osmanischen Reichs*, vii. 750.

SULTAN RESTORES ORDER.

of the principal cities of the empire which contained a considerable Greek population. At Adrianople, a deposed patriarch, Cyril, was put to death, and his execution served as a signal for the fanatics to plunder the Greeks in that city and in the neighbouring towns and villages. At Saloniki, at Cos, at Rhodes, in Crete, and in Cyprus, the Greeks were plundered and murdered with impunity. For several months during the year 1821, Greece and Turkey presented a succession of scenes so atrocious that no pen could venture to narrate their horrors. The Turks have always been a bloodthirsty race, indifferent to human suffering, and they had now terrible wrongs to avenge. The Greeks had by long oppression been degraded into a kind of Christian Turks. It is impossible to form a correct estimate of the number of Greeks who were massacred by the Turks: some have considered it as great as the number of Mussulmans murdered in Greece[1].

The sultan could not long forget that the wealth and intelligence of the Christian rayahs contributed to fill his treasury. He would not abstain from his revenge, but he wished to avoid weakening his own strength. The ingratitude of the dignified clergy and wealthy Phanariots on whom he had conferred high office, appeared to merit the severest punishment; but the cruel treatment of the common people compromised the order of society, and threatened to diminish the imperial revenues. He determined therefore to re-establish order and security of property; and the rare energy with which he carried his measures into immediate execution, enabled him to do so most successfully. He proved to the Christians that they could live in security, and continue to gain money, under his government; and he persuaded a considerable portion of the Greek race to separate themselves from the cause of the Revolution, and remain tranquil under his protection. While policy suggested that terror was the most effectual weapon for crushing rebellion, no monarch ever inflicted punishment with greater severity than Sultan Mahmud; but as soon as he felt satisfied that humanity would

---

[1] Humanity appears to have made little progress in the east since the Othoman conquest, when Drakul, the Christian prince of Vallachia, impaled women and children, and Giustiniani, the Venetian admiral, impaled and drowned his Turkish prisoners. Gobellinus, *Pii II. Pont. Max. Comment.* 296; Sismondi, *Républiques Italiennes*, v. 321.

enable him to combat the progress of the Greek Revolution with greater efficacy in those regions into which it had not yet spread, he acted both with moderation and prudence. Unfortunately, both the Turks and Greeks in arms considered that the results of their cruelty proved the wisdom of inhumanity. By destroying the native Mussulmans in Greece, the Christians had destroyed their most dangerous enemies, and converted what might have been a civil war into a national struggle for independence. The Turks, by cutting off the heads of the leading Greeks in their power, had checked the progress of the Revolution, and retained onehalf of the Greek population in subjection to the sultan.

A few examples of the manner in which the war was carried on will show the spirit of both the belligerents. The Othoman fleet, while passing near the island of Samothrace, embarked seventy of the inhabitants. They were accused of joining the Revolution, because the sailors of the Greek fleet had landed on the island, and collected a supply of provisions. Twelve of these poor islanders were hanged at Constantinople for the purpose of intimidation. It was impossible to suppose that they had committed any crime deserving so severe a punishment.

The Greek fleet, having captured some Turkish merchantvessels, sent one hundred and eighty prisoners to Naxos, where they were treated as slaves. For some time they were employed by the Greeks of the island as domestic servants or farm-labourers, and they were generally well treated by their masters. But one after another they were waylaid and murdered. As the Greek proverb expresses it, the moon devoured them; and when a French man-of-war arrived to carry off the survivors, only thirty were found alive.

About forty Turks, of whom five only were men, were allowed by the Greeks of Laconia to escape to Cerigo, where they expected to find protection under the English flag; but they were murdered in cold blood by the Ionian peasantry, who had no wrongs inflicted by Othoman tyranny to plead as an apology for the assassination of Mussulman women and children. The indignation of the British government was roused, and five Cerigots were tried, condemned, and executed for these murders.

During the whole period of the Revolution the Greeks

COMPLAINTS OF RUSSIA.   193

displayed a fiercer animosity to the Mussulmans than the Turks to the Christians. Gordon, a warm Philhellene, observes, 'Whatever national or individual wrong the Greeks may have endured, it is impossible to justify the ferocity of their vengeance, or to deny that a comparison instituted between them and the Othoman generals, Mehemet Aboulabad, Omer Vrioni, and the Kehaya Bey (of Khurshid), would give to the latter the palm of humanity. Humanity, however, is a word quite out of place when applied either to them or to their opponents[1].'

The Christian sovereigns who had ministers at the Porte, and especially the Emperor of Russia, who assumed that the treaty of Kainardji constituted him the protector of the orthodox subjects of the sultan, were reproached with their callousness to the sufferings of the Greeks. Several Europeans residing at Constantinople and at Smyrna were murdered by fanatics and brigands, yet the remonstrances of the ambassadors were treated with neglect by Sultan Mahmud. Under the circumstances it was thought by many that the Christian powers ought to have withdrawn their representatives from Constantinople. But these philanthropists overlooked a fact which forced itself on the attention of the Emperor Alexander I. It was, that the conduct of the Othoman government proved that the sultan's hand was heavy on the Greeks, not because they were orthodox Christians, but because they were rebels: and the policy of the Russian autocrat was quite as hostile to a democratic revolution as that of the sultan was. But the Baron Strogonoff, the Russian minister, did not allow the execution of the Patriarch Gregorios to pass without strong complaints. The Porte, however, replied, that he had been justly condemned and executed according to law; that his complicity in a conspiracy to overthrow the authority of his lawful sovereign had been proved by irrefragable evidence; and that he had been deposed from his ecclesiastical dignity with the usual forms before he had been punished for his crimes. To all this the Russian minister could offer no reply.

When the declaration published by the emperors of Russia and Austria and the king of Prussia at Laybach on the 12th

---

[1] *History of the Greek Revolution*, i. 313.

May 1821, against revolutionary principles, was made known to Sultan Mahmud, he viewed it as an engagement of these powers not to protect the Greek rebels. In this interpretation of the policy of the Christian powers he was confirmed by the assurances of several foreign ministers, and he availed himself of the opportunity which was thus afforded him of improving his position. He ordered all vessels quitting Othoman ports to be searched, in order to prevent the departure of Turkish subjects without passports. This, being entirely in accordance with the principles of police adopted by Christian states, admitted of no objection on the part of Russia. But at the same time an embargo was laid on all grain ships passing the Bosphorus, and the sultan insisted on enforcing his natural jurisdiction over all his Christian subjects who continued to reside in Turkey, even though they pretended to a foreign nationality, in virtue of passports obtained from foreign ambassadors. The Russian minister objected to these measures; and on the 18th July 1821 he presented to the Porte an ultimatum, in which the emperor demanded that the ill-treatment of the orthodox should cease, and that the churches which the Turks had wantonly destroyed should be rebuilt at the sultan's expense. No reply was vouchsafed to this document, which on some points exceeded the limits of international diplomacy. The Russian minister then broke off his relations with the Porte, and embarked for Odessa. This spirited conduct alarmed the Othoman ministers, who immediately sent an answer, which Baron Strogonoff declined receiving, as the Russian embassy had already quitted Constantinople. The reply to the Russian ultimatum was therefore transmitted to St. Petersburg.

In this reply the Porte argued that the Greeks, as well as all other orthodox Christians and the orthodox Church, had always been objects of the sultan's especial protection, that the treaty of Kainardji had not been violated by the Porte, and that rebellion must be punished by a sovereign, whether the rebels be Greeks or orthodox priests. The Emperor Alexander was reminded that his predecessor, Peter the Great, had put a patriarch to death; and the sultan now demanded, as a proof of the emperor's disapproval of the Greek rebellion and the lawless conduct of the Hetairists, that his imperial majesty should fulfil the engagement contained in the second article of the treaty of Kainardji, and deliver up the traitorous hospodar of Moldavia, Michael Soutzos, with the other traitors who had fled to Russia, in order that they might receive the merited punishment of their ingratitude and treason [1].

The Porte, however, was soon after induced by the influence of England and Austria to mollify the hostile feelings of Russia, and sought to avoid a war by removing the embargo on grain ships from Russian ports. Yet when Baron Strogonoff had an interview with the Emperor Alexander near Odessa, in the month of August, it was generally supposed by Russians as well as Greeks that a declaration of war would soon take place. The policy of the Russian cabinet at this time was misunderstood in the East. The Emperor Alexander was a man of warm feelings and a weak character, and his personal direction of the diplomacy of Russia placed his negotiations with Turkey, particularly when they related to Greek affairs, under the influence of two irreconcileable rules of conduct. His fear of revolutions, and his sincere conviction that the preservation of peace in Europe depended on the unanimity of the sovereigns who were members of the Holy Alliance, rendered him hostile to the Greek insurrection. Yet, on the other hand, as Emperor of Russia, he believed that it was his duty to enforce his claim to be recognized as the protector of the orthodox subjects of the sultan, and the traditions of his government placed him in a state of rivalry with Turkey on political as well as religious grounds. In conformity with his determination to uphold the authority of sovereigns, he abstained from war with the sultan, and in order to uphold his claim to protect the orthodox in Turkey and keep open a pretext for war, he vexed the Ottoman government with unceasing demands. As his estimate of the relative importance of his duty to the peace of Europe and to the dignity of his own empire was liable to continual change, his conduct was unsteady and his policy inconsequent. But for the present he took no further measures to coerce the sultan, and Russia did not resume her diplomatic relations with Turkey until George Canning brought the

---

[1] Baron Strogonoff's ultimatum, dated 6th (18th) July, 1821, and the reply of the Porte, dated 26th July, are printed in Lesur, *Annuaire historique pour* 1821, pp. 652, 656.

affairs of Greece before the cabinets of Europe, and succeeded in inducing Russia and France to co-operate with Great Britain in establishing peace between the Greeks and Turks.

The difficulties of Sultan Mahmud's position in 1821 would have terrified a man of a less determined character; and when he was about to commence operations against the insurgent Greeks, prudence might have suggested that a war with so powerful an enemy as Russia was to be avoided at every risk. But the sultan saw the importance of separating the cause of the Greek Revolution from the cause of the orthodox Church, and of defining clearly the political opposition which placed the principles of the Russian cabinet in hostility with those of the insurgent Greeks. He succeeded, however, more in consequence of the moderation of the Emperor Alexander than through his own sagacity or boldness. Yet for a considerable time he continued to be surrounded by other difficulties, and many persons well acquainted with the state of the Othoman empire considered these difficulties to be insurmountable. In his capital the janissaries were seditious, and the ulema discontented. The enthusiasm of the Mussulman feudatories required to be excited, and the bigotry of the Mussulman populace required to be restrained. The rebellion of Ali Pasha of Joannina still occupied a large portion of the naval and military forces of the empire. The pasha of Acre was in a state of rebellion. The Druses were in arms against the sultan's officers. An Othoman army was occupied in Vallachia and Moldavia, and the garrisons of the fortresses on the Danube required to be increased, on account of the threatening masses of troops which Russia had collected in her southern provinces. Amidst all these troubles, the true believers were appalled by the news that the holy cities of Mecca and Medina were threatened by an army of Wahabites; and the sultan, in this crisis, found himself obliged to declare war against the Shah of Persia, in consequence of repeated incursions into the eastern provinces of the Othoman empire.

Yet, with all these embarrassments, and with disorder in every branch of the public administration, Sultan Mahmud never swerved from his determination of crushing the Greek Revolution by force of arms. His first care was to strengthen his authority in Thrace and Macedonia, and to extinguish the flames of rebellion from Mount Athos to Olympus. The prudent measures adopted by Khurshid prevented many of the armatoli from joining their countrymen at the commencement of the Revolution, when their defection would have inflicted a severe wound on the power of the sultan. Khurshid saw immediately that, if the insurgent Greeks could succeed in engaging the Christian population of Agrapha to embark heartily in their cause, they would secure the co-operation of the whole of the armatoli of Pindus and Olympus, interrupt the communications of the Othoman army before Joannina with its supplies at Larissa and Thessalonica, compel him to raise the siege of Joannina, and allow Ali Pasha to place himself at the head of a revolution of the Mussulman Albanians. The fate of the Othoman empire depended as much on the prudence of Khurshid as on the firmness of Sultan Mahmud. Any error of the seraskier might have thrown all European Turkey into a state of anarchy, and compelled the Emperor Alexander to interfere for the protection of the lives of several millions of orthodox Christians of the Sclavonian race.

Khurshid augmented the garrisons of Prevesa and Arta, and by so doing he checked the progress of the Suliots, and kept open his communications with the Othoman fleet, and with the Ionian Islands. He stationed about two thousand men at Trikkala and Larissa, under the command of Mohammed Dramali, to support the derven-agas and hold the armatoli of Pindus and Olympus in check. The timely arrival of reinforcements of Mussulman Albanians in these districts prevented the Greek armatoli from taking up arms when they heard of the execution of the Patriarch Gregorios, and the massacres of their countrymen at Constantinople and Smyrna. The prudence of Khurshid, after the insurrection broke out, was as remarkable as his neglect of all precautions before its commencement.

During the year 1821, Sultan Mahmud succeeded in suppressing the revolutionary movements of the Greeks in most of the provinces in European Turkey beyond the limits of the present kingdom of Greece. The Christians took up arms in Agrapha, in the valleys of the Aspropotamos and of the river of Arta, on Mounts Pelion, Ossa, and Olympus, in the Macedonian mountains overlooking the plain of the Vardar, in the

Chalcidice of Thrace, and on Mount Athos. In all these districts the Greeks were defeated, compelled to lay down their arms, and induced to resume their ordinary occupations. The fact that they remained peaceful subjects of the sultan during the whole period of the revolutionary war, and that, when peace was established, and they obtained permission to emigrate to liberated Greece, they refused to avail themselves of the liberty of becoming subjects of King Otho, refutes the assertion of those Greek historians who declare that cruelty and oppression were the prominent features of Sultan Mahmud's government. The cruelty which represses anarchy is never considered to be intolerable by the agricultural population, to whom it secures the peaceable enjoyment of their property.

In Agrapha the insurrection commenced at the end of June. The Mussulman Albanians in garrison at Rendina were expelled by the armatoli, who, in company with the peasant proprietors of the district, descended into the plain of Thessaly, where they burned Loxada and some neighbouring villages inhabited by Koniarides, a Turkish agricultural tribe, which is said to have entered Europe as allies of the usurper Cantacuzene, and to have settled in this district when he was dethroned[1]. The Agraphiots were soon attacked by the Othoman troops in Larissa, and driven back into their mountains. The reinforcements sent by Khurshid enabled the Mussulmans to recover possession of Rendina, and to restore the state of things which existed before the outbreak. Stamati Gatsu was appointed captain of the Greek armatoli of the district. Though he had been one of the leaders in the foray into Thessaly, he remained faithful to the sultan. His loyalty was secured by liberal pay, and his conduct was closely watched by a derven-aga with a body of Mussulman Albanians.

The Vallachian villages of Syrako and Kalarites, in the valley of the river of Arta, were garrisoned by a body of Albanians under Ibrahim Premeti. The position is of great importance to those who wish to command the road from Metzovo to Joannina. The Vallachian population of this district consists of a sturdy, industrious, and wealthy race,

---

[1] *See* vol. i. p. 443. [Compare also vol. v. p. 125, *note.*]

but not of warlike habits. The people were instigated to take up arms, when they heard of the insurrection in Agrapha, by their primates, and by John Kolettes, a citizen of Syrako, who had been physician to Mukhtar Pasha, and who acquired celebrity as one of the most influential political leaders of the Greek Revolution. The primates of the Vallachian villages summoned to their assistance a body of armatoli, under the command of Rhangos, and succeeded in driving out the Albanians. But Khurshid, alarmed for his communications with Thessaly, sent the Mussulmans powerful reinforcements, which enabled Ibrahim Premeti to drive back the armatoli of Rhangos, and to regain possession of Syrako and Kalarites. The conduct of this Albanian officer was extremely prudent, and he succeeded in restoring tranquillity and order in the district over which his authority extended.

Nearly simultaneously with the insurrection of the Vallachian population in the valley of the river of Arta, the Vallachian population in the parallel valley of the Aspropotamos took up arms. About three thousand men, under the command of Nicolas Sturnari, prepared to invade Thessaly; but the armatoli of Agrapha, having already made their submission to the sultan, joined a body of Mussulman Albanians, and compelled the Vlachokhoria to remain at home on the defensive. In the mean time the Turks of Trikkala guarded the passes of Klinovo and Portais, and a body of Albanians detached from Khurshid's camp, reinforced by a portion of Ibrahim Premeti's troops, advanced into the valley of the Aspropotamos on the 12th of August. The Turks of Thessaly forced the pass of Portais at the same time. The Aspropotamites, surrounded on all sides, made their submission, delivered up their arms, and received tickets of protection from Khurshid, who declared a general amnesty, reinstated every man in his private property, and restored to the communities the full exercise of all their privileges. Considerable credit is due to the seraskier for his military combinations and political moderation during these operations; but his success in re-establishing the sultan's authority over the Christian population in the range of Pindus was unquestionably greatly assisted by the rapacity of the insurgent leaders and of the Greek troops who entered these districts. They plundered friends as well as foes, and carried off the working oxen of the Christian peasantry as well as their sheep and goats.

The progress of the Greek Revolution to the north was arrested quite as much by this shameful misconduct as by the prudent measures of Sultan Mahmud and the decisive operations of Khurshid Pasha. The Christian population of Mount Pindus, whether Greek, Albanian, or Vallachian, learned to look with aversion on the revolutionary troops, whom they designated as klephts or brigands, and not as armatoli or soldiers. At this period it was a maxim of the insurgents, that the people ought to be forced to take up arms by the destruction of their property, and they carried their maxim into practice in a revolting manner, by appropriating the property of the people to their own use in the process of destruction. Neither the civil nor military leaders of the Revolution reflected that the destruction of property must prove more injurious to the Greeks than to the Turks. The Greeks could only draw their resources from the land they occupied; the Turks could carry on the war with supplies brought from a distance. When, therefore, a desert frontier was created, that deserted line of country, which soon extended from Makronoros to Thermopylae, formed an impassable barrier to the progress of the Greeks northwards, while it afforded additional security to the sultan in maintaining his authority among the Greek population on the northern side of this line.

Zagora (Mount Pelion) was a prosperous district inhabited by Greeks, who enjoyed the privilege of local self-government and an elective magistracy. But about the commencement of the Greek Revolution it suffered much from the weight of taxation, and from the failure of the crops of silk and oil in the preceding year. The people were starving, and the population was dense. Twenty-four village communities on the mountain contained forty-five thousand inhabitants. Lekhonia alone contained some resident Turkish families. The town of Trikeri, situated on a rocky isthmus at the entrance of the Gulf of Volo, was inhabited by a hardy and prosperous maritime population of about two thousand souls, who owned many vessels engaged in the coasting trade between Greece, Saloniki, Smyrna, and Constantinople[1].

---

[1] *See* p. 167.

Anthimos Gazes, a leading member of the Hetairia, resided in Zagora as a teacher of Greek, and many of the inhabitants were initiated into the secrets of the society. When the Greek fleet arrived off the coast, the people immediately proclaimed their independence. On the 19th of May, a body of armed men entered Lekhonia, slew the aga, and put to death six hundred Mussulmans, murdering alike men, women, and children. But instead of marching instantly to surprise Volo, which might have been taken without difficulty, and the possession of which could alone secure the liberty of their country, they wasted their time quarrelling about the division of the property of the murdered Turks. The Greeks of Mount Pelion had been long a prey to party discord, and their municipal institutions had tended to nourish violent dissensions. The slaughter of the Turks animated all their evil passions, and harmony was banished from their counsels. They succeeded, however, after losing some precious time, in constituting a government, to which they gave the name of the Thessalo-Magnesian Senate, and at last assembled a military force to blockade Volo. The people, however, displayed neither enthusiasm in the cause of national liberty nor valour in defending their local independence.

The first operation of Dramali from his camp at Larissa, during the summer of 1821, was to attack the insurgents of Mount Pelion. He moved forward to relieve Volo, and the Greeks raised the blockade at his approach. About four thousand Turks then penetrated into the mountain and encamped in the principal villages, where they committed the direst cruelties, to avenge the slaughter of their countrymen murdered at Lekhonia, as well as to gratify their native ferocity. When they retired, they carried off many women and children, whom they sold in the slave-markets of Larissa and Saloniki. The men generally succeeded in concealing themselves in the ravines and forests, where the Turks did not venture to pursue them. Anthimos Gazes, and the leaders of the insurrection, escaped to Skiathos and Skopelos. Dramali allowed all the villages to make their submission, restored their local magistracies, and furnished the people with tickets of protection, for which, however, his officers often exacted considerable sums of money. Four villages on the cape of Trikeri set his authority at defiance, fortified the isthmus, and maintained their independence. Many armatoli and klephts sought refuge within these lines, and made frequent forays both against the Turks of Thessaly, and against their countrymen who had received pardon and protection from Dramali. The great expedition of the Turks from Thessaly into the Morea secured them impunity during the year 1822; and it was not until 1823 that Trikeri was subdued. The capitan-pasha then granted it an amnesty, on condition that it should surrender all its vessels and receive a Turkish garrison.

In no part of Greece were the facilities for commencing the Revolution, or for defending the national independence, greater than in the peninsula to the east of the Gulf of Thessalonica, called anciently Chalcidice. The population was almost entirely of the Greek race, and its villages enjoyed the title of the Free Townships (Eleutherokhoria), on account of their many privileges.

A confederation of twelve villages, called Mademkhoria, or mining villages, occupied the central and mountainous portion of the peninsula, stretching northward from the isthmus that connects Mount Athos with the Chalcidice. Silver mines were once worked on a considerable scale by the Othoman government in this district. Nisvoro was the seat of the local administration, and the residence of a Turkish bey, who dwelt in the Mohammedan quarter, with a guard of twenty-five soldiers. This Mohammedan quarter was about half a mile distant from the township occupied by the Christians, where the Greek magistrates of the district held their meetings, and where the bishop of Erissos, or, as he was usually called, of Aghionoros, resided.

A similar union of fifteen villages, in the more fertile region to the westward, was called the Khasikakhoria. Polygheros was the place where the deputies of this confederation held their meetings, for the repartition of taxes, and for carrying on the local administration.

The peninsula of Kassandra or Pallene formed another union of villages under the inspection of an Othoman voivode who resided at Valta.

The three peninsulas of Kassandra, Longos, and Athos, running out into the Aegean Sea, form three citadels, which might easily secure, to a maritime people like the Greeks, the complete command of the whole of the Chalcidice. Of these, the most remarkable is Mount Athos, now called Aghionoros, or the Holy Mountain. With very little exertion it might have been rendered impregnable by land; and it is almost inaccessible to an invader by sea.

No spot was better adapted to the operations of the Hetairists than the Holy Mountain, had the Hetairists really been men of counsel and action. But to command Basilian monks, some glow of religious enthusiasm and a sincere love of civil liberty was absolutely necessary. No counterfeits could escape detection among the ascetics; and, unfortunately, personal egoism, political ambition, and religious indifference were marked characteristics of the chiefs of the Hetairia. They never trusted the monks, and the monks never trusted them [1].

Mount Athos is a high wooded ridge of about thirty miles in length, running out into the sea, and rising at its extremity in a bold peak, towering over the Aegean to the height of six thousand three hundred and fifty feet. The isthmus that connects this rocky peninsula with the Mademkhoria is hardly a mile and a half broad; and the remains of the canal of Xerxes, which Juvenal thought fabulous, still afford considerable facilities for defending it. It might easily have been rendered impregnable against any attack of irregular troops, by constructing a few of the redoubts used by the Greeks and Turks in their warfare. Twenty large monasteries have been built round the base of the great peak [2]. Their walls are constructed with the solidity of fortresses, and within they contain large and well-filled magazines of provisions. Several have large courts flanked with towers, capable of defence, and covered communications with secluded creeks, where boats can find a shelter. The rocky coast and the sudden storms, like that which destroyed the fleet of Mardonius, render a blockade by sea extremely difficult. Some dependent monasteries and innumerable

---

[1] Πρὸς τούτοις μὴ δόσετε πίστιν μήτε εἰς τὸν ἁγιώτατον, ἀσκητικώτατον, καὶ φιλογενέστατον καλόγερον, οὔτε εἰς τοὺς στενοὺς φίλους αὐτῶν. Philemon, Ἑλλ. Ἐπαν. i. 62.

[2] [It would have been more accurate to say that they are built in various parts of the peninsula especially along the sea-board. Only three or four are in the immediate neighbourhood of the peak. ED.]

hermitages are scattered over the peninsula. A town of monks, called Karies, is situated near the centre, where the deputies of the great monasteries meet to manage the civil administration of the whole mountain community; and an Othoman governor, with a guard of only twenty soldiers, resided there, to perform the duties of police. A weekly market was held at Karies.

When the Revolution broke out, the Holy Mountain was regarded by the orthodox of the Levant as a seat of peculiar sanctity. It was celebrated in the traditions of the Bulgarians, Vallachians, Albanians, and modern Greeks as sacred ground, habitually trodden by blessed saints, and hallowed by a thousand miracles. In the minds of the common people in Greece it held a more revered place than the memories of Marathon and Salamis, for it moved their daily sympathies far more than the dull echoes of Hellenic history. When the Western traveller expressed his admiration of the ruins of Sunium to the Greek mariner, he was often astonished to hear him exclaim, 'What would you say if you saw the stupendous monasteries on the Holy Mountain?'

At the commencement of the Revolution about six thousand monks inhabited the mountain, but several hundreds were probably absent managing the farms which the monasteries possessed in the Chalcidice and other places, or travelling about collecting alms. Many had been initiated into the secrets of the Hetairia, in spite of the distrust inculcated by some of the leading Hetairists. It is not worth while to point out in detail the measures which ought to have been adopted to secure the independence of Mount Athos, to support the Revolution in the Chalcidice, to threaten Thessalonica, and to interrupt the communications of the Turks along the Thracian coast. The Greek population of the Chalcidice could have maintained eight thousand armed men. The monks might have added to these a body of two thousand enthusiastic warriors. Supplies of arms, ammunition, and provisions might have been prepared on the Holy Mountain. The Greek naval force commanded the sea, and the configuration of the peninsulas doubled the efficiency of a fleet composed of small vessels. Nothing was wanting to secure success but constancy and prudent leaders. The incapacity and presumption of the Hetairists, the selfishness of the leading primates, and the lukewarmness of the influential abbots, joined to the general aversion to military organization which springs from the intense egoism of the Greek character, neutralized all the advantages which this district offered to the insurgents.

The first revolutionary movements in the Chalcidice were mere acts of brigandage. As soon as the invasion of Moldavia by Hypsilantes was known, bands of armed Christians, sent out by the Hetairists, began to infest the roads. Mussulman travellers and Othoman couriers were plundered and murdered ; but the people did not take up arms and proclaim their independence until the month of May. Yussuf Bey of Saloniki, warned by the sultan of the danger of a general insurrection, demanded hostages from the Christian communities, and finding that his orders were disobeyed, sent troops to enforce his demand and conduct the hostages to Saloniki. When the Turkish soldiers approached Polygheros, the primates called the people to arms, and commenced the Revolution on the 28th of May, by murdering the Turkish voivode and his guards. Yussuf revenged this act by beheading the bishop of Kytria, and by impaling three proësti who were in durance at Saloniki. Many Christians in that city were imprisoned. The Mussulmans, and even the Jews, were invited to take up arms against the Greeks, who, it was said, were preaching a war of extermination against all who were not of their own religion.

The inhabitants of the Free Townships assembled an armed force, and compelled the Othoman troops to retire to Saloniki ; but they neglected to profit by their first successes, and did not even adopt any plan of defence.

In June, the Turks having received reinforcements from the Sclavonian Mussulmans in the north of Macedonia, attacked the Greek insurgents. Emmanuel Papas, who had assumed the title of General of Macedonia, acted as commander-in-chief. He had no military knowledge, and was defeated by the Mussulmans, who drove the Greeks from Vasilika and Galatista. The defeated troops fled within the peninsulas of Kassandra and Athos. Yussuf attempted to force the isthmus of Kassandra, which the insurgents had fortified with intrenchments, but was repulsed with some loss. Yussuf was as ignorant of war, and carried on his military operations with as little judgment, as Emmanuel Papas. He was superseded by Aboulabad, who was appointed pasha of Saloniki.

Aboulabad was a soldier who prepared his measures with some military skill and executed them with great energy. Yet he was unable to assemble a force sufficient to make a decisive attack on the Greek intrenchments at Kassandra until the month of November. He then carried them by storm. Most of the soldiers escaped with their leader, Captain Diamantes, on board the vessels anchored near the Greek lines. The people were abandoned to the mercy of the pasha, who captured about ten thousand souls, chiefly fugitives from the Free Townships. Of these it is said that the Turkish troops sold four thousand women and children as slaves. Many men were massacred in cold blood, but Aboulabad exerted himself with success to save the lives of the peasants. The sultan's commands were strict, and his own interest led him to avoid as much as possible depopulating a district which yielded a considerable revenue to his pashalik. During the whole period of his government he treated the peasantry with moderation, even in matters relating to taxation; but he indulged his cruelty, or what he called his love of justice, by torturing the chiefs of the insurgents who fell into his hands with inhuman barbarity.

The re-establishment of the sultan's authority over the religious communities of Mount Athos required to be effected by prudence rather than force. As soon as the monks joined the revolt of the Free Townships, they took into the pay of their community about seven hundred soldiers, and arms were found for about two thousand monks. Aboulabad knew that this force was sufficient to defend the isthmus against the troops he was able to bring into the field; and that, even should he succeed in forcing the isthmus, many of the large monasteries were strong enough to resist his attacks. He resolved, therefore, to try negotiation.

The leading monks favoured the Hetairia, because they had been induced to believe that it was a society countenanced by the Russian cabinet. When they discovered that they had been grossly deceived by the apostles, and that the insurrection was condemned by the patriarch, they ceased to wish well to the Greek Revolution. Like most established authorities possessing exclusive privileges, they were averse to change. They could not shut their eyes to the antiecclesiastical opinions of the political and military chiefs of the insurgents, nor to the fact that monks were losing favour with the people through the causes which produced the Revolution. The most influential members of the monastic community, consequently, ventured to suggest that the sultan was more likely to protect the ancient privileges of the Holy Mountain than the chiefs of the Greek republic. They contrasted the anarchy that prevailed wherever the Greeks commanded, with the order observed by the sultan's officers. Aboulabad had at this time acquired a great reputation for his clemency. Many of the Greek proprietors in the Free Townships owed their lives to his protection after the storming of Kassandra. He subsequently granted an amnesty to the inhabitants of Longos on their delivering up their arms. He now promised an amnesty to the monks of the Holy Mountain, if they would deliver up all the arms in their possession, engage to pay the sultan an annual tribute of two million five hundred thousand piastres, and admit an Othoman garrison to reside at Karies. These terms were accepted, and on the 27th of December 1821 the troops of Aboulabad took up their quarters on the Holy Mountain. This occupation put an end to the Greek Revolution in the Chalcidice and its three adjoining peninsulas.

The submission of Mount Athos enabled Aboulabad to turn his attention to the Greek population in the mountains between the mouths of the Haliacmon and the Axius. Zaphiraki, the primate of Niausta, was the most influential Greek in this district. He was a man of considerable wealth; he had opposed Ali Pasha in intrigue, and held his ground; and he had assassinated an apostle of the Hetairia, Demetrios Hypatros, to make himself master of secrets which might affect his interest. Aboulabad ordered him to send his son as a hostage to Saloniki. Zaphiraki had already concerted measures for taking up arms should he be driven to extremity. He now invited Gatsos and Karatassos, the captains of armatoli at Vodhena and Verria, to meet him. These three chiefs proclaimed the Revolution, and, as usual, commenced their operations by murdering all the Mussulmans on whom they could lay hands. At Niausta, men, women, and children were butchered without mercy. The Greek chiefs then marched out to call the Christian population to arms; but the Bulgarians, who form the great bulk of the agriculturists, showed no disposition to join the cause of the Greeks. The Revolution was therefore propagated in these mountains by burning down the houses of the Christian peasantry, and by plundering their property.

These insane proceedings were soon cut short. At the first rumour of the outbreak Aboulabad marched to Verria, and as soon as a sufficient supply of ammunition arrived, he pushed forward to attack Niausta. On the 23rd of April 1822 he dispersed the troops of Karatassos after some trifling skirmishing, and immediately summoned the town to surrender at discretion. His offers were rejected, and he carried the place by storm. Zaphiraki, Gatsos, and Karatassos, driven with ease from their ill-placed and ill-constructed intrenchments, fled with a few followers. Passing through Thessaly as armatoli, and avoiding notice, Karatassos and Gatsos succeeded in reaching Greece in safety. Zaphiraki attempted to conceal himself in the neighbourhood, but his cruelty had made him so many enemies, that few were willing to assist him, and he was tracked by the Turks and slain.

Aboulabad allowed his troops to plunder Niausta, and permitted the Mussulmans of the surrounding country to avenge the murder of their co-religionaries on the unfortunate inhabitants, who had been driven to revolt by their primate, and who had taken no part in the cruelties committed by the armatoli. On this occasion the Turks rivalled the atrocities committed by the Greeks after the capture of Navarin and Tripolitza. The cruelties perpetrated by Aboulabad were so horrid as to make the description sickening. The wives of Zaphiraki and Karatassos were tortured, in order to force them to become Mohammedans, with as much inhumanity as was ever perpetrated by the Inquisition. They resisted with unshaken firmness, and were at last murdered. The wife of Gatsos only escaped similar tortures by abjuring Christianity.

An expedition, sent by Prince Demetrius Hypsilantes from Greece to rouse the inhabitants of Mount Olympus to take up arms, arrived off the Macedonian coast a few days after the storming of Niausta. It was completely defeated by the troops of Aboulabad, who attacked the Greeks immediately after they landed [1].

Thus, early in the year 1822, the sultan succeeded in reestablishing his authority over the whole of the Greek population in European Turkey to the north of Joannina and Mount Pelion; and the insurgent districts, which were reduced to submission, were governed with so much moderation and firmness, that they never again showed any disposition to revolt, and during the whole course of the Greek Revolution they enjoyed as much tranquillity and prosperity as they had enjoyed before the rebellion of Ali Pasha.

The difficulties which Sultan Mahmud overcame at this period of his reign were certainly very great, and his success in maintaining the integrity of the Othoman empire is really wonderful. He was himself the sole centre of adhesion to the many nations, religions, and sects that lived under his sway. Not only the Greeks, the Albanians, the Servians, and the Vallachians, but even the Arabs and the Egyptians showed a disposition to throw off his authority. The old feudal institutions of the Turkish population had decayed. The sandjak-beys and the dere-beys were generally either rebels or robbers. The military organization of the Othomans was utterly corrupted. The janissaries were shopkeepers, and the spahis were tax-gatherers. The ulema had converted the administration of justice into an establishment for the sale of injustice. Universal discontent rendered the Mussulmans quite as rebellious as the Christians. Sultan Mahmud seemed to be the only man in Turkey who was labouring honestly to avert the ruin of the Othoman empire. No sense of duty, no patriotic feeling, no common interests, no social ties, and no administrative bonds, united the various classes of his subjects in such a way as to secure harmonious action. He could depend on no class even of his Mohammedan subjects, and during the whole course of the Greek Revolution he was unable to dispense with the political services of those Greeks who were willing to accept employment in the Othoman government. He was even compelled

---

[1] Tricoupi (ii. 186) mentions, that on this occasion the wife of Captain Diamantes and several other women were escaping with infants, whose cries, they feared, might reveal to the Turks their place of concealment. In order to escape, they strangled their own children.

to make use of the Greeks in civil and financial business, to arrest the progress of their insurgent countrymen, while he employed the Turks and Albanians to oppose them with arms. Yet in the midst of all the passions which bigotry and mutual atrocities had awakened, he succeeded, after one short burst of passion, in protecting the wealth of his Christian subjects from the avidity of the Mussulmans.

BOOK THIRD.

THE SUCCESSES OF THE GREEKS.

CHAPTER I.

THE ESTABLISHMENT OF GREECE AS AN INDEPENDENT STATE.

Victory of the Greeks at Valtetzi.—Capitulation of Monemvasia.—Capitulation of Navarin and massacre of the Turks.—Fraudulent division of the booty.—Taking of Tripolitza and capitulation of the Albanians.—The heroine Bobolina.—Sack of Tripolitza.—Anarchy it produced.—Cruise of the Othoman fleet in 1821.—Violation of neutrality at Zante.—Return of the Othoman fleet to Constantinople.—Kolokotrones prevented from besieging Patras.—Surrender of Corinth.—Resources of the Greeks for carrying on the war.—Administrative organization which arose with the Revolution.—Advantages and disadvantages of the communal system existing in Greece.—A Peloponnesian Senate formed.—Arrival, character, and conduct of Prince Demetrius Hypsilantes.—He claims absolute power.—Arrival of Alexander Mavrocordatos.—Organization of continental Greece.—The Greeks demand a central government.—Hypsilantes convokes a National Assembly.—The antagonistic positions of the National Assembly and the Peloponnesian Senate.—Prince Demetrius Hypsilantes deserts the popular cause.—The Peloponnesians make their Senate independent.—The constitution of Epidaurus.

THE numbers of the Christians who took up arms in Greece, enabled them immediately to blockade all the fortresses occupied by the Turks. And they endeavoured to gain possession of them by military operations as rude as those by which the Dorians attacked the Achaian cities in the heroic ages. Strong positions were occupied in the nearest mountains, and the defiles by which supplies could be obtained were closely watched, while, in the mean time, the country under the walls was laid waste by nocturnal forays. The improvidence of the besieged rendered this mode of attack effectual. Famine and sickness made terrible ravages in the ranks of the Mohammedans, crowded together without preparation and without precaution.

The first decisive victory of the insurgents was gained at Valtetzi, one of the blockading positions held by the Greeks to watch Tripolitza, but about eight miles distant from that city, and situated on the hills that overlook the south-western corner of the great Arcadian plain. The kehaya of Khurshid Pasha, Achmet Bey, had recently arrived at Tripolitza with a reinforcement of eight hundred cavalry and fifteen hundred infantry. He had marched from Patras along the southern shore of the Corinthian Gulf, penetrated through the Dervenaki to Argos, and crossed Mount Parthenius in defiance of the Greek troops. But when he reached Tripolitza he found the Turks in want of everything, and he saw that unless he could break up the blockade and open up regular communications with Messenia, the place would soon be untenable.

On the 24th of May 1821 he made a vigorous attack on the Greek post at Valtetzi, which was fortified with more than ordinary care. The Turkish force was supported by two guns, but the engagement in reality was nothing more than a severe skirmish of irregulars. The chief strength of the Turks consisted in a body of twelve hundred cavalry, and the rocky eminence on which the Greeks were intrenched rendered this force useless. The Albanian infantry was not much more numerous than the Greek troops they attacked, but they attempted to mount the hill crowned by the stone walls behind which their enemy was posted. A well-directed fire from marksmen, who aimed coolly from well-covered positions, compelled them to fall back with severe loss. The whole day was consumed in partial and desultory attacks, for the Albanians could not approach near enough to make any general attempt to carry the place by storm. The Turks were at last compelled to commence their retreat to Tripolitza. The Greeks, who had anticipated this movement, hastened to profit by it. They cut off the baggage from the cavalry, and hung on the flanks and rear of the infantry for some time, killing as many in the retreat as had fallen in the engagement.

In this affair about five thousand Turks and three thousand Greeks were engaged, and four hundred Turks and one hundred and fifty Greeks were killed. But the victory was so decidedly in favour of the Greeks that the battle of Valtetzi destroyed the military reputation of the Turks in the Morea, and broke the spirit of the garrison of Tripolitza. The Greeks followed up their success by occupying the rocky eminences called Trikorpha, which overlook Tripolitza, within rifle-shot of the western wall.

Monemvasia was the first fortress that capitulated. The place was impregnable : but want caused dissensions among its defenders, and the Turks made proposals for a capitulation. Prince Demetrius Hypsilantes (a younger brother of the great Hetairist), who had been appointed on his arrival in the Morea commander-in-chief of the Greek army, but who persisted in arrogating to himself the title of lieutenant-governor of Greece in the name of his brother, the unfortunate and incapable Alexander, sent Prince Gregorios Cantacuzenos to take possession of Monemvasia in his own name. To the style of this order the Peloponnesian Senate objected with justice, since it implied that Prince Alexander Hypsilantes was sovereign of Greece in virtue of his election to be the supreme head of the Hetairia, and that Prince Demetrius possessed greater powers than those conferred on him by the inhabitants of Greece. Now the blockade of Monemvasia had been carried on for four months entirely at the expense of the people, and neither Prince Alexander Hypsilantes and the Hetairists, nor Prince Demetrius, had assisted in reducing the place. The Senate, consequently, insisted that Monemvasia must be occupied in the name of the Greek government, and must be surrendered to the leaders of the blockading force conjointly with the officer deputed by Demetrius Hypsilantes, acting only as commander-in-chief of the Greek army. To this decision Hypsilantes was compelled to yield ; but he did not lay aside his viceregal pretensions and foolish vanity, and his injudicious conduct caused a feeling of distrust among the leaders of the blockading force, which produced very unfortunate consequences.

Monemvasia was surrendered to the Greeks on the 5th of August 1821. The Turks gave up their arms, and were allowed to retain their movable property. The Greeks engaged to transport them to Asia Minor in three Spetziot vessels, which had maintained the blockade by sea. The

Turks were bound to pay a fixed sum for their passage. In virtue of this capitulation, about five hundred souls were conveyed to Scalanova. But a body of Greek soldiers, principally Mainates, opposed the execution of the capitulation to the utmost of their power. They murdered several Turks who were on the point of embarking, and they plundered the property of families who had already embarked. Prince Gregorios Cantacuzenos and many officers present did everything in their power to put a stop to this violation of the first military convention concluded by the Greeks, but their interference was viewed with jealousy, and was only partially successful.

The surrender of Navarin followed, and was attended with far greater atrocities. Hypsilantes sent a Cephalonian civilian in his suite to act as his deputy. The Peloponnesian Senate sent Nikolas Poniropoulos. The agent of Hypsilantes was an honourable man, without ability or experience. Poniropoulos was an unprincipled intriguer—a type of the worst class of Moreot officials. He boasted some years later to General Gordon 'of his address in purloining and destroying a copy of the capitulation given to the Turks, that no proof might remain of any such transaction having been concluded [1].'

Before Navarin capitulated, many Turkish families had been compelled by hunger to escape out of the place, and throw themselves on the mercy of the Greeks of the neighbourhood, with whom they had once been connected by ties of mutual kindness. Sad tales are told concerning their fate.

On the 19th of August 1821, starvation compelled those who remained in the fortress to capitulate. They gave up all the public property in the fortress, and all the money, plate, and jewels belonging to private individuals. They were allowed to retain their wearing apparel and household furniture. The Greeks engaged to transport them either to Egypt or to Tunis. When the capitulation was concluded, the agent of Hypsilantes left the Greek camp to procure vessels; Poniropoulos remained to take advantage of his absence. A Greek ship engaged in the blockade anchored in the harbour, and the money and valuable property of the

---

[1] Gordon, i. 231, *note.*

Turks were carried on board. While this was going on, disputes arose concerning the manner in which the persons of females were searched for gold and jewels. A general massacre ensued; and, in the space of an hour, almost every man, woman, and child, who was not already on board ship, was murdered.

A Greek ecclesiastic, Phrantzes, who has left valuable memoirs of the events in the Morea during the first years of the Revolution, was present, and has given a description of the scenes he witnessed. Women, wounded with musket-balls and sabre-cuts, rushed to the sea, seeking to escape, and were deliberately shot. Mothers with infants in their arms were robbed of their clothes, and ran into the sea as the only place of concealment; yet while crouching in the water they were fired on by inhuman riflemen. Greeks seized infants from their mothers' breasts and dashed them against the rocks. Children, three and four years old, were hurled living into the sea and left to drown. When the massacre was ended, the dead bodies washed ashore, or piled on the beach, threatened to cause a pestilence. Phrantzes, who records these atrocities of his countrymen with shame and indignation, himself hired men to burn the bodies of the victims with the wrecks of some vessels in the harbour, in order to save the murderers from the effects of leaving so many bodies exposed to putrefaction under an autumn sun [1].

The Greeks having deliberately deceived the Turks by a treacherous treaty, immediately set to work to cheat one another. It had been stipulated that the spoil was to be divided into three equal parts; one-third for the national treasury, one-third for the troops, and one-third for the ships employed in the blockade. Both the government and the soldiers were defrauded of their shares. Two Spetziot vessels, belonging to Botases and Kolandrutzos, as soon as they had embarked the valuables of the Turks and a few of the wealthiest families, sailed off, and never gave any account of the greater part of the booty in their possession. This conduct caused much recrimination between the Greek soldiers and the Albanian sailors; but it was asserted that the Spetziots bribed the primates and the captains to

---

[1] Phrantzes, vol. i. p. 400.

abandon the cause of the national treasury and of the poor soldiers. The base conduct of their leaders damped the enthusiasm of the people of Messenia, who became so lukewarm in the cause of the Revolution, that they neglected to concert any effectual measures for blockading Modon and Coron, of which the Turks retained possession.

The surrender of Tripolitza was retarded by the measures which the chiefs of the blockading army adopted to get possession of the money and jewels of the Turks without being obliged to share the booty with the national treasury and the private soldiers. Their first speculation was to establish a trade in provisions, which they sold to the starving Turks at exorbitant prices, while they prolonged the negotiations for a capitulation. Kyriakuli Mavromichales, a brave and patriotic officer, put an end to these scandalous proceedings by bringing on a severe skirmish, and threatening to storm the walls. The soldiers also began to perceive the object of their leaders, and to clamour at their avarice.

If Prince Demetrius Hypsilantes had been present at the surrender of Tripolitza, as commander-in-chief of the Greek army, he would have gained the honour of the conquest, and his disinterestedness would, in all probability, have enabled him to protect the cause of order. He had some personal virtues which all men respected, and his probity and personal courage would have obtained for him the support of the best soldiers in the Greek army at this time. But, most unfortunately for the cause of Greece, Hypsilantes allowed himself to be persuaded to quit the camp before Tripolitza by the selfish Moreot leaders, just at the moment it became certain that the place could not hold out for many days. His object was to prevent the Turks landing within the Gulf of Corinth on the northern coast of the Morea. Most of the foreign officers in Greece accompanied him; and as soon as he departed, Kolokotrones and the greedy chieftains commenced separate negotiations with the Albanians, who formed part of the garrison of Tripolitza, and struck private bargains for selling their protection to wealthy Turks.

Petrobey became nominally the commander-in-chief of the besieging army after Hypsilantes' departure, but he possessed little authority. It was now known over all Greece that the fall of Tripolitza was inevitable, and crowds of armed peasants hurried to the camp to share in the plunder of the Turks. The booty gained by the crimes committed at Monemvasia and Navarin had demoralized the whole population. On the 27th of September, a conference was held to treat concerning a capitulation. The Greek chiefs offered to allow the Turks to retire with their families to Asia Minor on receiving forty millions of piastres, a sum then equal to £1,500,000 sterling. There was no possibility of collecting so large a sum; and as the Greeks demanded, moreover, that the Turks should deliver up their arms, the besieged, who could neither trust the promises of the chiefs nor the humanity of the people, felt that the possession of their arms alone gave them a chance of escaping the fate of their countrymen at Monemvasia and Navarin. The Turks therefore made a counter-proposition. They offered to give up everything they possessed, except their arms, and a small sum in money for the purchase of provisions, and demanded permission to occupy the passes of Mount Parthenium, in order to secure their safe retreat to Nauplia. The Greek chiefs refused these terms, for every hour of famine within the walls increased their profits. The kehaya-bey proposed to the garrison to cut its way through the besiegers and gain Nauplia; but the Moreot Mussulmans had no longer horses to carry off their families, and without their knowledge of the country the other troops feared to make the attempt.

The Greeks now concluded a separate capitulation with the Albanian Mussulmans under the command of Elmas Bey. These mercenaries were fifteen hundred strong, and they had suffered so little during the blockade that they were still fit for the severest service. The Greeks regarded them as dangerous enemies. They were experienced in mountain warfare, and would have preferred fighting their way home against any odds rather than surrendering their arms, or a single gold piece from the treasure they carried in their belts. To them the misery of the Turks was a matter of indifference. The great business of their lives was to amass money abroad, and to carry it back safely to their native villages in Albania.

While the negotiations with the Albanians were going on, the Greek chiefs employed the time in concluding separate bargains with wealthy Mussulmans, who delivered to them money and jewels on receiving promises of protection, ratified by the most solemn oaths. The widow of a Spetziot shipowner, named Bobolina, gained notoriety by her conduct in these bargains. She had displayed both energy and patriotism at the commencement of the Revolution; and a ship, of which she was the proprietor, was engaged in blockading Nauplia. She now came up to the camp before Tripolitza, to obtain a share of the booty at the surrender of the place. Petrobey and Kolokotrones allowed her to enter the city, in order to persuade the Turkish women to deliver up their money and jewels, as the only means of purchasing security for their lives and their honour. In the mean time the Greek chiefs treated with the Mussulmans for their respective districts, and the Mainates concluded private bargains with the Barduniots.

The Greek soldiers at last became aware that their chiefs were engaged in a conspiracy to defraud them of the booty which had been held out to them as a lure to prosecute the blockade for six months without pay. A feeling of indignation spread through the camp, and it was resolved by tacit consent to put an end to the treacherous proceedings of the chiefs by entering the place either by surprise or storm. An opportunity occurred on the 5th of October 1821. A few soldiers contrived to gain an entrance at the Argos gate, and to seize one of the adjoining towers, from which they displayed the Greek flag.

In a few minutes the whole Greek army rushed to the walls, which were scaled in several places and the gates thrown open. A scene of fighting, murder, and pillage then commenced, unexampled in duration and atrocity even in the annals of this bloody warfare. Human beings can rarely have perpetrated so many deeds of cruelty on an equal number of their fellow-creatures as were perpetrated by the conquerors on this occasion. Before the Greek chiefs could enter the place, the whole city was a scene of anarchy, and their misconduct had rendered them powerless to restore order, or to arrest the diabolical passions which their own avarice and dishonourable proceedings had awakened in the breasts of their followers.

When the tumult commenced, the Albanians under Elmas

SACK OF TRIPOLITZA.

[A.D. 1821.]

Bey formed under arms in the immense court-yard of the Pasha's palace. Their warlike attitude alarmed the Greek chiefs, who succeeded in preventing their falling on the dispersed Greeks, and persuaded them to march out of the place and take up their quarters at Trikorpha, in the strong position occupied by Kolokotrones during the blockade. They were supplied with provisions, and on the 7th October they commenced their march to Vostitza, where they crossed the gulf to Lepanto, and, hastening through Aetolia, reached Arta in safety[1].

The citadel of Tripolitza surrendered from want of water on the 8th of October, and Kolokotrones gained possession of all the treasure it contained. The official return of the artillery and ammunition found in the town and the citadel gives a contemptible idea of the military operations of this long siege. Of thirteen brass guns only two 6-pounders remained serviceable; and of seventeen iron guns, only three 9-pounders. There were found in the place only 855 shot of all calibres, and ten packets of grape; and the powder magazines were entirely empty.

Colonel Raybaud, a young French officer of talent, who commanded the Greek artillery during the siege, and who was the only foreigner of rank and character present when the Greek troops entered the place, has recounted the scenes of horror and disorder which prevailed for three days[2]. In a candid narrative he describes the acts of barbarity of which he was an eyewitness. Women and children were frequently tortured before they were murdered. After the Greeks had been in possession of the city for forty-eight hours, they deliberately collected together about two thousand persons of every age and sex, but principally women and children, and led them to a ravine in the nearest mountain, where they murdered every soul[3].

Prince Demetrius Hypsilantes returned to Tripolitza nine

---

[1] See p. 93. [2] Mémoires sur la Grèce, i. 463, 480.
[3] The writer saw heaps of unburied bones bleached by the winter rains and summer suns in passing this spot two years after the catastrophe; the size of many of which attested the early age of a part of the victims. See Raybaud, i. 483. and Gordon, i. 245. Speliades also describes these cruelties, and mentions that fifty Jewish families were exterminated. The manner in which he apologizes for and approves of these murders exhibits the state of public opinion in the better classes; for he was a man of education, and held high office during the presidency of Capodistrias. He recounts the inhuman murder of the Greek proëstos Soteros Kougias, who was tortured by Greek soldiers, i. 246.

days after the capture of the place. The Turks had made no attempt to effect a landing on the northern coast of the Morea, so that his absence had been unnecessary. He was laughed at for being out of the way by those who had profited by his absence, and his troops were discontented at being deprived of all share in the booty made at Tripolitza. His authority as commander-in-chief had been destroyed by his absence, and nobody henceforward would obey his orders, unless when they themselves thought fit to do so.

General Gordon, who returned to Tripolitza with Hypsilantes, and whose familiarity with the Turkish language enabled him to converse with those who were spared, estimates the number of Mussulmans murdered during the sack of the town at eight thousand souls[1]. Many young women and girls were carried off as slaves by the volunteers who returned to their native places, but few male children were spared.

The women of Khurshid Pasha's harem, and a few Turks of rank, were spared, in expectation of a high ransom. A few of the garrison, with some Moreot Turks, availing themselves of the confusion that prevailed among the Greeks, kept together under the kehaya-bey, and cutting their way through the conquerors, gained one of the gates, and marched off to Nauplia without being pursued.

The loss of the Greeks was estimated at three hundred slain in casual encounters. Many Turks surrendered on receiving a promise that their lives should be spared, but those who were capable of bearing arms were sent out of the city, under the pretence of quartering them in the neighbourhood, where greater facilities existed for obtaining provisions, and they were murdered during the night. Some prisoners were spared for a short time to bury the bodies of their slaughtered countrymen, which were putrefying by thousands in almost every house and garden. Even this precaution was too long neglected. The air was already tainted with deadly miasma, and a terrible epidemic soon broke out among the Greeks. The disease, generated by similar causes in other towns and villages, spread over all Greece; and, before the end of the year 1821, it is said to have carried off more Christians than fell by the hands of the Turks in the whole Othoman empire.

---

[1] Compare Gordon, i. 244 and 289.

The circumstances which accompanied the taking of Tripolitza neutralized all the advantages which might have resulted from the conquest of the capital of the Morea. Anarchy prevailed both in the civil and military affairs of the country. All respect for superiors, and all self-respect, ceased. Hypsilantes lost his personal as well as his military influence. During his short absence from the army, he had witnessed the destruction of the flourishing town of Galaxidhi from his camp on the Achaian hills without being able to succour the sufferers or avenge their losses. The troops lost all confidence both in his judgment and his good fortune. Kolokotrones, who, before the exhibition he made of his avarice and dishonesty in cheating the troops of the booty at Tripolitza, had a fair chance of becoming the leader of the Revolution, lost the moral influence he had accidentally gained, and relapsed into a klephtic captain and party chief. Most of the other leaders forfeited the confidence of the soldiers by similar conduct. When they defrauded their own followers, it is not astonishing that they were faithless to the Turks, to whom they sold promises of protection. The plunder obtained was very great, and some Moreot captains became chieftains by their success in appropriating to their own use the property of murdered Mussulmans. Mustapha Bey of Patras, and other opulent men, were known to have been murdered, after large sums had been extorted from them as a ransom for their lives[1]. The retribution for these crimes was immediate. Those who had despised every obligation of duty, morality, and religion, could no longer appeal to law and reason. Anarchy directed the future career of the Greek Revolution, and the struggle which a minority of honest men and sincere patriots sustained in favour of order, proved ineffectual; yet the mass of the people, though misguided and misgoverned, continued to defend their religious and political independence without faltering.

The Othoman fleet made a successful expedition during the summer of 1821. The Albanian islanders allowed their ships to return to Hydra and Spetzas in the month of August. This season is considered by the Turks as the most favourable

---

[1] Tricoupi (ii. 139) mentions that the few Turks who were spared at the taking of Tripolitza were murdered subsequently at Argos, on suspicion of being privy to the escape of one of their number.

for naval operations, as the winds in the Archipelago are fresh without being violent. The capitan-bey, Kara Ali, sailed from the Dardanelles with three line-of-battle ships, five frigates, and about twenty corvettes and brigs, but his force was soon increased by the junction of the Egyptian and Algerine squadrons. After throwing supplies of provisions and ammunition into the fortresses of Coron and Modon, which saved them from falling into the hands of the Greeks, he reached Patras on the 18th of September. The reinforcements with which he strengthened the garrison, enabled Yussuf Pasha to reduce the Lalliots to some degree of subordination, and to break up the blockade which the Greeks had formed.

On the 1st of October, Ismael Gibraltar, the commander of the Egyptian squadron, was sent into the Gulf of Corinth to destroy the vessels at Galaxidhi. It has been already mentioned that Prince Demetrius Hypsilantes witnessed this catastrophe[1]. The inhabitants of Galaxidhi were the principal shipowners on the western coast of Greece. They possessed about sixty vessels of various sizes, of which forty were brigs or schooners. At this time almost the whole Galaxidhiot navy was in port; and with the strange improvidence which characterized the proceedings of both Greeks and Turks in this war, no measures had been adopted to defend the town or the anchorage. The contempt which the Greeks entertained for the Turkish fleet, was not abated by the terrible disasters it inflicted on them. Their ignorance of the first elements of the art of war made them place far too much confidence in their knowledge of seamanship and naval manœuvres as a means of baffling the operations of the Othoman navy. They consequently neglected to defend their ports, and the Turks, profiting by their neglect, destroyed their fleets at Galaxidhi, Kasos, and Psara.

Ismael Gibraltar possessed sufficient naval skill to take advantage of the superiority of his artillery. He silenced the Galaxidhiot battery, and cannonaded the town without coming within the range of the Greek artillery, and his fire was on this account more than usually accurate. The soldiers whom the Galaxidhiots had hired to assist them in defending

---

[1] P. 221.

he beach, fled during the night, and the inhabitants were obliged to follow their example. The Algerines landed in the morning, plundered the houses, massacred most of those who had remained behind, and carried off a few prisoners. The town, the boats on the beach, and the vessels which were aground, were burned. But thirty-four brigs and schooners were found ready for sea, and were carried off by the Turks.

The season was now so far advanced that Kara Ali resolved to return to Constantinople in order to enjoy his triumph and exhibit his spoil. He quitted Patras and put into Zante for news, where he learned to his dismay that a Greek fleet of thirty-five sail had put to sea under Miaoulis, to attack him. He made the best arrangements in his power to prevent the Greeks retaking his Galaxidhiot prizes, and sailed with a firm determination to decline an engagement if possible.

On the 12th of October, an Algerine brig, having separated from the fleet, was surrounded by eighteen Greek brigs; but it refused to surrender, and made such a gallant resistance that the Hydriots did not venture to run alongside and attempt to carry her by boarding. The Algerines, aware that, if their ship became unmanageable, she would be burned and they would all perish, ran her ashore near the southern cape of Zante. The fight between the gallant Algerine and his numerous assailants had been witnessed by thousands of refugee Moreots and Zantiot peasants, who, when the Mussulmans landed, began to fire on them. Two English officers, with a guard of twenty men, had been sent from the town to enforce obedience to the quarantine regulations, which were then observed with great strictness by all the Christian powers in the Mediterranean. The Greeks were ordered to retire; but they refused, and, continuing to attack the Turks, they soon came into collision with the English. The officer commanding, hoping to intimidate the people, ordered his men to fire over the heads of the crowd. The Zantiots immediately replied by firing on the troops. The English were compelled to retire to a neighbouring house, leaving one man dead behind. The house was besieged, and a skirmish was kept up until fresh troops arrived. The Zantiots had two killed as the soldiers were forcing their way to the house, and they mangled the body of the English soldier which fell into their hands with frightful ferocity, to revenge this loss.

The Algerines said that they had been pursued by the Greek fleet, and that they had several men wounded after their vessel was ashore. The pursuit, however, did not prevent their landing a number of wounded men on a raft, which they constructed from spars and planks; and the violation of neutrality on the part of the Greek fleet was a trifling matter, and would have passed unnoticed had the Ionians not fired on the Turks.

The death of the two Ionians caused great animosity between the Greeks and the English in the Ionian Islands. The Ionians pretended that the neutrality which the English observed ought to have prevented their interfering in the combat between Greeks and Turks. For several years the conduct of the English government and of the English military was systematically calumniated by what was called the Philhellenic press over the whole continent of Europe, and most of the calumnies found a ready credence. The pride of English Philhellenes prevented their replying to the false accusations brought against their country and their countrymen, because those accusations generally assumed that the English character was deficient in honourable feeling, and that Englishmen were indifferent to the liberty of other nations. But it would have been impossible for the authorities in the Ionian Islands to have preserved order among a Greek population, inflamed with national enthusiasm, eager for revolution, and ready to resist the law, unless they had punished severely the death of an English soldier in the execution of his duty, and the wanton attack on the subjects of a friendly sovereign seeking protection on neutral territory. Martial law was proclaimed; five Zantiots were tried for firing on the English troops, convicted, and executed; a proclamation was issued by the Lord High Commissioner, forbidding the entry of either Othoman or Greek men-of-war into any Ionian port, unless driven in by stress of weather.

A day or two after the loss of the Algerine brig, the Greeks lost a brig which they were compelled to run ashore at Katakolo, and which the Turks succeeded in getting afloat and carrying off as a prize. The Turkish and Greek fleets engaged, and a great deal of ineffective cannonading ensued. Kara Ali, who would not risk losing any of his prizes, was driven back to Zante, where he embarked the survivors of

[A.D. 1821.]

the crew of the Algerine brig, and at last sailed with a favourable wind, which carried him safely through the Archipelago. He entered the port of Constantinople in triumph, towing his thirty-five Galaxidhiot prizes, and displaying thirty prisoners hanging from the yard-arm of his flag-ship. The sultan considered the results of this naval campaign as extremely satisfactory, though, when he compared the force of the capitan-bey with that under Miaoulis, he could not consider it as honourable to the Othoman navy. Kara Ali, who had hitherto only held the rank of capitan-bey, was rewarded with that of capitan-pasha.

Kolokotrones was the only man in the Morea who possessed the talent and energy to take advantage of the fall of Tripolitza for the national benefit; but his selfishness had destroyed his influence over the troops. Had his countrymen felt any confidence in his honour at this moment, he would have been raised to the chief command. Unfortunately, the trust was considered too great for his honesty, whatever it might be with reference to his capacity. He himself perceived that he had lost the public esteem, and he was anxious to regain his reputation. He claimed some credit for having persuaded the Albanians under Elmas Bey to desert the Turks. He asserted that he would be able to induce the Lalliots, with whom he had amicable relations, to abandon Yussuf Pasha, and perhaps to surrender the castle of Patras. He proposed, therefore, marching immediately to besiege that fortress. It is not improbable that, had Kolokotrones received proper support, his plan would have been successful, for the Lalliots were at open feud with Yussuf Pasha.

Kolokotrones marched from Tripolitza to invest Patras, which had been relieved from blockade by the arrival of the fleet under Kara Ali. His force, which consisted at first of only his personal followers, amounting to about a hundred men, was increased as he moved westward, until he mustered about two thousand in the plain of Elis[1]. A report was spread

---

[1] [Mendelssohn Bartholdy in his *Geschichte Griechenlands* (vol. i. p. 225 *note*) points out that this march of Kolokotrones is mythical, and arose from the misinterpretation of a passage in the Memoirs of Kolokotrones and Germanos, which found its way into Tricoupi's history. Kolokotrones never started on the expedition, though he wished to do so. ED.]

that Patras was on the eve of capitulating to Kolokotrones, and crowds of armed men hastened to share the expected plunder. The selfishness of the primates and captains, who had hitherto ineffectually attempted to blockade Patras, now thwarted him in all his projects. His own selfishness at Tripolitza was avenged by that of his rivals, and his feelings must have suggested thoughts which might have found expression in the words of Macbeth—

> 'This even-handed justice
> Commends the ingredients of our poisoned chalice
> To our own lips.'

The intrigues of Germanos, the Archbishop of Patras, and Andreas Zaimes, induced the Greek government to recall Kolokotrones, under the pretext that his services were more necessary elsewhere; and thus the only man who could have induced the Turks in Patras to capitulate was compelled to retire, precisely because it was supposed that he had been taught the value of a good character from experience, and possessed sufficient influence to cause a capitulation to be respected. The Achaians were soon punished for their selfishness. The Greek troops were defeated in an attempt to establish themselves amidst the ruined houses of the town, and the besieged were enabled to strengthen their position by completing the destruction of all the buildings in the vicinity of the castle which afforded any cover to the besiegers, or could interrupt the communications of the garrison with the sea.

The fortress of Corinth capitulated on the 22nd of January 1822. The Albanians of the garrison, who were only a hundred and fifty, had previously concluded a separate convention with the Greeks, which permitted them to retire from the place with their arms and baggage. They hired four vessels to transport them over the gulf, but they were plundered of their property during their passage, and many were murdered. The Turks who remained in the Acrocorinth gave up their arms and property to their besiegers on condition of being allowed to retain a small sum of money, and to hire neutral vessels to transport them to Asia Minor. On the 26th of January the Greek troops took possession of the Acrocorinth, and the Turks encamped at Kenchries to wait for shipping. Before neutral vessels arrived, they

SURRENDER OF CORINTH.

[A.D. 1821.]

were attacked by the Greeks and murdered. The conquerors had expected to find a considerable treasure in the Acrocorinth, for Kiamil Bey, who was the wealthiest Turkish landlord in Greece, was reported to have laid up there a fabulous amount of money. They were disappointed. If Kiamil Bey had ever possessed any very considerable hoard of ready money, it had been expended during the sieges of Tripolitza and Corinth. The Greeks, however, would not believe the word of the bey, and they tortured him in the cruellest manner.

The repeated examples of treachery on the part of the Greeks caused the Turks in the remaining fortresses to defend themselves with incredible fortitude. Convinced that no promises of the Christians would be kept, they determined to endure every privation rather than capitulate, and they now began to display unusual energy and sagacity in obtaining supplies of provisions.

In the Morea the Othomans still possessed the fortresses of Nauplia, Coron, Modon, and Patras, with the castle of Rhion.

The Greeks, from an insurgent populace, had now become an independent nation. They had assembled large bodies of armed men, and blockaded simultaneously a number of Othoman fortresses. The manner in which they were supplied with the resources necessary to keep a large force in the field, deserves to be described. In the first place, the improvidence of the Othoman authorities allowed an immense amount of public property to fall into the hands of the insurgents. A great part of this property was easily converted into money, and a large fund was thus placed at the disposal of those local leaders who assumed the command in different districts. In spite of the confusion that prevailed in Greece during the year 1821, the exports were considerably increased. The sums expended for military purposes escape the attention of the historian, from not being collected in a central treasury, or systematically employed on a general and preconcerted plan. Each locality collected and expended its own resources; and either from ignorance or selfishness, the local primates, proësti, and captains, took no steps to lay the foundation of an organized administration for that portion of civil, financial, and military business which requires a central direction. It was undoubtedly more from want of capacity and honesty in the clergy, the primates, and the military chiefs, than from any deficiency in a supply of men and money on the part of the people, that order, publicity, and responsibility were not introduced in the conduct of national business. The peasantry everywhere displayed zeal and disinterestedness in giving up all the Turkish property to be employed for the public service. Both peasants and private soldiers served for some months without pay; and both were for some time eager to see the public money employed in forming a corps of regular troops, and in purchasing a train of artillery. The terrible effects of Russian discipline and Russian artillery on the Othoman armies had been witnessed by many Greeks, and was the theme of many fabulous narratives in every Greek cottage. Had any man of ability and honesty succeeded in forming a corps of regular troops before the primates and captains had contrived to appropriate the revenues of their respective districts to their own purposes, such weak and ill-provided fortresses as Patras, Lepanto, Coron, and Athens, could not have held out many weeks, and must have fallen long before the end of the year 1821.

Unfortunately, the position in which the local authorities of the Greek population were placed at the first outbreak of the Revolution, rendered them averse to the formation of a central government. They feared that the Hetairists would obtain the direction of any general government that could then have been established, and in the Hetairists they had lost all confidence. The local authorities, trusting perhaps too much to their own abilities and good intentions, not only assumed the administration of the financial affairs of their districts, but also took the command of the troops enrolled in their neighbourhood. The result was, that the necessities of the Revolution enabled most of them very soon to become little dictators. They either commanded the armed force themselves, or appointed its officers and directed its movements without paying much attention to the orders of the central government which was at last constituted, and they collected the public and local revenues from the people, and expended them as they thought fit, without giving any account either to the government or the nation.

The rapid success of the Greeks during the first weeks of the Revolution threw the management of much civil and financial business into the hands of the proësti and demogeronts in office. The primates, who already exercised great official authority, instantly appropriated that which had been hitherto exercised by murdered voivodes and beys. Every primate strove to make himself a little independent potentate, and every captain of a district assumed the powers of a commander-in-chief. The Revolution, before six months had passed, seemed to have peopled Greece with a host of little Ali Pashas[1]. When the primate and the captain acted in concert—supposing they were not, as sometimes happened, the same person—they collected the public revenues; administered the Turkish property, which was declared national; enrolled, paid, and provisioned as many troops as circumstances required, or as they thought fit; named officers; formed a local guard for the primate of the best soldiers in the place, who were thus often withdrawn from the public service; and organized a local police and a local treasury. This system of self-government, constituted in a very self-willed manner, and relieved from almost all responsibility, was soon established as a natural result of the Revolution over all Greece. The sultan's authority, which had been the only link that bound together Christians and Mussulmans in the Othoman administration, having ceased, every primate assumed the prerogatives of the sultan. For a few weeks this state of things was unavoidable, and to an able and honest chief or government it would have facilitated the establishment of a strong central authority; but by the vices of Greek society it was perpetuated as an organized anarchy.

In the midst of this political anarchy, the communal institutions of Greece, which the Othoman government had used as an administrative engine for financial purposes, while they supported the power of the oligarchs, contributed also to preserve order among the people. There is, perhaps,

---

[1] Polybius (iv. 56. 13) gives the Greeks a bad character in money transactions; and I am afraid we must say of the primates and captains, in spite of their patriotism, what has been maliciously said of the American missionaries at Athens, in spite of their piety—
'Satan now is wiser than of yore,
And tempts by making rich, not making poor.'

no feature more remarkable in the Greek Revolution, and none so conclusive in proving that religious, more than political feeling, impelled the people to take up arms, than the fact that, during the whole period of the war with the sultan, the administrative organization of civil and financial business remained practically the same in free Greece as in Turkey. No improvement was made in financial arrangements, nor in the system of taxation; no measures were adopted for rendering property more secure; no attempt was made to create an equitable administration of justice; no courts of law were established; and no financial accounts were published. Governments were formed, constitutions were drawn up, national assemblies met, orators debated, and laws were passed according to the political fashion patronized by the liberals of the day. But no effort was made to prevent the government being virtually absolute, unless it was by rendering it absolutely powerless. The constitutions were framed to remain a dead letter. The national assemblies were nothing but conferences of parties, and the laws passed were intended to fascinate Western Europe, not to operate with effect in Greece.

The first administrative exigency of the Revolution was to supply the bodies of armed men who assembled to blockade the Turkish fortresses with regular rations and abundant stores of ammunition. The success of the Revolution would have been nearly impossible, unless an effective commissariat had arisen conjointly with the concentration of the blockading forces. This commissariat was found in the municipal authorities; its magazines consisted of an abundant provision of grain and other produce which existed in the public and private storehouses of the Turks all over the country. Ammunition was obtained by selling a portion of this produce. The waste that took place under this system of commissariat was incredible and unavoidable. During the first two months of the war, thousands of rations were issued to men where the presence of troops was useless, merely because a well-filled magazine of provisions existed in the district; and millions of cartridges were fired off at the public expense, where no Turk could hear the noise of these patriotic demonstrations.

But whatever may have been the inconveniences and

abuses of the communal system, there can be no doubt that the existence of a local Christian magistracy prevented the Greeks from being at first quite helpless, and it concentrated the strength of the population in countless energetic attacks on the dispersed Mussulmans. The attachment of the inhabitants, whether of the Greek or the Albanian race, to their native district, is the element of patriotism in Greece. The associations of family and tribe are strong; but unless orthodoxy coincides with nationality, the feelings of general patriotism are weak. The connection of the individual with his municipal chiefs was strongly marked and clearly defined. The reciprocal obligations and duties were felt and performed. Under this aspect, the conduct of the population of Greece during the early period of the Revolution is worthy of admiration; it displays great perseverance and unflinching patriotism. In the wider sphere of political and military action, the influence of the people unfortunately ceased, and we see ignorance, presumption, and selfishness in statesmen and generals rendering the energy of the people nugatory. From some circumstance which hardly admits of explanation, and which we must therefore refer reverentially to the will of God, the Greek Revolution produced no man of real greatness, no statesmen of unblemished honour, no general of commanding talent. Fortunately, the people derived from the framework of their existing usages the means of continuing their desperate struggle for independence, in spite of the incapacity and dishonesty of the civil and military leaders who directed the central government. The true glory of the Greek Revolution lies in the indomitable energy and unwearied perseverance of the mass of the people. But perseverance, unfortunately, like most popular virtues, supplies historians only with commonplace details, while readers expect the annals of revolutions to be filled with pathetic incidents, surprising events, and heroic exploits.

The active energy of the communal system, and the great authority it exercised over the people, offered an obstacle to the consolidation of any imperfect and defective scheme of governmental centralization; but these very circumstances would have increased the power of a central government which acquired the respect and confidence of the nation. A statesman of ability and honesty, if Greece had produced such a man, would have sought to lay the foundation of a central administration on the existing communal institutions. He would have embodied these into the fabric of the state, and would not, as Greek statesmen did, have sought to construct a powerful central authority by annihilating the influence of every communal magistracy.

Another disadvantage resulted from the communal institutions of Greece, which must, however, be attributed to the character of the Greeks who administered the system, and not to the system itself. The Greeks are ambitious, intriguing and presumptuous, and few are restrained by any moral principle in seeking self-glory and self-advancement. No men are, consequently, less adapted to bear sudden elevation, or to be entrusted with great power. When the Revolution, therefore, suddenly invested local magistrates with extraordinary powers, many communes became a scene of waste, peculation, and oppression. Civil contests arose, and open hostilities ensued. The low morality and unbounded ambition of political adventurers from Constantinople and other cities in Turkey increased these disorders. Bishops, primates, and captains began to imitate the pride and display the injustice of cadis, voivodes, and beys. The national revenues were diverted from carrying on the war, and expended in maintaining the households or the personal followers of these oligarchs. No petty archont could walk the streets of Tripolitza without being followed by a band of armed men.

The primates and higher clergy flattered themselves that the expulsion of the Turks would constitute them the heirs of the sultan's power. Their conduct soon isolated them from popular sympathy, and they saw the military officers, whom they had expected to employ as tools, invested with the greater part of the power they were desirous of seizing. They forgot that the Ottoman empire was a military government. The people became early clamorous for a legal government. Bold demagogues and intelligent patriots called for the creation of a responsible executive. The oligarchs were forced to yield. On the 7th of June 1821 a Peloponnesian Senate was constituted, and invested with dictatorial powers, which were to continue until the taking of Tripolitza. This Senate was nothing more than a committee of the oligarchs; it was appointed by a few of the most influential among the clergy and primates, with the co-operation of several of the most powerful military chiefs, at a meeting held in the monastery of Kaltetzi. No meeting of deputies popularly elected took place. The people who had taken up arms to conquer their independence were excluded from a share in electing their rulers. The consequence was, that the feelings of the people were deeply wounded, and the wound festered far more than politicians generally supposed. Nevertheless, even strangers who visited Greece in 1823 could observe that the central government of Greece was then generally regarded by the agricultural population as alien in sentiment, and unworthy of the nation's confidence.

The arrival of two Greeks of rank modified in some degree the consequences of the proceedings at Kaltetzi On the 22nd of June, Prince Demetrius Hypsilantes arrived at the Greek camp before Tripolitza, where he was welcomed as commander-in-chief by the whole army. Demetrius formed a favourable contrast to his brother Alexander, in his moral and military conduct; but he was inferior to him in personal accomplishments, and almost as deficient in judgment and political discrimination. His stature was small, his appearance insignificant, his voice discordant, his manner awkward, and his health weak; yet with these physical defects he had manly sentiments, undaunted courage, and sincere patriotism. His principles were those of an honourable man, and his feelings were those of a gentleman. Unfortunately, he had neither experience nor tact in conducting public business.

Prince Demetrius Hypsilantes laid claim to the authority of a viceroy in Greece. He assumed that his brother Prince Alexander, as supreme head of the Hetairia, had been appointed Prince of Greece, and he pretended to be empowered to act as lieutenant-governor of the country for his brother. The pretension was foolish, and it was put forward in a foolish way. Nevertheless, as he was supposed, when he arrived, to be the herald of Russian aid, he received an enthusiastic reception from the people and the troops. His inexperience and incapacity prevented his availing himself of that enthusiasm, either to consolidate his own power or to benefit the cause of Greece. He might easily have employed the authority it gave him with the people to compel the soldiers to receive some elementary organization, and the power it gave him over the soldiers to restrain the disorders of the captains. He might have created a central treasury for the payment of the troops on permanent duty before Tripolitza, and organized a central commissariat for ensuring regular supplies to at least thirty thousand men. Power was conferred on him, which, if wisely used, might have rendered him the Washington of Greece. Since 'vanquished Persia's despot fled,' no Greek had stepped into an easier path to true glory. But like a weak despot, instead of using the authority in his hands, he demanded additional powers, of which circumstances rendered it impossible for him to make any use, and of which in no circumstances could he have made a good use. He required that the Peloponnesian Senate should be formally abolished, and that the whole executive power should be placed in his hands as lieutenant-governor until the arrival of his brother. The Senate and the primates opposed these demands, which on the other hand were supported by the military.

Much intriguing ensued; the blockade of Tripolitza and the general interests of Greece were neglected by both parties. Men took to wrangling with so much good-will, that they neglected the subject of the contest in the pleasures of the dispute, and business seemed every day farther from any termination. At last Hypsilantes made a bold move to rouse the soldiers to declare that his cause was theirs, and thus put an end to all opposition. He suddenly quitted the camp before Tripolitza, declaring that all his efforts to serve Greece were useless, for they were paralyzed by the ambition and the selfishness of the senators and the primates. His departure, as he had foreseen, made the soldiers take up arms. Some of the primates were in considerable personal danger, and would have been murdered had they not been protected by the captains. The Senate yielded. A deputation was sent to invite Hypsilantes to return, and he was brought back in triumph from Leondari.

Prince Demetrius Hypsilantes was now in possession of all the power which could be conferred on him, but it soon became apparent that neither he nor those about him knew how to employ it. He made no attempt to give the troops any organization even with regard to their commissariat. He did not even create a central civil administration, which would have enabled him to keep the military power he had acquired over the captains in his own hands. At this moment the formation of a regiment of infantry, a squadron of cavalry, and a battery of light guns, would have enabled him to organize Greece, for he had the people and the soldiers devoted to his person, and eager to be ruled by a single chief. Everywhere he was saluted as the Aphendi, or lord of the country. The supreme authority of the Hetairia still exercised a magic influence over men's minds, and he was universally regarded as an agent of Russia; for it was argued that, unless the Russian government wished to support the Revolution, the Russian police would never have allowed him to pass the frontiers. Both Petrobey and Kolokotrones were disposed to act under his orders, and they might easily have been rendered most efficient, and at the same time responsible, supporters of his administration. But Hypsilantes was bewildered with the power he had assumed, and Kolokotrones, who soon discovered his incapacity, could not resist the temptation of profiting by it.

The advisers of Hypsilantes were men as destitute of practical experience as he was himself. The self-government which existed among the Greeks of the Morea was at variance with what they had heard and seen of administration in France and Russia. They excited dissatisfaction by openly expressing their contempt for what they called the Turkish system. Yet they were utterly incompetent to create a central system complete enough to supplant, or powerful enough to override, this despised system.

When Hypsilantes returned to the camp before Tripolitza, he was so imprudent as to allow the Peloponnesian senators to remain at Vervena. They soon recovered their previous authority, and, with the assistance of the other primates, began to undermine the power of the prince, who, with inexplicable ignorance, left all their agents and partizans in office over the whole country, and consequently permitted them to remain practically the only central executive authority. Partly by their intrigues, and partly by his ignorance of the duties of a ruler, before Hypsilantes had been six weeks at the head of the government, the camp was more than once without provisions. Hypsilantes could neither form nor execute any project to relieve himself from his difficulties. He waited for others to perform the duties of his station. Instead of acting himself, he wrangled with Germanos, the archbishop of Patras, Deliyani, and Charalambes, for infringing his authority. The military chieftains profited by his neglect. They acted in his name, and employed it to establish their own influence in different municipalities, from which they contrived to secure regular supplies to their own followers. Brigand chiefs and ignorant captains became in this way the possessors of those powers of which Hypsilantes had deprived the Senate and the primates, and which escaped from his own hands, from his incompetency to create a central administration. The original usurpation of the Peloponnesian Senate and this incapacity of Hypsilantes added strength to the causes of discord and internal anarchy which soon became a prominent feature of the Revolution. The thoughts of public men received a vicious direction, and public business was conducted in a secret and underhand manner.

An instructive comparison might be made between the prudence of Washington in his camp before Boston in 1775, and the ineptness of Hypsilantes in his camp before Tripolitza in 1821. The first requisite for military success is military discipline; and the man who cannot introduce and maintain this sufficiently to secure order, is unfit to command armies[1]. The difficulty of converting a national militia into a regular army is great; but enough has been said to show that many circumstances were favourable to the enterprise in the Morea. Washington flogged the citizens of the United States who infringed the laws of military order; Hypsilantes might have hanged primates and captains who disobeyed his orders: and had he known, like Washington, how to temper severity with justice and command the respect of his soldiers, he might have formed a Greek army, and saved Greece from anarchy.

Disorder and dissension were gaining ground when Alexander Mavrocordatos, then called Prince Mavrocordatos both by himself and others, arrived at the camp of Trikorpha on the 8th of August 1821. His long political career has

---
[1] Hypsilantes formed a small corps of regulars, but made no attempt to organize the irregulars as Capodistrias did.

rendered him the most celebrated statesman of the Greek Revolution. When he joined the Greeks, it required no great discrimination to observe that both Hypsilantes and the primates were acting unwisely, and advancing into false positions from which it would be difficult for them to retreat with honour. In such a complication Mavrocordatos would not act a subordinate part; and to escape from factions, whose errors he could not rectify, he obtained the political direction of the Revolution in Western Greece, and quitted the camp on the 9th of September. About the same time Theodore Negris, an active, able, intriguing, ambitious, and unprincipled Phanariot, was charged with the political organization of Eastern Greece.

When Mavrocordatos reached Mesolonghi, he convoked a meeting of deputies from the provinces of Acarnania, Aetolia, Western Locris, and that part of Epirus which had joined the Revolution. Negris held a similar meeting of deputies from Attica, Boeotia, Megaris, Phocis, and Eastern Locris, at Salona. At Mesolonghi a senate was constituted to conduct the executive government; at Salona a corresponding assembly was called the Areopagos. Both assemblies were under the guidance and direction of civilians, who knew very little of the existing institutions and first wants of the country they attempted to organize. Instead of strengthening the municipalities and disciplining the municipal authorities, they created new officers to represent the central power, vainly expecting to use the military chiefs as their subordinate agents. Several of the members of these senates were Greeks, educated in the universities of Western Europe; others were Phanariots, educated in the sultan's service. All placed more confidence in their own scientific maxims than in the practical experience of the local magistrates and captains. They were fond of talking, fond of writing, stiff in their opinions, and dilatory in their actions. Both demogeronts and captains soon perceived that they were eloquent in ignorance, that they carried on a mass of unnecessary and unintelligible correspondence, and that, when once they went wrong, they could never be set right.

In so far, however, as these assemblies were steps towards national union, and to the formation of a central government, they were useful. But their immediate tendency was to weaken the authority of any general government; for in the constitutions which they adopted provisions were inserted, encroaching on its necessary powers. Nor was this done on any systematic plan by which Greece might have been formed into a federal state. In the constitution of Western Greece Mavrocordatos attempted to conceal his ambition, by an article which declared in vague terms that the Senate, and the administrative arrangements it created, should cease as soon as a permanent general government was established. But in Eastern Greece the constitution boldly circumscribed the authority of the Greek government even in military matters. Both these constitutions were crude scholastic productions, ill suited to the temper of the people, to the actual state of civilization, to the existing institutions, and to the exigencies of the time. The enemies of Mavrocordatos and Negris justly blamed their legislation as a Phanariot manœuvre to gain political power, and as positively injurious to the liberties of the people, in so far as it elevated barriers between the municipal institutions of the country and the central executive.

In Western Greece the prudence of Mavrocordatos gained him many personal friends, and created a political party in his favour; but in Eastern Greece the restless ambition of Negris caused him to lose the support of his political associates. The invasion of the Turks also threw absolute power into the hands of unprincipled and rapacious military chiefs, like Panouria and Odysseus, and reduced the Areopagos to perform the duties of paymaster and commissary.

The four great divisions of liberated Greece—the Morea, the islands, the eastern and the western provinces of the continent—were compelled to meet the first demands of the Revolution by local arrangements. But the events of the year 1821 convinced all alike of the necessity of establishing a central government. The conquest of Tripolitza was the term fixed for the dissolution of the Peloponnesian Senate. But the weakness of Hypsilantes, the ambition of the primates and captains, and a general spirit of party, perpetuated the evils which had been fostered by the senators. The administration of the public revenues remained in the same hands, and they were diverted from carrying on the war against the Turks. Large bodies of men were kept under arms, but these men were engaged in supporting local governors and tax-gatherers.

In autumn, however, the Greeks demanded that a national assembly should be convoked, in a tone that enforced attention. Party intrigues absorbed the whole activity of the oligarchs, who were beginning to enjoy the fruits of partial success in the midst of serious danger. Germanos, the archbishop of Patras, made himself conspicuous by his luxury and pride. He strove to form a league of Moreot primates, who expected to rule the Peloponnesus by means of its own provincial administration.

Prince Demetrius Hypsilantes, seeing himself forsaken by the military chiefs, as well as opposed by the primates, now for the first time recognized the right of the people to a voice in the formation of their own government and laws. He supposed that the popular enthusiasm with which he had been welcomed still existed, forgetting all that he had done to forfeit the people's confidence. In virtue of the supreme authority he possessed, he issued a proclamation summoning a national assembly to meet at Tripolitza in November. But even in performing this popular act, he neutralized the favourable impression it might have produced, by signing the document as lieutenant-general of his brother Alexander, instead of issuing it as the elected chief of the Greek nation. The military misconduct and the disgraceful flight of his brother were already the theme of universal reprobation. But in spite of the strange perverseness of Demetrius Hypsilantes, the object of his proclamation coincided so completely with the wishes of the nation, that deputies were everywhere elected. Tripolitza was infested by the fearful epidemic which has been already mentioned. The meeting of the national assembly was transferred to Argos, where it took place in December 1821. But Argos was soon so crowded by the armed bands who followed the Peloponnesian oligarchs, that it was deemed an unfit place for a national assembly, which was transferred again to Piada, a small town about three miles west of the site of Epidaurus. In consequence of the fashion adopted by the modern Greeks of adorning their history with great names instead of noble deeds, this first national assembly is called the assembly of Epidaurus.

The primates and captains of the Morea were resolved to yield as little of the power they enjoyed to a central government as possible. They took their measures with promptitude, and carried them into effect with decision. Before the national assembly published the constitution of Greece, and elected an executive government, the oligarchs of the Morea reconstituted the Peloponnesian Senate, and enacted a local constitution, which invested it with a direct control over the financial and military resources of the Peloponnesus. They took a lesson from the proceedings of Mavrocordatos and Negris, who had created political influence by means of provincial constitutions; but their superior knowledge of the administrative machinery then in action, enabled them to draw up a more practical constitution, and establish a more efficient senate. Among other unconstitutional powers with which this senate was invested, it was authorized to name the deputies who were to represent the people of the Peloponnesus in the national assembly. It deserves to be noticed that the members from the rest of Greece did not protest against this violation of the principles of popular freedom.

It may, however, be doubted, whether the Peloponnesian oligarchs would have succeeded in this illegal proceeding, had Demetrius Hypsilantes not deserted the popular cause. His jealousy of Mavrocordatos at this time appears completely to have obscured the small portion of judgment he ever possessed, and to have concealed from him the iniquity of coalescing with men whom, in a public proclamation, he had recently accused of being eager to oppress the Greek people and to govern as Turkish officials. His conduct strengthened the Moreot primates and captains, but it entirely destroyed his own political influence, and greatly injured his personal reputation.

The organization of the Peloponnesian Senate forms an important and interesting feature in the history of the Greek Revolution. It was the immediate cause of the failure of the constitution of Epidaurus, and of the nullity of the executive government of Greece which that constitution created. The members of this Senate were really self-elected, and it circumscribed the legal powers of the central government under cover of arrangements to protect local liberties. The provincial constitution of the Peloponnesus pretended to create a subordinate provincial administration, but it really organized an independent executive government. It assumed an absolute control over the municipalities, and rendered all local authorities responsible for their financial and fiscal acts to the Peloponnesian Senate, not to the Greek government. This Senate was allowed to arrogate to itself the right of judging traitors, dismissing officials, ratifying the election of captains of the militia, whom the people were allowed to elect, and of appointing generals to command the troops of the Peloponnesus. With the concurrence of the captains and general thus named, it claimed the right of naming an archistrategos or commander-in-chief of the whole Peloponnesian forces, which in this way were kept as a distinct army, separated from the Romeliot armatoli, who formed the real military strength of liberated Greece. The ambition of Kolokotrones appears to have suggested this most unmilitary arrangement. It contributed, with other causes, to prevent the Peloponnesian armed bands from bearing almost any share in the warlike operations in continental Greece. The Senate also fixed the pay of the soldiers and officers of the Peloponnesian army, thus securing their obedience. It is true that the constitution required the nomination of the archistrategos to be submitted to the approval of the legislative assembly, but the consent of a legislative assembly to the appointment could only be regarded as a formal ratification. It could never be refused without the risk of a civil war.

Many of the objectionable provisions of the constitution of the Peloponnesian Senate were verbally transcribed from the constitution which Mavrocordatos had introduced in Western Greece, but the oligarchs of the Morea carried them into effect in a different spirit from that in which they had been drawn up. In Western Greece it was expressly stipulated that they were to cease when a central government was established; in the Peloponnesus, on the contrary, they were to operate as a check on the authority of the central government [1].

The worst feature of these local constitutions was common

---

[1] The laws and constitutions of Greece during the Revolution have been published by Mr. Mamouka, Under-Secretary of State, in eleven volumes. For the constitution of the Peloponnesus, see vol. i. p. 107; of Western Greece, i. 21.

to all. They all authorized provincial authorities to maintain armed bands to enforce their orders and defend their power. This provision perpetuated and legalized a state of anarchy. The Peloponnesian Senate carried this abuse to the greatest extent. It was empowered to keep up a guard of a thousand men at a moment when every man in Greece capable of bearing arms ought to have been sent to the banks of the Spercheus or the passes of Makronoros [1].

It is not necessary to enter into further details to explain how the Moreots paralyzed the national assembly at Piada, and rendered the constitution of Epidaurus and the executive government of Greece ineffectual. The primates and military chiefs, by their coalition with Demetrius Hypsilantes, were enabled to retain a complete command over the fiscal resources of the Morea, which then formed the great bulk of the national revenues. The executive government was comparatively powerless. Men of sagacity must have seen that the constitution of Epidaurus was a dead letter as long as the constitution of the Peloponnesus existed; yet Mavrocordatos and other men of talent allowed their ambition to blind them to the evil effects of promulgating a political constitution merely to witness its violation, and of acting as an executive body without exercising the powers of a national government. If they feared to make an appeal to the people in favour of representative institutions, lest the appeal should prove a signal for commencing a civil war, it was their duty to lay aside their ambitious schemes, to convert the Peloponnesian Senate into a national executive, by compelling it to undertake the conduct of the central executive of all Greece, and thus concentrate public attention on its proceedings. By taking a different course, they created two antagonistic administrations of nearly equal force.

Accidental circumstances diminished the personal influence of Mavrocordatos at the first assembly of the deputies of Greece, by bringing him on the scene under disadvantageous circumstances. He had just made himself ridiculous by an attempt to play the general. On quitting Mesolonghi to attend the national assembly, he crossed the gulf to the Greek camp before Patras. He arrived with a good deal of

---

[1] Mamouka, i. 117.

military parade, bringing with him some pieces of artillery and fifteen hundred stand of small-arms. He was attended by another Phanariot, Prince Constantine Karadja. The Achaians had already been successful in several skirmishes with the garrison of Patras, but Mavrocordatos, who knew nothing of military matters, did not know how to profit by these successes. The consequence was, that they rendered both him and the besiegers extremely negligent, and by alarming the Turks rendered them extremely vigilant. Suddenly, while Mavrocordatos was pluming himself on the favourable effect which his success in Western Greece had produced on the Moreots, the garrison of Patras made a general attack on the positions of the besiegers. The whole blockading army fled, and Mavrocordatos fled with it, leaving the artillery and arms which he had brought over from Mesolonghi, and the whole personal baggage of himself and his suite, in the hands of the Turks. He arrived at Argos in such a state of destitution as gave point to the sneers of his enemies, who attributed his disaster to his misplaced vanity in attempting to rival the military reputation of Hypsilantes.

The constitution of Epidaurus was proclaimed on the 13th of January 1822, the new year's day of Eastern Christians. It was the work of Mavrocordatos and Negris, who were assisted by an Italian refugee, named Gallina. It must be looked upon rather as a statement of the political principles of the new Greek state, as they were ratified by national consent, than as a practical organic law. Its provisions are excellent, but they are the enunciation of vague maxims. It does nothing to connect the existing institutions of the country with the central administration it created. Those who framed it probably thought more of its effect in Western Europe than of its operation in Greece. For practical government they trusted, with their national self-confidence, to their own talents. It has, however, the merit of proclaiming religious liberty, of abolishing slavery, and declaring that judicial torture was illegal. But it adopted no arrangements for enforcing financial responsibility on the municipal authorities who fingered public money, nor for restraining the fiscal rapacity of the proësti and the military exactions of the captains. No attempt was made to enforce responsibility on the rulers of the country, by furnishing the people with some information concerning the enormous amount of Turkish property which had become national, nor concerning the manner in which it was expended or administered.

The central government of Greece, established by the constitution of Epidaurus, consisted of a legislative assembly and an executive body. The names of several distinguished men appear neither in the one nor the other; there can be no doubt, therefore, that this National Assembly was employed to throw the power of which it could dispose into the hands of a party.

The executive body consisted of five members. Prince Alexander Mavrocordatos, after acting as president of the National Assembly, was named President of Greece. The executive was authorized to appoint eight ministers. The power of naming officials to civil, military, and financial employments was vaguely expressed in order to avoid a conflict of competency with the provincial senates and the government of the naval islands. A good deal was done by the Greeks at Epidaurus to deceive Europe; very little to organize Greece.

CHAPTER II.

THE PRESIDENCY OF MAVROCORDATOS.

The character and political position of Alexander Mavrocordatos.—Affairs of Euboea, and death of Elias Mavromichales. — Conduct of Odysseus at Karystos.—Affairs of Chios, and invasion of the island by the Samiots.— Prompt measures of the Sultan.—Massacres of the Chiots.—Greek fleet puts to sea.—Constantine Kanares burns the flag-ship of the capitan-pasha.—Devastation of Chios.— The President Mavrocordatos assumes the chief command in Western Greece.—Treachery of Gogos.—Defeat at Petta.—Effects of this defeat.—Death of Kyriakules Mavromichales.—Capitulation of Suliots.—Affairs of Acarnania.—Siege of Mesolonghi.—Defeat of the Turks.

A VAULTING ambition prompted Alexander Mavrocordatos to assume the supreme authority in Greece, when circumstances demanded greater abilities and a firmer character than he possessed, in order to execute the duties of the office with honour to the leader and advantage to the country. He has perhaps a better claim to be considered a statesman than any other actor in the Revolution; but even his claim to that high rank is very dubious. His conduct is recorded in the annals of the Revolution, and his conduct reveals his character. While in power he was always making a mystery of public business, and a parade of administrative knowledge in matters of no practical importance, but nations have no secrets in their proceedings, and the mists of adulation which once surrounded the first president of Greece have long vanished. Of him it can be said with great truth, *Major privato visus, dum privatus fuit, et omnium consensu capax imperii, nisi imperasset.*

The superiority of Mavrocordatos over the rest of his countrymen must have been really great; for, in his long political career, he has been five times called from an inferior or private station to occupy the highest rank in the administration of Greece. In every case he made shipwreck of his own reputation, and left public affairs in as bad a position as he found them, if not in a worse. It is, however, no inconsiderable honour to have been elected the first president of liberated Greece by the voice of a free people, and to have so comported himself that even when he forfeited the nation's confidence he retained a place in the people's esteem. This arose from the conviction that he was less influenced by a love of money than other politicians. And as dishonesty has been the vice most prevalent and most injurious in the conduct of public business in Greece, the unsullied reputation of Mavrocordatos has conferred on him a greater degree of popularity than his conduct would have obtained, had ministerial corruption and financial peculation not been considered the direct causes of most political evils by the Greeks.

The presidency of Mavrocordatos was a period of misfortune to himself and to the central government, and the misfortune was caused by misconduct and wilful errors. Yet the year 1822 was a period of glory to Greece; and had he known how to perform the duties of the presidency, some part of that glory would have been reflected on him and on the government of which he was the head. Partly from causes over which he had no control, his administration opened with disaster, and in consequence of his perverse and mistaken ambition, it terminated in calamity. The sad catastrophe of Chios cast a dark shade over the dawn of his government. The defeat of Petta brought disgrace on his personal administration. The first was an unavoidable misfortune, as far as Mavrocordatos was concerned, but for the second he was solely and entirely responsible. He deserted his duty, as President of Greece, to act as governor-general of its western provinces, and he assumed the command of an army to make political capital of military success, without possessing one single quality that fitted him for a soldier.

The first misfortune which happened to the Greeks in 1822 was the death of Elias Mavromichales, the eldest son of Petrobey. He was invited by the provincial government of Eastern Greece to take the command of the troops engaged in blockading the Acropolis of Athens; but when he arrived at the Athenian camp, he was persuaded to accept the chief command of an army destined to besiege Karystos. Elias preferred active operations in Euboea to the dull routine of watching the starving Turks at Athens. He marched to Kalamos, and crossed the channel to Kastelli, accompanied by his uncle Kyriakoules and six hundred Mainates.

Before his arrival at the camp of the Euboeans, the people of Kumi had elected Vasos to be their captain, a native of Montenegro, who, after passing his life in menial occupations, or as an ordinary klepht, had quitted Smyrna to join the Revolution and push his way as a soldier. Vasos was a man of a fine athletic figure, well suited to distinguish himself in personal brawls; but he was ignorant of military affairs, and never acquired any military experience beyond that which is required for a brigand chief. Elias Mavromichales displayed on this occasion far more generosity and patriotism than Hypsilantes and Mavrocordatos in similar circumstances. Without seeking to make his rank as a general appointed by the central government, and his invitation by a provincial committee of Euboea, a ground for insisting on receiving the chief command, he removed all cause of dissension by allowing Vasos, though a stranger and an untried soldier, to share his authority.

At the solicitation of the people of Euboea it was resolved to attack a body of Turks posted in the village of Stura without waiting for reinforcements which were hourly expected. The allurements of avarice prevailed over the suggestions of prudence. The Turks had collected considerable quantities of grain at Stura, which was occupied by only about a hundred men.

To insure success in this attack, it was necessary to occupy the pass over Mount Diakophti. This would have prevented Omer Bey of Karystos, an active and enterprising officer, from bringing assistance to the small garrison in Stura. The Greeks were fully aware of the importance of seizing this position; yet, in consequence of the utter want of military discipline, and the divided command, added to their natural habit of wasting the time for action in debate, the occupation of the pass was put off for a day. One body of troops marched to attack Stura, and another to occupy the pass of Diakophti.

Omer Bey had not lost a moment. As soon as he heard that a body of Greek troops had crossed the channel, he hastened to secure the pass, and the Greeks found him already intrenched in a strong position. After routing the troops opposed to him, he hastened forward to defend his magazines at Stura.

In the mean time Elias Mavromichales entered Stura, but the Turks in garrison had shut themselves up in the stone houses round the magazines, and made a determined resistance. While the skirmishing was going on, the advanced guard of the troops from Karystos arrived, and the Greeks were quickly driven out of the place. Elias, with a few men, kept possession of an old windmill, which he defended valiantly, expecting that his uncle and his colleague, Vasos, would be able to rally the fugitives and return to engage the Turks. In an hour or two, perceiving that the defeat was decisive, he attempted to cut his way through the enemy sword in hand, but was shot in the attempt. Two only of his followers escaped. This affair occurred on the 24th of January 1822.

The death of Elias Mavromichales was generally lamented. He had shown some military talent, as well as brilliant courage, which was a characteristic of many members of his house. No chief was more beloved by the soldiers, for no other was so attentive to their welfare and so disinterested in his personal conduct. He was strongly imbued with that youthful enthusiasm which seeks glory rather than power.

Shortly after the death of Elias Mavromichales, the fugitives were reinforced by the arrival of Odysseus from Attica with seven hundred men, many of whom were armatoli. The Greek army rallied under this new leader, and advanced to Stura, which was abandoned by the Turks. But the Greeks found the magazines empty; for Omer Bey, instead of pursuing his enemy, had prudently employed his time in conveying the grain at Stura within the fortress of Karystos.

The siege of Karystos was now formed, and the besiegers cut off the water which is conveyed into the town by an aqueduct. The Greek army was three thousand strong, and great expectations were entertained that Omer Bey would be compelled to capitulate. But about the middle of February, Odysseus, who had not been able to obtain the sole command, suddenly abandoned his position, and marched away without giving any previous notice of his movement to the other chiefs of the blockading army. He pretended that he was compelled to move because his troops were left without provisions; but the want of provisions certainly did not oblige him to keep his movements a secret. His desertion alarmed the remainder of the army, and the Greeks retired from before Karystos. The army of Euboea was soon after broken up. The Turks of Negrepont and Karystos, finding no troops in the field to oppose them, sallied out of these fortresses, and levied taxes and contributions over the greater part of the island during the year 1822.

The conduct of Odysseus was supposed to be the result of treasonable arrangements with Omer Bey. Like some other captains of armatoli, Odysseus felt doubts of the ultimate success of the Revolution, and had no enthusiasm for liberty. His feelings were those of an Albanian mercenary soldier, and he had no confidence in the talents of the Greek civilians who took the lead in public affairs. He entertained a settled conviction that the Revolution would terminate in some compromise; and as Ali of Joannina was his model of a hero, he pursued his own interest, like that chieftain, without submitting to any restraint from duty, morality, or religion. His character was a compound of the worst vices of the Greeks and Albanians. He was false as the most deceitful Greek, and vindictive as the most bloodthirsty Albanian. To these vices he added excessive avarice, universal distrust, and ferocious cruelty. The most probable explanation of his conduct at Karystos seems to be, that, on the one hand, he was jealous of the chiefs with whom he was acting, and that, on the other, he suspected some manœuvre of his enemy Kolettes, who was then acting as minister at war. He knew that Mavrocordatos was seeking to increase the power of the central government, and that the members of the Areopagos of Eastern Greece, which still continued to exist, were labouring to prevent his gaining a predominant influence in Attica. Odysseus had already formed the project of acquiring an independent provincial command in Eastern Greece corresponding to that once exercised, or supposed to have been exercised, by captains of armatoli. And he was inclined to leave it to the chapter of accidents whether he was to exercise this power as a general of Greece, or as an officer of the sultan. In spite of the military anarchy that reigned in Greece, public opinion was strong enough to derange his plans.

No calamity during the Greek Revolution awakened the sympathy and compassion of the civilized world more deservedly than the devastation of Chios. The industrious and peaceable inhabitants of that happy island were mildly governed, and they were averse to join the Revolution, in which, from their unwarlike habits, they were disqualified from taking an active part. By an insurrection against the sultan they had everything to lose, and nothing to gain. In both cases their local privileges would be diminished, if not entirely lost. Their municipal administration was already in their own hands; their taxes were light, and they were collected by themselves. The Chiots justly feared that the central government of Greece would increase the burden of taxation, and that Hydriots, Mainates, or Romeliot armatoli, would prove severer tax-gatherers than village magistrates. Even at the first outbreak of orthodox enthusiasm, when Russian aid was universally expected, the people refused to take up arms. Admiral Tombazes appeared off Chios with the Greek fleet during its first cruise, and vainly invited the inhabitants to throw off the Othoman yoke, and avenge the martyrdom of the Patriarch Gregorios.

This attempt of the Greek fleet to excite an insurrection alarmed Sultan Mahmud, and the Othoman government deemed it necessary to disarm the orthodox, and strengthen the Turkish garrison in the citadel, where the archbishop and seventy of the principal Greeks were ordered to reside as hostages for the tranquillity of the island. The fortifications were repaired, provisions and military stores were collected, and the citadel was put in a state of defence. Prudence now forbade the Greeks to invade Chios, unless they had previously secured the command of the sea; for it was impossible to take the citadel without a regular siege, since the vicinity of the continent rendered a blockade impossible even during the winter, when the Turkish fleet remained within the Dardanelles.

Unfortunately for the Chiots, their wealth excited the cupidity of many of the ruling men in Greece, and stimulated adventurers to undertake the conquest of the island. The inhabitants were stigmatized for their treachery to the national cause, and in an unlucky hour Prince Demetrius Hypsilantes authorized a Chiot merchant named, like very many other Chiot merchants, Ralli, to undertake an expedition to Chios in conjunction with Lykourgos, a man who had obtained considerable influence at Samos. Lykourgos, who had practised medicine at Smyrna, was a bold adventurer. Availing himself adroitly of the general ignorance of political and military affairs among his countrymen, he persuaded them to place the chief direction of public business at Samos in his hands. On the 2nd of January 1822, Hypsilantes, foreseeing that the presidency of Greece was about to pass into the hands of his rival Mavrocordatos, and perhaps deeming that the central government would be unable to support the expedition to Chios with sufficient energy, wrote a suggestion that it might be prudent to defer the enterprise. He only covered his own responsibility, without countermanding the expedition. To this suggestion in favour of delay, Lykourgos replied on the 1st of February, that he had put off the attack, but that he prayed fervently for a favourable opportunity for making the attempt, as he considered the conquest of Chios to be a sacred duty. The project was opposed, not only by the leading Chiots, but by the most intelligent Psarians.

Lykourgos had only delayed his enterprise because his preparations were incomplete. In order to deceive the Psarians and the Chiots, he gave out that he was going to attack Scalanova. The Turks, however, divined his object. Scalanova was secure, for it was occupied by a strong garrison. Fresh troops were therefore transported into the island of Chios, and Vehid Pasha found great difficulty in maintaining order among these bands, which were principally composed of volunteers, and who came, filled with Mussulman enthusiasm, to combat infidels, and, what was more pleasant, to plunder them. Vehid Pasha behaved with great prudence in his difficult position. He persuaded the Greeks to raise a monthly contribution of thirty-four thousand piastres, and he employed this sum in providing regular pay and liberal rations for the troops, and particularly for the volunteers. The Porte in the mean time ordered the pasha to send the three principal hostages to Constantinople, and to keep strict guard over the others.

As soon as Lykourgos had completed his preparations, he waited neither for the orders of Prince Demetrius Hypsilantes, the lieutenant-governor of the supreme chief of the Hetairia, nor of Prince Alexander Mavrocordatos, the President of Greece. On the 22nd of March 1822, he landed at Koutari with about twenty-five hundred men. After a trifling skirmish the invaders entered the town of Chios, where they burned the custom-house, destroyed two mosques, and behaved more like a band of pirates than a body of national troops. Their military dispositions consisted in occupying the houses nearest the citadel with riflemen, and beginning to form a battery on the commanding position of Turloti.

The time for invading Chios was extremely ill-chosen. The Turkish fleet had already quitted Constantinople. Lykourgos and his followers were nevertheless sure of gaining considerable booty by their expedition, though that booty could only be won by plundering the sultan's Christian subjects. They hoped that accident would enable them to get possession of the citadel of Chios, and in case they should be compelled to retreat, they trusted to their own ability and to the stupidity of the Turks for effecting their escape. The contempt with which the Greeks viewed the Turks at this period seems hardly credible to those who calmly look back at the events of the contest.

The siege of the citadel of Chios was commenced in form. Batteries were constructed not only on Turloti, but also on the beach of the port. They were, however, too distant to produce any effect, and the troops would not work at the trenches with sufficient regularity to make any progress with the attack. In the mean time the peasants crowded into the town from the villages in the mountains, and Lykourgos found himself at the head of a large force. But of that force he knew not how to make any use. Instead of devoting all his energy to the conquest of the citadel, he began to play the prince, and to organize a government. Taking up his quarters in the bishop's palace, he deposed the demogeronts, and appointed a revolutionary committee of seven ephors.

Lykourgos did nothing, the ephors had nothing to do, and the camp became a scene of anarchy.

It was soon evident that a more competent commander and a more powerful force was required to enable the Greeks to take the citadel. A deputation was therefore sent by the inhabitants to Corinth to solicit aid from Mavrocordatos. Mr. Glarakes, a man who had received his education in Germany, was at the head of this deputation [1]. The Greek government furnished the Chiots with a few heavy guns and some artillerymen. Several Philhellenes also accompanied these supplies, to assist in directing the operations of the siege. But no Greek fleet was sent to prevent Turkish troops from crossing over from the Asiatic coast. The ephors had only succeeded in hiring six small Psarian vessels to cruise in the channel, and watch the Turkish boats at Tchesmé. The disorderly conduct of the troops under Lykourgos compelled many of the wealthy Chiots to quit the island with their families. To prevent these desertions, as they were called, the officers imprisoned many wealthy individuals, threatened them with ill usage on the part of the soldiers, and made them pay large sums of money, as a bribe to purchase protection from the ill usage with which they were threatened at the instigation of these very officers.

The attack on Chios excited more indignation than alarm at Constantinople. The sultan felt it as a personal insult which he was bound to avenge. The ladies of the harem called for the extermination of the rebels who were plundering their mastic gardens. The divan was incensed at the boldness of the enterprise, and resolved to spare no exertions to preserve so valuable an appanage of the court as Chios then formed. The Porte suddenly became a scene of activity, which contrasted strongly with the apathetic indifference of the Greek government at Corinth. Sultan Mahmud commenced his operations in the true Othoman spirit, by ordering three of the Chiot hostages to be hanged, and a number of the wealthiest Chiot merchants in Constantinople to be thrown into prison.

---

[1] Glarakes would have been a valuable citizen in peaceful times. He was patriotic and honest, but misplaced in his career by the Revolution, yet he held the office of Secretary of State for a long time during the Revolution, and he was more than once a minister under King Otho.

The Othoman fleet put to sea. The pashas on the coast of Asia Minor were ordered to hold the best troops they could assemble ready for embarkation, and the officers at the ports nearest to Chios were instructed to pass over boat-loads of troops and provisions to the citadel at every risk as long as the Greeks remained in the island. Though the ordinary commands of a despotic government are frequently neglected, the extraordinary and express orders of a despotic master are promptly obeyed. The ports of Asia Minor were soon crowded with troops, and the citadel was maintained in a good state of defence.

The capitan-pasha, Kara Ali, arrived in the northern channel of Chios on the 11th April 1822. As he entered, a Turkish felucca belonging to his squadron got on shore, and was captured by the Greeks, who immediately put to death every soul on board. This act of barbarity was not sustained by the desperate courage which can alone excuse such a system of warfare. Next day, the capitan-pasha landed a body of seven thousand men to the south of the city. The Greeks made little exertion to prevent his landing, and fled from their intrenchments at the first approach of the Turkish troops. The victors plundered the town of whatever the lawless bands of Lykourgos had left, and a body of fanatic Mussulman volunteers, who had joined the expedition as a holy war against infidels, paraded the streets, murdering every Christian who fell into their hands.

Lykourgos showed as little courage in irregular warfare in the field as he had displayed military capacity in the camp. After a feeble attempt to defend the village of St. George to which he had retreated, he and his followers fled to the coast, and embarked in some Psarian vessels, abandoning the unfortunate Chiots whom they had goaded into rebellion, to the fury of the exasperated Turks. This fury, it must be mentioned, was increased by the deliberate murder of nearly all their prisoners by the Greeks during the whole period of the expedition.

Lykourgos returned to Samos. The failure of the expedition was attributed to his incapacity and cowardice, which perhaps only rendered an inevitable failure a disgraceful defeat. But no one appears to have upbraided him with his cruelty and extortion, which inflicted so many calamities on the unfortunate inhabitants of Chios. The Samiots deprived him of all authority, and drove him into exile. At a later period of the Revolution, however, he was reinstated in his authority by the primates of Hydra, who found it impossible to levy an assessment of three hundred thousand piastres which had been imposed on the Samiots as a contribution towards the maintenance of the Greek fleet. The local knowledge of Lykourgos, and his influence over the democratic party among his countrymen, pointed him out as the fittest man to bring about a peaceful arrangement; and as the defence of Samos was necessary for the safety of Greece, and the Greek fleet could alone save Samos from the fate of Chios, his nomination as governor was a prudent measure. He appears to have benefited by experience, for his conduct was firm and moderate.

The vengeance of the Turks fell heavy on Chios. The unfortunate inhabitants of the island were generally unarmed, but they were all treated as rebels and rendered responsible for the deeds of the Greeks who had fled. In the city the wealthier class often succeeded in obtaining protection from Turks in authority, by paying large sums of money. In the mean time the poor were exposed to the vengeance of the soldiers and the fanatics. The bloodshed, however, soon ceased in the town, for even the fanatic volunteers began to combine profit with vengeance. They collected as many of the Chiots as they thought would bring a good price in the slave-markets of Asia Minor, and crossed over to the continent with their booty. Many Chiot families also found time to escape to different ports in the island, and succeeded in embarking in the Psarian vessels, which hastened to the island as soon as it was known that the capitan-pasha had sailed past Psara.

Three thousand Chiots retired to the monastery of Aghios Minas, five miles to the southward of the city, on the ridge of hills which bounds the rich plain. The Turks surrounded the building and summoned them to surrender. The men had little hope of escaping death. The women and children were sure of being sold as slaves. Though they had no military leader, and were unable to take effectual measures for defending the monastery, they refused to lay down their arms. The Turks carried the building by storm, and put all within to the sword.

Two thousand persons had also sought an asylum in the fine old monastery of Nea Mone, which is about six miles from the city, secluded in the mountains towards the west. This monastery was built by Constantine IX. (Monomachos); and some curious mosaics, now almost entirely destroyed, still form valuable and interesting monuments of that flourishing period of Byzantine art[1]. The Turks stormed this monastery as they had done that of Aghios Minas. A number of the helpless inmates had shut themselves up in the church. The doors were forced open, and the Turks, after slaughtering even the women on their knees at prayer, set fire to the screen of paintings in the church, and to the wood-work and roofs of the other buildings in the monastery, and left the Christians who were not already slain to perish in the conflagration.

Kara Ali did everything in his power to save the island from being laid waste and depopulated. He was anxious to protect the peasantry, for he knew that his merit in having defeated the Greeks would be greatly increased in the eyes of the sultan if he could prevent any diminution in the amount of taxation. He would fain have confined the pillage of the fanatic volunteers to the city, where he could watch their proceedings, and deprive them of the slaves they might carry off when they quitted the island. On the 17th of April he invited the foreign consuls who remained in the island to announce an amnesty to the inhabitants, and on the 22nd the French and Austrian consuls conducted the primates of the mastic villages to the city. The primates delivered up the arms possessed by the Christians as a proof of submission, and Elez Aga, the voivode, engaged to prevent any of the irregular bands of volunteers from entering his district. By these arrangements the mastic villages, whose fate particularly interested the sultan's court, were saved from plunder. But in the rest of the island the power of the capitan-pasha, not being sustained by a well-organized body of soldiers like that under the orders of Elez Aga, proved insufficient to protect the people.

---

[1] A.D. 1042-1054.

As soon as Sultan Mahmud heard of the success of his admiral, he ordered the Chiot hostages to be executed as an expiation for the insurrection. Four hostages and several merchants were hung at Constantinople, and the archbishop and seventy-five persons were executed at Chios by express orders from the Porte. This cruelty on the part of the sovereign proves that the avarice of the Turkish soldiers, and not their humanity, saved the Christian women and children of Chios from the sad fate of the Mussulman women and children at Tripolitza.

The president Mavrocordatos, the Greek government, and the Albanian primates of Hydra, were accused of both incapacity and neglect in not sending the Greek fleet to oppose the entrance of the capitan-pasha into the channel between Chios and the main. No spot could have been found more favourable to the operations of the light vessels of the Albanian and Greek islanders, or for the use of fire-ships. At all events, the passage of irregular troops and constant supplies of provisions from the continent in small vessels would have been completely cut off.

It was only on the 10th of May that the Greek fleet put to sea. It consisted of fifty-six sail. The squadron of each of the naval islands had its own admiral, but the chief command over the whole fleet was conceded by common consent to Andreas Miaoulis, who, though he had not yet performed any remarkable exploit, had given such proofs of sound sense and prudent firmness that his character secured him universal respect; while the manner in which he displayed these qualifications, in combination with experience in seamanship, gave him a marked superiority over all the other captains in the motley assemblage of vessels called the Greek navy. Miaoulis deserved the place he obtained, and it reflects honour on the navy of Greece that the place was voluntarily conceded to him, and that he was steadily supported in it during all the vicissitudes of the war. But in the force under his command there was very little order and no discipline. Many of the captains performed their part as individuals bravely and honourably, but their ideas of their duty were founded on their experience as merchant adventurers, not as national officers. Captains and even crews frequently assumed the right of acting independently when the admiral required their co-operation, or of violating his commands when they ought to have paid implicit obedience to his orders.

The capitan-pasha passed the ramazan at Chios. On the 31st of May Miaoulis appeared off the north channel; and the Othoman fleet weighing anchor, an engagement took place at the entrance of the Gulf of Smyrna. The Greeks made use of fire-ships, but one which they directed against a Turkish line-of-battle ship was consumed ineffectually, and the battle terminated in an idle cannonade, which was renewed at intervals on the two subsequent days, without causing any damage to either party. The Greeks returned dispirited to Psara, and the capitan-pasha, elated with this trivial success, to his anchorage at Chios.

On the 18th of June, the last day of ramazan in the year 1822, a number of the principal officers of the Othoman fleet assembled on board the ship of the capitan-pasha to celebrate the feast of Bairam. The night was dark, but the whole Turkish fleet was illuminated for the festival. Two Greek ships, which had been hugging the land during the day, as if baffled by the wind in endeavouring to enter the Gulf of Smyrna, changed their course at dusk, when their movements could be no longer observed, and bore down into the midst of the Othoman fleet. One steered for the 80-gun ship of the capitan-pasha, the other for the 74 of the Reala bey. Both these ships were conspicuous in the dark night by the variegated lamps at their mast-heads and yards. The two Greeks were fire-ships. One was commanded by Constantine Kanares, the hero of the Greek Revolution. It is superfluous to say that such a man directed his ship with skill and courage. Calmly estimating every circumstance of the moment, he ran the bowsprit into an open port, and fixed his ship alongside the capitan-pasha, as near the bows as possible so as to bring the flames to windward of his enemy. He then lighted the train with his own hand, stepped into his boat, where all the crew were ready at their oars, and pushed off as the flames mounted from the deck. The sails and rigging, steeped in turpentine and pitch, were immediately in a blaze, and the Turkish crews were far too much astonished at the sudden conflagration to pay any attention to a solitary boat which rowed rapidly into the shade. The flames driven by the wind rushed through the open ports of the lower and upper decks, and filled the great ship with fire roaring like a furnace.

The other fire-ship was commanded by a Hydriot. This Albanian was less fortunate or less daring than his Greek colleague. His vessel was not so skilfully and coolly directed, or the train was fired with too much precipitation. Instead of holding fast to the line-of-battle ship against which she was directed, she drifted to leeward and burned harmlessly to the water's edge.

On board the capitan-pasha's ship the scene was terrible, A quantity of tents piled up on the lower deck, near the ports where the fire first entered, took fire so quickly, and the flames rushed up so furiously through the hatches, that all communication between the different parts of the ship was cut off. No effort could be made to arrest the conflagration, or to sink the ship. Those on board could only save their lives by jumping into the sea. The awning catching fire rendered it impossible to work even on the quarter-deck. The few boats which were alongside, or which could be lowered, were sunk by the crowds that entered them. The crews of the nearest ships were engaged in hauling off, and the progress of the flames was so rapid that when boats arrived they feared to approach. Fire was already rushing out of every port below, and blocks were beginning to fall from the rigging. The ship was crowded with prisoners; and the shrieks of those who could make no effort to escape struck all with horror who heard their cries. Kara Ali jumped into one of the boats that was brought alongside to receive him; but before he could quit the side of his ship, he was struck by a falling spar and carried dying to the shore.

The capitan-bey who succeeded to the command of the fleet, not thinking it safe to remain at Chios, and considering the naval operations terminated by the expulsion of the Greeks from the island, sailed for the Dardanelles. Though he was pursued by the Greek fleet, he stopped at Erisso, and visited Kydonies without sustaining any loss. On the 2nd of July he brought the Othoman fleet to anchor within the castles of the Dardanelles.

The prudence of Miaoulis, and the skill with which he

contrived to introduce some degree of order into the fleet under his command during this cruise, afforded hope of further improvements in the Greek navy which were never realized. The skill of the captains in handling their ships received well-merited praise from the naval officers of every nation who witnessed their manœuvres. But their ignorance of military science, and their awkwardness in the use of their imperfect artillery, did not allow them to derive any very decided advantage from their superior seamanship. The necessity of effecting a complete change in the naval system of the Greeks made a strong impression on an English officer who served as a volunteer at this time, and who made several proposals to attain the desired end by introducing steamships. His name was Frank Abney Hastings, and it will be our duty to record both his exploits and his death in the course of this work[1].

The cruelties of the Turks at Chios were renewed after the destruction of the capitan-pasha's ship. The mastic villages which had hitherto escaped invasion were now laid waste. For many months the slave-markets of the Othoman empire, from Algiers to Trebizond, were supplied with women and children from Chios. Fortunately for the wretched sufferers, their known character for honesty and docility secured a high price, and insured their purchase by wealthy families, where they generally met with better treatment than slaves often receive from Christian masters.

It is supposed that forty thousand persons were murdered or enslaved in the island of Chios during the year 1822, but this number must be exaggerated. About five thousand Chiots were absent from the island when it was invaded by the Samians. About fifteen thousand escaped before the arrival of the capitan-pasha. In the month of February 1822

---

[1] General Gordon says (i. 364), 'It was then that Frank Hastings commenced that course of honourable service which must ever connect his name with the emancipation of Greece.' See also p. 370, where it is mentioned that Hastings saved a vessel. He did so by going out on the bowsprit under a heavy fire of musketry (ii. 441). Gordon adds, 'If ever there was a disinterested and really useful Philhellene it was Hastings: he received no pay, and had expended most of his slender fortune in keeping the Karteria afloat for the last six months. ..... His ship, too, was the only one in the Greek navy where regular discipline was maintained.' The sum expended by Hastings in the cause of Greece eventually exceeded 7000l. A letter is inserted in Appendix III., in which Hastings complains of the reception he received on his arrival in Greece. The president Mavrocordatos then expected more support from France than England.

Chios was said to contain nearly one hundred thousand inhabitants; in the month of August it was supposed that it did not contain more than thirty thousand[1]. Most of the Greek islands were filled with fugitives from Chios; and many families who had lived in prosperous homes dragged out the remainder of their lives in abject poverty. Some who had succeeded in carrying off from their houses a few valuables, family jewels, and sums of money, were robbed by the Christian boatmen, who subsequently made a boast of having saved them from the Turks, and claimed rewards and gratitude from Greece.

The massacres of Chios excited just indignation in all Christian countries. It also opened the eyes of statesmen to the fact that the struggle between the Turks and Greeks was a war of extermination, which, if it continued long, would compel the governments of Christian Europe to interfere. Many impartial and enlightened persons already deemed it impossible for Mussulmans and Christians to live together any longer in peace under the Othoman government. Their mutual hatred was supposed to have produced irreconcileable hostility. The immediate effect, therefore, of the sultan's cruelties in this case was to interest the feelings of many liberal men and sincere Christians in favour of the independence of Greece, as the only means of establishing peace in the Levant. Greek committees were formed to aid the arms of Greece, and subscriptions were collected to assist the suffering Chiots. No charity could be more deserved, for no sufferers were ever more guiltless of causing the calamities which had overwhelmed them. For generations the unfortunate inhabitants of Chios had been the peaceable and obedient subjects of the sultan. As a community they had been remarkable for order and patriotism. In their families they were distinguished by mutual affection, and as private

---

[1] The accounts of the massacres at Chios differ chiefly in the numbers of those who are reported to have fallen victims to the cruelty of the Turks. Gordon says that fifteen thousand persons remained in the mastic villages. Tricoupi pretends that only eighteen hundred souls remained, which is a manifest error. It is always difficult, even when no feeling leads to exaggeration, to obtain accurate information concerning numbers. In 1853 the author was assured by persons at Chios who had access to the best means of information, that the population of the island did not then exceed forty-three thousand souls; but others of equal authority said the number was sixty-six thousand, and that ten thousand more were absent gaining their livelihood abroad.

individuals they were considered the most virtuous of the modern Greeks. Never, perhaps, had a better regulated society existed among so large a population, and never was a happy people suddenly struck with a more terrible catastrophe.

Soon after Mavrocordatos heard of the calamity which had laid Chios waste, he left the direction of the Greek government to any man who might succeed in assuming it; or, to speak more correctly, he left the Greek government without any direction, and set off on an ill-judged military expedition into Western Greece. As long as he retained the office of President of Greece, it was his duty to remain at the seat of government, and perform the business of a sovereign. If he considered that he could be more useful as a general on the frontier, it was his duty to resign his civil office, and support the administration of his successor with his military influence. Of all the blunders committed by Mavrocordatos in his long political career, this was the greatest and the most reprehensible. It was absurd to think of directing the administration of a country, without roads or posts, from a corner of the territory; and it was an unworthy and Phanariot ambition which induced him to retain possession of a high office merely in order to exclude a rival from the post, without taking into account the serious injury he inflicted on the cause of order and good government. Even had Mavrocordatos been an able general, his error must have produced bad consequences in Greece; but as he was destitute of every quality necessary to make a good soldier, his conduct brought disgrace on himself and calamity on the Greek government.

It was absolutely necessary for the Greek government to make every exertion to carry on the war vigorously in Western Greece. The death of Ali Pasha, and the suppression of the Revolution in Agrapha, in the chain of Pindus, in Thessaly, and in Macedonia, exposed Greece to be invaded by the whole of the Othoman troops under the command of the seraskier of Romelia. It became known early in spring that the sultan was assembling two powerful armies, in order to invade Eastern and Western Greece simultaneously. To direct these operations, Khurshid Pasha fixed his headquarters at Larissa, where he summoned all the ayans and timariots of Romelia to join his standard. An army composed in great part of Albanians, under the command of Omer Vrioni, was entrusted with the attack on Western Greece.

The first object of the Greek government was to support the Suliots, in order to enable them to keep possession of their native mountains, and thus retain a strong force on the flank of any Turkish army that might advance to force the pass of Makronoros, or attempt to cross the Ambracian gulf. After much precious time had been wasted, it was at last resolved to send large reinforcements to the Suliots, and to make a powerful diversion in their favour by invading Epirus. What was most wanted to give efficiency to the operations of the Greeks was order. Instead of endeavouring to introduce order, Mavrocordatos increased the disorder by assuming the command of the army—if indeed it is permissible to designate the undisciplined assemblage of armed men under a number of independent chiefs by the name of an army.

Before Mavrocordatos quitted Corinth, which was then the seat of government, a decree of the legislative assembly invested him with extraordinary powers as governor-general and commander-in-chief in Western Greece, but limited his absence from the seat of the central government to two months. On assuming the command of the army he was anxious to render his force efficient; but he was so ignorant of the first elements of military organization, that he neither knew what he ought to do nor what he ought to leave undone, so that his military operations were generally determined by accident.

Mavrocordatos quitted Corinth in high spirits, attended by a band of enthusiastic volunteers, ready to dare every danger. About one hundred foreign officers had arrived in Greece to offer their services; but in consequence of the neglect of military discipline on the part of the executive body, and indeed of the Greeks generally, they were allowed to remain unemployed. Not wishing to quit the country at the commencement of a campaign, they now offered to serve as simple soldiers, in order to teach the Greeks by their example the value of military discipline, and let them see what a small body of regular soldiers could perform. This noble offer was accepted without a due sense of its almost unexampled generosity. Mavrocordatos, who had as insatiable a rapacity for honours, or rather titles, as Kolokotrones for coined money, made himself colonel of this gallant band, which was called the corps of Philhellenes. The first Greek regiment, six hundred strong, under Colonel Tarella[1], a body of Ionian volunteers, and a band of Suliots under Marco Botzaris, also accompanied the president, who was joined at Mesolonghi by three hundred Moreots under the command of Geneas Kolokotrones, the second son of the old klepht, and by seven hundred Mainates. Kyriakules Mavromichales had already been sent forward to open a communication with the Suliots by sea.

Mavrocordatos marched from Mesolonghi with little more than two thousand men, and with only two light guns. His high-sounding titles and his dictatorial powers alarmed the captains of armatoli, who viewed his presence with jealousy, and showed little disposition to aid his enterprise. Some were already beginning to balance in their own minds the advantages to be gained by joining the cause of the sultan. Local interests directed the conduct of others. It was the season of harvest, and many soldiers and petty officers were obliged to watch the collection of the tenths and the rents of national property, in order to prevent the officers of the government, the primates, or the captains of armatoli, from cheating them of their pay. In a considerable part of Aetolia and Acarnania, some of the best soldiers in Greece were prevented from joining Mavrocordatos by the necessity of providing for their own subsistence.

The avowed object of Mavrocordatos was to assist the Suliots; and it must be remembered that, though this was wise policy, the cause of the Suliots was not then regarded by the people of Western Greece with any enthusiasm. That fierce Albanian tribe had not yet identified its cause with that of the independence of Greece.

The Greek troops advanced to the neighbourhood of Arta, and Mavrocordatos established his head-quarters at Kombotti. Gogos, the most influential chieftain in this district, had distinguished himself the year before, when the Turks

---

[1] Prince Demetrius Hypsilantes, with all his inactivity, formed the first regiment of regular troops in Greece. He found in Balestos an able officer to discipline and command it. Had Balestos been properly supported, a good body of regular troops might have been formed, but unfortunately everything in Greece was made a question of personal jealousy or party passion.

were repulsed in their attempts to force the pass of Makronoros. He now occupied the advanced position of Petta, on the left bank of the river of Arta, with about a thousand men. A blood feud existed between Gogos and Marco Botzaris; for Gogos was the cause of the death, if he was not the actual murderer, of Botzaris' father. But now a reconciliation was effected by the prudence of Mavrocordatos and the patriotism of Botzaris. Gogos, who was seventy years of age, was a brave soldier and an able captain of armatoli; but he was full of the passions nourished by a life spent in a tyrant's service, and, like most of the chiefs who had served Ali Pasha, he cared little for humanity, nationality, and liberty. He was also strongly imbued with Oriental prejudices. He hated all Franks, and disliked Mavrocordatos because he lived much in the society of European officers, wore the Frank dress, and made a show of introducing military discipline. He was acute enough to observe that the principles of centralization which Mavrocordatos put forward (often very unnecessarily in theory, when it was out of his power to introduce them in practice) would ultimately diminish the authority and the profits of the chiefs of armatoli. Gogos likewise distrusted the success of the Revolution; and this, added to his excessive selfishness, induced him to open communications with the Turks of Arta, so that he was already engaged in negotiations with the agents of Omer Vrioni before Mavrocordatos arrived at Kombotti. Mavrocordatos purchased the apparent submission of Gogos to his authority as governor-general of Western Greece, by tolerating a dangerous degree of independent action on the part of the veteran chieftain, and overlooking the secret correspondence which it was known that he carried on with the enemy.

The Turks made an attack on the Greeks in their position at Kombotti with a strong body of cavalry, but they were repulsed in a brilliant manner by the regular troops. Shortly after, General Normann, who acted as chief of the staff to Mavrocordatos, advanced with the regular troops, and occupied the position of Petta, while the commander-in-chief himself retired to the rear, and fixed his head-quarters at Langada, about fifteen miles from the main body of his army. Only a hundred men remained to guard Kombotti, though that place protected his line of communication. While the Greeks were changing their position, they beheld the first disastrous event of this campaign. As they marched along the hills, they saw three Turkish gunboats from Prevesa destroy the small Greek flotilla in the gulf.

The occupation of Petta was one of those ill-judged movements which incapable generals frequently adopt when they feel that their position requires immediate action, and yet are incapable of forming any definite plan. It rendered a battle inevitable, and yet no preparations were made for the engagement. Gogos seemed inclined to wait for the result of this battle to determine his future conduct. Until it was lost, he was therefore, to a certain degree, a supporter of the cause of Greece.

The Turks had assembled a large force at Arta, and Petta is only about two miles from the bridge over the river which flows under the walls of that city. A victory in such a position was not likely to bring any decided advantage to the Greeks; a defeat must inevitably insure the destruction of their army. The Turks had six hundred well-mounted cavalry to cover their retreat, and guns to defend the passage of the bridge. The Greeks had thrown forward the whole regular force into the advanced position of Petta, apparently with the intention of pushing forward a large body of irregulars to the relief of Suli. Yet when that project was abandoned, the regular troops, who formed the main body of the Greek army, were allowed to remain as its advanced guard, without being covered by a screen of irregulars.

General Normann, who commanded at Petta in consequence of the absence of Mavrocordatos, though persuaded that the position of the troops was very injudicious, would not order the regular troops to quit their position without an express order from the commander-in-chief. But as the position was exposed to be attacked hourly, he wished at least to construct some field-works for his defence. A small supply of tools was obtained with some difficulty, but it could hardly be expected that the corps of Philhellene officers should work at the spade under the burning sun of Greece in July, when the Greeks themselves seemed little disposed either to work or to fight. At this crisis the presence of Mavrocordatos at Petta might have smoothed every difficulty. He might have paid peasants, or, by his example, induced the Greek troops to labour; while the foreign officers, under such circumstances, would willingly have set an example to the regular regiment and the Ionian volunteers. The presence of Mavrocordatos was absolutely necessary in order to render Petta defensible, and Mavrocordatos was not present.

While the regular troops remained idle in their exposed and dangerous quarters, news reached the camp that the Suliots were reduced to extremity. Marco Botzaris determined to make a desperate attempt to cut his way through the Turkish posts at the head of his own little band, and encourage his countrymen to prolong their resistance until a decisive engagement should decide the movements of the Greek army. Botzaris obtained the consent of Mavrocordatos to his rash scheme, and he counted on receiving vigorous support from Varnakiottes, who had eight hundred armatoli under his orders. Varnakiottes, however, gave Marco Botzaris no assistance, and Gogos informed the Turks of his projected expedition; for Gogos hated the Suliots almost as much as he hated the Franks. The result was, that the attempt to penetrate through the Turkish lines was defeated, and the troops who accompanied Botzaris were compelled to return. He commenced his retreat from Plaka on the 12th of July.

This failure determined Gogos to draw closer his relations with the Albanians in Arta. His first overt act of treachery was a plot for separating the Philhellenes from the rest of the regular troops. The headlong courage and the well-managed rifles of these volunteers made them a redoubtable enemy; and in case of their absence from Petta, the Turks expected to carry the Greek position by storm without difficulty.

Colonel Dania, an experienced but rash officer, commanded the corps of Philhellenes as lieutenant-colonel. He would only take his orders directly from Mavrocordatos, and when he had no precise orders from the commander-in-chief, he assumed the liberty of acting on his own responsibility. He resolved to support the movement of Marco Botzaris, and neither the advice nor the commands of General Normann could prevent his listening to Gogos, who urged him to go off in pursuit of a body of Albanian troops, in order to prevent these Mussulmans from attacking the rear of the Suliots, who had advanced from the Greek camp. The Ionian battalion followed Dania's example. The Albanians were overtaken at Vrontza, on the road from Arta to Joannina; but the guides sent forward by Gogos gave sufficient warning to the enemy, by firing off their muskets, to allow them to decamp. Dania's troops, worn out by fatigue, and unable to obtain provisions, were now compelled to return, and they fortunately decided on effecting their retreat so promptly, and executed it with such celerity, that they forestalled all interruption. Their unexpected return to Petta rendered part of the treacherous scheme of Gogos abortive.

Geneas Kolokotrones chose this conjuncture to quit the head-quarters of Mavrocordatos at Langada. His desertion at this momentous crisis was not authorized by any orders from the central government. He abandoned the Greek army before the Turks, in order to serve the personal and party intrigues of his father in the Morea. The power of Mavrocordatos, as President of Greece, Governor-General of Western Greece, and Commander-in-Chief of the Greek forces in Epirus, was so completely nominal, that he could not prevent this petty chieftain from deserting the army on the eve of a battle.

Though a decisive engagement was now inevitable, it was evident that victory would bring little but glory to the Greek arms. The want of provisions rendered it impossible to advance to the relief of Suli, and the want of artillery rendered it impossible to attack Arta. On the other hand, defeat was sure to cause the total destruction of all the regular troops in the Greek service, who were imprudently thrown out in advance of the main body of the army. Prudence demanded that the Greeks should immediately fall back on the pass of Makronoros. A retreat, however, could only be ordered by Mavrocordatos, and he was already far in the rear.

The Turks in Arta were at this time commanded by Mehemet Reshid Pasha, well known to the Greeks during the war by the name of Kiutayhé[1]. On the 16th of July

---

[1] Reshid held a command at Kutaya (Cotyaeum) before coming into Epirus.

DEFEAT AT PETTA.

he marched out of the town at the head of five thousand infantry and six hundred cavalry to attack the Greek army, which did not exceed three thousand men. The whole force of the pasha was directed against the advanced position of the Greek regulars at Petta. General Normann, from a misplaced sense of honour, persisted in occupying the first line, in opposition to the opinion of several experienced European officers, who were supported by the advice of Marco Botzaris. It was argued that, if the Greek irregulars retarded the advance of the Turks by skirmishing in the usual way in front of the regulars, a favourable moment might be selected for a decisive attack on those who advanced as assailants. This plan was rejected, and the corps of Philhellenes, the Greek regiment, and the Ionian volunteers, remained in their advanced position, supported only by two guns. The irregulars occupied a ridge of hills rising behind Petta, of which Gogos held the key by occupying an elevation on the extreme right.

The Turks made their dispositions leisurely, and drew out their whole force in the plain, in order to attack the position occupied by General Normann on three sides at the same time. Their first assault was made with some vigour, but it was repulsed without the regulars suffering any loss. The assault was renewed in a series of desultory attacks for about two hours. During this time, Reshid Pasha was marching a large body of Albanians to turn the Greek position from the north. As the movement of these troops, though concealed from General Normann at Petta by intervening hills, was perfectly visible from the heights occupied by Gogos, this operation could only have been rendered successful by the treachery of that chieftain. A height visible from every part of the Greek position must have been left purposely unoccupied. This height was scaled by the Mussulmans, who planted the Othoman standard on its summit. As soon as they received an answer to their signal from the troops in the plain, they descended, to throw themselves on the rear of the regulars with loud shouts. The troops of Gogos, instead of attacking these Albanians on their flank, fled in the most shameful manner, and their flight spread a panic through the whole body of the Greek armatoli, who abandoned their positions in the wildest confusion. The small body of

Albanians was thus allowed to pass directly over the ground which had been occupied by the Greek irregulars, and to fall upon Petta in the rear.

On the other side, Reshid Pasha, as soon as he saw his Albanians in possession of the key of the Greek position, pushed forward strong bodies of infantry to attack Petta in front, and supported the assault by a brilliant charge of cavalry, which he led in person. The two field-pieces of the Greeks were taken; the Philhellenes were surrounded, and most of them were immediately shot down; but a few defended themselves for a short time, and twenty-five forced their way through the Turks with fixed bayonets. The rest fell gallantly. The Greek regiment under Tarella, and the Ionians under Panas, were both broken by the heavy fire of the infantry, followed up by charges of cavalry. More than half of their men lay dead on the field, and none allowed themselves to be taken prisoners. On this disastrous day four hundred of the best soldiers in Greece perished[1].

The defeat at Petta was a severe blow to the progress of order. It destroyed all confidence in political organization as represented by Prince Alexander Mavrocordatos, and in military discipline as represented by the corps of Philhellenes. Mavrocordatos made shipwreck of his political authority; art and science were banished from military operations, and the practices of brigandage henceforth regulated the tactics of the armies of Greece. The power of the central government ceased with the destruction of the regular troops. From this time until the arrival of Count Capodistrias, the whole public administration in liberated Greece was a scene of anarchy. The place of a central government was nominally held by the faction which could obtain possession of the largest share of the national revenues.

The fate of the regular troops had also the misfortune to lead the Greeks generally to form a false estimate of the value of discipline in military operations. They did not observe the real state of the case, which was, that two thousand Albanian infantry, supported by six hundred well-

---

[1] The best account of the battle is by Raybaud, and his map is better than that of Gordon. Tarella was slain at the side of Dr. Treiber, whose escape from the hospital is mentioned by Gordon. Treiber now holds the rank of chief of the medical staff of the Greek army, and enjoys the esteem of all who know him (1860).

mounted cavalry, by gaining a dominant position, were enabled to destroy three corps of regular troops, which, when united, did not exceed eight hundred men, and that this success was entirely due to the circumstance of five hundred infantry being unexpectedly brought to attack the rear of a position which was entrusted to the defence of two thousand Greek irregulars. But the enemies of political order, Romeliot captains of armatoli, Moreot primates, and chiefs of klephts, availed themselves of the blunders of Mavrocordatos as a general, and of the misfortune of the regulars at Petta, to persuade the Greeks generally that military science was inapplicable to Greek warfare. The adoption of the bayonet and the tactics of a battalion were supposed to be sure means of devoting Greek soldiers to slaughter. This false doctrine found a responsive echo in the breasts of many who were sincerely devoted to their country's cause. Mavrocordatos, without any military knowledge, supposed that he was a heaven-created general; others, who had studied philology and medicine, were satisfied that, though they knew nothing of the duties of a soldier, they were fully qualified to act as generals of irregulars. The Greek character is naturally averse to the restraints of discipline. Thus the rude military system of the Albanian race was imposed on the Greeks during their revolutionary war. The captains of armatoli reared by Ali Pasha, and the klephts of the Morea, men without any military training but that of robbers, became the virtual rulers of Greece. The Turks were allowed to precede the Greeks in reforming their military system, and their adoption of regular troops contributed to turn the tide of success in favour of Mohammedanism.

After their victory, the Turks occupied Kombotti, but did not immediately advance to seize the pass of Makronoros. Gogos attempted to conceal his treacherous conduct, and joined Mavrocordatos with the other fugitive captains of armatoli at Langada. But when the governor-general fled towards Mesolonghi, he openly deserted to the Turks, who confirmed him in his authority as captain of armatoli in the district of Arta.

Kyriakules Mavromichales, who had landed at Splanga, on the coast of Epirus, found it impossible to communicate with the Suliots. On the same day on which Reshid Pasha attacked the Greeks at Petta, Omer Vrioni ordered Achmet Bey and several other Albanian chiefs to attack the position of the Mainates. The day was marked as a fortunate one in the Turkish calendar. Kyriakules and Achmet Bey were both killed at the commencement of the engagement. The Greeks immediately abandoned their position, and, embarking the body of their leader, sailed to Mesolonghi, where the remains of Kyriakules Mavromichales were interred with due honour[1].

The defeats at Petta and Splanga, followed by the defection of Gogos, rendered the position of the Suliots desperate. They had wasted the immense magazines of provisions and military stores which Ali Pasha had deposited in the impregnable castle of Kiapha. Fortunately for them, Omer Vrioni, who was now pasha of Joannina, was so anxious to get quit of such dangerous neighbours that he granted them favourable terms of capitulation. The treaty was negotiated, and its faithful execution guaranteed by the British consul at Prevesa; for the Suliots had heard so much of the violation of treaties by the Greeks in the Peloponnesus, and they were afraid to trust the Turks. On the 16th of September 1822 they bade a final adieu to their native mountains. They received from the Turks the sum of two hundred thousand piastres, and retired with their families to the Ionian Islands, where they remained quietly for some time without taking part in the Greek Revolution. A few only departed secretly from Cephalonia, and joined Marco Botzaris and other Suliots already serving in Western Greece.

According to the plan of operations formed at the Porte, Reshid Pasha ought to have been able to co-operate with the Othoman fleet which visited Patras in July, to take on board Mehemet, who had been appointed to succeed Kara Ali as capitan-pasha. But the pasha of Arta had not been able to pass Makronoros; and it was not until the middle of August that he ventured to transport his little army over the Ambracian gulf, and occupy Lutraki. Very little skill and activity on the part of the Greeks would have frustrated this under-

---

[1] General Gordon, who was personally acquainted with Kyriakules, says, 'Greece lost in him one of her most skilful and dauntless warriors, and, by a singular coincidence, his old antagonist at Valtetzi, Achmet Kehaya, was killed in the same skirmish.' Vol. i. p. 393.

taking. A few gunboats would have insured to the Greeks the complete command of the Gulf of Arta, and the boats might have been manned by hardy fishermen from Mesolonghi. But there was no directing mind in Western Greece to employ the interval of inaction that followed the battle of Petta, while Omer Vrioni was forced to watch the Suliots, and Reshid was unable to act without his assistance.

The people of Acarnania, seeing that no preparations were made for their defence, fled to the Ionian Islands for protection. Thousands of families crossed over into the island of Kalamos, which the British authorities set apart as a place of refuge for the unarmed peasantry, who were allowed to enter it without being subjected to the expense and the embarrassments caused by the quarantine regulations, which were then enforced with great strictness in the Mediterranean. At a later period, when the devastations of the Albanians and the armatoli had rendered Acarnania almost a desert, and deprived its agricultural population of the means of subsistence, the British government distributed many thousand rations daily to the starving Greeks, and many soldiers as well as peasants owed their lives to the benevolence of the English at Corfu.

In the mean time, while Reshid Pasha was preparing to invade Greece, the captains and primates, instead of uniting to oppose the Turks, quarrelled among themselves for their shares of the national revenues. The district of Agrapha, or rather that portion which still adhered to the cause of the Revolution, was laid waste by the civil broils of Rhangos and Karaiskaki; the province of Vlochos was the scene of a struggle for power between Staikos and Vlachopulos; Kravari was pillaged alternately by Pillalas and Kanavos. Treachery also spread among the captains of armatoli. Varnakiottes, the captain of Xeromeros, Andreas Iskos, the captain of Valtos, Rhangos, and a primate called George Valtinos, all deserted to the Turks, and made their submission to Omer Vrioni. Mavrocordatos and John Tricoupi were cognizant of the dealings of Varnakiottes, which they authorized with the vain hope of profiting by a semblance of treachery. They were foiled at this dishonourable game. While they were flattering themselves that they were making use of Varnakiottes to cheat Omer Vrioni, that astute Albanian purchased the services of their agent, and showed himself an abler diplomatist than the wily Phanariot or the selfish Mesolonghiot.

Omer Vrioni, having at last finished his business with the Suliots, marched southward at the head of six thousand men. He occupied the pass of Makronoros, which he found unguarded, and was joined by Kiutayhé, who had now four thousand men under his command. The Othoman army reached the plain of Mesolonghi without meeting any opposition; but as the greater part of the country afforded no supplies, the Turks were dependent for their provisions on their magazines in Arta and Prevesa until they could open communication with Patras, and from thence with the Ionian Islands.

The siege of Mesolonghi was commenced on the 6th of November 1822. The aspect of affairs was extremely unfavourable to the Greeks. Gogos, Varnakiottes, Iskos, Rhangos, and Valtinos, had deserted their countrymen, and were serving the Turks. The people, however, everywhere remained true to the Revolution, and Mavrocordatos redeemed his previous errors by the resolute manner in which he encouraged them to defend Mesolonghi. When other civilians quitted the place on the eve of the siege, he declared that he would remain in the town as long as a man could be found to fight against the Turks. The garrison consisted of about six hundred soldiers, but the boatmen worked the guns in the batteries, and the people laboured to complete a line of fortifications. Mesolonghi was then protected by a low mud wall, with a ditch little more than six feet deep and about sixteen feet wide. Heavy rain had rendered the bottom of the ditch a soft mass of tenacious clay, which made it impassable to a man on foot. Fourteen guns were mounted on the ramparts; but the flanking defences were very imperfect, and to an unmilitary eye it seemed easy for the besiegers to carry the place by storm. It is not impossible that this would have happened, had the Turks made a bold attack immediately on their arrival, for it would have been easy to fill up the ditch with fascines. They delayed the assault, and by skirmishing before the wall, revealed to the Greeks the great advantage they derived from their low rampart of mud.

SIEGE OF MESOLONGHI.

Mavrocordatos was accompanied by several officers who were able to teach the Mesolonghiots how to avail themselves of the peculiar advantages which their defensive works afforded, and how to place their guns in the best positions. The houses in the town were too low to suffer from a cannonade, and the shells of the enemy generally sank harmless in the mud of the unpaved streets and courts. Not a single person was killed by their explosion.

The traitor chiefs who accompanied Omer Vrioni persuaded him that many Greeks in Mesolonghi were disposed to follow their example Reshid Pasha in vain urged him to try an assault, but the Albanian pasha preferred negotiation. The Greeks profited by his delay. While they treated with him, they opened negotiations at the same time with Yussuf Pasha of Patras, who had sent over some vessels to blockade Mesolonghi by sea.

On the 20th of November, the arrival of seven Hydriot brigs compelled the Turkish vessels to retire to Patras, and, three days after, one thousand men crossed over from the Morea under the command of Petrobey, Zaimes, Deliyani, and other leaders. The defenders of Mesolonghi then broke off their negotiations with the Turks, and sent Omer Vrioni a message, that if he really wished to become master of Mesolonghi, he might come and take it. He determined to make the attempt. The garrison was now increased to two thousand five hundred men, who were amply supplied with ammunition recently sent from Leghorn.

The Turkish army did not now amount to eight thousand men. The Greeks of Acarnania and Aetolia had assembled in their rear, and were beginning to attack and plunder their convoys. Provisions and military stores were becoming scarce in their camp. Omer Vrioni, convinced of the impossibility of continuing the siege through the winter, at last resolved to make an attempt to carry the place by storm, and in case of failure to raise the siege.

The assault was made on Greek Christmas day (6th January 1823), at the earliest dawn. The storming party expected to surprise the Christians at their church ceremonies, but the besieged, warned by a Greek fisherman in the pasha's service, were ready to receive their assailants. Two thousand two hundred well-armed men were either posted under cover on the ramparts, or concealed in the nearest houses to act as a reserve. The storming party consisted of eight hundred Albanian volunteers. One division of the assailants attempted to scale the wall on its eastern flank, while another endeavoured to penetrate into the town by wading through the shallow lagoon round the eastern extremity of the wall. The assault was masked by a heavy fire of musketry along the whole of the Turkish lines. The besieged cautiously watched the approach of the storming columns, which were allowed to advance within pistol-shot; they then poured a deadly volley into their ranks. The effect of this fire was decisive. The storming parties, which had expected to surprise the Greeks, were themselves surprised; they broke, and fled in confusion. Desultory attempts were made by the Turks to renew the attack, and for some hours there was an incredible waste of ammunition on both sides. The loss of the Turks in the assault was said to have exceeded two hundred men. Most of those who were wounded in the lagoon perished in the water. The Greeks lost only four men killed.

Six days after this defeat, Omer Vrioni broke up his camp and retired to Vrachori, from whence, after a short rest, he marched to Karvascrai unmolested by the armatoli. Indeed, in his retreat from Mesolonghi, he met with no obstacle except the swollen torrent of the Achelous. In the camp he abandoned the Greeks found ten guns, four mortars, and a small quantity of balls and empty shells, but he carried off all his powder.

Varnakiottes, distrusted both by the Turks and Greeks, fled to Kalamos, where he remained for some time under English protection. The other traitors, Iskos, Rhangos, and Valtinos, soon deserted Omer Vrioni, and again joined their countrymen.

CHAPTER III.

FALL OF ATHENS.—DEFEAT OF DRAMALI.—FALL OF NAUPLIA.

Preparations of Sultan Mahmud for reconquering Greece.—Defensive measures of the Greeks.—Their quarrels and intrigues.—Odysseus murders Noutzas and Palaskas.—Capitulation of Athens.—Massacre of men, women, and children.—Expedition of Dramali.—Corinth retaken.—Turkish plans of campaign.—First capitulation of Nauplia.—Flight of Greeks from Argos.—They defend the Larissa.—Patriotic conduct of Prince Demetrius Hypsilantes.—Numbers of the Greek forces in the field.—Defeat of Dramali.—Greeks retain possession of the Burdjé.—Operations of the hostile fleets.—Second capitulation of Nauplia.—Turkish population of Nauplia saved by Captain Hamilton of the Cambrian.—Kanares again destroys a Turkish line-of-battle ship.—State of the naval warfare between the Greeks and Turks.—State of affairs at Athens.—Odysseus gains possession of Athens.—Concludes an armistice with the Turks.

THE state of Sultan Mahmud's relations with Russia in 1822, and the destruction of Ali Pasha's power, allowed him to make his first great effort for reconquering Greece. The success of his measures in suppressing the revolutionary movements over Macedonia, Thessaly, and Epirus, persuaded him that the task would not be difficult, and the plan of campaign which he adopted was well devised.

The Greeks were blockading Nauplia, the strongest fortress in the Morea. Its relief was to be the first object of the campaign. A large army was assembled at Larissa, under the venerable Khurshid, seraskier of Romelia. A second army under Omer Vrioni, the pasha of Joannina, was instructed to co-operate with the movements of the principal force. We have already seen that Omer Vrioni was entirely occupied during the whole year by the Suliots and the affairs of Acarnania. The army of Khurshid was ordered to force the Isthmus of Corinth and advance to Nauplia, where it was to be joined by the Othoman fleet. After receiving the necessary supplies of provisions and military stores, it was to march on to Tripolitza, and establish its head-quarters in the great Arcadian plain. It was supposed that the fleet would have already thrown supplies and reinforcements into the fortresses of Coron, Modon, and Patras, and that the army would find no difficulty in establishing communications between these positions and the central camp. The Morea being thus cut up into several sections, and the population deprived of reciprocal support, it was thought they would be reduced to lay down their arms before winter arrived. The sultan overlooked the insuperable difficulties which the corruption of the Othoman administration presented to the execution of any plan which required activity and honesty on the part of many officials. The self-interest of each pasha suggested some modification in the execution of his instructions, and the subordinate officers sought to evade the performance of their duties, unless it was in their power to render the execution of them a means of gain.

As soon as the horses of the Othoman cavalry had eaten green barley in spring, according to the immemorial custom of the Turkish timariots, the seraskier ordered Dramali to advance into the valley of the Spercheus, and review the army. Before this was effected, the Greeks made an attempt to destroy the advanced guard of the Turkish army in Zeituni.

The Areopagus of Eastern Greece acted as a kind of executive committee of the central government. In the month of April 1822, it collected considerable supplies of provisions and ammunition, assembled about eight thousand men near Thermopylae, and hired thirty small vessels to act as transports in the Gulf of Zeituni. Odysseus was appointed commander-in-chief, and all the local chiliarchs and captains of municipal contingents either joined the army or held themselves ready to act as a reserve.

The central government at Corinth decreed that three thousand Peloponnesians should march to reinforce the Romeliot troops. But the central government made no arrangements for carrying its decree into execution; for the attention of Mavrocordatos was then absorbed by the preparations necessary for his own campaign as commander-in-chief in Western Greece. Only about seven hundred Moreots, under the command of Niketas, marched to join Odysseus.

The Greek army in Eastern Greece was divided into two bodies. The first division, under Odysseus and Niketas, embarked at Palaeochori, on the shore at the foot of Mount Knemis, and, crossing the gulf, occupied the villages of Stylida and Aghia Marina. Instead of pushing rapidly forward to attack the Turks, they wasted their time in idleness, without even throwing up proper field-works at Stylida. The Turks were more active; they marched down from Zeituni to attack their enemies, and compelled the Greeks to abandon Stylida, and concentrate their whole force at Aghia Marina, where they constructed an earthen redoubt, and remained inactive behind its mud walls for a fortnight.

The second division marched by land to Patradjik (Hypata), but only gained possession of about one half of the town, and from this it was soon expelled by the reinforcements which the Turks detached from Zeituni.

Odysseus, finding that he could not venture to advance beyond his lines at Aghia Marina, proposed to abandon that position. Niketas approved of his resolution, but the members of the Areopagus who accompanied the expedition opposed the evacuation of this useless post. An unseemly public discussion between Drosos Mansolas, a patriotic pedant, who knew nothing of military matters, and Odysseus, who, though he had no patriotism, had a good deal of military experience, took place on the deck of one of the transports. But the imprudence and the inutility of keeping a considerable force in the lagoons at Aghia Marina were so manifest that the Areopagus was compelled to yield. It had persisted, however, so long as to destroy its authority in the army. The soldiers asserted that it wished to abandon them to be attacked by the whole Othoman army, and they were eager to punish those who proposed that they should merit the glory of the Spartans and win the immortality of Leonidas by their actions. The members of the Areopagus saved themselves by flight, and the troops were relanded on the coast of Locris.

When the supplies of provisions collected by the Areopagus were exhausted, the soldiers ceased to receive either pay or rations, and the army dispersed. A few of the military chieftains who held commands as captains of districts, alone kept their contingents together, and took up their stations on the line of mountains which runs from Mount Oeta along the channel of Euboea.

The members of the Areopagus attempted to remove Odysseus from his command in Eastern Greece. He immediately resigned his commission as chiliarch in the army, and remained at the head of his troops as an independent chieftain. The central government sent officers to supersede him, but he took no notice of its proceedings, and maintained his men by compelling the ephors of districts and the demogeronts of villages to supply him with rations and money from the national revenues and public taxes[1].

Mavrocordatos and his partizans were guilty of a very mean intrigue, which brought discredit on their counsels, while it roused just animosities among their rivals. They elected Prince Demetrius Hypsilantes president of the legislative body. He possessed not one single qualification for the office, and he felt that the object was not to honour him, but to render him either useless or ridiculous. The prince was a brave soldier, and his rival was evidently desirous to exclude him from military employment, where it was certain he would not lose honour, and where he might recover power. Hypsilantes quitted the proffered office, and joined the army in Eastern Greece as a volunteer. On his way he acted with his usual imprudence, displaying the standard of the Hetairia, and not the flag of the Greek state adopted by the national assembly of Epidaurus. He also issued orders in his own name, as if he still arrogated power to himself from being the lieutenant-general of the Hetairia, in defiance of the executive government of Greece. These pretensions involved him in quarrels with the central authorities, and induced him to contract alliances with Odysseus, Niketas, and other military

---

[1] Speliades, in his Memoirs, represents Eastern Greece at this time as a scene of innumerable selfish intrigues. He reports that almost every political and military chief was engaged in a plot to supplant or to assassinate some rival. He enjoyed better opportunities of acquiring accurate information on these topics than Tricoupi or Gordon. Compare 'Απομνημονεύματα, i. 307, 314, 315, 346, 349-350.

CONDUCT OF THE GREEK LEADERS. 281

chiefs. Hypsilantes was a man of a very dull mind, and extremely slow in penetrating men's characters; he never could persuade himself that the Hetairia was already a vision of the past; nor could he believe that the Russian government was not on the eve of assisting the Greeks, and of assuming the direction of the Greek Revolution.

It is difficult to trace the mazes of the intrigues carried on by the principal men in Greece at this time. There were many actors; every actor had many projects, and each actor modified his plans and his conduct as circumstances and his personal views changed. Mavrocordatos, Hypsilantes, Kolokotrones, and Odysseus were pursuing adverse schemes. Every subaltern officer and secondary politician had his own ends to gain. No one in office seemed to watch the storm that was gathering in Thessaly; nor did any one appear to take any measures to ward off the blow which the Turks were about to strike at the independence of Greece.

Mavrocordatos chose this ill-timed moment to make efforts to extend the arbitrary power of the central government, and his efforts were so ill-judged that the contests he awakened were contests of persons, and not of principles. John Kolettes was acting as minister of war, and he employed in that office the lessons he had learned at Ali Pasha's court, working with imperturbable gravity and cunning to form a party which would adhere to him because it would require his assistance. His gravity and his portly figure gave him the appearance of a sagacious and honest man. To Mavrocordatos and his colleagues in the public administration he pointed out the evils of the Albanian military system, with which no man was better acquainted. To the captains and military chieftains with whom he transacted business as minister of war, he made himself appear both as a personal friend and as a defender of their cause. Negris, who was chief secretary of state, concealed the policy of Kolettes by thrusting himself forward as the champion of the central power.

To destroy the authority of Odysseus in Eastern Greece was the first object of the executive body. Alexis Noutzas and Christos Palaskas were sent to supersede him in the chief command, which he continued to exercise. These men were the friends of Kolettes, and were nominated by his influence. Noutzas was a man of considerable talent, and having been secretary of Ali Pasha, exercised some authority over many Greeks who had served at Joannina. Palaskas was the Suliot whose defection has been mentioned [1], and who had subsequently served both England and Russia. In the English service he attained the rank of captain; and when the Greek light infantry was disbanded in 1818, he settled at Joannina. Alexis Noutzas was now named civil governor of Eastern Greece by the central executive, and entrusted with the control over the finances and commissariat. Palaskas was destined to replace Odysseus in his military command. These appointments were kept secret, but Odysseus was perfectly informed of the intentions of the government to remove him from his command, and his suspicious nature persuaded him that Mavrocordatos and Kolettes had resolved to assassinate him. Noutzas and Palaskas, who were versed in the policy of Ali Pasha, seemed fit agents for this design. The two commissioners arrived at the camp of Odysseus at Drakospelia when they believed that chief was absent at Dadi. He had been duly informed of their movements, and he met them with polished hypocrisy, assuring them of a hearty welcome. After a banquet, under a magnificent wild pear-tree that grows near a small chapel of St. Elias, the commissioners retired to sleep in the building. The next morning was fixed for holding a conference at the head-quarters of Odysseus, but during the night Noutzas and Palaskas were both murdered. The assassins were well known. The crime spread alarm over all Greece. The report that Odysseus was about to join the Turks was generally believed. The members of the Areopagus sought refuge at Salona, where the spirit of the Galaxidhiots placed a check on the tyranny of Panouria. Hypsilantes was summoned by the government to return to the Peloponnesus, and obeyed the order.

Public attention was diverted from the crimes of Odysseus, and the anarchy which these crimes produced in Eastern Greece, by the conquest of Athens. The capitulation of the Acropolis was an event of great moral and military importance to the Greek cause at this moment. The name of Athens magnified the success throughout the whole

[1] P. 51.

civilized world, and the possession of a fortress on the flank of the Turks, who might venture to invade the Peloponnesus, would enable the Greeks to embarrass their assailants.

Omer Vrioni had relieved the Acropolis in the autumn of 1821. Before leaving Attica he supplied the garrison with provisions and military stores. But the besieged neglected to take proper precautions for securing a supply of water. They did not clean out their cisterns during the winter, and they trusted to the imperfect enclosure of the Serpendji for the defence of the only good well they possessed[1]. The winter proved extremely dry. The Greeks drove the Turks from the Serpendji; so that when the supply of water in the cisterns was exhausted, the garrison was forced to capitulate.

The capitulation was signed on the 21st of June 1822. The Turks surrendered their arms, and the Greeks engaged to convey them to Asia Minor in neutral ships. The Turks by the treaty were allowed to retain one-half of their money and jewels, and a portion of their movable property. The bishop of Athens, a man of worth and character, who was president of the Areopagus, compelled all the Greek civil and military authorities to swear by the sacred mysteries of the Oriental Church that they would observe strictly the articles of the capitulation, and redeem the good faith of the nation stained by the violation of so many previous treaties.

The Mussulmans in the Acropolis consisted of 1150 souls, of whom only 180 were men capable of bearing arms, so obstinately had they defended the place. After the surrender of the fortress, the Mussulman families were lodged in extensive buildings within the ruins of the Stoa of Hadrian, formerly occupied by the voivode. Three days after the Greeks had sworn to observe the capitulation, they commenced murdering their helpless prisoners. Two ephors, Andreas Kalamogdartes of Patras and Alexander Axiottes of Corfu, had been ordered by the Greek government to hasten the departure of the Turks. They neglected their

---

[1] The Serpendji is the enclosure indicated in Colonel Leake's plan, lying between the rock of the Acropolis, the Odeon of Herodes Atticus, and the theatre of Bacchus.

duty. The Austrian and French Consuls, Mr. Gropius and M. Fauvel, on the other hand, did everything in their power to save the prisoners. They wrote to Syra during the negotiations to request that the first European man-of-war which touched at that port should hasten to the Piraeus. Unfortunately, before any ship of war arrived, the news reached Athens that the Othoman army had forced the pass of Thermopylae. Lekkas, an Attic peasant, whose courage had raised him to the rank of captain, but who remained a rude Albanian boor, excited the Athenian populace to murder their Turkish prisoners, as a proof of their patriotic determination never to lay down their arms. The most disgraceful part of the transaction was, that neither the ephors nor the demogeronts made an effort to prevent the massacre. They perhaps feared the fate of the mollah of Smyrna[1]. A scene of horror ensued, over which history may draw a veil, while truth obliges the historian to record the fact. The streets of Athens were stained with the blood of four hundred men, women, and children. From sunrise to sunset, during a long summer day, the shrieks of tortured women and children were heard without intermission. Many families were saved by finding shelter in the houses of the European consuls. But the consuls had some difficulty in protecting the fugitives; their flags and their persons were exposed to insult; and the Greeks were threatening to renew the massacre when two French vessels, a corvette and a schooner, entered the Piraeus and saved the survivors.

Three hundred and twenty-five persons who had found an asylum in the French consulate were escorted to the Piraeus by a party of marines with loaded muskets and fixed bayonets. The party was surrounded by Greek soldiers on quitting the town, who brandished their arms and uttered vain menaces against the women and children whom the French protected, while crowds of Athenian citizens followed the soldiers shouting like demoniacs. When this party of prisoners was safely embarked and the French vessels sailed, the Greeks appeared suddenly to become sensible of the baseness of their conduct. Shame operated, and all the Turks who remained in the Austrian and Dutch consulates

---

[1] P. 190.

were allowed to depart unmolested. England, being only represented by a Greek, was helpless on this occasion. Lekkas, who was the first to urge this massacre, was taken prisoner by the Turks when visiting Attica as a spy, after the capitulation of the Acropolis in 1827, and was impaled at Negrepont.

Sultan Mahmud invested Dramali with the command of the army destined to invade Greece, and to increase his authority he created him seraskier. This promotion displeased the veteran Khurshid, who desired to retain the supreme direction of the whole Othoman force as the only commander-in-chief, and from the moment that Dramali was elevated to an equal rank and held an independent command, he became indifferent to the fate of his rival. Khurshid has been reproached with not giving the army of the Morea sufficient support; but we must remember that Dramali marched from Thessaly at the head of a force amply sufficient for all the objects of the campaign. Eastern Greece submitted to his authority, and he had it in his power to take proper measures for keeping open his communications with Zeituni and Larissa. The envy of Khurshid did not cause the negligence of Dramali.

The Othoman army, when it mustered on the banks of the Spercheus, amounted to more than twenty thousand men. Of these about eight thousand were cavalry, composed chiefly of feudal militia, under the command of five pashas and several Sclavonian Mussulman beys of Macedonia and Thrace. A considerable portion of the infantry had served at the siege of Joannina. Abundant supplies of provisions and military stores were collected at Zeituni, and ample means of transport were provided. A member of the great feudal house of Kara Osman Oglou was appointed to superintend the commissariat.

The army moved from Zeituni in the beginning of July 1822; and since the day when Ali Kumurgi crossed the Spercheus to reconquer the Morea from the Venetians in 1715, Greece had not witnessed so brilliant a display of military pomp. But in the century which had elapsed the strength of the Othoman empire appeared to have melted away. Ali Kumurgi was attended by a corps of military engineers, who opened roads for his artillery, and who constructed bridges for his ammunition-waggons. Dramali moved only with such baggage as could be transported over rugged limestone paths on the backs of mules and camels. Ali Kumurgi enforced the strictest discipline[1]; Dramali could not prevent every Albanian buloukbash from laying waste the country.

The ill-timed disputes of the central government with Odysseus left Eastern Greece without defence. Even the troops sent to guard the passes over Mount Geranea fell back and fled from the great derven before the Turks arrived. The defence of the Acrocorinth had been entrusted to a priest, Achilles Theodorides, because he belonged to the faction of the Notaras family, not because he had the slightest knowledge of military matters. He murdered the Turkish prisoners in his hands, and abandoned the impregnable fortress of which he was the commandant, though it was amply supplied with provisions. On the 17th of July, Dramali took up his quarters in Corinth, where he was joined by Yussuf Pasha from Patras.

The Turkish leaders held a council of war to decide on their future operations. The seraskier was a man of a sanguine disposition and haughty character, ignorant of mountain warfare, and full of contempt for the Greeks. The ease with which he had marched through Eastern Greece and the flight of the garrison of Corinth increased his confidence. The terror which his presence seemed to have inspired, the facility with which he had obtained forage for his cavalry, and the certainty, as he supposed, of being joined by the Othoman fleet at Nauplia, induced him to believe that he was destined to overrun the Morea with as much ease as Ali Kumurgi. He proposed, therefore, to march with his whole army to Nauplia. The pashas under his immediate orders, who looked to him for promotion, warmly supported his opinion. The beys who commanded the feudal cavalry agreed to this plan, as it promised a speedy termination of the campaign.

Two men alone maintained a different opinion. Yussuf Pasha, and Ali Pasha, a great landlord of Argos, both knew the country and the enemy. They proposed making Corinth

---

[1] *See* vol. v. p. 222.

the head-quarters of the Othoman army, and forming large magazines of provisions and military stores under the protection of its impregnable citadel. A Turkish squadron already commanded the Gulf of Lepanto; by fortifying Kenchries a second squadron might be maintained in the Saronic Gulf. The insurgents in the Morea would then be cut off from all communication with the armatoli in Romelia. They also recommended dividing the Othoman army into two divisions. The main body under the seraskier would be amply sufficient to relieve Nauplia and recover possession of Tripolitza. The second division might march securely along the Gulf of Lepanto, supported by the Turkish ships which had brought Yussuf to Corinth. It would compel the inhabitants of Achaia to submit to the sultan, and secure for the Turks all the profits of the currant crop, and of the custom-duties on the exportation of Greek produce. These divisions of the army, when established firmly at Tripolitza and Patras, could then concert their ulterior movements in co-operation with the garrisons of Coron and Modon, and with the Turkish fleet. This judicious plan was rejected, and the seraskier advanced without even waiting to form magazines at Corinth.

The direct road from Corinth to Nauplia and Argos passes through a narrow defile called the Dervenaki (anciently Tretos), but there is another difficult road parallel to this at a short distance to the east. There are also two other roads, —one making a circuit to the west by Nemea and the village of St. George, and the other passing considerably to the east by Aghionoros and the pass of Kleisura. Dramali passed the defile of the Dervenaki without encountering opposition; and with inconceivable rashness and stupidity he left no guard to keep possession of the pass, and neglected to occupy the villages of St. George and Aghionoros, to secure his flanks, and prevent his communications with Corinth from being interrupted. He established his head-quarters in the town of Argos on the 24th of July, having sent forward Ali Pasha, attended by 500 cavalry, to assume the command of the garrison of Nauplia, immediately on entering the plain.

Had the Greeks acted with good faith, they would have gained possession of Nauplia before Dramali reached Argos. At the end of June, the garrison was reduced to such extremities by hunger, that the Turks signed a capitulation, saying that it was better to be quickly massacred than to die slowly. This capitulation stipulated that the Turks should surrender the fortress, and deliver up their arms and two-thirds of their movable property, on condition that the Greeks should allow them to hire neutral vessels to transport them to Asia Minor, and supply them with provisions until the arrival of these vessels. Hostages were given by both sides for the exact fulfilment of the treaty, and the Greeks were put in possession of the small insular fort that commands the port, called the Burdjé.

The Greek government immediately sent secretaries into Nauplia to register the property of the Turks, and these officials were accused of behaving like Bobolina and the agents of Kolokotrones at Tripolitza. Both parties soon considered it for their advantage to retard the execution of the capitulation. The members of the Greek government contrived to make large sums of money by secretly purchasing the property of the Turks, by selling them provisions, and promising to aid them in escaping with their families. After Mavrocordatos had abandoned the presidency of Greece to play the general in Epirus, the members of the executive body and the Greek ministers enjoyed little confidence, and deserved even less. They pretended that no money could be raised to pay the freight of the neutral vessels necessary for transporting the Turks in Nauplia to Asia Minor; but the allegation was a mere pretext for enabling their secretaries in the fortress to make larger profits by bargains with the wealthy families in the place. It was well known that, when the Turks signed the capitulation, they were so anxious to escape that they would have deposited the sum necessary to pay the freight of neutral vessels within twenty-four hours. But when they obtained regular rations from the Greek government, and succeeded in purchasing supplies of every necessary from private persons, they endeavoured to prolong their stay until the arrival of Dramali's army, which was known to be on its march to relieve them. They also expected that the place would be revictualled by the Othoman fleet.

Things were in this state when Ali of Argos entered Nauplia to assume the command. His first care was to secure all the hostages, and arrest the secretaries sent into the place by the Greek government. He asserted that the Greek government had repudiated the treaty by neglecting to fulfil its conditions, and he retained the hostages as pledges for the safety of the Turkish hostages in the hands of the Greeks. In this case, self-interest induced both parties to listen to the voice of humanity. Ali's next object was to prepare for a long defence, but Dramali had conducted his operations with such improvidence that he could obtain only scanty supplies from the Othoman commissariat. The fate of Nauplia depended on the fleet, and all hopes of immediate assistance from that quarter were destroyed by the news that it had passed round the Morea, in order to take on board Mehemet, the new capitan-pasha, who was then at Patras. The convoy destined for Nauplia, which it was escorting, could not be expected for some weeks.

This proceeding of the Othoman fleet entailed ruin on the expedition of Dramali. As he had brought with him very scanty supplies of provisions and ammunition, common prudence required him to remain at Corinth until he was informed that the fleet had landed supplies for his army in Nauplia. And when he found himself at Argos without provisions, it was so evident that he could not advance farther into the Morea, that he ought immediately to have fallen back on Corinth, and sent to Patras for a few transports to proceed up the gulf and replenish his magazines. Yet though he could throw no supplies of provisions into Nauplia, he wasted his time uselessly at Argos, ashamed to admit that he had done wrong in not listening to the counsels of Yussuf Pasha.

The conduct of the Greek government was not wiser than that of the seraskier. Some of its political leaders, particularly the Zinzar Vallachian, Kolettes, and the Ionian exile Metaxas, were men whose names in future years were connected with the worst party proceedings that stained the Revolution. They now showed themselves utterly unfit for their high station. Greece at this conjuncture was saved by the constancy and patriotism of the people, not by the energy of the government or the valour of the captains. The members of the government fled from Argos as the advanced-guard of Dramali issued from the Dervenaki. In their hurried flight, the ministers abandoned the national archives and a large quantity of plate which had just been collected from churches and monasteries for the public service. The military followers of ministers and generals, who had swarmed into Argos to share the plunder of Nauplia, took advantage of this moment of confusion to plunder their countrymen.

The reign of anarchy was established. During the night cries of alarm were raised, and fire-arms were discharged in the quarter of Argos near the road that leads into the town from Corinth. Men shouted that the Turks were entering the place. Thousands of the inhabitants, particularly the refugees from Smyrna, Kydonies, and Chios, rendered more timid than others by the calamities they had witnessed, rushed from their houses in frantic terror, leaving all their property behind. The roads to Lerna and Tripolitza exhibited scenes of confusion and of misery which would fill a volume. Crowds pressed blindly forward without knowing what direction they had taken; family followed family for hours in sad procession; men hurried along carrying bundles snatched up at the moment of flight, or bending under the weight of sick parents; women and children, suddenly roused from sleep and half clad, strove to keep up with the crowd of fugitives, but many sank exhausted by the roadside, weeping, praying, and awaiting death at the hands of their imaginary pursuers.

In the mean time the houses they quitted were plundered with remorseless rapacity. Horses, mules, and working oxen were carried off from the stables of the peasants, and laden with booty at the houses of the citizens. The residence of the executive body, the property of the members of the legislative assembly, and most of the private dwellings in the town, were sacked by bands of Greek klephts before the Turks entered it. The small but choice library of Theodore Negris, the secretary of state, was carried off on a stolen horse by a Mainate soldier. The horse fell lame; the Mainate then sold it for two dollars to an officer who bought it to carry water to his soldiers, who were posted on the hill above Lerna; to his surprise he found himself in possession of a library. Some days after, the books came into the possession of Captain Hastings, who informed Negris of the fate of his library; but that restless politician never expressed a wish to repossess them, perhaps never afterwards had a place where he thought them safe.

Amidst these disorders, some of the local magistrates of the Albanian population of Argolis took prompt and prudent measures for defending their country. Before they retreated, they burned all the grain and forage which they could not carry off, and filled up some of the wells. Nikolas Stamatelopulos, the brother of Niketas, who had commanded the principal body of troops employed in the long blockade of Nauplia, distinguished himself as much by his judgment at this period as he had previously done by his personal valour. He retired to the eastward, and took up his post in the plain of Iri.

When Dramali established his head-quarters in Argos, he had about ten thousand men under his immediate orders, and nearly one-half of this force consisted of cavalry. While the ministers, senators, and chieftains of Greece were escaping on board the vessels anchored at Lerna, and their followers were plundering the town, a body of volunteers threw themselves into the ruined castle on the Larissa, where the ancient acropolis of Argos stood. The patriotic conduct of these men during the general panic was so meritorious that the name of every one ought to be handed down to the gratitude of Greece. They defended the exposed position they occupied with great firmness, and their success revived the courage of the troops who had posted themselves at Lerna, and emboldened them to return and occupy the line of the Erasinus.

On this occasion Prince Demetrius Hypsilantes regained the esteem of his countrymen by displaying unwonted activity in addition to his usual courage. The members of the legislative body, from mean jealousy, summoned him to take his place on board the ship in which they had sought refuge, and act as their president. He despised the summons of the cowards, and remained among the people, where they ought to have been. Though he had personal reasons for being dissatisfied with the conduct of Kolokotrones, who had treated him with rudeness and insolence after the taking of Tripolitza, he now hastened to confer with that influential chieftain, in order to urge him to immediate action. The energy and patriotism of Hypsilantes electrified everybody he addressed. Petrobey, the nominal commander-in-chief in the Peloponnesus, and Krevatas, a primate of Mistra, caught something of his enthusiasm. The Peloponnesian Senate stepped forward and assumed the duties of government which the executive body had abandoned. The people had flown to arms without waiting for the call of their official leaders. Captains and primates were carried along by the general impulse. The patriotism of Greece was completely roused.

Hypsilantes returned to the mills of Lerna, where, finding that the body of volunteers in the Larissa was hard pressed, he boldly threw himself into the castle, accompanied by several young chiefs. The force in the Larissa was now increased to one thousand men, but it was scantily supplied with provisions and water. The Turks kept the place closely invested, and defeated two attempts of the Greeks at Lerna to throw in additional supplies. But the object of the volunteers who first occupied the place was gained. The progress of the Othoman army had been arrested, until the delay had given time to a Greek force to assemble strong enough to meet it in the field. Hypsilantes and the greater part of the garrison of the Larissa withdrew, therefore, in the night, but a few of the original band of its defenders determined to keep possession of the place until they had finished their last loaf. Their escape then became extremely difficult, but on the night of the 1st of August they succeeded in forcing their way through the Turkish line of blockade. A Mainate officer, Athanasios Karayanni, boasted of being the first to enter the place, and the last who quitted it.

The position of the Greeks was now improving rapidly, while that of the Othoman army was becoming untenable. Upwards of five thousand troops were assembled at the mills of Lerna. The position was fortified by low walls, and flanked by the artillery of several Greek vessels. The Erasinus, which issues in a large stream from a cavern about two miles from Argos, confines the road leading to Lerna and Tripolitza between a rocky precipice and several dilapidated artificial channels formed to conduct the water to turn mills, or to irrigate plantations of maize and cotton. Lower down, towards the sea, the plain is intersected with ditches and planted with vineyards. The line of the Erasinus consequently offered ground well suited to the operations of the irregular infantry of the Greeks, and almost impracticable for the Turkish cavalry. On this line numerous skirmishes took place, and the Greeks at last gained a decided superiority.

Other strong bodies of Greeks assembled on all the mountains which overlook the plain of Argos. The season was singularly dry. The Turkish horsemen found great difficulty in procuring forage, and they were often obliged to skirmish with their enemy while watering their horses. Provisions grew scarce, and the soldiers dispersed in the vineyards, and devoured grapes and unripe melons. Disease soon weakened the army, and before Dramali had occupied Argos a fortnight, he found himself compelled to fall back on Corinth.

On the 6th of August he sent forward the first division of his army to occupy the passes. The Greek force in the field now exceeded the Othoman army in number. About eight thousand men, nominally under the command of Kolokotrones, who had been elected generalissimo or archistrategos, but really under the immediate orders of a legion of chiefs, occupied the hills from Lerna to the Dervenaki. Another corps of two thousand men had established itself at Aghionoros under Niketas, the archimandrite Dikaios, and Demetrius Hypsilantes; and a third body of about two thousand sturdy Albanians from Kranidi, Kastri, and Poros, had joined the troops of Nikolas Stamatelopulos, and advanced to watch Nauplia. The want of system which reigned wherever Kolokotrones commanded, or pretended to command, prevented the Greeks from occupying permanent stations and erecting redoubts, which would have compelled the army in Argos to submit to any conditions the Greeks might have thought fit to impose. Had Kolokotrones possessed any military capacity, he might have cut off Dramali's retreat, and secured the immediate surrender of Nauplia. Every hour added to the numbers of the Greeks. Almost every village sent a contingent of armed men to the spot which some local chief considered the best position for cutting off a portion of the seraskier's baggage.

The advanced-guard of the Othoman army consisted of one thousand Albanians. These men, who had studied the country as they advanced with the instinct of warlike mountaineers, took the western road by the plain of Nemea, and kept so good a look-out that they contrived to pass the troops of Kolokotrones, stationed at St. George, without even a skirmish. It is difficult to ascertain whether the Moreots mistook these Albanians for a body of Greek troops on account of the similarity of their dress, or whether they avoided an encounter with veteran warriors, and allowed them purposely to pass unmolested.

A body of Dramali's cavalry, sent forward about the same time to occupy the Dervenaki, found the Greeks intrenched in the pass. The first division of the Turks, therefore, took the road by Aghio-Sosti. The leading horsemen had almost gained the open valley below the village of St. Basili, when Niketas, who had hastened to meet them from Aghionoros, fell on their flank, and threw himself into the valley before them. Niketas seized a position commanding the junction of the road of Aghio-Sosti with that issuing from the Dervenaki. The rest of the Greek troops who followed Niketas, under Dikaios and Hypsilantes, attacked the right flank of the Turks. The Othoman cavalry charged boldly to the front, but recoiled under the steady fire of the select body of marksmen on the low eminence occupied by Niketas. The little hill overlooked a ravine, through which the Turks were forced to pass. A fierce struggle took place at this spot. The Delhis attempted to force their way onward with desperate valour, but the Greeks encumbered the passage through the ravine by shooting a number of horses, and then heaping over them the bodies of their riders. The attack was renewed several times, and at last such numbers pressed forward from behind that retreat became impossible. A desperate body of well-mounted horsemen then dashed past the Greeks, and, gaining the open ground in the plain of Kortessa, reached Corinth without further opposition. Above the ravine the scene of slaughter was terrible. Confusion spread along the whole Turkish line. The Greeks who attacked it in flank covered the road with dead and wounded. Their principal object was to cut off the baggage, shoot baggage-mules, and secure the booty. The Turks fled in every direction, leaving their baggage to arrest the pursuit of their enemy. Few could make much progress up the side of a rugged mountain, and armed men seemed to spring up out of every bush to attack them. Many abandoned their horses, and succeeded in finding their way to Corinth during the night. Long trains of baggage-mules and camels, and a number of richly-caparisoned horses, were captured. The booty gained was immense.

The conduct of Niketas on this occasion received well-merited praise. He executed a judicious manœuvre with rapidity and courage. He also gained the prize of personal valour in the combat, by rushing sword in hand on a body of Turkish infantry which was endeavouring to form a mass in order to attack his position. His soldiers gave him the name of Turkophagos (the Turk-eater), as the legionaries of Rome saluted their general Imperator; and the title was adopted by all the Greeks. Kanares, Miaoulis, Marco Botzaris, and Niketas, were men whose valour and patriotism raised them above envy.

This defeat stupified Dramali : he remained a whole day inactive. But as it was impossible to continue in the plain of Argos, he moved forward on the 8th of August by the road of Aghionoros. This road was guarded by the archimandrite Dikaios. As the Turks slowly wound their way up the steep ascent of the Kleisura, the archimandrite opposed them in front, and Niketas and Hypsilantes, who had marched to his support from Aghio-Sosti and Aghio-Basili, assailed them on their left flank. The Turks were soon thrown into confusion. The Greeks on this occasion directed their attention exclusively to gaining possession of the baggage; and while they were occupied in cutting it off from the line of retreat, a chosen troop of Delhis succeeded by a brilliant charge in clearing the front, and enabled Dramali, with the main body of the cavalry, to escape to Corinth. But the seraskier purchased his personal safety by abandoning his military chest and the whole baggage of his army to the Greeks.

Had the Greeks combined their movements with skill, not a man of the Turkish army could have escaped. The seraskier's retreat was foreseen several days before it commenced, and each leader took measures for securing to himself and his followers as large a share of booty as possible; but no general measures were adopted for destroying the Turkish army, and no information was transmitted of the enemy's movements from one corps to another. The honours of victory are often obtained by those who have little share in the fight. In the present case, though the troops under the immediate orders of Kolokotrones had no share in the glories of the two days' combat, they gained a considerable share of the booty, and Kolokotrones, because he was called the commander-in-chief in the Peloponnesus, was supposed to be the conqueror of Dramali. Thousands of Moreots returned to their native villages enriched with the spoil they had gained, and they attributed their good fortune to the generalship of Kolokotrones. The imaginary tactics of the old klepht were said by his ignorant partizans to have caused the destruction of a mighty army of thirty thousand men. History, which is too often the record of party passions and national prejudices, has repeated the fable.

The great success of the Greeks on this occasion, like the great disaster at Petta, increased the popular aversion to military discipline, and strengthened the general conviction that patriotism could conduct military operations better than science. Tactics were supposed to be useless against the Turks, whom the orthodox believed God had delivered into their hands.

The remains of Dramali's army melted away at Corinth. The seraskier himself died there in December 1822.

Nauplia had now nothing to rely on but the Othoman fleet. The Greeks retained possession of the small insular fort called the Burdjé, while Dramali's army occupied Argos, and after his departure they made some efforts to gain possession of the fortress. A French officer, Colonel Jourdain, offered to burn all the houses in the town with incendiary balls fired from the guns in the Burdjé. The destruction of the houses in which the wealthy Turks had accumulated considerable stores of provisions during the armistice, would have compelled the garrison to surrender in a short time. There were, however, still some officers and soldiers in the Greek army who opposed this measure, because they thought it would diminish their share of the long-expected plunder to be obtained at the surrender of the fortress.

When Ali of Argos entered Nauplia and assumed the command of the garrison, there were only about twenty Albanians of Kranidi in the Burdjé, and their captain was a boatman, ignorant of the very elements of gunnery. Colonel Jourdain was ordered by the Greek government to enter the place and put his plan into execution. He contrived to excuse himself from remaining in it, but Captain Hastings, assisted by two young artillery officers—Hane, an Englishman, and Animet, a Dane—volunteered to make the attempt to burn Nauplia with the colonel's combustible balls. A noisy cannonade was kept up between the batteries of Nauplia and this little insular fort, which was situated under the guns of the fortress, and ought to have been knocked into a heap of broken stones and mortar in six hours. The firing on both sides continued for several days without inflicting much loss on either party. Jourdain's balls, when thrown into the town, made a vast deal of smoke, but set nothing on fire. The Turkish shot generally flew past the Burdjé without hitting it. But what with the stray shots that did not miss, and the concussion of the artillery in the place, the walls were so shaken that it became dangerous to fire the heaviest guns, which were alone of any effect against Nauplia. Fortunately, just as things reached this state, the retreat of Dramali's army induced the garrison of Nauplia to stop their fire. The Kranidiots then intimated to Hastings and his companions that their presence was no longer necessary; that they could not expect a share of the booty in Nauplia; and that no rations would in future be supplied to them. Hastings was not a man to remain in a place where there was no danger, when his presence was considered unnecessary.

On the 20th September, the Othoman fleet, consisting of eighty sail, including transports, was descried from the beacon of Hydra, and on the following morning the capitan-pasha stood in towards the island of Spetzas with a fair wind, and the Gulf of Nauplia open before him. The Greek fleet, consisting of sixty sail, chiefly brigs of from eight to fourteen guns, stood out to engage the Turks. A distant cannonade ensued; but it was in the power of the capitan-pasha to have sent on his transports to Nauplia under the escort of his corvettes and brigs, while with his heavy ships he opposed the Greeks. The weather was fine, the wind very light, and the capitan-pasha both fool and coward. The Christians acted with timidity as well as the Turks, and the firing was carried on at such a distance that neither party sustained any damage. In the evening the wind died away.

For three days the Othoman fleet remained manœuvring idly off Spetzas. The capitan-pasha did not venture to approach near enough to the Christians to use his heavy guns with effect. The Albanians of Hydra and Spetzas showed neither skill nor daring in the employment of their fire-ships. Kanares was not present. On the night of the 23rd the wind blew into the gulf, a circumstance rather rare at this season of the year; but the capitan-pasha, instead of pressing all sail, hove to during the night. At the time there was not a single Greek ship near enough to prevent the transports from reaching Nauplia. The cowardice of the capitan-pasha prevented him from profiting by this favourable opportunity. On the morning of the 24th the Othoman fleet proceeded up the gulf with a light breeze.

The Greek fleet was then nine miles distant, hugging the island of Spetzas. Twenty-three men of war and five fire-ships were in advance. The breeze freshened, and had the Turks done their duty, Nauplia would have been relieved without difficulty or danger. But the capitan-pasha sent forward only an Austrian merchantman, without the escort of a single man-of-war. He appears to have trusted to the protection of the Austrian flag. A Greek vessel detached near the head of the gulf issued from her place of concealment and captured this hired transport. After this abortive attempt the capitan-pasha made no further effort to throw supplies into Nauplia. He quitted the gulf, and sailed for Suda on the 26th of September.

The naval skirmishes in the Gulf of Nauplia were disgraceful to the Turks, and by no means honourable to the Greek navy. The Albanian seamen of Hydra and Spetzas showed very little enterprise on this trying occasion. Their exertions were probably paralyzed by their ignorance of naval tactics, and by their fear to move far from their own islands, which they had neglected to put in a proper state of defence. The captains of a few ships displayed some boldness, but in general the crews were neither steady nor obedient. In spite of the incapacity of the Turks, the only serious loss sustained by the Othoman fleet was the result of accident. An Algerine frigate bore down on a Greek fire-ship, mistaking it for a brig of war. The crew set fire to the train before taking to their boats, and the flames burst out as the Algerine ran alongside to board it. The sails of the frigate caught fire, and fifty men perished before the flames could be extinguished and the fire-ship set adrift.

The approach of the capitan-pasha so terrified the Kranidiot garrison in the Burdjé that the fort was abandoned, and for nearly forty-eight hours that fort was only occupied by a Hydriot who had served in the French artillery, by a Spetziot sailor, and by Hane, the young English artillery officer, who had returned a few days before. After this interval, twenty Ionians arrived to replace the Kranidiots, and shortly after the garrison was reinforced by a party of Albanian Christians from the Chimariot mountains, under the command of an officer who had served in the Albanian regiment of Naples. On the 24th of September, when the Turks in Nauplia felt sure of immediate relief from the capitan-pasha, they opened a heavy fire on the Burdjé from every gun which could be brought to bear on it; but when the Othoman fleet retired, their fire ceased, and was never again renewed.

The defence of Nauplia was now prolonged only from fear of treachery on the part of the Greeks. In the beginning of December children were frequently found dead in the streets; women were seen wandering about searching for the most disgusting nourishment, and even the soldiers were so weak from starvation that few were fit for duty. The fortress on the high rock of Palamedes, which towers above the town, was abandoned by its garrison. No one could carry up provisions. The soldiers descended to obtain food, and were too weak to remount the long ascent. The Greeks, hearing of their retreat, entered the place before daybreak on the 12th December 1822.

The conquest of the Palamedes was announced to the Greek troops, who guarded the passes towards Corinth, by volleys of the whole artillery of the place. Kolokotrones soon arrived; other captains quickly followed. A negotiation was opened with the Turks in the town, and a capitulation was at last concluded.

The Greeks engaged to transport all the Mussulmans in Nauplia to Asia Minor, and to allow them to retain a single suit of clothes, a quilt for bedding, and a carpet for prayer.

Kolokotrones and the captains hindered all soldiers, except their own personal followers, from entering the place. To the mass of the soldiers who clamoured for admittance, they pleaded the orders of the Greek government, and the necessity of preventing a repetition of the massacres of Monemvasia, Navarin, Tripolitza, and Athens. The soldiers replied that Kolokotrones paid no attention to the orders of government unless when it suited his purpose; that the previous massacres had been caused by the faithlessness and avarice of the captains who cheated the troops; and they declared that they would not allow Kolokotrones and his confederates to appropriate to themselves everything valuable in Nauplia. Large bodies of soldiers assembled before the land-gate, and threatened to storm the place, murder the Turks, and sack the town. The avarice and faithlessness of Kolokotrones and the military chiefs had done more to make the Greek army a mere rabble than the absence of all military discipline.

On this occasion Greece was saved from dishonour by the arrival of an English frigate on the 24th of December. The Cambrian was commanded by Captain Hamilton, who was already personally known to several of the Greek chiefs then present. His frank and decided conduct won the confidence of all parties. He held a conference with Kolokotrones and the Moreot chieftains, whose Russian prejudices induced them to view the interference of an English officer with great jealousy. He was obliged to tell them in strong language, that if, on this occasion, they failed to take effectual measures for the honourable execution of the capitulation, they would render the Greek name despicable in civilized Europe, and perhaps ruin the cause of Greece. The chiefs respected Hamilton's character; the wild soldiers admired his martial bearing and the frankness with which he spoke the whole truth. He took advantage of the feeling he had created in his favour to act with energy. He insisted on the Greek government immediately chartering vessels to embark the Turks, and to facilitate their departure he took five hundred on board the Cambrian[1]. He thus saved the Greeks from the dishonour of again violating their plighted faith, but he inflicted a great sacrifice on England. Sixty-seven of the Turks embarked on board the Cambrian died before reaching

---

[1] Nine hundred were embarked in the Greek transports.

CONDUCT OF CAPTAIN HAMILTON. 301

Smyrna. The typhus fever, which they brought on board, spread among the crew, and several fell victims to the disease. Captain Hamilton was the first public advocate of the Greek cause among Englishmen in an influential position, and he deserves to be ranked among the greatest benefactors of Greece.

Ali of Argos and Selim were the two pashas who commanded in Nauplia, and as both refused to sign the capitulation, they were detained as prisoners by the Greeks.

Public opinion among the Greeks at this time was not generally favourable to Captain Hamilton's conduct, though the contrary has been subsequently asserted. The journal of a Philhellene who was at Tripolitza observes that the Greeks were in great choler against the English for having insisted on the immediate embarkation of the Turks. Captain Hastings confirms this also in his journal[1].

The capitan-pasha, after remaining a short time at Suda, sailed through the Archipelago unmolested, and anchored between Tenedos and the Troad. The contingents of the Greek fleet from the Albanian islands remained inactive in the ports of Hydra and Spetzas, and neglected to take advantage of the well-known inactivity and cowardice of Mehemet Pasha. But another brilliant exploit of Kanares threw a veil over their shortcomings. By his persuasion, the community of Psara fitted out two fire-ships.

On the 10th of November 1822 the Othoman fleet was riding at anchor without a suspicion of danger. At daybreak, Kanares and his companion approached without exciting any attention. Two line-of-battle ships were anchored to windward of the rest of the fleet. Kanares undertook the more difficult task of burning the leeward ship. The breeze which brought up the Greek fire-ships had hardly reached the Turks, who, under the influence of the current of the Hellespont flowing through the channel of Tenedos, were not swinging head to wind. Kanares, with his cool sagacity, observed

---

[1] Hastings went on board the Cambrian on the 5th January, 1823, and saw five hundred Turks embarked. He adds: 'Much difference of opinion exists among the Greeks on the conduct of Captain Hamilton; but I feel convinced that he saved the lives of the Turks by his prompt measures, and thus did a great service to Greece.' A few days after, at Hydra, he writes: 'I found here, as at Nauplia, various opinions concerning Captain Hamilton's conduct, but respectable people here were in his favour.'

this circumstance, and ran his enemy aboard abaft the fore-chains on the larboard side. The fire-ship was to windward, the sails nailed to the masts, the yards were secured aloft by chains, and everything was saturated with turpentine, so that in an instant the flames blazed up higher than the main-top of the seventy-four, and enveloped her deck in a whirlwind of fire. There was no time for the crew to escape. Those who leaped into the sea perished before they could reach the distant shore. The ships at anchor cut their cables and made sail. The loss of the Turks is said to have reached eight hundred men.

The flag-ship of the capitan-pasha, which Kanares had left as a sure prey to his companion, escaped. It was already swinging to the breeze when the Greek ran his fire-ship under its bowsprit. In consequence of this ill-judged position, the fire-ship fell off and drifted away to leeward. The employment of fire-ships seems to have required the cool judgment and unflinching determination of Kanares to insure success. The Othoman fleet, which dispersed in its first access of terror, soon reassembled at the Dardanelles; but one corvette went on shore on Tenedos, and another was abandoned by its crew, and found floating a complete wreck in the Archipelago. Constantine Kanares and the crews of the two fire-ships returned safely to Psara in their boats. The hero was received by his countrymen with universal enthusiasm. Envy for once was speechless in Greece. By the hand of one man, the sultan had lost two line-of-battle ships and nearly two thousand men during the year 1822. Yet the naval operations of the year revealed to a scientific observer like Frank Hastings that the Greek navy, in its actual state, was unable to continue a prolonged contest with the Othoman fleet.

The sultan could not send to sea a more incapable officer than Mehemet Pasha; nor was it likely that worse manned ships would ever quit the port of Constantinople than those he commanded. Yet, under these disadvantages, the Othoman fleet had thrown supplies into the fortresses of Coron, Modon, Patras, and Lepanto, and had twice navigated the Archipelago, without sustaining any loss which could not be easily repaired. Sultan Mahmud had obtained the conviction, that all the skill and enterprise of the Greeks could not secure for their light vessels any decided advantage over the inert masses of the Turkish ships. A prolonged naval war must therefore exhaust the resources of Greece, while it would be sure to improve the efficiency of the Turkish seamen. Some modification in the naval forces of the Greeks was evidently necessary to give them a decided victory. Hastings urged them to adopt the use of steam, heavy artillery, and shells fired horizontally, in order to confound their enemy with new engines and new tactics. His advice was rejected by the men of influence among the Greeks, who believed that their own fire-ships would secure them the victory. But this could only have happened if every Greek fire-ship had found a Kanares to command it, and if every Othoman fleet should be sent to sea with a capitan-pasha as incapable as Mehemet [1].

The greatest losses inflicted on the Turks this year were by the desultory expeditions of the Psarians and Kasiots. The Psarians cruised incessantly along the coast of Asia Minor, from the Dardanelles to Rhodes. The Kasiots infested the coasts of Karamania, Syria, and Egypt. Hardly a single Turkish coaster could pass from one port to another. On one occasion all the vessels in the port of Damietta were plundered, and three ships laden with rice, which were on the eve of sailing to supply the Pasha's fleet at Alexandria, were carried off to Kasos. These daring exploits, however, only enriched the captains and crews of the privateers engaged, and they weakened the Greek navy, by alluring some of the best ships and sailors to seek their private gain instead of serving the public cause.

The misconduct of the central government and the crimes of Odysseus left Eastern Greece in a state of anarchy during the summer of 1822. Even at Athens order was not established, though the social condition of the inhabitants afforded peculiar facilities for organizing a regular administration. There were no primates in Attica who exercised an influence like Turkish beys or Christian Turks—no men who, like Zaimes and Londos in Achaia, could waste the national revenues in maintaining bands of armed followers far from the scene of actual hostilities; nor was there any military influence powerful enough to reduce the province to the condition of an armatolik. The Greek population of the city

---

[1] See the Memorandum by Captain Hastings, in Appendix.

of Athens was unwarlike. The Albanian population of Attica served in several bands under local captains of no great distinction. Many of the native soldiers, both citizens and peasants, were small landed proprietors, who had a direct interest in opposing the introduction of the irregular military system, to which Greece was rapidly tending. They united with the local magistrates and the well-disposed civilians in striving to organize a local militia capable of preserving order. Power was very much divided, and administrative talent utterly wanting. Every man who possessed a little influence aspired at command, and was indifferent to the means by which he might acquire it. Athens, consequently, became a hotbed of intrigue; but it would be a waste of time to characterize the intriguers and to describe their intrigues. Something must nevertheless be told, in order to explain the result of their folly and selfishness.

An Athenian citizen employed by the central government to collect the public revenues was murdered by the soldiery, who wished to seize the national resources, and make Attica a capitanlik of armatoli. An Athenian captain gained possession of the Acropolis, and displayed more insolence and tyranny than had been recently exhibited by any Turkish disdar. He was driven from power by another Athenian; but against the authority of his successor constant intrigues were carried on. The shopkeepers of the city at last imagined that, like the Turkish janissaries at Constantinople, they could unite the occupations of hucksters and soldiers, and under this delusion they undertook to garrison the Acropolis themselves, instead of forming a corps of regular troops. As might have been foreseen, each man did what seemed good in his own eyes, anarchy prevailed, and the persons possessing anything to lose sent a deputation to Prince Demetrius Hypsilantes, inviting him to come and take the command of the Acropolis. He arrived at Megara, but the soldiery in the Acropolis refused to receive him as their leader, and in order to secure a powerful patron, they elected Odysseus as their general, and offered to put him in possession of the fortress. He hastened to seize the prize, and hurrying to Athens with only a hundred and fifty men, was admitted into the Acropolis on the 2nd of September 1822. The authority of Odysseus was recognized by the

Athenians as the speediest way of putting an end to a threatening state of anarchy.

Attica was thus lost to those who, from their opinions and interests, were anxious to employ its resources in consolidating civil order and a regular central administration, and was thrown into the scale of the Albanian military system, which soon extended its power over all liberated Greece.

As soon as Odysseus found himself firmly established as captain of Attica, he persuaded the people of Eastern Greece to form a provincial assembly at Athens, where he held the members under his control. This assembly dissolved the Areopagus, and appointed Odysseus commander-in-chief in Eastern Greece. Without waiting for his confirmation by the central executive, he assumed the administration of the revenues of Attica, and compelled the municipality of Athens to sell the undivided booty surrendered by the Turks at the taking of the Acropolis. This money he employed in paying his followers, and in laying up stores of provisions and ammunition in the Acropolis, which all parties had hitherto neglected. He subsequently added a strong angular wall to the Acropolis, in order to enclose a well situated below the northern wing of the Propylaea.

But while he was making these prudent arrangements, he also gratified his malicious disposition by a cruel as well as a vigorous use of his power. Three persons were brought before him accused of treasonable correspondence with the Turks. The truth was, that they favoured the government party; but the accusation afforded Odysseus a pretext for revenging private opposition. He remembered the lessons of his old patron, Ali of Joannina. Two of the accused were hung, and the third, who was a priest, was built up in a square pillar of stone and mortar. As the mason constructed the wall which was to suffocate him, the unfortunate man solemnly invoked God to witness that he was innocent of the crime laid to his charge.

The defeat of Dramali did not cause Khurshid Pasha to relax his efforts for reconquering Greece, but the disasters of the Othoman army in the Morea produced so much discontent in Macedonia, that he could only send forward about eight thousand men to occupy Zeituni and secure the line of the Spercheus. A portion of this force advanced to Salona by the road of Gravia without encountering any serious resistance from Panouria. Mehemet Pasha, who commanded the Turks, after burning a part of Salona fell back to Gravia, in order to form a junction with a body of Albanians which had endeavoured to penetrate to Salona by Daulis and Delphi.

A skirmish took place between the Greeks and Turks near Gravia on the 13th of November, which ended in the defeat of the Greeks. Odysseus lost several officers, and was in danger of falling into the hands of the Albanians in the Othoman army. The season was fortunately too far advanced for Mehemet Pasha to profit by his victory. The country between Gravia and Thebes had been laid waste, and abandoned by the inhabitants. The Greek troops, however, who knew the places to which the people had retired with their cattle, would have hung on the flanks of the Turks, and cut off their communications with Zeituni. Odysseus was nevertheless terrified lest Mehemet Pasha should push boldly forward into Attica, trusting to obtain supplies of provisions from Negrepont. Such a movement might have induced the garrison of the Acropolis to join with the citizens in electing a new commander-in-chief.

From this difficulty Odysseus extricated himself with his usual perfidy. He sent his secretary to Mehemet Pasha to propose an armistice, offering to make his submission to the sultan on condition that he should be recognized as captain of armatoli, and he engaged to persuade the other captains in Eastern Greece to submit on the same conditions. Mehemet had as little intention of executing these conditions as Odysseus, but he accepted them, because they afforded him a pretext for returning to Larissa, where the death of Khurshid rendered his presence necessary.

The long and not inglorious career of Khurshid Pasha had been suddenly terminated by a sentence of death, and his honourable service could not save him from falling a victim to Sultan Mahmud's determination to sweep away every man of influence who adhered to the traditional system, and supported the old administrative organization which he was resolved to destroy.

At the end of November 1822 the Turks withdrew all their troops from Eastern Greece, south of Thermopylae, and took up their winter-quarters in Zeituni. The peasantry commenced sowing their fields, with the expectation of reaping their crops before their enemy could return. The armistice concluded by Odysseus saved them from ruin; and, as they knew nothing of its conditions, they approved highly of his proceedings, and became generally attached to his party.

It is curious to observe by what accidents two men so depraved and morally worthless as Kolokotrones and Odysseus became the objects of hero-worship to the Greeks. The temple of fame is not always 'a palace for the crowned truth to dwell in.'

CHAPTER IV.

THE CONDITION OF GREECE AS AN INDEPENDENT STATE.

Firmness of Sultan Mahmud.—He adopts a conciliatory policy.—A great fire at Constantinople destroys his armaments in 1823.—Plan of campaign for 1823.—Negligence of the Greek government.—Olympian armatoli plunder Skiathos and Skopelos.—Operations of the Turks.—Death of Marco Botzaris.—Advance of the Turkish army.—Siege of Anatolikon.—Operations of the Greek and Turkish fleets.—Escape of eight Psarian sailors.—Violation of Ionian neutrality.—Misconduct of the sailors on board the Greek fleet.—Surrender of the Turks in the Acrocorinth.—Lord Byron in Greece.—First Greek loan contracted in England.—First civil war.—Mohammed Ali engages to assist the sultan.—The political state of Greece in 1824.—Position of Kolettes.—Of Mavrocordatos.—Second civil war.—Evil consequences of the two civil wars.—Wasteful expenditure of the two loans.—Anecdotes.—Military expenditure.—Naval expenditure.

THE successes of the Greeks during the year 1822 established Greece as an independent state, and forced even those who were hostile to the Revolution to acknowledge that the war was no longer a struggle of the Porte with a few rebellious rayahs. The importance of the Greek nation could no longer be denied, whatever might be the failings of the Greek government. The war was now the battle of an oppressed people against a powerful sovereign. The inhabitants of Greece, whether of the Hellenic or the Albanian race, fought to secure their religious liberty and the independence of their country. Sultan Mahmud fought to maintain Othoman supremacy and the divine right of tyranny. Both were supported by strong feelings of religious and national antipathy; but the strength of the Greek cause lay in the hearts of the people, and that of the Turkish in the energy of the sovereign. Between such enemies there could neither be peace nor truce.

THE GREEKS AND THE SULTAN. 309

To the friends of civil and religious liberty the cause of Greece seemed sure of victory. A nation in arms is not easily conquered. Holland established her independence under greater difficulties than those against which the Greeks had to contend, for the power of Philip II. in the seventeenth century was much greater than that of Sultan Mahmud in the nineteenth. Switzerland was another example of the success of patriotism when the people are determined to be free. The people in Greece had adopted that determination, and they neither counted the cost of their struggle, nor shrank from encountering any hardships to gain their end.

The noble resolution of the Greeks and of the Christian Albanians in Greece to live or die free, encountered a firm determination on the part of Sultan Mahmud to re-establish his authority even by the extermination of the inhabitants of liberated Greece. When his fleets were defeated and his armies destroyed; when Russia threatened his northern frontier, and Persia invaded his eastern provinces; when, to meet his expenditure, he was cheating his subjects by debasing his coinage; when the janissaries revolted in his capital, and the timariots and spahis refused to march against the rebellious infidels; when rival pashas fought with one another instead of marching against the Greeks; and when all Turkey appeared to be a scene of anarchy, the inflexible sultan pursued steadily his great object of preserving the integrity of the Othoman empire. While most European statesmen regarded him as a frantic tyrant, he was already revealing to the keen observation of Lord Stratford de Redcliffe the sagacious policy which raised that skilful diplomatist to his profound mastery of Eastern questions. The shattered fabric of the falling empire was for some years upheld by the profound administrative views, the unwearied perseverance, and the iron character of Sultan Mahmud. He was an energetic, if not a great man, and his calm melancholy look was an index to his sagacious and saturnine intellect.

The spectacle of a duel between such a sovereign and the resuscitated Demos of Greece, was a spectacle that deservedly excited the attention of civilized nations. Mohammedanism and Christianity, tyranny and liberty, despotism and law, were all deeply compromised in the result. The massacres at Chios and the defeat of Dramali were considered proofs that the sultan could not reconquer the Greeks, and Christendom could not allow him to exterminate a Christian people. Public opinion—the watch-dog whose bark sounds as an evil omen in the ear of monarchs—began to growl a warning to Christian kings not longer to neglect the rights of Christian nations, and statesmen began to feel that the sympathies of the people in Western Europe were at last fairly interested in the cause of Greece. But the friends of the holy alliance still argued that anarchy was inflicting hourly more misery in Greece than the sultan's government inflicted annually on the Greeks in Turkey; that the extortions of Kolokotrones and Odysseus, and the misgovernment of Mavrocordatos, produced greater evils than the faults of pashas and the errors of Sultan Mahmud; and that the power and resources of the Othoman empire rendered the success of the Greek Revolution hopeless. The friends of Greece, on the other hand, replied, that if the Greek chiefs were worthless, and the Greek government weak, the will of the people was strong, and the nation would prove unconquerable. The Greeks, they said, might yet find a government worthy of their cause, and the liberties of Greece might find a champion like William of Orange or Washington; or, if liberty produced no champion, war might give the nation a chief like Cromwell or Napoleon.

The animosity of the belligerents was never more violent than at the commencement of 1823, but the resources of both were for the time exhausted. The sultan, finding that his indiscriminate cruelty had only strengthened the Greeks in their determination to oppose his power, changed his policy, and began to treat them with mildness. Many who had been thrown into prison merely as hostages, were released, and the Greek communities generally were allowed to enjoy their old municipal privileges, and manage their own financial affairs. Strict orders were transmitted to all pashas to act equitably to the Greek subjects of the Porte. Some slight concessions were also made in order to conciliate Russia, and negotiations were opened with Persia, which eventually terminated the war with that power[1]. Even the sympathy of

---

[1] The treaty of peace between Turkey and Persia was signed on the 28th July, 1823, but it was not published at Constantinople until the month of October, and not ratified by the Shah of Persia until January, 1824.

Western nations in the Greek cause was not overlooked. Sultan Mahmud knew little of public opinion, but he was not ignorant of the power of popular feeling. The early events of his life, and the state of his capital, had taught him to fear insurrections. He was persuaded by his own judgment, as well as by foreign ambassadors and his own ministers, that Christian nations might force kings and emperors to defend the Greeks, and that it would be wise to avert a combination of the Christian powers for such a purpose. He therefore ordered the new capitan-pasha, Khosref Mehemet, called Topal, to assure the English ambassador and the Austrian internuncio, that the Othoman fleet would not lay waste the defenceless islands of the Archipelago, and that terms of submission would be offered to all Christians who had taken up arms.

The sultan's preparations for the campaign of 1823 were suddenly paralyzed by a great disaster. The arsenal and cannon-foundry at Tophana were destroyed by fire. An immense train of artillery had been prepared for the army of Thessaly; twelve hundred brass guns were ready to arm new ships in the port; an extraordinary supply of ammunition and military stores was packed up for service: all these materials were destroyed by one of the most terrible conflagrations ever witnessed, even by the inhabitants of Constantinople. Besides the artillery arsenal, fifty mosques and about six thousand houses were destroyed. A large part of Pera was reduced to ashes.

This fire was attributed by public rumour to the malevolence of the janissaries, and that rumour was believed by Sultan Mahmud. Fifteen ortas were under orders to march against the Greeks. They dared not refuse marching against infidels, but without the materials of war, destroyed by this conflagration, their departure was useless. They had now gained time to organize an insurrection, and their discontent alarmed the sultan to such a degree that, contrary to the established usage of the empire, he did not appear in public on several occasions. But neither his personal danger, nor the destruction of his artillery, abated his energy. A small fleet was fitted out, and, instead of making a decisive attack on the Greeks, it was resolved to harass them with desultory operations. The capitan-pasha hoisted his flag in a frigate, and his fleet was unencumbered by a single line-of-battle ship. The financial difficulties of the Turkish government were met by a new issue of debased money, which was at that time the substitute for a loan. By the old plan of debasing the coinage, the loss fell on the sultan's own subjects; by the new plan of borrowing money, it is sure to fall on strangers, and in all probability on the subjects of Queen Victoria.

The sultan's plan of campaign was as usual well devised. An army was destined to invade the Morea. Instead of entering the peninsula by the Isthmus of Corinth, it was to cross the gulf at Lepanto, and establish its head-quarters at Patras. The garrison of Corinth was to be provisioned and strengthened by the Othoman fleet. Elis and Messenia offered facilities for the employment of the Turkish cavalry. Abundant supplies of all kinds might be obtained from the Ionian Islands to fill the magazines of the army at Patras, Modon, and Coron.

Yussuf Berkoftzali, who was well known to the Greeks by his exploits in Moldavia, was ordered to advance from Thessaly through Eastern Greece, with a strong body of cavalry. The main army, consisting of Gueghs under Mustaï Pasha of Scodra, and Tosks under Omer Vrioni, pasha of Joannina, was ordered to advance through Western Greece. A junction was to be effected either at Lepanto or at Patras, where the Othoman fleet was to meet the army.

Mavrocordatos had been driven from office by his own mismanagement. His successors at the head of the Greek government were too ignorant to adopt measures for retarding the advance of the Turks, and too selfish to think of anything but their personal interests. The people stood ready to do their duty, but the popular energy was left without guidance. The captains and best soldiers were far from the frontier, collecting and consuming the national revenues. The Morea was filled with well-paid troops; but few were disposed to quit the flesh-pots of the districts in which they had taken up their quarters; so that, when the campaign opened, Greece had no army in the field.

Reshid Pasha (Kiutayhé) commenced the military operations of the year 1823, by treading out the ashes of the Revolution that still smouldered on Mount Pelion. He subdued Trikeri in conjunction with the capitan-pasha, and drove the Olympian armatoli from their last retreat in Thessaly[1].

The Olympian armatoli escaped to Skiathos and Skopelos, where they maintained themselves by plundering the inhabitants, while Yussuf Berkoftzali was laying waste Eastern Greece. In the month of July, the inhabitants of Skiathos were driven from their houses by these Greek troops, who took possession of the town, and consumed the grain, oil, and wine which they found stored up in the magazines. Parties of soldiers scoured the island, and seized the sheep and goats as if they had been in an enemy's country. The inhabitants fled to an ancient castle about five miles from the town, with as much of their property as they could save, and defended this strong position against their intrusive countrymen. The armatoli were so much pleased with their idle life, varied with goat hunts and skirmishes with the natives, that they refused to obey the orders they received from the Greek government, to join a body of troops in Euboea. Admiral Miaoulis visited Skiathos on the 11th of October, and found the inhabitants in great distress. They were shut up in the castle, and their supplies were exhausted, while the soldiers were consuming the last remains of their property in the town. The authority, the solicitations, and the reproaches of Miaoulis, were employed in vain to expel the armatoli from the island, and the lawless soldiery did not quit Skiathos until they had consumed everything on which they could lay their hands.

While the Olympian armatoli were ruining Skiathos and plundering Skopelos, Yussuf Berkoftzali was laying waste Phocis and Boeotia. Many villages, and several monasteries on Parnassus and Helicon, which had hitherto escaped devastation, were plundered and burned. Kastri, the village which occupies the site of Delphi, was pillaged; but instead of establishing himself at Salona, opening communications with Lepanto, and co-operating with the army of Mustaï Pasha, Berkoftzali fixed his head-quarters at Thebes, sent his infantry to Negrepont, and pushed forward his foraging parties into the plain of Athens.

Kolettes, like Mavrocordatos, was eager for military glory,

---

[1] *See* p. 201.

and even more unfit for military command. He now persuaded the other members of the government to appoint him commander-in-chief of a Greek army which he was to assemble in Euboea. He had no military qualifications but a portly frame and the Albanian dress; but these physical and artificial advantages induced the stout Zinzar Vallachian to despise the moral courage and the patriotic disinterestedness of his Phanariot rival, whose frame, though smaller, was far more active. When the Turks appeared, Kolettes fled and abandoned Euboea to its fate. Odysseus, however, who commanded the Greek force in the southern part of the island, defeated the Mussulmans in a skirmish near Karystos. As a trophy of his victory, he sent fifty heads and three living Turks to Athens. The modern Athenians deliberately stoned these three unfortunate prisoners to death.

Mustaï Pasha assembled his army at Ochrida. It consisted of five thousand Mohammedan Gueghs, and three thousand Catholic Mirdites. These Catholics, who speak the Guegh dialect of the Albanian language, boast of their descent from the Christians who fought against the Turks under their national hero Skanderbeg, or George Castriot. But their hatred of the orthodox Greeks has long since bound them in a closer alliance with the Mussulman tribes in their neighbourhood, than with any body of Christians. On the present occasion, the Mirdites formed the advanced guard of Mustaï's army. They upheld the military glory of their race, and ridiculed the vanity of the Greeks, who attempted to filch from them the glory of Skanderbeg.

The Greeks made no preparations to oppose Mustaï. Mavrocordatos had quitted Mesolonghi. While he remained there, he concentrated in his own person the three offices of President of Greece, Governor-General of the Western Provinces, and Commander-in-Chief of the Aetolian army; but when he departed he left three persons to execute the duties of commander-in-chief. This absurd arrangement would doubtless have created anarchy had it not already existed, and it tended to increase the disorders that prevailed. Almost every chief, both in Aetolia and Acarnania, engaged in quarrels with his neighbours. Sometimes they fought in order to decide who should march to encounter Mustaï's army, and the prize of victory was liberty to stay at home and plunder the peasantry. In most cases their proceedings were an inexplicable enigma; and their most intelligent countrymen could only tell strangers, what indeed was very evident without their communication, that the conduct of the captains and primates was ruining the people.

The army of Mustaï Pasha marched by the plain of Nevropolis, descending the valley of the Aspropotamos, and reached Karpenisi by traversing Agrapha and crossing the mountains to the westward of Veloukhi. Its advance was signalized by one of the most brilliant exploits of the war. The first division of the Othoman force consisted of four thousand men, Catholics and Mussulmans, under the command of Djelaleddin Bey. It encamped in the valley of Karpenisi, near an abundant fountain of pure water, which forms a brook as it flows from its basin, shaded by a fine old willow-tree.

At midnight on the 21st of August 1823 the orthodox Tosks surprised the camp of the Catholic and Mussulman Gueghs. Marco Botzaris, at the head of three hundred and fifty Suliots, broke into the midst of their enemies and rushed forward to slay the bey. The Othoman troops, roused from sleep, fled with precipitation, leaving their arms behind. Had the Greek captains descended with the armatoli of Aetolia and Acarnania from the villages in which they were idly watching the flashes of the Suliot arms, they might have annihilated the Turkish force. But Greek envy sacrificed the Albanian hero. The bey of Ochrida had pitched his tent in a mandra or walled enclosure, built to protect bee-hives or young lambs from badgers and foxes. Botzaris reached this wall, and, not finding the entrance, raised his head to look over it, in order to discover a means of entering it with his followers. The alarm had now roused Djelaleddin's veterans, who were familiar with nocturnal surprises. Several were on the watch when the head of Botzaris rose above the wall, and showed itself marked on the grey sky, and a ball immediately pierced his brain. Even then a few hand-grenades would have driven Djelaleddin's guard from the enclosure, and completed the defeat of the Turkish force; but the Suliots had learned nothing of the art of war during their long intercourse with the Russians, French, and English in the Ionian Islands. Like most warlike savages, they despised the improvements of science; and the consequence was, that their victorious career was now stopped by a rough wall, built as a defence against foxes and badgers. But before retiring with the body of their leader, they collected and carried off their booty. No attempt was made to interrupt their retreat to Mikrokhorio, where they arrived accompanied by a train of mules caught in the camp, and laden with spoil. Horsehair sacks filled with silver-mounted pistols, yataghans, and cartridge-cases, were fastened over pack-saddles like bags of meal, and long Albanian muskets were tied up in bundles like fagots of firewood. The booty was very great, but the death of Marco Botzaris cast a gloom over their spirits. The Greek soldiers in the neighbouring villages of Tranakhorio and Nostimo, when it was too late, became ashamed of their inactivity, and reproached their captains for causing the death of the bravest chief in the Greek army. As the news of the loss spread, the whole nation grieved over the noble Suliot.

The affair at Karpenisi is one of the examples of the secondary part which the rival dominant races of Othomans and Greeks often bore in the war of the Greek Revolution. The Othomans who accompanied the army of Mustaï were still in the plain of Thessaly. The Greeks were encamped idly on the hills. The battle was fought between the Catholic Gueghs and the orthodox Tosks.

The troops of Djelaleddin remained in possession of the field of battle, and buried their dead on the spot. Two English travellers who passed the place during the following summer saw a number of small wooden crosses fixed over the graves of the Mirdites.

The Suliots who bore a part in this memorable exploit near the fountain and the old willow-tree, were long distinguished by the richly ornamented and strangely mounted arms they wore; but many regretted their dearly-purchased splendour, and thought the night accursed on which it was obtained, saying, that it had been better for them and for Greece had Markos still lived, and they had continued to carry the plain rifles of their fathers.

The success of the Suliots did not retard the advance of Mustaï. His Gueghs pressed on, eager to avenge their losses and wipe off the stain on their military reputation. The

Greeks abandoned their positions at Tranokhorio, and made an unsuccessful attempt to defend the valley between the two precipitous mountains of Khelidoni and Kaliakudi.

The road from Karpenisi to Vrachori runs through a succession of frightful passes and giant rocks. It may be compared with the most difficult footpaths over the Alps. The great mountain Kaliakudi closes the entrance by a wall of precipices, broken by one chasm, through which the river of Karpenisi forces its passage to join the Achelous. In this pass a skirmish took place, and the Greeks boast of an imaginary victory at Kaliakudi. To any one who has visited the monastery of Bruso, it must be evident that three hundred men, inspired with the spirit of Markos Botzaris, might have stopped an army as numerous as that of Xerxes or of Brennus. But the Albanians of Mustaï drove the Greek armatoli before them through the sublime valleys which diverge from Bruso. It has been said that Mustaï sowed distrust among the Greek chiefs, by promising capitanliks to some venal leaders. He could hardly have ventured to march through the pass of Bruso, had he not been assured that he should find no enemy to oppose him.

At Vrachori Mustaï found Omer Vrioni with an army of Mussulman Tosks. The dialects of the Gueghs and Tosks do not afford a better means of communicating than those of the Irish and the Scotch Highlanders. The dress of the two tribes is as dissimilar as their speech. The white kilt of the Tosk forms as strong a contrast with the red tunic of the Guegh, as the grey top-coat of Paddy with Sandy's checkered plaid. The followers of the two pashas quarrelled, and the pashas did not agree.

In October 1823 their united force attacked Anatolikon, a small town in the Aetolian lagoons, about five miles west of Mesolonghi. The Greeks had only a mud battery, mounting six guns, to defend the place. In the hour of need they allowed William Martin, who had deserted with another seaman from an English ship, to constitute himself captain of a gun[1]. He dismounted the only piece of artillery the

---

[1] Martin's companion died of typhus fever at Mesolonghi shortly after Mustaï's defeat. Martin was left without either pay or rations, and imprisoned by the Greeks for insubordination. From his own mouth the author learned that he must have died of want had he not been relieved by Mr. Blackett.

Turks placed in battery. The pashas found it impossible to do anything but bombard the place from a couple of mortars, which they planted out of reach of the fire of the Greeks. Their shells did little damage, and only about twenty persons were killed and wounded. On the 11th of December Mustaï raised the siege, and retired to Epirus, through the unguarded pass of Makronoros. Before commencing his retreat, he buried some guns which arrived too late to be of any use, and in order to conceal them from the Greeks, he surrounded them with a low wall of masonry, and ornamented the place like a Turkish cemetery. The Greeks showed the spot with pride, boasting of the beys who had fallen under their deadly fire; but when Kiutayhé besieged Mesolonghi in 1825, he commenced operations by digging up the brass guns in the tombs of the beys.

The new Othoman admiral Khosref, called Topal or the lame pasha, was a man of a courteous disposition and considerable ability—far better suited to be minister of foreign affairs than capitan-pasha. He was not more of a sailor, and quite as great a coward, as his unworthy predecessor Kara Mehemet, but he knew better how to make the officers of the fleet obey his orders. He issued from the Dardanelles at the end of May with a fine fleet, composed of fourteen frigates and twenty corvettes and brigs, attended by forty transports. On the 4th of June he landed three thousand Asiatic troops at Karystos, and sent several transports laden with military stores to Negrepont. He then sailed past Hydra, threw supplies into Coron and Modon, and landed a body of troops and a large sum of money at Patras on the 20th of the same month. Instead, however, of remaining on the western coast of Greece, to support the operations of Mustaï, who was still at Ochrida, he hastened back to the Dardanelles.

The Albanians of Hydra and Spetzas displayed neither activity nor zeal during the year 1823. The Greeks of Psara, Kasos, and Samos, on the contrary, were never more active and enterprising. The Psarians made a descent on the Asiatic coast at Tchanderlik, on the site of Pitane in Aeolis, where they stormed a battery, burned the town, and carried off the harem of a bey belonging to the great house of Kara Osman Oglou of Magnesia. The booty gained by plundering the town was increased by the receipt of ten thousand dollars as ransom for the bey's family. The shores of the gulf of Adramyti were then plundered, and contributions were levied on the Greeks of Mytilene. The ravages committed on the coast of Asia Minor caused the Mussulman population to break out into open revolt. The sultan was accused of sparing the Giaours to please the Christian ambassadors at Constantinople, and the people called on all true believers to avenge the slaughter of the Turks who had been murdered at Tchanderlik and other places. In many towns the Christians were attacked by fanatical mobs, and at Pergamus several hundred Greeks perished before the Othoman authorities could restore order.

During the autumn Miaoulis sailed from Hydra with a small fleet. On his return he complained bitterly of the misconduct of those under his command. Some of the ships of Hydra delayed joining him. At Psara quarrels occurred between the Albanian and Greek sailors; and on the 5th of October the Psarians, in defiance of Miaoulis, seized some Turkish prisoners on board a Hydriot brig, and carried them on shore. Several were publicly tortured before the town-hall of Psara, and the rest were murdered in the streets. When the fleet reached Skiathos fresh disorders broke out. The efforts of the admiral to expel the Olympian armatoli, who were plundering the island, proved ineffectual, as has been already mentioned, partly in consequence of the misconduct of the Albanian sailors. A fight took place on shore between the Hydriots and Spetziots, in which three Spetziots were killed and eight wounded. These dissensions rendered all co-operation between the ships of the three islands impossible, and Miaoulis returned to Hydra on the 16th of October almost in a state of despair.

The conduct of the sailors had been insolent and mutinous during the whole cruise. They landed at Lithi, on the west coast of Chios, without orders, robbed the poor Greek peasants of their oxen, plundered the men of their money, and violated the women. Complaints of these acts were laid before Miaoulis, but he was unable to punish the offenders.

Admiral Miaoulis and six brigs were exposed to great danger off Mount Athos on the 27th of September. A Turkish squadron, consisting of five frigates and four sloops-of-war, gained the wind of the Greeks while their ships lay in a calm.

A cannonade of three hours and a half ensued, in which several thousand shot were fired; but as the Turks declined engaging their enemy at close quarters, the Hydriots escaped through the Turkish line with the loss of only eight men killed. The Turks declared that they did not lose a single man; and it is not improbable that they never ventured within range of the smaller guns of the Greek ships.

A romantic event during this cruise deserves to be recorded. On the 1st of October the Psarian admiral picked up a boat with eight of his countrymen on board, who were drifting about in the Archipelago without either provisions or water. They had encountered strange vicissitudes during the previous fortnight. An Austrian schooner had seized them in the gulf of Smyrna, where they were looking out for prizes without papers from the Greek government. They were delivered to the Turkish authorities as pirates, and put on board a small vessel bound for the Dardanelles. At the lower castles they were transferred to a boat manned by fifteen Turks, which was to convey them to the bagnio at Constantinople. They proceeded to Tchanak-kalesi, as the Asiatic town at the Dardanelles is called by the Turks, where most of the Turkish boatmen slept ashore. The Psarians contrived to kill those who remained on board without noise, and, casting loose the moorings, they were carried by the current beyond the lower castles before daybreak. There they were met by a contrary wind, without provisions and with only one jar of water. In this difficulty they were forced to put into a secluded creek in Tenedos, and two of their number, who were dressed like the Greek sailors who serve in the Turkish fleet, walked to the town to purchase bread and carry back two jars of water. One of them had fortunately succeeded in concealing a small gold coin in the upper leather of his slippers before he was searched by the lynx-eyed janissaries of Smyrna. The two Psarians remained all day in a Greek wine-shop kept by an Ionian, as the safest place of concealment, bought bread, and procured water. In the evening they walked back to their companions, who had found water, but were famished with hunger. At midnight they left Tenedos; but before they could reach any Greek island the wind became calm or contrary, and they had been rowing incessantly for thirty-six hours, endeavouring to reach Psara, when they were picked up by Admiral Apostoles.

A Greek squadron was sent to relieve Anatolikon, when it was besieged by Mustaï Pasha. Before the Hydriot and Spetziot sailors would embark they insisted on receiving a month's pay in advance. The primates made their mutinous behaviour during the previous cruise a pretext for refusing to make any advance. The Greeks of Psara, with more patriotism, immediately sent a few brigs and a fire-ship to Hydra, where their promptitude to serve the cause of their country was regarded as an offence. The Hydriots, who were intent only on the question of pay, attacked the Psarian sailors, in order to punish them for giving a bad example to the rest of the Greek navy. Several Psarians were cruelly beaten, and a civil war was on the point of breaking out. Shame, and the expectation of being speedily repaid by Lord Byron, at last induced the Hydriot primates to advance the sum required to fit out seven vessels and two fire-ships. The fire-ships of Hydra were generally prepared as jobs, and were rarely of any service. One of these could not go farther than Navarin. The Hydriot squadron was joined by five Spetziot brigs and a fire-ship. Miaoulis, disgusted with the insubordination displayed in the preceding cruise, remained on shore, and the command was given to Captain Pinotzi, who hoisted a broad pennant, for the Greeks mimicked the external signs of naval organization, though they neglected the essentials of discipline and tactics. Mavrocordatos embarked to resume his dictatorship in Western Greece, expecting to find a firm support in the influence of Lord Byron, who had recently arrived at Cephalonia.

On the 11th of December 1823 this squadron fell in with a Turkish brig off the Skrophes. Five Greek ships came up with her, and raked her with their broadsides until she was in a sinking state. None of these vessels ventured to run alongside and carry her by boarding, so that she was enabled to reach Ithaca, where the Turks expected to find protection under the English flag. This brig mounted twenty-two six-pounders, and carried a crew of eighty men, besides twenty passengers. She had sailed from Prevesa the day before with a large sum of money for the garrison of Patras.

The Greeks had too often violated their most solemn

treaties to care much about violating Ionian neutrality, when it appeared that they could do so with impunity. The sailors landed on Ithaca, and murdered the Turks who attempted to defend their ship. The brig was seized as soon as she was abandoned by her crew, and the treasure on board was transferred to the Greek ships. The captain, who refused to quit the deck, was slain. The brig presented a terrible spectacle to her captors. Upwards of forty Turks had been killed during the action, and their dead bodies were found piled up between decks, in order that they might be taken ashore for burial. While some of the Greek sailors were plundering the stranded vessel, others were shooting down the Turks on shore, whose flight was impeded by the people of the island. The arrival of a company of English soldiers saved thirty-five men, who were carried to the lazaretto. Every one of these had received severe wounds.

The English government was justly indignant at this conduct on the part of a Greek fleet, claiming the rights of an organized force, and sailing under a broad pennant. It seemed intolerable that a navy which pretended to enjoy all the advantages accorded to Christian governments, should commit atrocities that would have disgraced Algerine pirates. The behaviour of the Greeks was on this occasion peculiarly offensive, for the neutrality of the Ionian Islands had been rendered by the British government extremely advantageous to Greece. Kalamos was at that very time serving as a refuge to the population of Acarnania and Aetolia, which had fled from the armies of Omer Vrioni and Mustaï. Karaiskaki, a distinguished captain, was receiving not only protection, but also medical assistance gratis, and hundreds of families of Greek armatoli were then fed by the British government; yet the newspapers of the continent afford evidence that at this time the Greeks were calumniating England over all Europe from Marseilles to St. Petersburg.

Among the wounded Turks who were carried into the lazaretto of Ithaca, there was one man of a noble aspect and of dignified manners, who had been left for dead all night on the beach. In the morning he was found breathing, and carried to the lazaretto to die. But after his wounds were dressed, his face and hands washed, and his green turban arranged on his head, he muttered a few words of thankfulness in Greek, and made signs for a pipe. He smoked one or two pipes, and the two English surgeons who were attending him thought it not improbable that he would die smoking. The pipes, however, appeared to restore him, and he gradually recovered. His convalescence was long; and during the time he remained in Ithaca, the fluency with which he spoke Greek, and the good sense he displayed in his conversation, made him a favourite. He had been cadi of Tripolitza just before the Revolution broke out, but had accompanied Khurshid's army to Thessaly. This man considered the Othoman empire on the verge of ruin; but he ridiculed the idea of its being replaced by a Greek kingdom. He feared a coalition of the Christian powers.

The Greek vessels returned to Mesolonghi with their booty, and quarrelled about the division of the spoil. A schooner, with several chests of treasure on board, attempted to escape, but was brought back by force, and anchored in the midst of the Hydriot brigs. Mavrocordatos, who was an involuntary spectator of these disgraceful scenes, attempted in vain to persuade the Hydriots to make an honourable division of their dishonest gains. On the 17th of December a scheme of division, modelled on the system of shares in the mercantile operations of the islanders, was adopted. The share of one of the Hydriot ships, which had sailed shamefully undermanned, with only forty-eight seamen on board, but which drew shares for seventy-one, amounted to 77 okas of paras, measured by weight, and 267 gold mahmudiés in coin, besides other plunder, estimated at 770 piastres [1].

No sooner was the division of the treasure terminated than the crews demanded pay for a second month in advance. Application was made to Lord Byron, but he considered it impolitic to purchase the service of such ill-manned ships, and hopeless to expect honourable service from such disorderly and mutinous crews. The Hydriots quitted Mesolonghi, and they so timed their voyage that they made Hydra on the 29th December, the very day on which the month paid in advance ended.

The Ionian government forgot its dignity in avenging the

---

[1] An English gentleman, once a midshipman in the navy, was accidentally on board the Hydriot squadron as a volunteer, and witnessed the events above narrated.

injury it had received. The Lord High Commissioner issued a violent proclamation, upbraiding Mavrocordatos in rather unseemly terms for calling himself a prince, which certainly was no violation of Ionian neutrality. The sultan called upon the Ionian government for indemnification for the loss he had sustained in consequence of their neglect to enforce neutrality, and his demand was immediately recognized. The Greek government foolishly refused to refund the money, until the British government, losing patience, ordered Captain Pechell in H.M.S. Sybille to enforce the claim. Several Greek ships were then seized, and not released until an indemnity of forty thousand dollars was refunded.

The Greeks had regained possession of the Acrocorinth before the Albanian pashas raised the siege of Anatolikon. The Turks capitulated on the 7th November 1823. On this occasion the firmness and honourable conduct of Niketas, supported by the soldiers under his immediate orders, prevented Greece from being stained by another infamous massacre. But all the energy and activity of Niketas could not prevent four or five Turks from being murdered on the way from Corinth to Kenchries. The indifference shown by Kolokotrones to the disorderly conduct of the Greek troops under his command on this occasion, induced many to believe that he would have willingly seen a repetition of the massacres of Tripolitza.

In the autumn of 1823 Lord Byron directed the attention of all Europe to the affairs of Greece by joining the cause. He arrived at Mesolonghi on the 5th of January 1824. His short career in Greece was unconnected with any important military event, for he died on the 19th of April; but the enthusiasm he awakened perhaps served Greece more than his personal exertions would have done, had his life been prolonged. Wherever the English language was known, an electric shock was felt when it was heard that

> 'The pilgrim of eternity, whose fame
> Over his living head like heaven was bent,
> An early but enduring monument,'

had died 'where his young mind first caught ethereal fire.'

The genius of Lord Byron would in all probability never have unfolded either political or military talent. He was not disposed to assume an active part in public affairs. He regarded politics as the art of cheating the people, by concealing one-half of the truth and misrepresenting the other; and whatever abstract enthusiasm he might feel for military glory was joined to an innate detestation of the trade of war. Both his character and his conduct presented unceasing contradictions. It seemed as if two different souls occupied his body alternately. One was feminine, and full of sympathy; the other masculine, and characterized by clear judgment, and by a rare power of presenting for consideration those facts only which were required for forming a decision. When one arrived the other departed. In company, his sympathetic soul was his tyrant. Alone, or with a single person, his masculine prudence displayed itself as his friend. No man could then arrange facts, investigate their causes, or examine their consequences, with more logical accuracy, or in a more practical spirit. Yet, in his most sagacious moment, the entrance of a third person would derange the order of his ideas,—judgment fled, and sympathy, generally laughing, took its place. Hence he appeared in his conduct extremely capricious, while in his opinions he had really great firmness. He often, however, displayed a feminine turn for deception in trifles, while at the same time he possessed a feminine candour of soul, and a natural love of truth, which made him often despise himself quite as much as he despised English fashionable society for what he called its brazen hypocrisy. He felt his want of self-command; and there can be no doubt that his strongest reason for withdrawing from society, and shunning public affairs, was the conviction of his inability to repress the sympathies which were in opposition to his judgment[1].

No stranger estimated the character of the Greeks more correctly than Lord Byron. At Cephalonia he sometimes smiled at the enthusiasm of Sir Charles Napier, and pointed out where the soldier's ardour appeared to mislead his judgment. It may, however, be observed, that to nobody did the Greeks ever unmask their selfishness and self-deceit so candidly. Almost every distinguished statesman and general sent him letters soliciting his favour, his influence, or his

---

[1] [This sketch of Lord Byron's character was drawn from close personal observation. During two months that Mr. Finlay remained at Mesolonghi about this time, he passed almost every evening in Byron's company. Ed.]

money. Kolokotrones invited him to a national assembly at Salamis. Mavrocordatos informed him that he would be of no use anywhere but at Hydra, for Mavrocordatos was then in that island. Constantine Metaxa, who was governor of Mesolonghi, wrote, saying that Greece would be ruined unless Lord Byron visited that fortress. Petrobey used plainer words. He informed Lord Byron that the true way to save Greece was to lend him, the bey, a thousand pounds. With that sum not three hundred but three thousand Spartans would be put in motion to the frontier, and the fall of the Othoman empire would be certain. Every Greek chief celebrated his own praises and Lord Byron's liberality, but most of them injured their own cause by dilating too eloquently on the vices and crimes of some friend or rival. Lord Byron made many sagacious and satirical comments on the *chiaroscuro* of these communications. He wrote: 'Of the Greeks, I can't say much good hitherto, and I do not like to speak ill of them, though they do of one another.' He knew his own character so well, that he remained some time at Cephalonia, not venturing to trust himself among such a cunning and scheming set, fearing lest unworthy persons should exercise too much influence over his conduct. This feeling induced him to avoid familiarity with the Greeks, even after his arrival at Mesolonghi, and with Mavrocordatos his intercourse was not intimate. Business and ceremony alone brought them together. Their social and mental characteristics were not of a nature to create reciprocal confidence, and they felt no mutual esteem.

Lord Byron did not overlook the vices of the Greek leaders, but at the same time he did not underrate the virtues of the people. The determined spirit with which they asserted their independence received his sincere praise, even while the rapacity, cruelty, and dissensions of the military weighed heavily on his mind. Nothing, during his residence at Mesolonghi, distressed him more than the conduct of the Suliots whom he had taken into his pay. He saw that he had degraded himself into the chief of a band of personal followers, who thought of nothing but extorting money from their foreign leader. Three hundred Suliots were enrolled in his band; of these upwards of one hundred demanded double pay and triple rations, pretending to be officers, whose dignity would not allow them to lounge about the coffee-houses of Mesolonghi unless they were attended by a henchman or pipe-bearer. Lord Byron, annoyed by their absurd pretensions, remembered Napier's plans for the formation of a small regular military force, and lamented his own inability to carry them into execution. Colonel Leicester Stanhope (the Earl of Harrington) increased his irritation by appearing as the agent of the Greek committee, and giving in to all the pedantic delusions of the literati. The typographical colonel, as Lord Byron sarcastically termed him, seemed to think that newspapers would be more effectual in driving back the Othoman armies than well-drilled troops and military tactics.

The political information which Lord Byron extracted from Mavrocordatos in their personal interviews, and the proceedings of that statesman in the conduct of the public administration, revealed the thousand obstacles to the establishment of an honest government in Greece. A mist fell from Lord Byron's eyes. He owned that his sagacity was at fault, and he abandoned all hope of being able to guide the Greeks, or to assist them in improving their administration. Not long before his death, he frequently repeated, that with Napier to command and form regular troops, with Hastings to arm and command a steamer, and with an able financier, Greece would be sure of victory. Then, too, he began to express doubts whether circumstances had authorized him to recommend the Greek loan to his friends in England. He was struck by the fact that a majority of the Moreot captains and primates opposed pledging the confiscated Turkish property as a security to the lenders. He feared that the proceeds of a loan might be misspent by one party, and the loan itself disowned by another. Bowring and the bankers, he said, would secure their commissions and their gains, but he feared many honest English families might lose their money by his Philhellenism.

Lord Byron's knowledge of the prominent defects of the Greek character, his personal experience of their rapacity, and his conviction that selfishness was the principal cause of a civil war in Argolis which broke out about the time of his arrival at Mesolonghi, made him an advocate for the formation of a strong central government. Order was, in his opinion, the first step to liberty. The Earl of Harrington talked as if he considered Lord Byron's desire for order a proof of his indifference to liberty. Lord Byron was, however, a far wiser counsellor than the Colonel, and, had he lived, might have done much to arrest the factious madness and shameless expenditure which rendered the English loans the prize and the aliment of two civil wars.

The first Greek loan was contracted early in 1824. The Greeks received about £300,000, and they engaged to pay annually £40,000 as interest, as the capital of the debt created was £800,000 at five per cent. The lenders risked their money to deliver Greece, and they have never received a shilling of interest or a syllable of gratitude from the thousands whom their money saved and enriched. Indeed, the Greeks generally appear to have considered the loan as a small payment for the debt due by civilized society to the country that produced Homer and Plato. The modern Greek habit of reducing everything to a pecuniary standard, made Homer, Plato, & Co. creditors for a large capital and an enormous accumulation of unpaid interest.

A worse speculation, in a financial point of view, than the Greek loan, could not have been undertaken. Both the loan contractors and the members of the Greek committee knew that the revenues of Greece in 1823 fell short of £80,000. Yet with this knowledge they placed the absolute control of a sum equal to nearly four years' revenue of the country in the hands of a faction engaged in civil war. Foreigners were amazed at this display of financial insanity on the London Stock Exchange. Future years have proved that the disease returns in periodical fits, which can only be cured by copious bleeding.

The contractors of the Greek loan, when they paid over its proceeds to a government engaged in civil war, could not be ignorant that the money would be diverted from carrying on war against the Turks, in order to be employed against domestic rivals. When it was too late, however, they considered it to be their duty to check its wasteful expenditure, and during the year 1824, Sir Henry Lytton Bulwer, afterwards her Majesty's ambassador at Constantinople, visited Greece at their request, 'to see if the nature of the Greek government warranted the payment of the portion not yet advanced.' Sir Henry stated the following observations for the benefit of his countrymen, as the result of his experience: 'We (the English) have generally busied ourselves about the government of Greece, which really was no business of ours; while the management of our money, in which we might be thought concerned, has been left entirely in the hands of the Greeks[1].' General Gordon was subsequently invited to return to Greece, which he had left shortly after the fall of Tripolitza, in order to watch over the expenditure of the second loan; but he wisely refused to have anything to do with the business when he read the instructions on which he was to act. He has recorded his deliberate opinion of the men who were entrusted with the expenditure of the English loans in very strong terms: 'With, *perhaps*, the exception of Zaimes, the members of the executive are no better than public robbers[2].' The internal history of Greece, from the defeat of Dramali to the arrival of King Otho, attests the truth of this severe sentence. The country was ruined by intestine broils, originating in private rapacity. Amidst these disorders, two civil wars stand out with disgraceful prominence, as having consumed the proceeds of the English loans, abandoned Psara and Kasos to be conquered by the Turks, and prepared the Morea to be subdued by Ibrahim Pasha.

The first of these civil wars was called the war of Kolokotrones, because that old chieftain was its principal author. It commenced in November 1823, and finished in June 1824. It was concluded as soon as the news reached the belligerents that an instalment of the first English loan had arrived at Zante. Panos, the eldest son of Kolokotrones, who held possession of Nauplia, immediately surrendered it to the executive body on receiving a share of the English money. This transaction took place on the 5th of June 1824.

While the Greeks were fighting among themselves, Sultan Mahmud was smoothing away the obstacles which impeded the co-operation of his powerful vassal, Mohammed Ali, pasha of Egypt, in attacking them. By his prudent arrangements he secured the zealous support of the Egyptian pasha. Mohammed Ali was already disposed to chastise the Greeks for the losses he had sustained from their cruisers. He also feared that a prolonged contest with the insurgent Christians

---

[1] *An Autumn in Greece*, by H. Lytton Bulwer, Esq. 8vo. London, 1826.
[2] *History of the Greek Revolution*, ii. 72.

might end in bringing a Russian fleet into the Mediterranean. He therefore received the proposals made to his political agent at Constantinople in the most conciliatory spirit. The sultan invested his son Ibrahim with the rank of vizier of the Morea, and wrote a flattering letter to the great pasha himself, calling him the champion of Islam. Mohammed Ali received this letter with the warmest expressions of pleasure, and engaged to send a powerful fleet and army to attack the Greeks. He had not yet been inspired by French intrigue with delusive visions of becoming the founder of an Arab empire.

The Greeks heard with indifference of the preparations which were going on at the dockyards of Constantinople and Alexandria. They treated the rumoured co-operation of the sultan and the pasha as impossible. They insisted on supposing that Mohammed Ali reasoned like themselves. They thought that the pasha must want his own money for his own schemes, and deluded themselves with the idea that he was more likely to act against the sultan than for him. They argued that he must be more anxious to establish his own independence than to destroy theirs. Their whole souls were absorbed in party contests for wealth and power, until they were awakened from their dreams by a series of terrible calamities.

It has been mentioned that the civil war of Kolokotrones embittered the last months of Lord Byron's life, by doubts of the propriety of entrusting the Greeks with large sums of money. He foresaw that selfishness would find more nutriment in foreign loans than patriotism.

The executive government which defeated the rebellion of Kolokotrones was supported by a majority in the legislative assembly. It cannot be said that the members of this assembly were freely chosen by the people; yet, on the whole, its feelings represented those of the best portion of the Greek population. Many were well-meaning men, who could clothe their thoughts in energetic and eloquent language, but few had any experience in legislation and politics. Their deliberations rarely conducted them to practical resolutions, and their incapacity prevented their exercising any control over the financial affairs of their country. The consequence of this inaptitude for business was, that George Konduriottes and Kolettes exercised absolute power in the name of the executive body.

The government which vanquished the faction of Kolokotrones was formed by a coalition of three parties: the Albanian shipowners of Hydra and Spetzas; the Greek primates of the Morea; and the Romeliot captains of armatoli. The chief authority was conceded to the Albanian shipowners; George Konduriottes of Hydra was elected president of Greece, and Botasses of Spetzas, vice-president. It is necessary to record the sad truth, that two more ignorant and incapable persons were never entrusted with the direction of a nation's affairs. The Greeks are the most prejudiced of all Europeans when there is a question of the purity of the Hellenic race, and no people regards education with more favour; yet with all this nationality and pedantry they entrusted their public affairs, in a period of great difficulty, to two men who could not address them in the Greek language, and whose intellectual deficiencies prevented them from expressing their thoughts with clearness even in the corrupt Tosk dialect which they habitually used. The descendants of Pericles and Demosthenes submitted tamely to these aliens in civilization and race, because they were orthodox and wealthy.

The interest of the president and vice-president was identical with that of the shipowners of Hydra and Spetzas, and it was directly opposed to the formation of a national navy. The money placed at their disposal was wasted in paying inefficient ships, and hiring the support of mutinous sailors; and they refused to purchase and arm a single steamer at the recommendation of Captain Hastings, when such a vessel might have frustrated the operations of Mohammed Ali, and prevented Ibrahim Pasha from landing in the Morea. Had they possessed a very little naval knowledge and a small share of patriotism, they might have obtained the glory of initiating the change in naval warfare which is in progress throughout all maritime nations [1].

The party of the Moreot primates was next in importance to that of the naval islanders; but this party soon forfeited its influence and fell into contempt by the unprincipled selfishness of its leading members. Had the Moreot primates

---

[1] The memoir which Hastings laid before Konduriottes' government is subjoined in Appendix I.

supported the just demands of the people for a system of publicity in financial business, they might have become the guardians of the liberties of Greece, and the founders of their country's constitution. They were, perhaps, the only persons capable, from their administrative experience, of placing the existing municipal institutions in harmony with the action of the central government.

The Romeliot captains of armatoli, though they already possessed great territorial and political influence when the government of Konduriottes entered on office, had not yet constituted themselves into a distinct party in the state. Kolettes now succeeded by his schemes in uniting them together, and allying them with himself by the ties of a common interest. He purchased their services by securing to them a large share of the English loans; and he taught them to maintain themselves in provincial commands, in imitation of the old system of armatoliks. Kolettes acted as their agent and representative in the executive body. That astute Vallach was the first to perceive how their political influence might be rendered supreme in liberated Greece, by imitating the administrative practice of Ali of Joannina, with which he was well acquainted. He conducted their bargains for pay and rations with the central government; he assisted them in obtaining contracts for farming the taxes of the provinces of which they had obtained the military command; and he regulated with them the number of the personal followers they were to be permitted to charge on the public revenues as national troops.

The position which Kolettes created for himself by these arrangements rendered him the most influential politician in the government, and nothing but his want of personal courage and honesty prevented him from being the first man in Greece. It has been already said that he was a Zinzar Vallachian, and not a Greek, and all the moral and physical peculiarities of that race were strongly marked both in his mind and his personal appearance. Both contrasted with those of the Greeks and Albanians by whom he was surrounded. He exhibited neither the boorish pride of the Albanian islanders, nor the loquacious self-sufficiency of the Greek logiotati. With patience and stolid silence he profited by the blunders of his colleagues, always himself doing and saying as little as possible. He trusted that others, by their restless intrigues and precipitate ambition, would ruin their own position, and leave the field open for him. His policy was crowned with success. Hypsilantes, Mavrocordatos, Konduriottes, and Zaimes, all ruined their own personal position by exhibiting more ambition than capacity.

The second civil war, called the War of the Primates, constituted Kolettes the leader of the Romeliot military faction, and victory rendered that faction the most powerful party in Greece [1].

In England, Mavrocordatos was supposed to be at the head of a powerful constitutional party. If this had ever been possible, he had destroyed that possibility by abandoning the presidency of Greece to play the commander-in-chief at Petta. The testimony of English Philhellenes and well-informed foreigners was, however, unavailing to undeceive the British public. The delusion appears to have originated among the Greeks settled in Western Europe, who believed that Mavrocordatos was the most disinterested statesman in Greece, and that a strong constitutional party ought to exist in a free country. But Mavrocordatos, by his grasping ambition, his schemes for governmental centralization, his personal mismanagement, and his political indecision, had ruined his influence before the year 1824. Feeling his position changed, and ill satisfied unless he was the first man at the seat of government, he lingered at Mesolonghi during the whole of the important year 1824, and allowed all parties to learn that public business could go on as well without him as when he was present.

In Western Greece his administration, after Lord Byron's death, was neither honourable to himself nor advantageous to the country. A civil war broke out in the district of Vlochos between two rival captains, Staikos and Vlachopulos. Its continuance was ascribed to his imprudence and indecision. His civil administration was unpopular. He gave his support

---

[1] Kolettes was sent to the court of Louis Philippe as minister by Count Armansperg in 1835 to get him out of the way. Those who saw and conversed with General Kolettes, as he was called at Paris, could hardly refrain from applying to him Fox's celebrated observation on the first appearance of Lord Thurlow on the woolsack: 'That fellow is a humbug; no man can be as wise as he looks.' Kolettes wore the wise look well, and had the sense to speak little, but as he was not always silent, his tongue bewrayed him.

to John Soutzos, the eparch of Venetico, who was stigmatized as the most corrupt and rapacious Phanariot in Greece.

Before quitting Mesolonghi to return to the seat of government, Mavrocordatos convoked an assembly of captains and eparchs, to concert measures for defending the country against the incursions of the Turks, and for reforming internal abuses. His dictatorial authority authorized him to take this step, but he ought to have perceived its imprudence. Its effect was to legalize the system of capitanliks, which had been tacitly revived, and to consolidate the personal independence of the military chiefs, who learned to act in concert whenever it was their interest to resist the central government. The peasants were not blind to the effect of Mavrocordatos' conduct. They saw that it would perpetuate a state of anarchy, and many were so alarmed that they fled to Kalamos, declaring that the prince, as they still called their governor-general, had assembled a pack of wolves to debate how the sheep could be preserved from the eagles and reserved for their own eating.

The second civil war, or war of the primates, was not of long duration. Zaimes was the principal author of this iniquitous movement, and his object was to deprive Konduriottes and those who supported his government of the wealth and influence they enjoyed, by disposing of the proceeds of the English loans.

In appearance and manners Andreas Zaimes was a perfect gentleman. His disposition was generous, and his private conduct upright; but his position as a hereditary primate made him ambitious, while nature had made him neither energetic nor courageous. He thrust himself forward as a statesman and military chief, but he was too weak for a political leader, and utterly unfit for a soldier.

Andreas Londos was next in rank and influence among the conspirators. He was a warm personal friend of Zaimes, and the constant affection which the two Andreas showed to one another in prosperity and adversity was most honourable to both. It proved that they had virtuous stuff in their hearts. Londos was brave and active. His personal courage, however, proved of no use to his party, for, instead of establishing order and enforcing discipline among his followers, he allowed them to commit as great depredations on the property of the Moreot peasants, as were committed by the most lawless chief of Romeliot armatoli. Londos was at this time addicted to riotous debauchery[1].

Both Zaimes and Londos had assumed the position of Turkish beys, and the Greek government allowed them to collect the taxes and administer the greater part of the public affairs of their respective districts. They pretended to employ the revenues for the public service, and in maintaining troops to blockade Patras. But it was too evident that they surrounded themselves with bands of personal followers withdrawn from the armies of Greece, and that Patras was hardly blockaded at all.

Sessini of Gastuni was another influential man in the party of the primates. He was descended from a Venetian family, and had studied medicine in his youth. Shortly after the retreat of the Mussulmans from Lalla, he contrived to assume a position in Elis between that of a voivode and a pasha. He became receiver-general of taxes, paymaster of troops, and farmer-general of confiscated Turkish estates. He adopted the pride and many other vices of the Osmanlis. His household was maintained with considerable pomp. The courtyard was filled with well-caparisoned horses; the galleries were crowded with armed followers. He never quitted his dwelling without a suite of horsemen, armed guards on foot, and grooms leading Persian greyhounds. His sons were addressed as beys; and Ibrahim Pasha, when he occupied Gastuni, was much amused by the tales he heard from the peasantry, who said they had been compelled to fall down on their knees whenever they addressed a word to the medical primate, even in reply to the simplest question[2].

---

[1] Lord Byron used to describe an evening passed in the company of Londos at Vostitza, when both were young men, with a spirit that rendered the scene worthy of a place in *Don Juan*. After supper, Londos, who had the face and figure of a chimpanzee, sprang upon a table, which appeared to be a relic of the Venetian domination, and whose antiquity rendered the exploit a dangerous enterprise, and commenced singing through his nose Rhiga's Hymn to Liberty. A new cadi, passing near the house, inquired the cause of the discordant hubbub. A native Mussulman replied, 'It is only the young primate Londos, who is drunk, and is singing hymns to the new panaghia of the Greeks, whom they call Eleftheria.'

[2] Many stories were current concerning the manner in which Sessini had collected his wealth; one may be mentioned, relating to the loss of a part of his ill-gotten riches. Whether true or false, it excited much amusement at Zante. Madame Sessini resided in that island, and acted as her husband's agent. Before

Notaras, Deliyannes, and Kolokotrones, all joined the war of the primates, which broke out in November 1824.

Kolettes was at this time the most active member of Konduriottes' government. In six weeks he marched an overwhelming force of Romeliot armatoli into the Morea, and crushed the rebels. Had the Greek government displayed similar energy in arraying equal forces against the Turks during the years 1823 and 1824, the war might have changed its aspect. Panos Kolokotrones, the eldest son of the old klepht, after plundering the peasants of Arcadia like a brigand, was slain in a trifling skirmish. Old Kolokotrones and Deliyannes were made prisoners, and confined in a monastery at Hydra. Sessini sought safety at Zante; but the English government was determined to discountenance the unprincipled civil broils of the Greeks, and refused him permission to land. He had no resource but to submit to the clemency of the executive body, and join Kolokotrones in prison. Zaimes, Londos, and Niketas fled to Acarnania, where Mavrocordatos allowed them to hide themselves, and where they were protected by Zongas.

Konduriottes and Kolettes used their victory with impolitic barbarity. Their troops plundered innumerable Greek families who had taken no part in the civil war of everything they possessed. The working oxen of the peasantry were carried off, and in many villages the land remained unsown. The

---

the war of the primates commenced, he wished to place some of his treasure where it would be secure against the Greek government in case of defeat. He wished, however, to do this with great secrecy, for many valuable jewels had been deposited with him by Turkish families who had been obliged to escape in a hurry to Patras at the outbreak of the Revolution. His enemies accused him of intending to declare that these deposits were lost in the civil war. Sessini wrote to inform his wife that he would send the most valuable jewels in his possession to her in a cheese and skin of butter, with peculiar marks. The letter miscarried; and when the cheese and the skin of butter arrived, the lady, having a large supply of both, sold them to a bakal or grocer, who had often purchased previous consignments which she had received from old Sessini. A few days passed before the lost letter arrived. When it reached the lady she hastened to the bakal, but he denied all knowledge of the jewellery. He showed her a cheese with the mark for which she sought untouched, and a skin of butter unopened. The accounts of the custom-house showed that he had only imported cheese and butter. Lawyers and justice could not aid her. The bakal kept the treasure, and the world laughed at Madame Sessini and her rapacious husband. But it was said that the bakal proved himself a better man than the primate, and that he restored a valuable jewel to a Turkish family who had entrusted it to the keeping of Sessini, when that family passed by Zante on its way to Alexandria. The whole story may be the creation of an idle brain, but it deserves notice as a specimen of popular rumour. *Se non è vero, è ben trovato.*

sheep and goats having been also devoured by the armatoli, the people were left to starve. The progress of Ibrahim Pasha in the following year was greatly facilitated by the misgovernment of Konduriottes, the barbarity of Kolettes, and the inhuman ravages of the Romeliot troops.

The two civil wars are black spots in the history of the Greek Revolution. No apology can be offered for those who took up arms against the government in either case, but in the second civil war the conduct of the primates was peculiarly blamable. Patriotism had certainly nothing to do with a contest in which Zaimes and Londos were acting in concert with Kolokotrones. Ambition and avidity were the only motives of action. The coalition of the primates and military chiefs was based on a tacit pretension which they entertained of forming a territorial aristocracy in the Morea. The leaders of the rebels knew that the great body of the people was discontented, and eager to constitute a national representation capable of controlling the executive body and enforcing financial responsibility. Zaimes and Kolokotrones attempted to make this patriotism of the people a means of binding them with fresh fetters. Had the primates given a thought to the interests of their country, they would have supported the demands of the people in a legal way, and there can be no doubt that they would have soon secured a majority in the legislative assembly, even as it was then constituted. Their rebellion inaugurated a long period of administrative anarchy, wasted the resources of Greece, and created a new race of tyrants as despotic as, and far meaner than, the hated Turks.

The victors in the civil wars were as corrupt as the vanquished had been rapacious. The members of the executive wasted the proceeds of the loans with dishonesty as well as extravagance; and the anomalous condition to which Greece was reduced by the stupidity of its government, cannot be exhibited in a clearer light than by tracing the way in which the money was consumed.

The first sums which arrived from England in 1824 were absorbed by arrears due on public and private debts. The payments made had no reference to the necessities of the public service, they were determined by the influence of individual members of the government. The greater part of the first loan was paid over to the shipowners and sailors of what was called the Greek fleet; and the lion's share was appropriated to the Albanians of Hydra and Spetzas. The civil wars engulfed considerable sums. Romeliot captains and soldiers received large bribes to attack their countrymen. No inconsiderable amount was divided among the members of the legislative assembly, and among a large body of useless partizans, who were characterized as public officials. Every man of any consideration in his own imagination wanted to place himself at the head of a band of armed men, and hundreds of civilians paraded the streets of Nauplia with trains of kilted followers, like Scottish chieftains. Phanariots and doctors in medicine, who, in the month of April 1824, were clad in ragged coats, and who lived on scanty rations, threw off that patriotic chrysalis before summer was past, and emerged in all the splendour of brigand life, fluttering about in rich Albanian habiliments, refulgent with brilliant and unused arms, and followed by diminutive pipe-bearers and tall henchmen. The small stature, voluble tongues, turnspit legs, and Hebrew physiognomies of these Byzantine emigrants, excited the contempt, as much as their sudden and superfluous splendour awakened the envy, of the native Hellenes. Nauplia certainly offered a splendid spectacle to any one who could forget that it was the capital of an impoverished nation struggling through starvation to establish its liberty. The streets were for many months crowded with thousands of gallant young men in picturesque dresses and richly ornamented arms, who ought to have been on the frontiers of Greece.

To the stranger who saw only the fortress of Nauplia filled with troops, Greece appeared to be well prepared to resist the whole force of the Othoman empire. Veteran soldiers and enthusiastic volunteers were numerous. Military commands were distributed with a bountiful hand. Rhodios, the Secretary of State, who had studied medicine, was made colonel of the regular troops. It is needless to say that the appointment soon made them as irregular as any other troops in Greece. Military chiefs were allowed to enrol under their private banners upwards of thirty thousand men, and pay was actually issued for this number of troops from the proceeds of the English loans. But over these troops

EXPENDITURE OF THE LOANS.

the Greek government exercised no direct control. No measure was taken even to verify the numbers of the men for whom pay and rations were furnished. Everything was left to the chiefs, who contracted to furnish a certain number of men for a certain amount of pay and a fixed number of daily rations. Amidst this lavish military expenditure, Modon, Coron, Patras, and Lepanto were left almost unwatched, and without any force to keep up a regular blockade.

The illegal gains made by drawing pay and rations for troops who were never mustered, quite as much as the commissions of colonel given to apothecaries, and of captain to grooms and pipe-bearers, demoralized the military forces of Greece. The war with the sultan seemed to be forgotten by the soldiers, who thought only of indulging in the luxury of embroidered dresses and splendid arms. This is the dominant passion of every military class in Turkey, whether Greeks, Albanians, or Turks. The money poured into Greece by the loans suddenly created a demand for Albanian equipments. The bazaars of Tripolitza, Nauplia, Mesolonghi, and Athens were filled with gold-embroidered jackets, gilded yataghans, and silver-mounted pistols. Tailors came flocking to Greece from Joannina and Saloniki. Sabres, pistols, and long guns, richly mounted, were constantly passing through the Ionian Islands as articles of trade between Albania and the Morea. The arms and dress of an ordinary palikari, made in imitation of the garb of the Tosks of Southern Albania, often cost £50. Those of a chiliarch or a strategos, with the showy trappings for his horse, generally exceeded £300. These sums were obtained from the loans, and were abstracted from the service of the country. The complaint that Greece was in danger of being ruined by this extravagant expenditure was general, yet everybody seemed to do his utmost to increase the evil by spending as much money as possible in idle parade. Strange stories were current at the time concerning the large sums of money which individuals contrived to amass. The Arabs, who took Sphakteria and slew the henchman of Mavrocordatos, were said to have found about £300 in his belt, in English sovereigns and Venetian sequins. This man had been appointed an officer in the Greek army, though he knew nothing of military service, and had learned to carry a gun, as a municipal guard, when it was his duty to protect the vineyards of Vrachori from the hostilities of the dogs of the Turkish quarter and the invasions of the foxes of the neighbouring hills.

Makrys was for a time the hero of Mesolonghi, and the captain of the neighbouring district, Zygos. He was a brave man, but a lawless, and, consequently, a bad soldier. His early years were passed as a brigand, and he often recounted how he had lived for many days on the unbaked dough he had prepared from pounded Indian-corn. He first gained wealth by participating in the plunder and massacre of the Jews and Turks of Vrachori. The English loans increased his treasures, which the exaggerations of the people of Mesolonghi swelled to a fabulous amount. Yet, with all his wealth, he was in the habit of drawing pay and rations for five hundred men, when he had only fifty under arms.

Amongst the literary Greeks it has been the fashion to talk and write much concerning the patriotic spirit and the extraordinary military exploits of the klephts, as if these robbers had been the champions of Greek liberty. But the truth is, that these men were mere brigands, who, both before the Revolution, during the revolutionary war, and under the government of King Otho, have plundered the Greeks more than they were ever plundered by the Turks.

It is not to be supposed that military anarchy was established without some opposition on the part of many patriotic Greeks. But its opponents were civilians, and men generally without either practical experience or local influence. The treatment which the few who ventured to make any efforts to put some restraint on the frauds and peculations of the military chiefs received at the hands of the soldiery, prevented this kind of patriotism from finding imitators. Before the siege of Mesolonghi by the army of Reshid Pasha, a patriotic commissary made an attempt to force the chiefs in the Greek camp to muster their followers, in order that no more rations might be issued than were really required, as he found that a large sum was expended by the Greek government in transporting provisions to the camp, while the chiefs who received these provisions as rations for their soldiers, compelled the peasants to carry them back to Mesolonghi. The soldiers of Makrys, instigated by their leader, declared that to muster troops was an arbitrary and despotic act, and pronounced that the reforming commissary was an enemy to constitutional liberty. The troops resolved that the rights of the military should not be violated by this undue assumption of power on the part of the central government, and they carried their resolution into effect by beating the patriotic commissary, and plundering the public magazine. The unfortunate man was confined to his bed for several days, and, if his patriotism was not diminished, we may be sure that he was more prudent and reserved in exhibiting a virtue which had proved so distasteful to the defenders of his country, and so calamitous to himself. His friends gave him no consolation during his convalescence. They reproached him with not commencing his reforms by cutting off the extra rations which were issued to Katzaro, the captain of the body-guard of Mavrocordatos, who drew fifty rations, and did duty with only seven armed followers; or with General Vlachopulos, who pretended to be the leader of four hundred soldiers, but who was said to be unable to muster more than about eighty. These abuses were universal. Mr. Tricoupi informs the world that the veteran Anagnostaras, who fell at Sphakteria, marched against the enemy with only seventeen armed peasants, though he was paid by the Greek government to enrol seven hundred men[1]. Ghoura subsequently drew twelve thousand rations, when he commanded only from three to four thousand men[2]. It is vain for historians and orators to tell us that true patriotism existed in the hearts of men so wanting in common honesty. Men who combine heroism and fraud ought to be praised only in French novels.

The waste of money on the navy was even greater than on the army. Ill-equipped and dull-sailing vessels were hired to take their place in the Greek fleet, because their owners belonged to the faction of Konduriottes and Botasses. Fire-ships were purchased and fitted out at an unnecessary expense, because their proprietors wished to dispose of useless vessels. The great number of fire-ships belonging to the island of Hydra, which were consumed during the years 1824 and 1825 without inflicting any loss on the Turkish

---

[1] Tricoupi, iii. 2c6. Phrantzes considers Anagnostaras, the archimandrite Dikaios, and Odysseus, as the three principal corrupters of the Greek soldiery. Vol. ii. p. 343, *note*.
[2] Gordon, ii. 231, 267; Phrantzes, ii. 403, *note*.

fleet, attest the mal-administration which took place in this department of the naval service. The sailors, who were spectators of the jobs of the primates and captains, became every month more insolent and disorderly. They landed at Santorin, and, not content with carrying off large supplies of grapes and figs, they deliberately plundered the cotton plantations, and sent boat-loads of cotton on board their ships, as if they had conquered a lawful prize in an enemy's territory.

Yet all these disorders, abuses, waste, and extravagance seem hardly sufficient to explain the rapidity with which the proceeds of the loans disappeared ; and indeed it required the assistance of equal extravagance and similar jobbing in London and New York to empty the Greek treasury. But the thing was done quickly and effectually. Early in the year 1826, the government at Nauplia had spent every farthing it could obtain, and made a vain attempt to raise a loan of 800,000 dollars among the Greeks themselves, which was to be immediately repaid by the sale of national lands. These lands had been pledged only a short time before by the same government to the English bondholders as a security for the second loan. The Greeks, who were better informed concerning the proceedings and bad faith of their countrymen than strangers, would not advance a single dollar. The dishonesty of the government, the rapacity of the military, and the indiscipline of the navy, were forerunners·of the misfortunes of the nation.

BOOK FOURTH.

THE SUCCESSES OF THE TURKS.

CHAPTER I.

NAVAL SUCCESSES.—IBRAHIM IN THE MOREA.

Destruction of Kasos.—Destruction of Psara.—Expedition of Mohammed Ali.—The Bairam at Makri.—Naval battles off Budrun.—Failure of the Turks at Samos.—Ibrahim driven back from Crete.—Ibrahim lands in Greece.—Greeks unprepared for defence.—Defeat of the Greek army.—Egyptians take Sphakteria.—Escape of the brig Mars.—Capitulation of Navarin.—Success of Miaoulis at Modon.—Kolokotrones general in the Peloponnesus.—Defeat of the Greeks and death of the archimandrite Dikaios at Maniaki.—Defeat of Kolokotrones at Makryplagi.—Ibrahim repulsed at Lerna.—Defeat of Kolokotrones at Trikorpha.—Ibrahim ravages the Morea.—Receives orders to aid in the siege of Mesolonghi.

THE tide of success which had hitherto borne the Greeks onward to glory and independence began to ebb in 1824. Sultan Mahmud studied the causes of the disasters of his fleets and armies, and laboured with stern industry to remedy their defects. He observed that his own resources were not diminished by his losses, while those of the Greeks were daily declining, and were sure to be utterly exhausted if he could prolong the contest for a few years. He therefore changed his plans. Instead of invading Greece, where the great mass of the population was determined to defend its liberty with desperate courage, he resolved to destroy all the outlying resources of his enemies before attempting to attack the centre of their power.

He saw that the first step to reconquering Greece was to recover the command of the sea. This, he soon discovered, was easier than was generally supposed. The Greeks were not in a condition to replace the loss of a few ships; the Othoman empire could rebuild a fleet every year. The destruction, therefore, of a single Greek ship and a few sailors, was cheaply purchased by the conflagration of a Turkish line-of-battle ship or a frigate; the ruin of a Greek naval island by the sacrifice of an Othoman fleet. The sultan selected Psara and Kasos as the first objects of attack. They were the most exposed naval stations of the Greeks. Their cruisers inflicted the most extensive losses on the Turkish population, and their destruction would be more popular in the Othoman empire than any victory either by land or sea. Psara was the cause of intolerable evils to the Mussulmans in Thrace and Asia Minor; Kasos was an eyesore and a torment to Syria and Egypt. Mahmud and Mohammed Ali concerted their operations to attack the two islands suddenly and simultaneously with two fleets. Their plans were framed with skill and executed with vigour.

The commercial activity of Kasos adds another to the proofs already mentioned that the principles of the sultan's policy were better than the administration of his authority. Christians or Mussulmans, Yezidis and Nestorians, Druses and Maronites, were often prosperous and contented under the sultan's government, but rarely either the one or the other when their affairs were conducted by Othoman officials. Secluded valleys, like the valley of the river of Arta, were carefully cultivated; barren rocks, like Hydra, were peopled by active seamen. The Vallachs of Kalarites and Syrako, and the Albanians of Hydra, administered their own affairs without being controlled by a pasha or a voivode.

Kasos afforded a striking example of the advantages to be derived from the sultan's protection, when it could be obtained without the evils of the Othoman administration. This island is about twelve miles long, and in its aridity and iron-bound coast resembles Hydra. It also has no secure port; yet at this time it contained seven thousand inhabitants, who owned fifteen square-rigged vessels and forty smaller craft, which had for three years been employed in plundering the islands of Crete, Rhodes, and Cyprus, and ravaging the coasts of Karamania, Syria, and Egypt. It was said that the Kasiots usually murdered their captives at sea; and there is reason to fear that the accusation is well founded, for few Turkish prisoners were ever brought to the island. Indeed, during the years 1821 and 1822 the inhabitants had difficulty in procuring bread for themselves, and could not feed their enemies. Mercy, it must be owned, was a virtue as little practised by the Christian as by the Mussulman combatants at the commencement of the Greek Revolution, and few lives were spared from motives of humanity.

Sultan Mahmud expected to paralyze the Greeks with terror, by destroying Kasos and Psara at the same time. But the Egyptian fleet was ready for action before that of the capitan-pasha could leave Constantinople. The force destined by Mohammed Ali to attack Kasos consisted of three frigates and ten sloops of war, under the command of Ismael Gibraltar Pasha. On board this squadron three thousand Albanians were embarked under Hussein Bey Djeritli, an able officer, who fell afterwards at Mesolonghi.

Kasos was ill fortified, and the inhabitants neglected every precaution which common prudence ought to have suggested for their defence. The Albanians effected their landing on the 19th of June 1824, during the night, not far from the usual landing-place, and scaled the rocks that commanded the Kasiot batteries without encountering any resistance. The surprise was complete. The islanders dwelt in four villages situated high in the mountain. The troops of Hussein climbed the rugged ascent in silence, and fell unexpectedly on the villagers. The men capable of bearing arms were slain without mercy. The old women shared their fate, but the young women and children, who were deemed suitable for the slave-market of Alexandria, were carried on board the ships. The Kasiots posted in the batteries near the beach stood firm. But the Albanians, experienced in mountain warfare, occupied the higher grounds, and crept forward, under the cover of rocks and stones, until they could shoot the islanders at their guns. Fourteen square-rigged vessels and about thirty small craft were captured, and five hundred Kasiot seamen were slain. The Albanians lost only thirty killed and wounded. Upwards of two thousand women and children were carried on board the ships. The Albanians were allowed twenty-four hours to plunder and collect slaves. The instant that term was expired, Ismael Gibraltar and Hussein took effective measures to restore order, and gave protection to every Greek who submitted to the sultan's authority.

The news of this sad disaster spread consternation through all Greece. It was a forewarning of the vigour of their new enemy; but the admonition was given in vain.

A greater calamity followed. Khosref Pasha sailed from the Dardanelles in the month of May, before the Greeks had any cruisers out to watch his movements. After a feint attack on Skopelos, the Othoman fleet returned to Mytilene, where it was soon joined by transports carrying three thousand janissaries. The capitan-pasha then embarked four thousand Asiatic troops and sailed for Psara. His force consisted of thirty-eight frigates, corvettes, and brigs, and forty transports, with about eight thousand soldiers.

Psara is a high rocky island, smaller than Kasos. Its northern and eastern sides are precipitous and were considered unassailable. The town is situated in the south-western part. Below it, to the west, there is a good roadstead sheltered by a rocky islet, called Antipsara. A small port to the south of the town also affords shelter to a few vessels. The native Psarians amounted to seven thousand souls; but in the year 1824 there were so many refugees from Chios, Kydonies, and Smyrna, residing in the island, that the population exceeded twelve thousand. About a thousand of the Romeliot armatoli, who had plundered Skiathos, were now engaged to defend Psara. Every point where it was supposed that the Turks would attempt to land was fortified. The Psarians unfortunately overrated their own knowledge of military affairs, and greatly underrated the skill and enterprise of their enemy. Two hundred pieces of artillery were mounted in ill-constructed and ill-placed batteries.

Extraordinary success in privateering had rendered the Psarians presumptuous. They spoke of the Turks as cowards, and of Sultan Mahmud as a tyrant, a fool, and a butcher. Foreigners who possessed military knowledge in vain pointed out to them the defects of their batteries; all advice was treated with contempt. Their domineering conduct was insupportable to their countrymen in the Archipelago; they were the tyrants of the Greek islands on the Asiatic coast, and seemed to emulate the insolence of the ancient Athenians. To complete the similarity, they commenced hostilities with the Samians, who refused to receive a Psarian governor and a Psarian tax-collector. Samos was blockaded, and the Turks of Asia Minor were relieved from the depredations of the Greeks, while the privateers of Psara were pursuing and plundering the privateers of Samos. The Psarians were also accused of neglecting to aid the brave inhabitants of Trikheri in their last struggle with the Turks, and of pillaging the Greeks of Mount Pelion, who by their neglect had been compelled to acknowledge the sultan's authority.

Unlike the Athenians of old, the Psarians placed more confidence in their stone batteries than in their wooden walls. As sailors, they knew the inferiority of their ships; their utter ignorance of the art of war made them fancy that their batteries were impregnable. They laid up the greater part of their ships in the roadstead of Antipsara, and employed the crews as gunners on shore. The island was defended by four thousand well-armed men, but these men were without discipline and without a leader; they were consequently little better than an armed mob.

The safety of Psara depended on the activity of the Greek fleet, and on the skill of the Psarians in using fire-ships. Unfortunately for Greece, the plan of defence adopted by the local government threw away the best chance of success. Upwards of fifteen hundred seamen, who had acquired great naval skill, some degree of discipline, and some knowledge of marine artillery when embarked in small vessels, were rendered of little use by being employed on shore in ill-constructed batteries without artillery officers, and mixed up with undisciplined armatoli.

The capitan-pasha consumed six weeks in making preparations which ought to have been completed in as many days. The Greek government had, therefore, ample time to send a fleet to meet him in the narrow seas, to oppose his embarking troops at Mytilene, and to attack his transports when he attempted to effect a landing at Psara. The avarice of the Hydriot primates and the self-sufficiency of the Psarians prevented Greece from profiting by the delay.

The attack on Psara was skilfully conducted. Khosref

with ten ships opened a heavy cannonade on the batteries, while he detached a part of his fleet in a direction which rendered it visible from the town, and induced the Psarians to believe that the object was to debark troops. The attention of the islanders was diverted by this simple stratagem. In the mean time a body of Arnaouts and Asiatics landed at a small open beach and stormed a battery manned by fifty armatoli. They then climbed the mountain, concealing themselves as much as possible from observation until they reached the heights above the town. On gaining that point they unfurled the Turkish flag, and announced their success to the capitan-pasha and the astonished Greeks by a discharge of fire-arms. At a signal from the Othoman flag-ship a hundred boats, filled with troops, immediately pushed off, and attacked simultaneously all the batteries at the roadstead. After a short engagement the Turks were everywhere victorious. Terror seized both the armatoli and the Psarians. All who saw a chance of escape fled. Those whose retreat was cut off made a desperate resistance, and no Psarian laid down his arms. What yesterday had been insolence and pride to-day was converted into patriotism. But the valour which, under the guidance of discipline and science, might have repulsed the Turks, could only secure an honourable death. Eight thousand persons were slain or reduced to slavery; about four thousand, chiefly Psarians, succeeded in getting on board vessels in the port and in putting to sea while their enemies were engaged in the sack of the town. The victorious Turks slew every male capable of bearing arms, and the heads of the vanquished were piled into one of those ghastly pyramidal trophies with which Othoman pashas then commemorated their triumphs. One hundred vessels of various sizes fell into the hands of the capitan-pasha. Only twenty vessels escaped.

The Turks of Asia Minor were frantic with joy, and their cruelty might have equalled that of the Greeks at Navarin and Tripolitza, had their avarice not induced them to spare the women and children for the slave-markets of Smyrna and Constantinople. Great were the festivities on the coasts of Thrace and Asia Minor when it was known that the dwellings of the Psarians were desolate, and the sailors who had plundered the true believers were slain.

EXPEDITION OF MOHAMMED ALI.

The Albanians of Hydra and Spetzas had been slow to aid the Greeks of Kasos and Psara. This neglect was not caused by any prejudice of race, but by ignoble feelings of interest. When the terrible catastrophe of Psara was known at Hydra, fear for their own safety inspired the islanders with a degree of activity, which, if displayed a few weeks earlier, might have saved both Kasos and Psara. Both at Hydra and Spetzas, soldiers were hired to defend the islands during the absence of the sailors, who hastened on board their ships, and the whole Greek fleet put to sea.

The capitan-pasha had returned to Mytilene with the booty and slaves captured at Psara before Miaoulis appeared; so that the Greek fleet could only save the fugitives who had concealed themselves in caverns and in secluded ravines. Two transports with captives on board were also captured in the port. Khosref celebrated the Courban Baïram at Mytilene. It was his intention to attack Samos, and, had he carried that project immediately into execution, it would have had a good chance of success. The blockade of Samos by the Psarians had thrown the affairs of that island into confusion, and the people were ill-prepared for defence. But the month which the capitan-pasha wasted at Mytilene was not left unemployed. The fate of Kasos and Psara awakened all the energies of the Samians, and when the Greek and Turkish fleets appeared in the waters of Samos at the same time, the capitan-pasha did not venture to make an attempt to land troops. After some manœuvring, he bore up for Budrun, where he was to effect his junction with the Egyptian fleet.

Mohammed Ali, having resolved to become the sultan's agent for reconquering the Morea, prepared for the enterprise with prudence and vigour. He had been previously engaged in forming a fleet, of which one of the finest ships, called the Asia, had been recently fitted out at Deptford. A fleet of twenty-five sail was now prepared for sea, and a hundred transports were collected in the port of Alexandria to receive troops, provisions, and military stores. Everything necessary for a long voyage was supplied in profusion; eight thousand men and a thousand horses were embarked. An experienced English seaman who was present, declared that the stores were carefully packed, and that the transports could not have embarked the same number of men and the same amount of material in less time in most English ports, though the operation would of course be performed at home with less noise and fewer men. This service, like all other military and naval business in Egypt at this time, was organized and directed by French and Italian officers who had served in the armies of Napoleon I.

Ibrahim sailed from Alexandria on the 19th July 1824. The difficulty of getting clear of the Egyptian coast during the strong north winds which prevail in summer, forced the transports to beat up in small squadrons; and the whole sea between Egypt, Cyprus, and Crete was crowded with ships. A few Greek cruisers might have made great havoc, and secured valuable prizes—perhaps frustrated the expedition. But, at this time, the supineness and civil wars of the Greeks formed a discouraging contrast with the activity and harmony of the Turks.

On the 2nd of August Ibrahim put into the gulf of Makri, where he found two of his frigates repairing the damage they had sustained in a gale of wind. Many of the transports had already reached this rendezvous. The pasha landed the troops to celebrate the feast of Baïram, and the ceremonies of this great Mohammedan festival were performed in a very imposing manner. In the afternoon the whole army was drawn up on the beach. When the sun went down, bright-coloured lanterns were hoisted at the mast-heads of all the ships, and a salute was fired from every gun in the fleet. The troops on shore followed the example, firing by platoons, companies, and battalions as rapidly as possible, until their fire became at last a continuous discharge of musketry along the whole line, which was prolonged in an incessant roar for a quarter of an hour. The spectacle was wild and strange, in a deserted bay, overlooked by the sculptured tombs of the ancient Telmessus. Ibrahim seemed to be rivalling the folly of Caligula. Suddenly, when the din of artillery and musketry had swelled into a sound like thunder, every noise was hushed, and, as the smoke rolled away, the thin silver crescent of the new moon was visible. A prolonged shout, repeated in melancholy cadence, rose from the army, and was echoed back from the fleet. A minute after, a hundred camp-fires blazed up as if by enchantment. The line was broken, and the busy hum of the soldiers hastening to receive their rations of pilaf, reminded the spectator that the pageant on which he had gazed with delight was only a transient interlude in a bloody drama.

The Egyptian fleet, after quitting Makri, proceeded to Budrun. In passing Rhodes it was ordered to bear up and come to anchor. The reason for this strange order was never known. Ibrahim's frigate gave the signal, and let go its anchor in sixty fathoms. Another frigate, in her zeal to obey the signal, let go her anchor in a hundred and fifty fathoms, and of course lost anchor and cable. A day or two after, Ibrahim's frigate drove into deeper water, and her crew being unable to get up the anchor, the pasha ordered her captain to be bastinadoed on the quarter-deck. There can be no doubt that if Miaoulis had possessed the power of applying the cat-o'-nine-tails to the backs of his mutinous sailors, the Greek fleet would have been a more dangerous adversary to the Egyptian than it proved.

Ibrahim joined the capitan-pasha at Budrun on the 1st of September. Their united fleets consisted of a seventy-four bearing the flag of Khosref, twenty frigates, twenty-five corvettes, and forty brigs and schooners, with nearly three hundred transports of all sizes and shapes. Great improvements had been made in the Othoman fleet during the preceding winter, but it was far from being in good order. The ships were in general so over-masted, and so heavily rigged, that they could not have carried their spars for an hour during a heavy gale in the Channel. Even in their own seas, the miltems, or summer gales, often drove them from their course, and English seamen correctly described the cruises of the capitan-pasha's fleet by speaking of the Othoman navy as being adrift in the Archipelago.

The Greek fleet, consisting of between seventy and eighty sail, mounting eight hundred and fifty guns, and manned by five thousand able seamen, appeared in the channel between Cos and the island of Kappari on the 5th of September. The Turkish fleet got under weigh and stood out to engage it. The capitan-pasha, though a man of some administrative capacity, was a coward. He fancied every Greek brig was a fire-ship prepared to blow him up, like his predecessor Kara Ali, and, to avoid that fate, he always contrived that some accident should prevent his ship from getting into danger. On this occasion, he carried away his maintop-sail and his topgallant-yard while in stays, and then ran behind Orak to refit.

The Greeks endeavoured to throw their enemies into confusion, hoping that when the ships were crowded together a favourable opportunity would occur for using their fire-ships. This object seemed nearly gained, when four frigates stood boldly on to gain the weather-gauge of the Greeks, and endeavoured to force Miaoulis and the leading ships of the Greek fleet under the guns of the fort of Cos. The naval skill of the Hydriots baffled this manœuvre. An Egyptian corvette at the same time engaged a Greek pretty closely for ten minutes, and did not haul off until her captain was killed. The frigates of Ibrahim and Ismael Gibraltar ran along the Greek line firing with steadiness, but at too great a distance to do much damage, and quite out of range of the smaller guns of their opponents. A fire-ship was directed against Ibrahim's frigate, but it drifted past, and consumed itself harmlessly in the midst of the Othoman fleet. The Egyptians succeeded in forcing another fire-ship under the guns of Cos, where it was abandoned by its crew with such precipitation, that it fell uninjured into the hands of the Turks, who examined its construction with the greatest interest. These two failures diminished the fear with which the Greek fireships had been hitherto regarded.

The first battle off Budrun was more favourable to the Turks than to the Greeks. A long day was spent by the hostile fleets in an incessant cannonade, and much powder was wasted beyond the range of any guns. To the Turks this was of use as practice; and if we take into account the number of ships engaged, the inexperience of the crews and officers, and the advantage which the narrow channel afforded to the light ships and naval skill of the Greeks, it is surprising that the Turks escaped with so little loss. Among the Constantinopolitan division of the fleet there was often considerable disorder. Several ships ran foul of each other. Most fired their broadsides as the guns were laid before getting under weigh, so that when the Greeks were to windward the shot were seen flying through the air like shells, and when the enemy was to leeward the broadsides lashed the sea into a foam at a hundred yards from the muzzles of the guns, while the Greeks were a mile distant. The day ended in a much greater loss of jib-booms and spars than of men on the part of the Turks. The Greeks lost two fire-ships. It is supposed that not twenty men were killed on both sides. Ibrahim was extremely proud of his exploits. It was his first naval engagement. He had baffled one Greek fire-ship and captured another. Half-a-dozen such battles would give him the command of the sea.

The Greek fleet anchored in the bay of Sandama. On the 10th of September the Turks again stood out of Budrun. Their object was to force a passage to Samos. Several ships endeavoured to get to windward of the Greeks by standing out to Leros, and for a time it seemed probable that Miaoulis, who lay becalmed near the rock Ataki with a dozen brigs, would be cut off from the rest of the fleet, and be surrounded by the enemy[1]. The breeze, which had hitherto only favoured the Turks, at last reached the Greeks, who knew how to employ it to the best advantage. A confused engagement ensued, in which both parties suffered several disasters. A Greek fire-ship was dismasted, but was burned by its own crew before it was abandoned. Three fire-ships, manned by Albanian islanders, were successively launched against an Egyptian brig, which disquieted the Greeks by the skill and daring of its manœuvres. For a moment the brig seemed to be enveloped in flames, and the report was spread through the Greek fleet that it was destroyed. This was a mistake. The little brig emerged from the flames uninjured, while the three fire-ships, drifting away, burned harmless to the water's edge. The sight of four fire-ships consumed in vain, inspired the Turks with unusual boldness. The Tunisian commodore led his squadron to attack the Greeks with more courage than caution. Two Hydriot fire-ships bore down upon him, and one grappled his frigate, which was blown up. The crew consisted of four hundred men, and she carried

---

[1] Gordon (ii. 154) by some mistake writes Zatalia instead of Ataki. Tricoupi, who habitually transposes the ancient and modern names of his authorities, misled by the word, supposes that the fleets were off Attalcia, which is at least two hundred miles distant. Tricoupi, iii. 164. Gordon's information concerning the naval operations in 1824 was in part drawn from the journal of an Englishman in Ibrahim's fleet, which was lent to him by the Author on his complaining that he had found great difficulty in obtaining accurate accounts of the movements of the Greek fleet from the Greek islanders.

two hundred and fifty Arab regular troops. The commodore, the colonel of the troops, and about fifty men, were picked up by Greek boats. All the rest perished at the time, and most of those then saved were subsequently murdered at a massacre of Turkish prisoners in Hydra [1]. A Turkish corvette was also destroyed by a Psarian fire-ship. These losses so terrified the Turks that they hauled off, and both fleets returned to their former anchorages.

In this second engagement the Egyptians remained almost inactive. Ibrahim and Gibraltar, who were neither of them deficient in courage, were not disposed to expose their ships to secure victory for a capitan-pasha who kept always at a distance from the enemy. Jealousy also prevailed between Ibrahim and Khosref. The superior rank of the capitan-pasha had enabled him to assume airs of superiority, which had mortified the Egyptian. It was now necessary to secure the cordial co-operation of Ibrahim, since it was evident that it would be impossible for the Othoman fleet alone to effect a debarkation at Samos. After a few days had been passed in negotiations and ceremonious visits, Ibrahim consented to send all his frigates to assist the Turks, and encamped his own troops at Budrun until the capitan-pasha's operations should be finished.

It may be here observed, that if the Greeks had endeavoured to learn the truth concerning their enemies, they might easily have ascertained that they were now about to encounter a much more dangerous enemy than any who had previously attacked them. While the Egyptian regulars remained at Budrun they maintained strict discipline. Neither in the town nor in the neighbouring country were the Christians molested in any way by Ibrahim's soldiers, though two thousand Albanians, whose services had been transferred by the capitan-pasha to the Egyptian expedition, could hardly be prevented from plundering Mussulman and Christian alike.

---

[1] Sir James Emerson Tennent, in *A Picture of Greece in* 1825, by James Emerson (vol. i. 244) gives an account of this massacre, of which he was an eye-witness. Two hundred innocent and helpless prisoners were butchered like sheep in the public square of Hydra, and no primate or captain made an effort to save their lives. This unparalleled act of atrocity was caused by a mere rumour that a Hydriot vessel had been blown up by a Turkish slave, though it was as probable that it was destroyed by the carelessness of its crew. The Author saw a Psarian captain smoking in his cabin, when it contained many boxes of cartridges which he was transporting to the army.

Ibrahim had accepted their services in order to keep them as a check on the Turks in the Cretan fortresses.

The Greek and Turkish fleets met again between Icaria and Samos. Some severe skirmishing ensued, in which the Greeks compelled the capitan-pasha to abandon the project of landing on Samos. Heavy gales during the latter part of September dispersed both fleets, and the capitan-pasha returned to the Dardanelles early in October, leaving several Othoman frigates and corvettes with the Egyptian fleet.

The Greek fleet was about the same time weakened by the departure of the Psarians, but Miaoulis continued to harass the Egyptians. An engagement took place off Mytilene, in which Nicodemos, the only Psarian who remained with the Greek fleet, burned a Turkish corvette, and two other fire-ships destroyed an Egyptian brig. Again, however, a Hydriot fire-ship was burned uselessly in consequence of the timidity, the indiscipline, or the inexperience of the crew. Ibrahim was so dissatisfied with the conduct of his captains in this engagement, that he expressed his displeasure in strong terms. He ordered the captain of the brig which had been burned to be strangled for abandoning his ship too precipitately, and he ordered another captain to be bastinadoed on his own quarter-deck, for running foul of a frigate in order to escape a Greek fire-ship.

The season was far advanced before the Egyptians returned to Budrun. Most of the Greek ships, without waiting for orders, sailed for Hydra and Spetzas. Miaoulis remained with twenty-five sail, and continued to watch the enemy with indefatigable zeal. Ibrahim lost no time in embarking his army in order to reach Crete, where a considerable number of men and a large amount of military stores had already arrived direct from Alexandria.

On the 13th of November 1824, while the whole Egyptian fleet was approaching Crete, about twenty Greek brigs hove in sight, and bore down on the transports, which were far ahead of the men-of-war. A single frigate, which was much to windward of the others, was surrounded by five Greek brigs, and might easily have been carried by boarding her from stem and stern, had the Greek islanders ventured to come to close quarters. Their timid manœuvres allowed her to escape, which she did in the most unseamanlike way, by running towards the middle of the transports with all her studding-sails set. The Greeks, who outsailed her, passed successively under her stern, and raked her with their broadsides. A fire-ship was also sent down on her, and her studding-sails caught fire, but they were cut away, and the fire was prevented from spreading to the other sails. The aversion of the Hydriots to encountering the Turks sword in hand, prevented their taking advantage of the confusion produced by the conflagration. A bold attack would have insured either the capture or the destruction of the frigate. In the afternoon all the transports had retired behind the men-of-war, and Ibrahim Pasha, his admiral Ismael Gibraltar, with nine more frigates, formed a line to protect them. The Greek force before night was increased to forty sail. Two fire-ships were directed against one of the Egyptian frigates, but she avoided them without much trouble. The night came on dark and squally, and the Egyptians were ordered to bear away between Crete and Kasos.

Next morning a number of transports assembled under the lee of Karpathos, where they found Ibrahim's frigate. They then made sail for Rhodes; but as that island affords no anchorage during the winter, the bay of Marmorice, on the opposite coast, was fixed on for the general rendezvous. In the engagement of the 13th the Greeks captured only seven or eight transports, but they dispersed the convoy so completely that many vessels bore away for Alexandria. A few, however, by holding on their course, gained Suda in safety. At Marmorice Ibrahim degraded eleven captains for neglecting to keep to windward of the transports according to orders.

The Greeks allowed themselves to be deluded into a belief that Ibrahim would not dare to renew his voyage to Crete during the winter. They returned to Hydra with their prizes, and the persevering pasha sailed from Marmorice on the 5th of December, and reached Suda before the end of the year 1824, where he observed to one of the European officers of his suite, 'As we have now outmanœuvred the Greeks at sea, we shall certainly find little difficulty in beating them on shore.'

A calm survey of the campaign of 1824 at last convinced the Greeks that their navy was inadequate to obtain a decisive victory over the Turks. The expedition against Samos had indeed been frustrated, and seven Turkish ships had been destroyed. But to obtain these successes, twenty-two Greek fire-ships had been consumed. On the other hand, the Turks had to boast of the destruction of Kasos and Psara, and of having captured nearly a hundred and fifty Greek vessels, and slain about four thousand Greek seamen. The Greeks could only hope for ultimate success by changing their system of warfare. Captain Hastings again urged them to purchase steam-ships, arm them with heavy guns, and make use of shells and hot shot. Had his proposition been promptly accepted, and its execution entrusted to his zeal and activity, Greece might still have been saved by her own exertions.

When Ibrahim Pasha quitted Alexandria in July 1824, he made a vow not to put his foot on shore until he landed in Greece. On the 24th of February 1825, he debarked at Modon with four thousand regular infantry and five hundred cavalry. His fleet immediately returned to Crete, and soon came back, bringing the second division of his army, consisting of six thousand infantry, five hundred cavalry, and a strong corps of field artillery. On the 21st of March the Egyptian army encamped before Navarin.

After the unfortunate battle of Petta, the Greeks banished every semblance of military discipline from their armies in the field. At the beginning of 1825 no words were strong enough to express their contempt for the regular troops of the Egyptian pasha. They said that the Arabs would run away at the sight of the armatoli, who had always been victorious over the bravest Mussulmans in the sultan's empire. This self-confidence had prevented them taking any precautions against an enemy they despised. For more than six months the Greek government had known that Navarin would be the first fortress attacked, but no measures had been adopted for putting it in a state of defence. Yet a small sum would have rendered it capable of a prolonged resistance, and nothing was so likely to disgust Mohammed Ali with the war in Greece as a long and expensive siege. The siege of a maritime fortress would also have afforded the Greek navy frequent opportunities of cutting off the supplies of the besieging army.

At this crisis of the Revolution, the president of Greece, George Konduriottes, showed himself utterly unworthy of the high trust he had received from the nation, and Kolettes proved himself ignorant and incapable. The Greek government had for several months been paying thirty thousand men, who were called soldiers; when it now became necessary to march against the invaders of the Morea, ten thousand men could not be collected. The sycophants who surrounded Konduriottes persuaded him to take the command of the army. The president departed from Nauplia with great pomp, mounted on a richly-caparisoned horse, which he hung over as if he had been a sack of hay, supported by two grooms. His ungraceful exhibition of horsemanship was followed by a long train composed of secretaries, guards, grooms, and pipe-bearers. 'As he passed under the lofty arched gateway of Nauplia on the 28th of March, the cannon from the ramparts and from the fortress above pealed out their loud salutations, and were answered by the batteries on the shore and the shipping in the harbour[1].' Mavrocordatos, whose presidency had been characterized by a similar attempt to play the generalissimo, accompanied Konduriottes as a cabinet counsellor. An old Hydriot sea-captain, named Skourti, who had displayed some skill as a sailor, and some courage on the quarter-deck, was named lieutenant-general of the Greek army. So little idea had the president of the real point where danger was to be apprehended, that he proposed besieging Patras. When he reached Tripolitza, he found that a storm had burst on another quarter. The natural imbecility of Konduriottes got the better of his pride, and he could not conceal his incapacity to form any resolution. He felt that he ought to hasten in person to Navarin, and he set out; but instead of taking the direct road, he turned off to Kalamata, lingered there a moment, and then regained the seat of government without ever seeing an enemy.

The simplicity with which Ibrahim Pasha took the field formed a striking contrast to the pomp affected by the Hydriot president and the Greek captains. The aspect of the two armies was equally dissimilar. The gold of the English loan glittered profusely in the embroidered jackets and richly ornamented arms of the Greek soldiers, while in the Egyptian army the dress and the arms were plain and

---

[1] *Historical Sketch of the Greek Revolution*, by Dr. S. G. Howe, who was an eye-witness, p. 226.

simple. The Greek officers were equipped for show; the Egyptian for service. The Greek camp seemed to contain an accidental crowd of armed men. The Egyptian camp exhibited strict discipline and perfect order. One half of the regular troops was engaged in constant exercise or unceasing labour, while the other half reposed. The artillery and material for a siege were brought up from Modon with order and celerity.

The first attempt of the Greeks to interrupt Ibrahim's operations was made by the veteran chieftain Karatassos, and it was defeated with severe loss. The armatoli found to their surprise that the Arab boys, who had been disciplined by Ibrahim, were more dangerous enemies than the bravest Arnaouts the Greeks had ever encountered. Karatassos stated that this was the case to the executive government. His opinion was disregarded. It was said that he praised the discipline of the Egyptians to excuse his defeat, and he had conducted his attack carelessly because he was envious of the honour conferred on Captain Skourti, and wished to be named commander-in-chief.

Ibrahim formed the sieges of Navarin and of the old castle on the ruins of Pylos at the same time. Navarin contained a garrison of sixteen hundred men; Pylos of eight hundred. The flower of the Greek army advanced to relieve these two places, with the intention of falling on the rear of the besiegers, who were divided into two separate bodies, and compelled to keep up communications with Modon. The Greeks were commanded by Skourti. Their force exceeded seven thousand, and was composed of Romeliot armatoli, choice Moreot troops, and a band of Suliots. Ibrahim, who divined the plan of his enemy, did not allow him to choose his point of attack. On the 19th of April he attacked the Greek position at the head of three thousand regular infantry, four hundred cavalry, and four guns. The Suliots under Djavella and Constantine Botzaris, the armatoli under Karaï-skaki, and the Albanians of Argolis under Skourti, received the Egyptians in positions which they had themselves selected for their encampment. They were supported by a body of irregular cavalry, consisting in great part of Servians and Bulgarians. The leader, Hadji Christos, made a gallant show. He was surrounded by a retinue in imitation of a pasha of three tails, with kettledrums, timbileks, and a topuz-bearer.

After a short halt, which Ibrahim employed in reconnoitring the Greek position, the first regiment of Arabs was ordered to charge the Suliots and armatoli with the bayonet. The regulars marched steadily up to the Greek intrenchments under a heavy fire without wavering, though many fell. As they approached the enemy their officers cheered them on in double-quick time to the assault; but the best troops of Greece shrank from their encounter, and after a feeble resistance fled in every direction. A few round shot and a charge of cavalry dispersed the rest of the army and completed the victory. The vanquished Greeks fled in wild confusion, leaving six hundred men dead on the field. The Egyptians, particularly the cavalry, collected a rich booty; and silver-mounted arms, which had been thrown away by the Turks after their defeats at Valtetzi and Dervenaki, were now in like manner abandoned by the fugitive Greeks to insure their escape. This affair at Krommydi—for it cannot be called a battle—convinced every military friend of Greece that the best Greek irregular troops were unfit to encounter the most ordinary disciplined battalions in a pitched battle in the plain.

A few days after this victory, Hussein Djeritli, the conqueror of Kasos, arrived at the Egyptian camp with reinforcements. Hussein had the eye of a soldier, and he immediately pointed out to Ibrahim that his engineer, Colonel Romey, had not selected the best position for the batteries he had constructed against Navarin. Without having read Thucydides, Hussein also observed that the island of Sphakteria was the key of Navarin. It commanded the port, and its possession would render the defence of both Navarin and Pylos impracticable. He proposed to change the whole plan of attack. Ibrahim followed his advice, and entrusted him with the direction of the operations against Sphakteria.

When Ibrahim opened his trenches before Navarin, that fortress was ill supplied with provisions and ammunition. The neglect both of the government and the officers commanding in the place had been so great, that when the Egyptians cut off the water of the aqueduct half the cisterns were empty. Even Sphakteria had been left without defence. At last an effort was made to prevent the island from being occupied by the enemy. Eight brigs were at anchor in the harbour. Tsamados, who commanded the Mars, landed three eighteen-pounders, which he had embarked at Nauplia, and constructed a battery on the southern point of Sphakteria, in order to prevent the Egyptian ships from entering the port[1]. Though it was evident that this battery could oppose no obstacle to a landing of the Egyptians in other parts of the island, it was only with great difficulty that several foreign officers in Navarin could persuade the Greeks to take more effectual measures for the defence of Sphakteria. Mavrocordatos, who possessed more moral courage as well as more activity and ability than Konduriottes, fortunately visited Navarin to concert measures for its relief when the president fled back from Messenia. Mavrocordatos, Sakturi, the governor, and Tsamados, succeeded by their co-operation in getting four more guns in battery on the island, to protect the only spot where it was supposed that the Egyptians would attempt to land[2].

On the 8th of May 1825, the Egyptian fleet, carrying three thousand troops, stood out from Modon, and on reaching Sphakteria opened a cannonade on the Greek batteries. Under cover of the smoke, a regiment of Arab regulars and a body of Moreot Turks, who had volunteered to lead the attack, effected a landing. Hussein Bey led them on to charge the Greeks who defended the guns, but Romeliots, Moreot klephts, and artillerymen, all fled at his approach, and abandoned the batteries without offering any resistance. The Arab bayonet swept all before it. Tsamados, who had landed with a few of his crew to assume the direction of a carronade belonging to his ship, stood his ground, and died bravely at his post. He was a member of the Hydriot aristocracy, and had shown himself more inclined to the introduction of discipline in the Greek fleet, and to avail himself of scientific improvements, than the rest of his countrymen. He commanded his own brig, and on several occasions he had displayed a degree of naval skill and personal courage which had obtained for him warm praise from Miaoulis. His amiable

---

[1] These guns were intended by the Greek government for the siege of Patras.
[2] Collegno (*Diario dell' Asedio di Navarino*, p. 54) says there were twelve guns in battery on the 7th of May, but other authorities equally well informed agree in giving the number as only seven.

character, his youth, his enlightened views, and his true patriotism, rendered his death a national calamity at this moment.

The veteran Hetairist, Anagnostaras, who had forfeited a good name won at the siege of Tripolitza by his subsequent avarice and rapacity, was recognized by a Moreot Mussulman, and slain to avenge the blood of the slaughtered Turks. The victor carried the rich arms of Anagnostaras during the whole campaign of 1825.

Count Santa Rosa, a Piedmontese exile, fell also in this affair. No man's death was more sincerely regretted, and none fell to whom death was so welcome. The Greek deputies in London, at the suggestion of some of the liberal counsellors by whom they were surrounded, invited Santa Rosa to serve in Greece. On his arrival at Nauplia he found that the members of the Greek government turned from him with pride. Everything he said was treated with contempt, and he himself with neglect. Yet, as he understood much better than Mavrocordatos, Kolettes, and Rhodios the extent of the danger to which Greece was then exposed, he deemed it dishonourable to abandon her cause at such a crisis. His services not having been accepted, he was serving at Sphakteria as a volunteer. After receiving a severe wound, he refused to surrender, and was killed by an Arab soldier, who found a small sum of money and a seal in his possession. The sight of this seal enabled a friend in the Egyptian camp to learn his fate[1].

Three hundred and fifty Greeks were killed, and two hundred taken prisoners, at Sphakteria. The victorious Arabs gained considerable booty, for the majority of the slain wore silver-mounted arms, and their belts were lined with English gold. Sovereigns soon circulated in the bazaar of Modon, and the war became extremely popular in the Egyptian army.

---

[1] This seal was given to the Author by a Philhellene who was taken prisoner a few days later. Collegno accompanied Santa Rosa to Greece. Like every foreigner, his feelings were wounded by the treatment his friend received, and he reproaches the Greeks with their ingratitude. Tricoupi gave a strong example of this national vice. His funeral oration in memory of those who fell at Sphakteria, amidst much hyperbole concerning Greek courage, omitted all mention of Santa Rosa's name, though he and many of his hearers knew well that Santa Rosa was one of the very small number who fell honourably fighting. The neglect was the more disgraceful, because the orator was personally acquainted with Santa Rosa, and knew his virtues. Collegno, *Diario*, p. 118.

There were five brigs remaining in the harbour of Navarin when Hussein Bey stormed the island. They immediately stood out to sea, one only lingering at the entrance of the port. This was the Mars, which sent its boats to bring off the captain. Mavrocordatos and Sakturi escaped in these boats, and brought on board the news that Tsamados had refused to abandon his post, and had fallen doing his duty. Sakturi did not think of returning to his post at Navarin. He abandoned his government, and remained on board the Mars, which in order to escape was obliged to pass through the Egyptian fleet, and receive the broadsides of several frigates, yet she lost only two men killed and seven wounded, so trifling was the danger in the severest naval engagement during this war, unless when fire-ships were successful. Lord Byron, who witnessed the firing of two Turkish men-of-war endeavouring to prevent the Greeks from taking possession of a stranded brig, quaintly observed, 'These Turks would prove dangerous enemies if they fired without taking aim.'

Three days after the conquest of Sphakteria, Pylos capitulated. The garrison, consisting of seven hundred and eighty-six men, laid down its arms, and the Greeks were allowed to depart uninjured.

Navarin was feebly defended. The Romeliot troops in the place were eager to capitulate. George Mavromichales, who afterwards assassinated Capodistrias, displayed great determination, and urged his countrymen to defend the place to the last. He harangued the soldiers, and opposed all terms of capitulation. It was evident, however, that the fortress could not hold out many days, since all hope of relief, both by land and sea, was cut off.; Ibrahim offered honourable terms of capitulation. He was desirous of winning the Greeks to submit to his government, and for this purpose he was eager to exhibit proofs of his humanity. He had established his military superiority; he wished now to place his civil and financial administration in contrast with that of the Greek government. He expected by his treatment of the garrison of Navarin to facilitate his future conquests. A capitulation was arranged after a good deal of negotiation, for the besieged could not forget the scenes which had followed the capitulation of the Turks. The Greeks laid down their arms and surrendered all their property. The field-officers alone were allowed to retain their swords. The whole garrison was transported to Kalamata in neutral vessels, under the escort of a French and Austrian man-of-war. Ibrahim, who thought that the British government showed undue favour to the Greek cause, refused to allow any mention of an English escort to be inserted in the capitulation.

On the 21st of May the Greeks marched out of Navarin to embark in the transports prepared for their reception. A crowd of Moreot Mussulmans from Modon and Coron, excited by a few survivors of the massacre of Navarin, assembled to waylay the Christians as they were embarking. But Ibrahim was a man of a firmer character and more enlarged political views than the primates and chieftains of Greece. He had foreseen the attempt, and he adopted effectual measures for preventing any stain on his good faith. A body of regular cavalry prevented the Turks from approaching the ground; and the unarmed Greeks marched securely to the ships between lines of Arab infantry with fixed bayonets. George Mavromichales and Iatrakos of Mistra were detained as hostages for the release of the two pashas who were detained by the Greeks after the capitulation of Nauplia. George Mavromichales, like Ali of Argos, had refused to sign the capitulation. The exchange was soon effected.

We have often had occasion to observe that the Greek fleet arrived too late to avert disaster. It mattered little whether the Greek government was destitute of money or rolling in wealth, whether the scene of danger was near or far off, the same supineness and selfishness always characterized the proceedings of the Albanian islanders. At Chios, at Kasos, at Psara, at Sphakteria, and at Mesolonghi, the neglect of the Greek government and the sordid spirit of the Hydriots were equally conspicuous. A small squadron put to sea when the news of Ibrahim's landing in the Morea reached Hydra, but it was so weak that Miaoulis could not prevent Hussein Bey from conquering Sphakteria, and gaining possession of the magnificent harbour of Navarin, where the Egyptian fleet was anchored in safety, even before the fortress capitulated. But when Miaoulis reached Modon, he observed that a part of the Egyptian fleet was still at that place, and by instant action he hoped to inflict such a loss on Ibrahim as might delay the fall of Navarin, and perhaps save the place.

On the 12th of May he sent six fire-ships simultaneously into the midst of the Egyptian squadron as it lay at anchor. The attack was well planned and promptly and boldly executed. The conflagration was terrible, and accident alone prevented it from being more extensive. A fine double-banked frigate, the Asia, which, it has been mentioned, was fitted out at Deptford, three sloops of war, and seven transports, were destroyed; but on shore the fire was prevented from destroying anything but a magazine of provisions[1]. The explosion of the powder-magazines of the ships of war was heard both in Ibrahim's camp and in Navarin; and for some time a report prevailed that all the transports and military stores had been destroyed. Successive couriers soon brought exact accounts of the real loss sustained. Ibrahim was satisfied that it was not sufficient to interrupt his operations for a single hour. The Greeks considered this affair of Modon as a brilliant achievement; with equal justice, the Egyptians regarded it as an insignificant disaster[2].

Even the fall of Navarin did not entirely awaken the Greeks from the lethargy into which they had sunk. The government did everything in its power to conceal the defeats sustained by the army, and the people were willing to be deceived. The news of the capitulation spread slowly, and was in some degree neutralized by fabricated reports of imaginary successes[3].

Ibrahim advanced towards the centre of the Peloponnesus before the Moreots made any general effort to repel his invasion. Selfishness and party animosity were more powerful than patriotism. But the timid Konduriottes observed with alarm many signs of his own declining influence, and of the reviving power of the Peloponnesian primates and chieftains. The departure of the Romeliot troops, who had quitted the Morea when they heard of the invasion of Western Greece by Kiutayhé, left the executive body without a strong military force on which it could depend. The

---

[1] The Egyptians reported their loss as one frigate, two brigs, and eight transports. Collegno, Diario, 75.
[2] Two eye-witnesses give accurate information concerning the siege of Navarin—Collegno in his Diario, and Dr. Millingen in Memoirs of the Affairs of Greece.
[3] Some time elapsed before the Greek newspapers alluded to the fall of Navarin, and the private journals of many Philhellenes which the Author has examined record reports of victories which, though generally circulated, were entirely without foundation.

nullity of Konduriottes, the administrative ignorance of Kolettes, the licentiousness of the archimandrite Dikaios, and the shallow presumption of Rhodios, added to the fiscal corruption of the civil officials and the rapacity and dissensions of the military, enabled the municipal authorities to recover some portion of their former power. They raised a cry for the deliverance of Kolokotrones and the other chiefs and primates imprisoned at Hydra; and the people soon supported their demand in a voice which the government did not dare to disobey.

It was necessary to raise a new army in order to replace the armatoli who had abandoned the defence of the Peloponnesus. Kolokotrones was the only man whom the Moreots were inclined to follow to the field. There was therefore no alternative but to reinstate him in his former position as general-in-chief of the Peloponnesian forces, to release all who were in prison for their share in the second civil war, and to conciliate the two primates, Zaimes and Londos, who had returned from exile, and declared their wish to serve their country and forget past dissensions. Konduriottes' government proclaimed a general amnesty: thanksgivings were offered up in the churches of Nauplia for the happy change which had taken place in the hearts of the rulers of Greece; harangues in praise of forgiveness and concord were now uttered by men who had hitherto been the most violent instigators of discord and vengeance. By these timely and politic concessions, Konduriottes, Kolettes, and Rhodios purchased immunity for the violence and peculation which had characterized their public administration. Kolokotrones resumed his former power and his old habits. The severe lesson he had learned, and the calamities he had brought on his country, had not moderated the egoism of his ambition. His administrative and military views were as confined as ever, and his avarice remained insatiable.

The archimandrite Dikaios (Pappa Phlesas) was still Minister of the Interior. He was the most unprincipled man of his party, and had been, with Kolettes, the most violent persecutor of the Moreot chiefs. The universal indignation now expressed at his conduct convinced him that it would be dangerous for him to remain at Nauplia, where his licentious life and gross peculation pointed him out as the first object of popular vengeance, and the scapegoat for the sins of his colleagues. The archimandrite was destitute of private virtue and political honesty, but he was a man of activity and courage. Perhaps, too, at this decisive moment a sense of shame urged him to cancel his previous misdeeds by an act of patriotism. He asked permission to march against the Egyptians, boasting that he would vanquish Ibrahim or perish in the combat. The permission was readily granted, though little confidence was felt in his military conduct. He quitted Nauplia with great parade, attended by a body of veteran soldiers; and when he reached the village of Maniaki, in the hills to the east of Gargaliano, his force exceeded three thousand men.

The bold priest possessed no military quality but courage. He posted his troops in an ill-selected position and awaited the attack of Ibrahim, who advanced in person to carry the position at the head of six thousand men on the 1st of June. Many of the archimandrite's troops, seeing the superior force of the Egyptians, deserted during the night, and only about fifteen hundred men remained. The pasha's regulars were led on to storm the Greek intrenchments in gallant style, and a short and desperate struggle ensued. The Greeks were forced from their position before they fled. The affair was the best contested during the war, for a thousand Greeks perished by the Arab bayonets, and four hundred Arabs lay dead on the field[1]. In spite of the defeat and the severe loss sustained by the Greeks, they gained both honour and courage by the battle of Maniaki. The national spirit, which had been greatly depressed by the flight of the Romeliots, and by the ease with which the Egyptians had taken Sphakteria, again revived at seeing so great a loss inflicted on Ibrahim's army by a body of men consisting in great part of armed Moreot peasants. Very little had been expected from Dikaios as a military leader. He had selected his position ill, and he had not known how to construct proper intrenchments, but he had given his followers an example of brilliant courage, and died nobly at his post. The result induced the Greeks to expect a great victory when the Moreot soldiery took the field under their tried champion Kolokotrones.

---

[1] Phrantzes, ii. 347-351.

The indefatigable Ibrahim lost no time in profiting by his victory. After allowing his troops to plunder the town of Arcadia, he marched to occupy Nisi and Kalamata, which the Mainates, who called themselves Spartans, abandoned at his approach. On the 10th of June he made a short incursion into Maina, but, seeing the mountaineers prepared to dispute his progress, he advanced no farther than Kitries.

Kolokotrones was now in the field. It is said that he wished to destroy the walls and citadel of Tripolitza, but that the executive body refused to sanction this measure, fearing lest it should tend more towards rendering Kolokotrones master of the Morea than towards defending the country against Ibrahim Pasha [1]. Kolokotrones made his dispositions for defending the passes between Messenia and Arcadia by establishing magazines at Leondari, and fixing his headquarters at Makryplagi, where his troops constructed their tambouria or stone intrenchments to cover the defile. His force was considerable, but he was incompetent to employ it to advantage. A thousand Greeks were posted at Poliani, a village which commands a difficult passage over the northern slopes of Mount Taygetus. But in spite of the advantage of the ground, Kolokotrones made his dispositions so ill that he allowed the Egyptians to turn his flank. The general-in-chief of the Peloponnesus always appeared to be more ignorant of Greek topography than the Egyptian pasha. The troops at Poliani were left without provisions. Their officers, who usually derive a considerable profit from the extra rations they draw, hastened to Makryplagi to upbraid Kolokotrones with his neglect, which they ascribed to his avarice. Ibrahim profited by this misconduct. Advancing along an almost impracticable mountain track, he gained possession of Poliani, and on the 16th June compelled the Greeks to abandon the pass of Makryplagi. The superiority of Ibrahim to Kolokotrones as a general, and the inferiority of the irregular Greek troops to the regular Arab battalions, were never exhibited in a more decisive manner. The Greeks had selected their own positions in an almost impracticable country, with which they were well acquainted. They were routed by a foreign force which could make no use of its cavalry and artillery, and

---

[1] Phrantzes, ii. 356.

on ground where even regular infantry was compelled to act in loose order as skirmishers. Kolokotrones was perhaps a better military chief than Dikaios, but he wanted his bravery and patriotism.

The Greek army fled to Karitena, leaving the road to Tripolitza without defence; and Ibrahim on reaching that city found it abandoned by its inhabitants and garrison. It contained large stores of provisions, which the officers commanding in the place neglected to destroy. Without losing a moment, the pasha pushed on to the plain of Argos with about five thousand men, hoping to gain possession of Nauplia either by surprise or treachery.

On the 24th of June he reached the mills of Lerna. Nauplia was thrown into a state of the wildest confusion by his unexpected appearance. A report of treason spread among the citizens, and several persons were accused of holding correspondence with the enemy. Among these was George Orphanides, a friend of Kolettes, who was tried and acquitted[1]. The patriotism of the people awakened with a sense of the magnitude of the danger to which their country was exposed. Captain Makryannes and Constantine Mavromichales, who afterwards assassinated Capodistrias, with about three hundred and fifty soldiers, hastened over to defend the mills of Lerna as soon as the Egyptians were descried on the hills. Prince Demetrius Hypsilantes and several Philhellenes followed as volunteers. A large quantity of grain for the supply of Nauplia was stored at Lerna. Its loss would have endangered the safety of that fortress.

The mills of Lerna were surrounded by a stone wall, flanked by the celebrated marsh and a deep pond. The garrison was supported by two gunboats anchored within musket-shot of the shore. There was, however, a small break in the wall, which the Greeks, with their usual carelessness, had neglected to repair. Through this space a company of Arabs attempted to force an entrance into the enclosure. They crowded over the breach, and attempted to form in the court; but before they could get into order, they were charged by Makryannes and a band of Greeks and Philhellenes sword in hand, who cut down thirteen on the spot,

---

[1] Tricoupi, iii. 221.

and drove the rest back over the breach. The Greeks then occupied the wall of the enclosure, and opened loop-holes. Ibrahim, finding that the garrison was prepared for a desperate defence, and was constantly receiving reinforcements, did not venture to renew the attack. He marched on to Argos to pass the night; and after remaining there a day or two, and reconnoitring the environs of Nauplia, he returned with his little army to Tripolitza on the 29th of June, without the Greeks venturing to attack him on the way.

As Ibrahim carried with him no provisions on this expedition, it has been inferred that he trusted to some secret intelligence, and expected to gain an entrance into Nauplia by treachery. It seems, however, that he counted rather on surprise and intimidation. The arrival of Captain Hamilton in the Cambrian, accompanied by another frigate and a sloop of war, appears to have hastened his departure. Hamilton landed at Nauplia with a number of his officers, and held a private conference with the members of the Greek government. He encouraged them, and every person with whom he spoke, to put the place in the best state of defence; and he took up such a position with his ships as induced both the Greeks and the Egyptians to infer that he proposed aiding in the defence of the fortress. A report was spread and generally believed at the time, that, in case of an attack, the Greeks were authorized to hoist the English flag, and place their country under British protection[1]. Ibrahim, who was informed of all that passed, retired immediately; but he drew off his troops without precipitation, and took such precautions to secure his flanks that Kolokotrones, with the whole forces of the Morea, did not attempt to make the Kakeskala of Mount Parthenius a scene of triumph to the Greeks like the defile of Dervenaki. The army of Ibrahim received considerable reinforcements shortly after his return to Tripolitza.

Early in July Kolokotrones had assembled upwards of ten thousand men on the hills overlooking the great Arcadian plain[2]. He then occupied Trikorpha, and began to make preparations for blockading Tripolitza. Ibrahim, on the 6th of July, anticipated his design by making a simultaneous

---

[1] Tricoupi, iii. 224.
[2] Phrantzes, ii. 367; and Tricoupi, iii. 226.

attack on all his positions. The pasha directed the attack on Trikorpha in person. Kolokotrones made a feeble resistance, but the Greeks lost two hundred men, most of whom were killed in their flight after they had abandoned their intrenchments[1]. The Greek army was completely defeated, but the soldiers felt that they had been worsted in consequence of the bad dispositions of their chiefs, and they did not disperse. They rallied in the mountain passes that lead into the great Arcadian plain, and showed by their activity and perseverance that they only required an abler chief to keep Ibrahim blockaded in Tripolitza. After his defeat, Kolokotrones invited the Mainates to hasten to his assistance, declaring that he had still four thousand men under arms at Karitena and three thousand at Vervena[2].

Kolokotrones, with his usual military incapacity, neglected to fortify the mills of Piana, Zarakova, and Davia, from which the garrison of Tripolitza obtained the necessary supplies of flour. The siege of Tripolitza by the Greeks ought to have taught him the importance of keeping possession of these mills; but even experience could not teach him foresight where his own personal interests were not directly and immediately concerned. The Egyptian pasha profited by his enemy's neglect. He seized and fortified these mills, and secured their communications with Tripolitza by a line of posts which he established in the mountains. His foraging parties then covered the plains of Arcadia from Mantinea to Megalopolis, and collected large quantities of grain.

On the 8th of August Ibrahim drove Hypsilantes and Mavromichales from the camp at Vervena, established a strong garrison at Leondari, and returned to Modon on the 13th. Soon after his departure from Arcadia, the Greeks surprised the post at Trikorpha, and recovered possession of the mills of Piana and Zarakova; but when Ibrahim returned to Tripolitza, before the end of the month they were again driven from their conquests.

Ibrahim then led his troops through Tzakonia to Monemvasia, laying waste the country in every direction. The Greeks nowhere opposed him with vigour. Their spirit

---

[1] Phrantzes, ii. 370.
[2] Phrantzes, ii. 372, who gives Kolokotrones' letter. It proves that Phrantzes assigns an erroneous date to the affair of Trikorpha.

seemed broken, and they contented themselves with following on his flanks and rear to waylay foragers and recapture small portions of his plunder[1]. He was now intent on destroying the resources of the population. The Egyptians carried on a war of extermination; the Greeks replied by a war of brigandage. The ultimate result of such a system of warfare was inevitable. The invaders were fed by supplies from abroad; the country could not long furnish the means of subsistence to its defenders. Famine would soon consume those who escaped the sword.

During the expedition to Tzakonia, Colonel Fabvier, who had been appointed to command a body of Greek regulars, made an attempt to surprise Tripolitza. It failed, in consequence of the irregulars under Andreas Londos not making the concerted diversion.

On returning to Tripolitza, and finding everything in good order, Ibrahim marched to Arcadia (Cyparissia), carrying off all the provisions from the districts through which he passed, and laying waste the towns of Philiatra and Gargaliano. The campaign of 1825 terminated when he reached Modon on the 30th of September.

Mohammed Ali was induced by the sultan to send large reinforcements to Ibrahim about this time, and to order him to co-operate with Reshid Pasha in the siege of Mesolonghi.

---

[1] Tricoupi says, τοὺς ἐχθροὺς ἔβλαπτον κλεπτοπολεμοῦντες (iii. 233); and no great injury could they inflict by such contemptible warfare.

CHAPTER II.

THE SIEGE OF MESOLONGHI.

Operations of Reshid Pasha.—State of Mesolonghi.—Number of its garrison and of its besiegers.—Arrival of the Othoman fleet.—Arrival of the Greek fleet.—Difficult position of Reshid.—He constructs a mound.—Treason of Odysseus.—Military operations in continental Greece.—Reshid withdraws to a fortified camp.—Operations of the Turkish and Greek fleets.—Ibrahim arrives before Mesolonghi.—Lethargy of the Greeks and of their government. —The Turks take Vasiladi and Anatolikon.—Offers of capitulation rejected. —Turkish attack on Klissova repulsed.—Defeat of the Greek fleet under Miaoulis.—Final sortie.—Fall of Mesolonghi.

THE second siege of Mesolonghi is the most glorious military operation of the Greek Revolution: it is also the most characteristic of the moral and political condition of the nation, for it exhibits the invincible energy of the people in strongest contrast with the inefficiency of the military chiefs, and the inertness and ignorance of the members of the government. Never was greater courage and constancy displayed by the population of a besieged town; rarely has less science been shown by combatants, at a time when military science formed the chief element of success in warfare.

Greek patriotism seemed to have concentrated itself within the walls of Mesolonghi. Elsewhere hostilities languished. While the citizens of a small town, the fishermen of a shallow lagoon, and the peasants of a desolated district, sustained the vigorous attack of a determined enemy, the fleets and armies of Greece wasted their time and their strength in trifling and desultory operations. An undisciplined population performed the duty of a trained garrison. Here, therefore, the valour of the individual demands a record in history. Yet, though private deeds of heroism were of daily occurrence, the historian shrinks from selecting the acts of heroism and the names of the warriors that deserve pre-eminence. All within the town seemed to be inspired by the warmest love for political liberty and national independence, and all proved that they were ready to guarantee the sincerity of their feeling with the sacrifice of their lives.

Reshid, pasha of Joannina, or as he was generally called, Kiutayhé, had distinguished himself at the battle of Petta, and when he assumed the command of the Othoman forces destined to invade Western Greece in the year 1825, much was expected by the sultan from his known firmness and ability. On the 6th of April he seized the pass of Makronoros, which the Greek chieftains neglected to defend, and where the Greek government had only stationed a few guards under the command of Noti Botzaris, a veteran Suliot. No three hundred Greeks were now found to make an effort for the defence of this western Thermopylae[1]. The Turks advanced through Acarnania without encountering any opposition. The inhabitants fled before them, and many, with their flocks and herds, found shelter under the English flag in Calamo, where the poor were maintained by rations from the British government; others retired to Mesolonghi, and formed part of the garrison which defended that place[2]. On the 27th of April, Reshid established his head-quarters in the plain, and two days afterwards opened his first parallel against Mesolonghi, at a distance of about six hundred yards from the walls[3]. His force then consisted of only six thousand men and three guns.

Mesolonghi was in a good state of defence. An earthen rampart of two thousand three hundred yards in length extended from the waters of the lagoon across the promontory on which the town was built. This rampart was partly faced with masonry, flanked by two bastions near the centre, strengthened towards its eastern extremity by a lunette and a tenaille, and protected where it joined the lagoon to the west by a battery on an islet called Marmaro, distant about two hundred yards from the termination of the wall. In

---

[1] Tricoupi, iii. 281.
[2] There is a tribute of gratitude to England in the newspaper published at Mesolonghi. *Hellenic Chronicles*, 4th April, 1825, p. 2.
[3] Gordon, ii. 233; Tricoupi, iii. 287.

front of the rampart a muddy ditch, not easy to pass, separated the fortress from the adjoining plain. Forty-eight guns and four mortars were mounted in battery. The garrison consisted of four thousand soldiers and armed peasants, and one thousand citizens and boatmen. The place was well supplied with provisions and ammunition, but there were upwards of twelve thousand persons to feed within the walls.

The army of Reshid never exceeded ten thousand troops, and a considerable part of it never entered the plain of Mesolonghi, for he was obliged to employ about two thousand men in guarding a line of stations from Makronoros and Kravasara, on the Ambracian Gulf, to Kakeskala on the Gulf of Patras, in order to keep open his communications with Arta, Prevesa, Lepanto, and Patras. But in addition to his troops, Reshid was accompanied by three thousand pioneers, muleteers, and camp-followers [1]. It was not until the commencement of June that the besiegers obtained a supply of artillery from Patras, which increased their force to eight guns and four mortars. For several weeks, therefore, Reshid trusted more to the spade than to his artillery, and during this time he pushed forward his approaches with indefatigable industry. Early in June he had advanced to within thirty yards of the bastion Franklin, which covered the western side of the walls. But his ammunition was then so much reduced that he was compelled to fire stones from his mortars instead of shells [2].

While the Turks were working at their approaches, the Greeks constructed traverses and erected new batteries.

Little progress had been made in the active operations of the siege, when a Greek squadron of seven sail arrived off Mesolonghi on the 10th of June. It encouraged the besieged

---

[1] Compare Gordon, ii. 233; and Tricoupi, iii. 281. Reshid's commissariat distributed twenty-five thousand rations at the commencement of this campaign. A deduction of one-third must be made in estimating the number of men then actually under arms. A few weeks of actual service usually reduced a Turkish army to one-half of the number of the rations issued. It must also be observed that Reshid detached two thousand men under his kehaya to dislodge the Greeks from Salona.

[2] Gordon, Tricoupi, and Fabre (*Histoire du siège de Missolonghi, suivie de pièces justificatives*. Paris, 1827), all indicate the position and nature of the defensive works of Mesolonghi with sufficient accuracy. The bastion Franklin to the west, and the bastion Botzaris to the east, formed the centre. Between them was the battery Koraës. Against these the principal attack of Reshid was directed.

by landing considerable supplies of provisions and ammunition, and by announcing that Miaoulis would soon make his appearance with a large fleet. The garrison, confident of success, began to make frequent and vigorous sorties. In one of these, Routsos, a native of Mesolonghi, was taken prisoner by the Turks, and was terrified into revealing to the enemy the position of the subterraneous aqueducts which supplied the town with water. The supply was immediately cut off, but fortunately the besieged found fresh water in abundance by digging new wells, so that very little inconvenience was felt from the destruction of the aqueducts, even during the greatest heat of summer. The besiegers, who had pushed on their operations with great activity, at last made an attempt to carry the islet of Marmaro by assault, which was repulsed, and entailed on them a severe loss.

The besieged now met with the first great trial of their firmness. They were eagerly awaiting the arrival of the fleet under Miaoulis, which they fondly expected would compel Reshid to raise the siege. On the 10th of July several vessels were descried in the offing. Their joy reached the highest pitch, and they overwhelmed the advanced-guard of the besiegers, which consisted of Albanians, with insulting boasts. Soon, however, fresh ships hove in sight, and it was evident that the fleet was too numerous and the ships too large to be Greek. The red flag became visible on the nearest brigs, and gradually the broad streaks of white on the hulls and the numerous ports showed plainly both to Greeks and Turks, that this mighty force was the fleet of the capitan-pasha. The besieged were greatly depressed, but their constancy was unshaken.

Reshid now assumed the offensive with great vigour. He introduced a number of flat-bottomed boats into the lagoon, gained possession of the islands of Aghiosostis and Prokopanistos, which the Mesolonghiots had neglected to fortify, and completely invested the place both by sea and land. On the 28th of July he made a determined attack on the bastion Botzaris, and on the 2nd of August he renewed the assault by a still more furious attempt to storm the bastion Franklin, in which a breach had been opened by his artillery; but both these attacks were gallantly repulsed.

Before the assault on the bastion Franklin, Reshid offered

ARRIVAL OF GREEK FLEET.

terms of capitulation to the garrison of Mesolonghi. His offers were rejected, and, to revenge his defeat, he ordered Routsos and some other prisoners to be beheaded before the walls. The cruisers of the capitan-pasha informed him that the Greek fleet was approaching, before this was known to the besieged, and he made the assault on the 2nd of August with the hope of carrying the place before its arrival.

The Greek fleet, consisting of forty sail of the best ships which Greece still possessed, under the command of Miaoulis, Saktures, Kolandrutzos, and Apostoles, was descried from Mesolonghi on the 3rd of August. Next day the Othoman fleet manœuvred to obtain an advantageous position. The Hydriot squadron in the end succeeded in getting the weather-gauge of the advanced ships of the Turks; yet the Greeks, in spite of this success, could not break the line of the main division, which consisted of twenty-two sail. Three fire-ships were launched in succession against the capitan-pasha's flag-ship; but this mode of attack no longer threw the Turks into a panic terror, and they manœuvred so well that the blazing vessels drifted harmless to leeward without forcing them to break their line of battle. Khosref was, nevertheless, so intimidated by the determined manner in which the Greeks directed their attacks against his flag, that he avoided a second engagement. He claimed the victory in this indecisive engagement merely because he had escaped defeat, and he made his orders to effect a prompt junction with the Egyptian fleet a pretext for sailing immediately for Alexandria. His cowardice left the flotilla of Reshid in the lagoon without support, and as the Greeks captured one of the transports laden with powder and shells for the army before Mesolonghi, the besiegers were again inadequately supplied with ammunition for their mortars.

The command of the lagoons was of vital importance to the besieged. It was necessary to secure their communication with the fleet, and to prevent their being deprived of a supply of fish which formed a considerable portion of their food. The Turks were not deprived of the advantages they had gained without a severe contest, but the skill of the Mesolonghiot fishermen, who were acquainted with all the passages through the shallow water and deep mud, secured the victory, and with the assistance of some Hydriot boats sent by Miaoulis to their aid, the flotilla of Reshid was destroyed, and his Albanians driven from the posts they had occupied in the islands. Five of the flat-bottomed boats were captured, and the Greeks recovered the command of the whole lagoon[1]. The fleet then sailed in pursuit of the capitan-pasha, leaving eight ships to keep open the communications between the besieged and the Ionian Islands, and prevent any supplies being sent by sea to the besieging army.

Reshid was now placed in a very difficult position. He received his supplies of provisions with irregularity, both from Patras and Prevesa. His stores of ammunition were so scanty that he could not keep up a continuous fire from his guns, and was compelled to abandon the hope of carrying the place by an artillery attack. He had no money to pay his troops, and was unable to prevent great numbers of the Albanians from returning home, though he allowed all who remained double rations[2]. On the other hand, the prospects of the besieged were very favourable. They felt confident that Reshid would be forced to raise the siege at the approach of winter, for they daily expected to hear that a Greek army had occupied the passes in his rear. It seemed therefore to be certain that if he persisted in maintaining his position, his army must perish by want and disease. The armatoli of Romelia, who had quitted the Peloponnesus after their defeats at Navarin, were said to be marching into the mountains behind Lepanto, whose rugged surface is familiar to classic readers from the description which Thucydides has left us of the destruction of the Athenian army under Demosthenes[3].

Reshid weighed his own resources and estimated the activity of the Greek irregulars with sagacity. His guns could not render him much service, but he still believed that the spade would enable him to gain possession of Mesolonghi before winter. To effect his purpose he adopted a singular, but under the circumstances in which he was placed, by no means an ill-devised method of covering the approach of a large body of men to the counterscarp of the ditch.

---

[1] Tricoupi (iii. 303) says seven.
[2] Tricoupi, iii. 305. Yet only twelve thousand rations were now issued daily in Reshid's camp.
[3] Thuc. iii. 97.

He set his army to raise a mound by heaping up earth, and this primitive work was carried forward to the walls of the place in defiance of every effort which the besieged made to interrupt the new mode of attack. So strange a revival of the siege operations of the ancients excited the ridicule of the Greeks. They called the mound 'the dyke of union,' in allusion to the mound which Alexander the Great constructed at the siege of Tyre. It was commenced at about a hundred and sixty yards from the salient angle of the bastion Franklin, and made an obtuse angle as it approached the place. Its base was from five to eight yards broad, and it was so high as to overlook the ramparts of the besieged. By indefatigable perseverance, and after much severe fighting in the trenches, the Turks carried the mound to the ditch, filled up the ditch, and stormed the bastion Franklin. Even then they could not effect an entry into the place, for the Greeks cut off this bastion from all communication with the rest of their defences, and soon erected batteries which completely commanded it. They then became the assailants, and after a desperate struggle drove the Turks from their recent conquest. On the 31st of August all the ground they had lost was regained, and preparations were commenced for a great effort against the mound. Several sorties were made in order to obtain exact knowledge of the enemy's trenches. At last, on the 21st of September, a great sortie was made by the whole garrison. The Turkish camp was attacked in several places with such fury that Reshid was unable to conjecture against what point the principal force was directed. He was in danger of seeing his batteries stormed and his guns spiked. After a bloody struggle the Greeks carried the works that protected the head of the mound, and maintained possession of their conquest until they had levelled that part of it which overlooked their defences. While every spade in Mesolonghi was employed in levelling the mound, bodies of troops cleared the trenches, and prevented the enemy from interrupting the work. As the Greeks had foreseen, rain soon rendered it impossible for Reshid to repair the damage his works had sustained.

The garrison of Mesolonghi received considerable reinforcements after the capitan-pasha's departure. At the end of

September it still amounted to four thousand five hundred men, and was much more efficient than at the commencement of the siege. Hitherto the fire of the Turkish artillery had been so desultory and ill directed, that not more than one hundred persons had been killed and wounded in the place. This trifling loss during a six months' siege induced the Greeks to form a very erroneous idea of the efficiency of siege-artillery; while the facility with which provisions and ammunition had been introduced inspired them with a blind confidence in their naval superiority. The only severe loss they had suffered had been in their sorties, and in these they had hitherto been almost invariably the victors.

The operations of the Greek army to the north of the Isthmus of Corinth were feeble, desultory, and unsuccessful. The leaders could not be prevailed upon to act in concert. Party intrigues, personal jealousies, and sordid avidity, prevented them from combining at a time when it was evident that a vigorous effort would have delivered Mesolonghi. Northern Greece was then occupied by a numerous body of armatoli. Even in the year 1830, after the losses sustained at Mesolonghi and Athens, Capodistrias assembled six thousand veterans belonging to this army[1]. By a bold advance, the communications of Reshid with his resources in Arta, Prevesa, and Joannina might have been cut off. The treason of Odysseus has been urged as an apology for the inactivity of the Romeliots at the opening of the campaign of 1825, but it ought to have excited them to increase their exertions, as it rendered their services more necessary. But very little patriotism was displayed this year by the armatoli, either before or after the treason of Odysseus.

Odysseus was a man of considerable ability, but he was too selfish to become a dangerous enemy to a national cause; and when he became openly a traitor, his career was soon terminated. In trying to overreach everybody, he overreached himself, remained without support, and was easily overpowered.

The treason of Odysseus is the most celebrated instance of treachery among the Greeks during their Revolution. But

---

[1] *Parliamentary Papers*: Communications with Prince Leopold relating to the sovereignty of Greece; Count Capodistrias to Prince Leopold, 25th March (6th April), 1830, p. 42.

it derives its importance more from the previous fame of the traitor, and from his tragic end in the Acropolis of Athens, than from the singularity or the baseness of his conduct. Many chiefs of armatoli, who, like Odysseus, had been bred up in the service of Ali of Joannina, felt like Albanian mercenaries rather than Greek patriots. Several committed acts of treason; Gogos, Varnakiottes, Rhangos, Zongas, Valtinos, and the Moreot captain Nenekos, were all as guilty as Odysseus, and the treachery of Gogos on the field of Petta inflicted a deeper wound on Greece.

Odysseus never attached any importance to political independence and national liberty. His ambition was to ape the tyranny of Ali in a small sphere, and his conduct from the commencement of the Revolution testified that he had no confidence in its ultimate success. He viewed it as a temporary revolt, which might be rendered conducive to his own interests. His cunning taught him at times to make use of popular feelings which he did not understand, and whose strength he was of course unable to estimate. His opinions prepared him to act the traitor, but he was so far from being a man of a daring character, that a prudent government might have retained him in its service, and found in him an useful instrument, for he possessed more administrative capacity than most of the Romeliot chiefs. Kolettes' influence caused Konduriottes' government to leave him without employment, and to stop the pay and rations of the soldiers who followed his banner. When he saw chiefs of inferior rank, who had previously served under his orders, named captains of districts, and observed that every soldier who quitted his band received a reward, he became alarmed for his personal safety. He believed that Kolettes designed to treat him as he himself had treated Noutzas and Palaskas, and fear was the immediate cause of his last treasonable acts. By his negotiations with the Turks he hoped to secure to himself the possession of a capitanlik in Eastern Greece like those held by Gogos and Varnakiottes in Western Greece, but the Turks would not trust him unless he joined them openly. When forced to choose his side, it was fear of Kolettes which decided his conduct, and induced him to declare in favour of the Turks, who then sent a small body of Mussulman Albanians to his aid. But his movements had been long watched, and he was quickly surrounded by superior numbers at Livanates, before he could effect a junction with the Turkish forces either at Zeitouni or Chalcis. Finding that all his intrigues were baffled, and that resistance was impossible, he surrendered himself a prisoner to Goura, his former lieutenant, from whom he expected some favour in requital for former benefits[1]. Goura did not deliver him up to the vengeance of the members of the government. He was kept prisoner in the Acropolis until the disastrous measures of Konduriottes and Kolettes roused general indignation. Goura then feared that his prisoner might escape, and regain his former power. Interest prevailed over gratitude, and Odysseus was murdered on the night of 16th July. After the murder, his body was thrown from the Frank tower in the southern wing of the Propylaea, in order to give credit to the assertion that he perished by a fall in attempting to escape. Thus one of the most astute of the Greek chiefs fell a victim to the policy of a rude Albanian soldier whom he had raised to a high rank[2]. And the son of that Andrutsos, who first raised the standard of revolt against the Othomans in 1769, is the traitor at whose name the finger of scorn is pointed by every Greek. Odysseus perished like his patron and model, Ali of Joannina, a sacrifice to his own selfishness; and he will be execrated as long as the memory of the Greek Revolution shall endure.

On the 17th April 1825, Abbas Pasha crossed the Spercheus with two thousand men and two guns, but the surrender of Odysseus, who had been expected to make a vigorous diversion, prevented this small force from advancing southward until the kehaya of Reshid marched into the heart of Aetolia with about the same number of chosen Albanians. The kehaya routed the Greek captain Saphaka, who attempted

---

[1] He surrendered on the 19th April, 1825.
[2] Tricoupi mentions that Goura tortured his benefactor to learn where his treasures were concealed (iii. 240). Odysseus fortified a cavern near Velitza (Tithorea), of which Trelawney, who married his sister, kept possession until he was severely wounded by Fenton and Whitcombe, who were suborned by agents of the Greek government to assassinate him. Tricoupi erroneously supposes this cavern to be the Corycian cave, and quotes Pausanias, who proves that the Corycian cave was on the other side of Parnassus. The Author passed two months during the spring of 1824 with Odysseus and Negris, moving about in Phocis and Boeotia, and arrived at Argos in their company just in time to witness the defeat of Kolokotrones' attempt to gain possession of the mills at Lerna, and the termination of the first civil war in the Morea.

to oppose his progress, occupied Vetrinitza, defeated the Greeks a second time at Pentornea, and entered Salona in triumph, where he was joined by Abbas Pasha at the end of May.

About the same time, the Romeliot troops, who had abandoned the Morea after their defeat by Ibrahim, formed a camp at Distomo, round which large bodies of Greek troops rallied. This force arrested the advance of the Turks, who were inferior in number. But the dissensions of the Greek leaders rendered their superiority of no avail. Abbas Pasha was allowed to establish himself at Salona, and no attempt was made to raise the siege of Mesolonghi. The military operations of the Greeks in continental Greece during the whole campaign of 1825 were conducted in the same desultory and feeble manner as in the Peloponnesus.

Goura was commissioned by the Greek government to enrol six thousand veteran soldiers. He assumed the chief command at Distomo, where the troops under his orders drew daily eleven thousand six hundred rations, though their number hardly ever exceeded three thousand men[1]. A trade in provisions was openly carried on both by the officers and the soldiers. They sold their surplus rations to the families of the peasants, whom patriotism had induced to abandon their villages rather than submit to the Turks.

While the advanced-guard of the army of Eastern Greece skirmished with the Turks at Salona, a body of troops under Karaïskaki and Djavellas marched into Western Greece. Karaïskaki threw himself into the rear of Reshid's position. Djavellas forced his way into Mesolonghi on the 19th of August[2]. The summer was consumed in trifling skirmishes, in struggles for booty, or in contests of military rivalry. The country was laid waste, and truth compels the historian to record that the cultivators of the soil suffered quite as much from the rapacity of their countrymen who came to defend them, as from the Turks who came to plunder them[3]. The Turks occupied Salona until the 6th of November, when it is the immemorial custom of the Albanian and Turkish militia

---

[1] Compare Tricoupi, iii. 249, with Captain Humphrey's Journal, p. 312.
[2] Gordon (ii. 240) mentions that Djavellas entered Mesolonghi with only twenty-five men, yet he drew rations for one thousand.
[3] The armatoli were truly ἀρνῶν ἠδ' ἐρίφων ἐπιδήμιοι ἁρπακτῆρες.

to return home, for the habits of the timariot system are still preserved[1].

The victory which the garrison of Mesolonghi obtained over the besiegers on the 21st of September, convinced Reshid that he must think rather of defending his own position from the attacks of the Greeks than of prosecuting the siege. Before he had matured his plans, a vigorous sortie inflicted a severe loss on his army, and accelerated his retreat from the trenches[2]. He immediately selected a position for a camp at the foot of Mount Zygos, which he fortified with great care, and on the 17th of October withdrew the remains of his army to this new station. His cavalry enabled him to keep open his communications with Krioneri, where his supplies of provisions were usually landed. He now anxiously awaited the return of the capitan-pasha, and the arrival of the reinforcements which Ibrahim Pasha was about to bring. But with all his vigour and ability, had the Greeks employed the superiority which they possessed at this time with skill, courage, and unanimity, his position might have been rendered untenable long before assistance could arrive. He had not now more than three thousand infantry and six hundred cavalry fit for service. The garrison of Mesolonghi was more numerous, and a considerable body of Greek troops under Karaïskaki and other captains occupied strong positions in his rear. Nothing but the irreconcileable jealousies of the Greek chieftains and their military ignorance, which prevented their executing any combined operations, saved Reshid's army from destruction. The pasha remained for a month in this dangerous situation, liable to be attacked by an overwhelming force at any moment, but determined to persist in his enterprise—to take Mesolonghi, or perish before its walls.

The Greeks in Mesolonghi amused themselves with destroying the works of the besiegers; but their confidence in their ultimate success was so great that they executed even this

---

[1] The troops of the Othomans then took the field on St. George's Day (5th May), after the horses of the spahis had eaten their green barley, and broke up their camp to return home on St. Demetrius' Day (7th November), in order to superintend the cultivation of their property by their Christian tenants. It deserves notice that the spring is much later in Macedonia and Greece than in corresponding latitudes in Italy and Spain.

[2] On the 13th October, 1825.

triumphant labour with extreme carelessness. And at the same time, the Greek government committed a blamable oversight in not transporting to Mesolonghi a large supply of grain, collected as land-tax in the plains of Elis and Achaia, and deposited in magazines on the western coast of the Morea. The sea was open, and these supplies might have been removed without difficulty.

The Othoman fleet, which returned to Patras on the 18th of November, saved Reshid's army from starvation, and furnished it with some reinforcements and ample supplies of ammunition. The Greek fleet ought to have engaged the Othoman before it entered the waters of Patras, but it did not reach the gulf until the capitan-pasha had terminated the delicate operation of landing stores at Krioneri.

A series of naval engagements then took place, in which the Turks baffled all the attempts of the Greeks to cut off their straggling ships and capture their transports. Both parties claimed the victory—the capitan-pasha because he kept open the communications between Patras and Krioneri, and Miaoulis because he succeeded in throwing supplies into Mesolonghi and in keeping open its communications with the Ionian Islands. But the real victory remained with the Turks, whose fleet kept its station at Patras, while the Greeks retired from the waters of Mesolonghi on the 4th December 1825, and returned to Hydra.

Shortly before the departure of the Greek fleet, a new and more formidable enemy appeared before Mesolonghi. The campaign in the Peloponnesus had proved that neither the courage of the armatoli nor the stratagems of the klephts were a match for the discipline and tactics of the Egyptians; and Ibrahim advanced to attack the brave garrison of Mesolonghi, confident of success. He encountered no opposition in his march from Navarin to Patras. The pass of Kleidi was left unguarded, and he captured large magazines of grain at Agoulinitza, Pyrgos, and Gastouni, which ought either to have been previously transported to Mesolonghi or now destroyed. These supplies proved of great use to Ibrahim's army during the siege [1].

A council of war was held by the Othoman pashas at

---

[1] Phrantzes, ii. 358, *note*.

Lepanto, to settle the plan of their operations[1]. The capitan-pasha, Ibrahim, Reshid, and Yussuf were present, and they agreed to prosecute the siege with redoubled energy, to act always with perfect unanimity, and mutually to support one another with all the means at their command. They kept these promises better than the Greek chiefs usually kept similar engagements. Yussuf at this meeting pointed out the measures which had enabled him to defend Patras for nearly five years. He soon after quitted Greece, being raised to the rank of pasha of Magnesia as a reward for his prudence and valour[2].

The month of December was employed by Ibrahim in forming magazines at Krioneri, and bringing up ammunition to his camp before Mesolonghi. Heavy rains rendered it impossible to work at the trenches. The whole plain, from the walls of the town to the banks of the Fidari, was either under water, or formed a wide expanse of mud and marsh. The Egyptian soldiers laboured indefatigably, and the order which prevailed in their camp astonished Reshid, who was said to have felt some irritation when he found that Ibrahim never asked him for any assistance or advice, but carried on his own operations with unceasing activity and perfect independence. A horrid act of cruelty, perpetrated by Reshid, was ascribed to an explosion of his suppressed rage. A priest, two women, and three boys, who were accused of having conveyed some intelligence to their relatives in the besieged town, were impaled by his order before the walls[3].

The Greek government became at last sensible that it had too long neglected the defence of Mesolonghi. It had often announced that Reshid was about to raise the siege, and, believing its own assertions, it had neglected to do anything to force him to retreat. It now learned with surprise that Reshid's camp was well supplied with provisions; that the garrison of Mesolonghi was in want of ammunition; and that the Greek troops sent to cut off the supplies of the Turks were in danger of starvation. An attempt was made to raise

---

[1] 29th Nov. 1825. [2] Gordon, ii. 244; Tricoupi, iii. 325.
[3] Gordon (ii. 253) and Tricoupi (iii. 331) both say that several children suffered. They were boys above twelve years of age. Children under that age would have been compelled to embrace Mohammedanism. Reshid, who was religious as well as inhuman, would have seized the opportunity of making forced converts, had the law of Mahomet allowed it.

money by selling national lands; but as these lands were already mortgaged to the English bond-holders, and the sale of national lands was expressly prohibited by national assemblies, the bad faith of the members of the government was too apparent for any Greek to part with his money on such security. The conduct of the members of the executive body was in this case both impolitic and dishonest. It proved that they were dishonourable enough to violate a national engagement, and so incapable as to make a display of their bad faith without securing any advantage. A sum sufficient to enable a Greek fleet to put to sea was raised by private subscription. Individual patriotism has displayed itself on every emergency in Greece, when not thwarted by the action of the government. Many Greeks who were not wealthy subscribed largely; ministers of state, shipowners, chieftains, and officials, who had enriched themselves with the produce of the English loans, or by farming taxes, endeavoured to conceal their wealth by their illiberality[1].

The sums collected equipped twenty Hydriot and four Psarian ships. On the 21st of January 1826 these vessels, reinforced by three Spetziot brigs which had remained in the waters of Mesolonghi, forced the Turkish cruisers to retire under the guns of Patras, and enabled the besieged to communicate directly with the Ionian Islands, and lay in stores of provisions and ammunition for two months. The crews of the Greek ships were paid in advance for a single month. The spirit of patriotism was not then powerful in the Albanian islands; and the Hydriot sailors, in order to escape being obliged to give their services to their country for a single hour gratuitously, sailed from Mesolonghi, after remaining in its waters only a fortnight[2].

---

[1] Dr. Howe, the well-known philanthropist of Boston, Mass., who was present, records the manner in which the people expressed their feelings when Professor Gennadios addressed an appeal to their patriotism at a public meeting in the square of Nauplia (*Historical Sketch of the Greek Revolution*, p. 329):—' Gennadios threw down his purse. "There is my all; I give it to my country as freely as I would to my child. I am ready to serve in any occupation for a year, and pay the whole salary I receive into the public treasury." The crowd was moved to tears. Many voices were raised offering money. The public excitement forced the chiefs and rich men to come forward, though unwillingly, and a scornful laugh was raised as their names were called out.' Compare the vauntings of Tricoupi, iii. 332. The letter of the President soliciting subscriptions is given in the Hydriot newspaper, Ὁ Φίλος τοῦ Νόμου, December 14 (26), 1825.

[2] It is curious to read the accounts which were given of the deplorable condition of the Egyptians and Turks before Mesolonghi at this time in the Greek

Three weeks after the departure of the Greek ships, Ibrahim commenced active operations. On the 25th of February he opened his fire from batteries mounting forty pieces of artillery, and on the 27th and 28th two unsuccessful attempts were made to storm the walls by the united forces of the Turks and Egyptians. The gallant resistance of the besieged convinced Ibrahim that it would cost too much to take the place by storm, unless he could attack it by sea as well as by land. In a short time he launched a flotilla of thirty-two flat-bottomed boats, which gave him the complete command of the lagoons, and on the 9th of March he stormed the fort of Vasiladi, which defends the entrance to Mesolonghi from the sea. Anatolikon capitulated on the 13th.

The Greeks now perceived that the progress of the besiegers, although not very rapid, would soon render the place untenable. The supplies of provisions received in January, added to what was then in the public magazines, ought to have furnished abundant rations to the whole population until the end of April; but these stores were wasted by the soldiery[1]. Ibrahim and Reshid contrived to be well informed of everything that was said or done within the walls of Mesolonghi, and they learned with pleasure that watchfulness and patience would soon force the Greeks to surrender the place or die of hunger.

The moment appeared favourable for offering a capitulation, but the besieged rejected all negotiation with disdain. Sir Frederic Adam, the Lord High Commissioner in the Ionian Islands, convinced that the loss of Vasiladi and Anatolikon rendered the fall of Mesolonghi inevitable, endeavoured to prevent farther bloodshed. He visited Krioneri in a British ship-of-war, and offered his mediation. But the two pashas were now sure of their prey, and as the Greeks refused to treat directly with them, they refused all mediation, and Sir Frederic was obliged to retire without effecting anything,—an example of the folly of too much zeal in other

---

newspapers, and in the MS. journals of Philhellenes. The Arab regulars of Ibrahim's army in particular were supposed to be then enduring a series of calamities which would exterminate them in a few weeks.

[1] Gordon (ii. 267) states this in his usual candid manner:—'We have one reproach to address to the Suliot chiefs, and particularly to Noti Botzaris; it is, that, whenever things wore a favourable aspect, they did not bridle their incurable improvidence and love of peculation.'

people's business. As soon as he was gone, Ibrahim and Reshid, pretending that the Greeks had expressed a wish to learn what terms of capitulation could be obtained, sent a written summons to the garrison offering to allow all the Greek troops to quit Mesolonghi on laying down their arms, and engaging to permit the inhabitants who desired to leave the town to depart with the garrison; at the same time they declared that all those who wished to remain should be allowed to retain possession of their property, and should enjoy ample protection for themselves and their families. To this summons the Greeks replied, that they had never expressed any wish to capitulate; that they were determined to defend Mesolonghi to the last drop of their blood; that if the pashas wanted their arms they might come to take them; and that they remitted the issue of the combat to the will of God[1].

The only post in the lagoon of which the Greeks held possession, was the small islet of Klissova, about a mile from Mesolonghi, to the south-east. This post was defended by a hundred and fifty men under Kitzo Djavellas. The Greeks were advantageously posted, and protected by a rampart of earth from the artillery of their assailants; while a low chapel, with an arched roof of stone, served them as a magazine and citadel. On the 6th of April the Albanians of Reshid attacked Klissova. The shallow water prevented even the flat-bottomed boats of the Turks from approaching close to its shore, so that the attacking party was compelled to jump into the sea and wade forward through the deep mud. While the gunboats fired showers of grape, the Greeks crouched in a ditch close to their earthen rampart; but as soon as the Albanians jumped into the water, they rose on their knees, and, resting their long guns on the parapet, poured such a well-directed volley on their enemies, that the foremost fell dead or wounded, and the rest recoiled in fear. Several officers were standing up in the boats directing the landing: they offered a conspicuous mark to the best shots among the Greeks, and most of them fell mortally wounded. The Albanians retired in confusion.

---

[1] The summons was dated the 2nd of April, 1826. Both it and the reply of the Greeks are curious and characteristic documents. They are printed by Tricoupi, iii. 401, 402.

Ibrahim then ordered his regular troops to renew the attack. The result was similar; but the Egyptians were led back a second time to the attack, and again retreated under the deadly fire of the Greeks. Seeing the advantage which the defenders of Klissova derived from their position, Ibrahim ought to have abandoned the assault and kept the islet closely blockaded until he could bring up a few mortars. But he was eager to prove that his regulars were superior to the Albanians of Reshid. He therefore ordered Hussein, the conqueror of Kasos, Sphakteria, and Vasiladi, to make a third attack. Hussein led his men bravely on, but as he stood up in his boat giving orders concerning the formation of the storming parties, he was struck by a musket-ball, and fell down mortally wounded. The steady fire of the Greeks prevented the regulars from completing their formation. The men turned and scrambled back into the boats in complete disorder. After this repulse the pashas drew off their troops. Five hundred men were killed or wounded in this vain attempt to storm a sandbank defended by a hundred and fifty good marksmen.

The victory of Klissova was the last success of the Greeks during the siege of Mesolonghi. Provisions began to fail, and rations ceased to be distributed to any but the men who performed service. Yet as relief by sea was hourly expected, the garrison remained firm. At last the Greek fleet made its appearance, but the hope it inspired was soon disappointed. The Turks were in possession of the lagoon, and Miaoulis arrived without any flat-bottomed boats to enable him to penetrate to Mesolonghi. A feeble attempt was made by the Hydriots on the 13th of April to penetrate into the lagoon by the channel of Petala; but it was easily repulsed, and never renewed. The naval skill of the Greeks no longer insured them the command of the sea, nor did they now possess the heroic enterprise which they had often displayed during the first years of the Revolution. They had refused to adopt any scientific improvements either in their ships or their artillery; the Turks had improved both. Miaoulis entered the waters of Mesolonghi with the same ships as those with which he had combated Kari Ali; the Turkish fleet, which stood out of the Gulf of Lepanto to engage him, was very different in construction and armament from the

FAILURE OF THE GREEK FLEET.

fleets that sailed from Constantinople in 1821 and 1822. The Turks kept their line of battle, and held their position to windward of the Greeks, exchanging broadsides, and frustrating all the manœuvres of their enemy to bring on a general action or cut off straggling ships.

On the 15th of April, while the Turks still held their position between the Greek fleet and the town, and completely closed the communications with the lagoons, Miaoulis attempted to throw their line into confusion by sending down a fire-ship on two frigates; but the exposed vessels tacked, kept the weather-gauge, and allowed the blazing brulot to drift away to leeward and consume itself ineffectually. Fire-ships had ceased to inspire terror. The Greek fleet at this time consisted of only thirty sail, and the Turkish of sixty; but at the commencement of the war this disparity would have hardly enabled the Othomans to keep the sea. It now insured them a decided victory. Miaoulis, baffled and unable to open communication with the besieged, was driven out to sea, and the besieged town was abandoned to its fate. The glory of the Greek navy was tarnished by its spiritless conduct on this occasion. It declined to close with the enemy, and retreated without an effort to emulate the heroism of the defenders of Mesolonghi.

The magazines of Mesolonghi did not contain rations for more than two days. The garrison had now to choose whether it would perish by starvation, capitulate, or cut its way through the besiegers. It resolved to face every danger rather than surrender. The inhabitants who were unable to bear arms, the women, and the children, showed as much patience and courage in this dreadful situation as the veteran soldiers hardened in Turkish warfare. A spirit of heroism, rare in the Greek Revolution—rare even in the history of mankind—pervaded every breast. After deliberate consultation in a numerous assembly, it was resolved to force a passage for the whole population through the besieging armies. Many would perish, some might escape; but those who fell and those who escaped would be alike free. A well devised plan was adopted for evacuating the town, but its success was marred by several accidents.

About sunset on the 22nd of April 1826 a discharge of musketry was heard by the besieged on the ridge of Zygos.

This was a concerted signal to inform the chiefs in Mesolonghi that a body of fifteen hundred armatoli, detached from the camp of Karaïskaki at Platanos, was ready to attack the rear of the Turks and aid the sortie of the besieged. The garrison was mustered in three divisions. Bridges were thrown across the ditch, and breaches were opened in the walls. There were still nine thousand persons in the town, of whom only three thousand were capable of bearing arms. Nearly two thousand men, women, and children were so feeble from age, disease, or starvation, that they were unable to join the sortie. Many of the relations of these helpless individuals voluntarily remained to share their fate. The non-combatants, who were to join the sortie, were drawn up in several bodies, according to the quarters in which they resided, or the chiefs under whose escort they were to march. The Mesolonghiots formed themselves into a separate band. They were less attenuated by fatigue than the rest; but being collected from every quarter of the town, their band was less orderly than the emigrants from the country, who had been disciplined by privation, and accustomed to live and act together. Most of the women who took part in the sortie dressed themselves in the fustanella and carried arms, like the Albanians and armatoli; most of the children had also loaded pistols in their belts, which many had already learned to use.

At nine o'clock the bridges were placed in the ditch without noise, and a thousand soldiers crossed and ranged themselves along the covered way. Unfortunately a deserter had informed Ibrahim of the projected sortie, and both he and Reshid, though they gave little credit to the information, that the whole population would attempt to escape, adopted every precaution to repulse a sortie of the garrison. When the non-combatants began to cross the bridges, the noise revealed to the Turks the positions in which crowds were assembled, and on these points they opened a terrific fire. Crowds rushed forward to escape the shot. The shrieks of the wounded and the splash of those who were forced from the bridges were unnoticed; and in spite of the enemy's fire the greater part of the inhabitants crossed the ditch in tolerable order. The Mesolonghiots still lingered behind, retarded by their interests and their feelings. It was no easy sacrifice to quit their homes and their relations. For a considerable time the garrison waited patiently for them under a heavy fire. At last the first body of the Mesolonghiots crossed the ditch, and then the troops sprang forward with a loud shout and rushed sword in hand on the Turks.

Never was a charge made more valiantly. The eastern division of the garrison, under Noti Botzaris, struggled forward to gain the road to Bochori; the central division, under Kitzos Djavellas, pushed straight through the enemy's lines towards the hills; and the western division, under Makry, strove to gain the road to the Kleisura. All three intended, when clear of the Turks, to effect a junction on the slopes of Zygos, where the road ascends to the monastery of St. Simeon.

Almost at the moment when the garrison rushed on the Turks, that portion of the Mesolonghiots which was then on the bridges raised a cry of 'Back, back.' Great part of the Mesolonghiots stopped, fell back, and returned into the town with the military escort which ought to have formed the rearguard of the sortie. The origin of this ill-timed cry, which weakened the force of the sortie and added to the victims in the place, has excited much unnecessary speculation. It evidently rose among those who were in danger of being forced into the ditch. Their cry was repeated so loudly that it created a panic.

The three leading divisions bore down all opposition. Neither the yataghan of Reshid's Albanians, nor the bayonet of Ibrahim's Arabs, could arrest their impetuous attack; and they forced their way through the labyrinth of trenches, dykes, and ditches, with comparatively little loss. Only some women and children, who could not keep up with the column as it rushed forward over the broken ground, were left behind. Had it not been for the information given by the traitor, the greater part of the defenders of Mesolonghi would have escaped. In consequence of that information, Ibrahim and Reshid had taken the precaution to send bodies of cavalry to watch the roads leading to Bochori, St. Simeon, and Kleisura. The horsemen fell in with the Greek columns when they were about a mile beyond the Turkish lines, and were beginning to feel secure. The division of Makry was completely broken by the first charge of the cavalry. The others were thrown into confusion. All suffered severely, yet small bands of the garrison still kept together, and, by keeping up a continuous fire, enabled numbers of women and children to rally under their protection. At last the scattered remnants of the three divisions began to recover some order on reaching the slopes of Zygos, where the irregularities of the ground forced the cavalry to slacken the pursuit.

The fugitives prepared to enjoy a short rest, and endeavoured to assemble the stragglers who had eluded the swords of the horsemen. They were confident that the fire they had kept up against the cavalry would draw down the fifteen hundred men of Karaïskaki's corps to their assistance. While they were thus engaged in giving and expecting succour, a body of Albanians, placed in ambuscade by Reshid to watch the road to the monastery of St. Simeon, crept to their vicinity unperceived, and poured a deadly volley into their ranks. Instead of friends to assist them, they had to encounter one thousand mountaineers, well posted, to bar their progress. The Greeks, surprised by these unseen enemies, could do nothing but get out of the range of the rifles of the Albanians. The Albanians followed and tracked them in order to secure their heads, for which the pashas had promised a high price. The loss of the Greeks was greater at the foot of the hills, where their own troops ought to have insured their safety, than it had been in forcing the enemy's lines and in resisting the charges of the cavalry. Most of the women and children who had dragged themselves thus far, were so exhausted that they were taken prisoners.

About midnight small parties of the garrison, and a few women and children, succeeded in reaching the post occupied by the Greek troops; but instead of fifteen hundred men they found only fifty, with a very small supply of provisions to relieve their wants. Here they learned also, with dismay, that the camp at Platanos was a prey to the ordinary dissensions and abuses which disgraced the military classes of Greece at this period. The weary fugitives, in order to escape starvation, were soon compelled to continue their march to Platanos. Even there they obtained very little assistance from the chiefs of the armatoli; and when they had rested about a week, they resumed their journey to Salona. Many perished from wounds, disease, and hunger on the road. About fifteen hundred reached Salona during the month of May, straggling thither generally in small bands, and often by very circuitous roads, which they followed in order to procure food. Of these about thirteen hundred were soldiers; there were several girls in the number of those who escaped, and a few boys under twelve years of age [1].

As soon as Ibrahim and Reshid found that the greater part of the garrison had evacuated Mesolonghi, they ordered a general assault. Their troops occupied the whole line of the walls without encountering resistance. But it was not until morning dawned that the Turkish officers allowed their men to advance into the interior of the town, though several houses near the walls had been set on fire during the night. A whole day was spent by the conquerors in plundering Mesolonghi. The Greek soldiers who were prevented from accompanying their comrades either by wounds or sickness, intrenched themselves in the stone buildings best adapted for offering a desperate resistance. The party which occupied the principal powder-magazine, when closely attacked, set fire to the powder and perished in the explosion. A second powder-magazine was exploded by its defenders, who also perished with their assailants. A windmill, which served as a central depôt of ammunition, was defended until the 24th of April, when its little garrison, having exhausted their provisions, set fire to the powder. All the soldiers preferred death to captivity.

The loss of the Greeks amounted to four thousand. Ibrahim boasted that the Turks had collected three thousand heads; and it is probable that at least one thousand perished from wounds and starvation beyond the limits which the besiegers examined. The nearest points where the fugitives could find security and rest, were Petala, Kalamos, and Salona. The conquerors took about three thousand prisoners, chiefly women and children. About two thousand escaped;

---

[1] Tricoupi (iii. 353) says that all the women who took part in the sortie perished except seven, and all the children except three or four. This is merely rhetorical arithmetic, for in 1827 M. Tricoupi himself received thirty barrels of flour from Mr. Miller, the agent of the American committee, expressly for the relief of non-combatants—natives of Mesolonghi who had survived the siege; and about the same time M. George Constantinides was sent to relieve twenty-seven who were at Aegina, chiefly women and children. It is impossible to fix the number of those who escaped with precision. See *The condition of Greece in* 1827 *and* 1828, by Col. Jonathan Miller, of Vermont, New York, 1828, pp. 80, 245.

for besides those who reached Salona, a few found refuge in the villages of Aetolia, and some of the inhabitants of Mesolonghi and of the surrounding country evaded the Turkish pursuit by wading into the lagoon, and ultimately reached Petala and Kalamos, where they received protection and rations from the British government.

Many deeds of heroism might be recorded. One example deserves to be selected. The Moreot primates have been justly stigmatized as a kind of Christian Turks; and, as a class, their conduct during the Greek Revolution was marked by selfishness. Yet a Moreot primate displayed a noble example of the purest patriotism at the fall of Mesolonghi. Papadiamantopulos of Patras, a leading Hetairist, was one of the members of the executive commission intrusted with the administration of Western Greece. In the month of February he visited Zante to hasten the departure of supplies. His friends there urged him to remain. They said that as he was not a soldier he could assist in prolonging the defence of Mesolonghi more effectually by remaining at Zante, to avail himself of every opportunity of sending over supplies, than by serving in the besieged town. But the noble old gentleman silenced every entreaty by the simple observation: 'I invited my countrymen to take up arms against the Turks, and I swore to live and die with them. This is the hour to keep my promise.' He returned to Mesolonghi, and died the death of a hero in the final sortie [1].

John James Meyer, a young Swiss Philhellene, also deserves to have his name recorded. He came to Greece in 1821, married a maiden of Mesolonghi, and at the commencement of the siege was elected a member of the military commission that conducted the defence. He was an enthusiastic democrat in his political opinions, and a man of indefatigable energy; acting as a soldier on the walls, as a surgeon in the hospital, as an honest man in the commissariat, and as a patriot in the military commission. A short time before it was resolved to force a passage through the Turkish lines, he wrote his last letter to a friend which contains these words, 'Our labours and a wound in the shoulder (a prelude to one which will be my passport to eternity) have prevented my

---

[1] Gordon (i. 266) and Tricoupi (iii. 356) both mention the conduct of Papadiamantopulos with just praise.

writing lately. We suffer horribly from hunger and thirst; and disease adds to our calamities. In the name of our brave soldiers of Noti Botzaris, Papadiamantopulos, and in my own, I declare that we have sworn to defend Mesolonghi foot by foot, and to accept no capitulation. Our last hour approaches.'

In the final sortie he reached the foot of the hills, carrying his child and accompanied by his wife. He was there slain, and his wife and child were made prisoners. Meyer entertained a firm conviction that constancy on the part of the Greeks would eventually force Christian nations to support their cause, and he deemed it to be his duty to exhibit an example of the constancy he inculcated. Greece owes a debt of gratitude to this disinterested stranger who served her before kings and ministers became her patrons[1].

The conduct of the defenders of Mesolonghi will awaken the sympathies of freemen in every country as long as Grecian history endures. The siege rivals that of Plataea in the energy and constancy of the besieged; it wants only a historian like Thucydides to secure for it a like immortality of fame.

---

[1] *See* Gordon, ii. 268. Meyer was the editor of the Greek newspaper commenced at Mesolonghi in 1824, 'Ελληνικὰ Χρονικά. It was printed with types sent to Greece by the London committee. The brother of General Vlachopoulos was beside Meyer when he fell.

In my first edition I omitted to mention Meyer, but his title to a place in the history of the Greek Revolution, which Gordon recognized with his usual candour and judgment, was forced on my attention by my being requested to name the twelve Greeks and four Philhellenes most deserving of record on a public monument. Those selected were Khiga, the Patriarch Gregorios, Hypsilantes, Diakos, Mavromichales, Miaoulis, Mavrocordatos, Kanares, Marco Botzaris, Karaïskakes, Kolokotrones, Kapodistrias, Byron, Fabvier, Santa Rosa, Meyer. The fame of Byron gives him precedence over Gordon, the earliest, and Hastings, the best, of English Philhellenes.

CHAPTER III.

THE SIEGE OF ATHENS.

Ibrahim's operations in the Morea during 1826.—Reshid's operations in continental Greece.—Commencement of the siege of Athens, and battle of Khaidari.—Death of Goura.—Grigiottes throws himself into the Acropolis.—Karaïskaki's operations to raise the siege.—Fabvier throws himself into the Acropolis.—State of Greece during the winter 1826-27.—Expeditions for the relief of Athens under Gordon, Burbaki, and Heideck.—General Sir Richard Church.—Lord Cochrane (Earl of Dundonald).—Election of Count Capodistrias to be president of Greece.—Naval expedition under Captain Hastings.—Greek traders supply Reshid's army with provisions.—Operations of Church and Cochrane before Athens.—Massacre of the garrison of the monastery of St. Spiridion.—Karaïskaki's death.—Defeat of Sir Richard Church at the Phalerum.—Evacuation of the Acropolis.—Conduct of Philhellenes in Greece, England, and America.—Lord Cochrane's naval review at Poros.—Sufferings of the Greeks.—Assistance sent from the United States.

AFTER the conquest of Mesolonghi, the Othoman fleet returned to Constantinople, and the Egyptian to Alexandria. The Greeks, with their reduced naval strength, were therefore again left masters of the sea.

Ibrahim Pasha returned to the Morea in order to complete the conquest of his own pashalik. After reviewing his troops at Patras, he found himself compelled to open the campaign of 1826 at the head of only four thousand infantry and six hundred cavalry. With this insignificant army he marched against the Greeks, laid waste the fields of that part of the population of Achaia which had not submitted to his authority, and drove the inhabitants into the inaccessible regions of Mount Chelmos, where the snow still lay thick on the ground. During this foray he captured many prisoners, and carried off large herds of cattle and innumerable flocks of sheep.

A small detachment was sent to reconnoitre the monastery of Megaspelaion; but at this time no attack was made on it. The monks imagined a miracle. They recounted that a high wall stood up before the Egyptian troops, and closed the road by which they endeavoured to reach the holy building. Terrified by this proof that God opposed their undertaking, they marched back to Kalavryta[1].

From Kalavryta Ibrahim marched to Tripolitza. Near Karitena he was joined by considerable reinforcements from Modon. The summer was employed in a series of expeditions for laying waste the country and starving the population into submission. The crops being generally ready for the sickle, or already reaped, were either destroyed or carried off. Great quantities of grain were burned, and great quantities were transported to Tripolitza. From the 15th of May to the 14th of November 1826 the Egyptian troops carried on the work of destruction almost without interruption. Achaia, Elis, Arcadia, Messenia, and Laconia were devastated, villages were burned to the ground, cattle were driven away, and the inhabitants, when captured, were either shot or sold as slaves. The desolation produced was so complete, that during the following winter numbers of the peasantry, particularly women and children, died of actual starvation.

During the summer Ibrahim made two attempts to penetrate into Maina—the first from the pass of Armyros on the west side, the other from Marathonesi on the east coast. Both were repulsed by the Mainates, who availed themselves of the natural difficulties which the precipitous gorges of Mount Taygetus offer to the advance of an invader.

The military operations of Kolokotrones and the other Peloponnesian chiefs were conducted without union, vigour, or judgment. An abortive attempt had been made to surprise Tripolitza, while Ibrahim was absent besieging Mesolonghi[2].

---

[1] The ecclesiastic Phrantzes boasts of his own belief in this miracle, which took place on the 7th May, 1826. On the 6th July, 1827, Ibrahim reconnoitred the monastery in person, and made an attack on it. The monks were prepared, and the monastery was garrisoned by Greek troops, who repulsed the attack, which Ibrahim did not renew. The monks were generally suspected of having entered into a secret arrangement with the Egyptian pasha, but Phrantzes assures us that this was not the case. Phrantzes, ii. 441, *note* 1, and 495.

[2] See a boasting extract from a despatch of Kolokotrones in Fabre, *Histoire du Siège de Mesolonghi*, 331. The disorder that prevailed in the Greek armies is well described in the graphic dialect of the old klepht, as reported in Διήγησις Συμβάντων τῆς 'Ελληνικῆς Φυλῆς, Athens, 1846.

After Ibrahim returned to the Morea, the faculties of Kolokotrones appeared to have been paralyzed. The only success he obtained was carrying off a few mules from the Egyptian convoys, and recovering a small portion of the booty taken from the peasantry, which he employed to feed his own followers.

At the end of the year Ibrahim found his troops so worn out by fatigue and disease, that he was compelled to suspend his operations until he received fresh reinforcements from Egypt[1]. Mohammed Ali showed some hesitation in prosecuting the war against the Greeks at this time. He was watching the progress of the negotiations between the sultan and the courts of Great Britain and Russia, and he wished to learn whether his son would be allowed to complete the conquest of the Morea, and retain permanent possession of it, before expending more money in the undertaking.

In the mean time Reshid Pasha laboured strenuously to re-establish the sultan's authority in continental Greece. His road to fame and power lay in his absolute devotion to Sultan Mahmud's interests, and his faithful execution of the orders he received from the Porte.

During the month of June 1826 he fixed his head-quarters at Mesolonghi, and many of the Greek chieftains submitted to him, and publicly recognized the sultan's authority. Rhangos, Siphakas, Dyovuniottes, Kontoyannes, and Andreas Iskos all owned allegiance to the Porte, accepted the rank of captains of armatoli, and forgot the heroism of the defenders of Mesolonghi.

As soon as the affairs of Western Greece were settled on a footing that promised at least a temporary security for the restoration of order, Reshid marched into Eastern Greece, occupied the passes over Oeta, Knemis, Parnassus, and Parnes, strengthened the garrison of Thebes, and organized regular communications by land between Larissa and Chalcis in Euboea. He entered Attica before the crops of 1826 were gathered in.

The exactions of Goura exceeded those of Odysseus, for Odysseus, like his patron, Ali of Joannina, allowed no extortions but his own, while Goura permitted his mercenaries to glean after the harvest of his own rapacity had been

---

[1] See the plan of campaign proposed by Sir C. Napier in Appendix.

gathered in. A great proportion of the Attic peasantry was driven to despair, and the moment Reshid's forces appeared in the Katadema, or hilly district between Parnes and the channel of Euboea, they were welcomed as deliverers. On advancing into the plain of Athens, they were openly joined by the warlike inhabitants of Menidhi and Khasia, who vigorously supported Reshid's government as long as he remained in Attica.

The contributions which Goura levied under the pretext of preparing for the defence of Attica were exclusively employed for provisioning the Acropolis, and in garrisoning that stronghold with four hundred chosen mercenaries in his own pay. These men were selected from those whom the civil war in the Morea had inured to acts of tyranny, and they were taught to look to Goura and not to the Greek government for pay and promotion. The citizens of Athens were distrusted by the tyrant, and not allowed to form part of the garrison of their own citadel.

The Turks took possession of Sepolia, Patissia, and Ambelokepos without encountering serious opposition. On the 28th of June Reshid arrived from Thebes, and established his head-quarters at Patissia. His army did not exceed seven thousand men, but his cavalry, which amounted to eight hundred, was in a high state of efficiency, and he had a fine train of artillery, consisting of twenty-six guns and mortars. The siege of Athens was immediately commenced. The hill Museion was occupied, and batteries were erected at the little chapel of St. Demetrius, and on the level above the Pnyx.

Reshid soon obtained a brilliant victory over the Greeks. About four thousand armatoli had been concentrated at Eleusis. The Greek chiefs who commanded this army proposed to force their way into Athens, and expected to be able to maintain themselves in the houses. Reshid divined their object, and forestalled them in its execution. On the night of the 14th of August he stormed the town, and drove the Athenians into the Acropolis, into which Goura could not refuse to admit them.

The Greek troops persisted in advancing from Eleusis, though their generals seem to have formed no definite plan. Their numbers were insufficient to hold out any reasonable probability of their being able to recover possession of Athens. The irregulars amounted to two thousand five hundred under the command of Karaïskaki, the regulars to one thousand five hundred under Fabvier. The Greek force crossed the mountains by a pathway which leaves the Sacred Way and the monastery of Daphne to the right, and took up a position at a farmhouse with a small tower called Khaïdari. Instead of pushing on to the Olive Grove, and stationing themselves among the vineyards, where the Turkish cavalry and artillery would have been useless, they awaited Reshid at Khaïdari. On the 20th of August the attack was made, and the Greeks were completely defeated. The two leaders endeavoured to throw the whole blame of the disaster on one another, and they succeeded in convincing everybody who paid any attention to their proceedings that both of them had displayed great want of judgment. Nobody suspected either of them of want of personal energy and daring, but both were notoriously deficient in temper and prudence [1].

Karaïskaki soon regained his reputation with his own soldiers, by sending a large body on a successful foray to Skourta, where they captured a numerous herd of cattle destined for the use of the Turkish army.

Fabvier withdrew his corps to Salamis.

Reshid bombarded the Acropolis hotly for some time, but seeing that his fire did the besieged little injury, he attempted to take the place by mining. Though he made little progress even with his mines, he persisted in carrying on his operations with his characteristic perseverance.

A body of Greek troops, consisting of Ionians and Romeliots, made two unsuccessful attempts to relieve the besieged. The summer dragged on without anything decisive. The soldiers in the Acropolis manifested a mutinous spirit in consequence of the ineffectual efforts made to relieve them, and many succeeded in deserting during the night, by creeping unobserved through the Turkish lines. To prevent these desertions Goura passed the night among the soldiers on guard, and in order to secure the assistance of the enemy in preventing the escape of his men, he generally brought

---

[1] The best account of this affair is by Friedrich Müller, *Denkwürdigkeiten aus Griechenland*, 17. See also Gordon, ii. 336.

DEATH OF GOURA.

on a skirmish which put them on the alert. On the 13th of October, while exchanging shots with the Turkish sentinels, he was shot through the brain. His opponent fired at the flash of the powder in the touch-hole of his rifle [1]. The death of Goura drew public attention to the dangerous position of the garrison, and to the neglect of the Greek government.

A cry of indignation at the incapacity and negligence of its members was now raised both in Greece and the Ionian Islands. Greece had a numerous body of men under arms in continental Greece, yet these troops were inactive spectators of the siege of Athens. General Gordon, who had recently returned to Greece, records that these troops were condemned to inaction by the bickerings of their leaders [2]. Some attempts were at last made to interrupt Reshid's operations. Fabvier advanced into Boeotia with the intention of storming Thebes; but being deserted by his soldiers, he was compelled to fall back without attempting anything. Reshid, who was well informed of every movement made by the Greeks through the Attic peasants who acted as his scouts, sent forward a body of cavalry, which very nearly succeeded in occupying the passes of Cithaeron and cutting off Fabvier's retreat to Megara. On his return, Fabvier was left by the Greek government without provisions; and attempts being made in the name of Karaïskaki and Niketas, perhaps without their authority, to induce his men to desert, he found himself obliged to withdraw the regular corps to Methana in order to prevent its dissolution [3].

Karaïskaki advanced a second time to Khaïdari. This movement enabled Grigiottes to land unobserved in the Bay of Phalerum, near the mouth of the Cephissus, and to march up to the Acropolis, into which he introduced himself and four hundred and fifty men without loss.

As Athens was now safe for some time, Karaïskaki moved off to Mount Helicon, where a few of the inhabitants still

---

[1] Sourmeles, 164; Tricoupi, iv. 74. Goura's widow was killed, with ten female companions and attendants, three months later, by the roof of the Erechtheion falling in. The Athenian historian Sourmeles says that she was already betrothed to Grigiottes, by the persuasion of her intriguing brother Anastasios Loidorikes, who had induced her to lay aside her widow's weeds. He exclaims, Ἰδοὺ ἀπιστία γυναικὸς καὶ ἀναίδεια (p. 189).
[2] Gordon, ii. 343.
[3] Friedrich Müller, 22.

remained faithful to their country's cause. He expected to succeed in capturing some of the Turkish magazines in Boeotia, and in intercepting the supplies which Reshid drew from Thessaly by the way of Zeituni.

The Acropolis was now garrisoned by about one thousand soldiers, but it was encumbered by the presence of upwards of four hundred women and children. The supply of wheat and barley was abundant, but the clothes of the soldiers were in rags, and there was no fuel to bake bread. Reshid, who determined to prosecute the siege during the winter, made arrangements for keeping his troops well supplied with provisions and military stores, and for defending the posts which protected his communications with Thessaly.

The Turks neglected to keep a naval squadron in the channel of Euboea, though it would always have found safe harbours at Negrepont and Volo. The Greeks were therefore enabled to transport a large force to attack any point in the rear of Reshid's army. It was in their power to cut off all the supplies he received by sea, and, by occupying some defensible station in the northern channel of Euboea, to establish communications with Karaïskaki's troops on Mount Helicon, and form a line of posts from this defensible station to another of a similar kind on the Gulf of Corinth. Talanta and Dobrena were the stations indicated. But instead of attempting to aid the army, the Greek navy either remained idle or engaged in piracy. Faction also prevented a great part of the Greek army from taking the field, and the assistance which the Philhellenic committee in Paris transmitted to Greece was employed by its agent, Dr. Bailly, in feeding Kolokotrones' soldiers, who remained idle in the Morea, without marching either against the Egyptians or the Turks. Konduriottes and Kolokotrones, formerly the deadliest enemies, being now both excluded from the executive government, were banded together in a most unpatriotic and dishonourable opposition to a weak but not ill-disposed government, composed of nearly a dozen members, many of whom were utterly unfit for political employment of any kind[1]. Some feeble attempts were made to organize attacks

---

[1] General Gordon, who served under this executive, thought more favourably of it than the Author of this work, who watched its proceedings as a volunteer under Captain Hastings. The General says, 'The president, Zaimes, had considerable

on Reshid's rear; but each leader was allowed to form an independent scheme of operations, and to abandon his enterprise when it suited his convenience.

The command of one expedition was entrusted to Kolettes, a man destitute both of physical and moral courage, though he looked a very truculent personage, and nourished a boundless ambition. The feeble government was anxious to prevent his allying himself with Konduriottes and Kolokotrones, and to effect that object he was placed at the head of a body of troops destined to destroy the magazines of the Turks in the northern channel of Euboea. Nobody expected much from a military undertaking commanded by Kolettes, but the selfish members of the executive body, as usual, consulted their personal and party interests, and not their country's advantage, in making the nomination.

Kolettes collected the Olympian armatoli who had been living at free quarters in Skiathos, Skopelos, and Skyros for two years. The agents of the French Philhellenic committees supplied the expedition with provisions and military stores, and Kalergi, a wealthy Greek in Russia, paid a considerable sum of money into its military chest. Kolettes' troops landed near Talanti in order to gain possession of the magazines in that town, but the Turks, though much inferior in number, defeated them on the 20th November 1826. The armatoli escaped in the ships, and Kolettes abandoned his military career, and returned to the more congenial occupation of seeking importance by intriguing at Nauplia.

Karaïskaki about the same time began active operations at the head of three thousand of the best troops in Greece. Though he was compelled to render all his movements subordinate to the manner in which his troops could be supplied with provisions, he displayed both activity and judgment. His object was to throw his whole force on the rear of Reshid's army, master his line of communications, and destroy his magazines. The diversion, which it was expected would be made by Kolettes' expedition, would

---

merit. and the government contained several men of fair talent and business-like habits' (ii. 300). Their names were—Zaimes, president, Petrobey of Maina, A. Deliyannes, Tsamados, Hadji Anarghyros, Monarchides, Tricoupi, Vlachos, Zotos, Demetrakopulos. This government removed from Nauplia, where it felt too much under the control of the Moreot military faction, to Aegina, on the 23rd of November, 1826.

enable Karaïskaki's troops to draw supplies of provisions and ammunition from the channel of Euboea through Eastern Locris, as well as from Megara and the Gulf of Corinth. The victory of the Turks at Talanti occurring before the Greek troops entered Phocis, Karaïskaki determined to cut off the retreat of Mustapha Bey, who, after defeating Kolettes, proposed falling back on Salona. Both Turks and Greeks endeavoured to be first in gaining possession of the passes between Mounts Cirphis and Parnassus. Karaïskaki sent forward his advanced-guard with all speed to occupy Arachova, and his men had hardly established themselves in the village before they were attacked by a corps of fifteen hundred Mussulman Albanians. Mustapha Bey had united his force with that of Elmas Bey, whom Reshid ordered to occupy Arachova and Boudonitza, in order to secure his communications with Zeituni.

The beys endeavoured to drive the advanced-guard of the Greeks out of Arachova before the main body could arrive from Distomo to its support, but their attacks were repulsed with loss. When Karaïskaki heard of the enemy's movements, he took his measures with promptitude and judgment. He occupied the Triodos with a strong body of men, to prevent the Albanians falling back on Livadea; and he sent another strong body over Mount Cirphis to take possession of Delphi, and prevent them from marching on to Salona. While the beys lingered in the hope of destroying the advanced-guard of the Greeks, they found themselves blockaded by a superior force. They were attacked, and lost the greater part of their baggage and provisions in the engagement. During the night after their defeat they made a bold attempt to escape to Salona by climbing the precipices of Parnassus, which the Greeks left unguarded. The darkness and their experience in ambuscades enabled them to move off from the vicinity of Arachova unobserved, but a heavy fall of snow surprised them as they were seeking paths up the rocks. At sunrise the Greeks followed them. Escape was impossible, for the only tracks over the precipices which the fugitives were endeavouring to ascend, were paths along which the shepherd follows his goats with difficulty, even in summer. They were all destroyed on the 6th of December. Their defence was valiant, but hopeless; quarter was neither asked nor given. Many were frozen to death, but three hundred, protected by the veil of falling snow, succeeded in climbing the precipices and reaching Salona. The heads of four beys were sent to Aegina as a token of victory.

Karaïskaki was unable to follow up this success; want of provisions, more than the severity of the weather, kept his troops inactive. Reshid profited by this inaction to strengthen his posts at Livadea and Boudonitza. Part of the Greek troops at last moved northward to plunder his convoys, while the rest spread over the whole country to obtain the means of subsistence which the Greek government neglected to supply. The Turks intrenched themselves at Daulis. Omer Pasha of Negrepont at last attacked the Greek camp at Distomo, and this attack compelled Karaïskaki to return and recall the greater part of his troops. After many skirmishes the Turks made a general attack on the Greeks at Distomo on the 12th of February 1827, which was repulsed, and the pasha was soon after compelled to retire to Chalcis. But the country was now so completely exhausted that Karaïskaki was compelled to abandon his camp and fall back on Megara and Eleusis, where the presence of his army was deemed necessary to co-operate in a direct attack on Reshid's force before Athens.

After Goura's death, several officers in the Acropolis pretended to equal authority. Grigiottes was the chief who possessed most personal influence. All measures were discussed in a council of chiefs, and instability of purpose was as much a characteristic of this small assembly of military leaders as it was of the Athenian Demos of old. One of the chiefs, Makriyannes, who distinguished himself greatly when Ibrahim attacked the mills at Lerna, was deputed to inform the Greek government that the supply of powder was exhausted, and that the garrison was so disheartened that succour must be sent without delay. Makriyannes quitted the Acropolis on the 29th November 1826, passed the Turkish lines, and reached Aegina in safety. His appearance awakened the deepest interest. He had distinguished himself in many sorties during the siege, and he was then suffering from the wounds he had received. His frank and loyal character inspired general confidence. The members of the executive government felt the necessity of immediate action.

Colonel Fabvier, who had brought the regular corps into some state of efficiency at Methana, was the only officer in Greece at this time capable of taking the field with a force on which the government could place any reliance. He was not personally a favourite with the members of the executive body. They feared and distrusted him, and he despised and distrusted them[1]. Fortunately the news of Karaïskaki's victory at Arachova rendered him extremely eager for immediate action. The fame of his rival irritated his jealous disposition and excited his emulation. He therefore accepted the offer to command an expedition for the relief of Athens with pleasure, and prepared to carry succour to the Acropolis with his usual promptitude, and more than his usual prudence.

Fabvier landed with six hundred and fifty chosen men of the regular corps in the Bay of Phalerum, about midnight on the 12th December 1826[2]. Each man carried on his back a leather sack filled with gunpowder. The whole body reached the Turkish lines in good order and without being observed. They were formed in column on the road which leads from Athens to the Phalerum, a little below its junction with the road to Sunium, and rushed on the Turkish guard with fixed bayonets, while the drums sounded a loud signal to the garrison of the Acropolis to divert the attention of the besiegers by a desperate sortie. Fabvier cleared all before him, leading on his troops rapidly and silently over the space that separated the enemy's lines from the theatre of Herodes Atticus, under a shower of grape and musket-balls. To prevent his men from delaying their march, and exchanging shots with the Turks, all the flints had been taken out of their muskets. A bright moon enabled the troops of Reshid to take aim at the Greeks, but the rapidity of Fabvier's movements carried his whole body within the walls of the Acropolis, with the loss of only six killed and fourteen wounded. In such enterprises, where the valour of the soldier and the activity of the leader were the only qualities wanted to insure success, Fabvier's personal conduct shone to the greatest advantage.

---

[1] Dr. Howe (*Historical Sketch*, 294) says that Fabvier 'treated the government with a degree of rudeness that was neither gentleman-like nor soldier-like.'
[2] Friedrich Müller, 25.

His shortcomings were most manifest when patience and prudence were the qualities required in the general.

His men carried nothing with them into the Acropolis but their arms, and the powder on their backs. Even their great-coats were left behind, for Fabvier proposed returning to the vessels which brought him on the ensuing night. The garrison of the Acropolis was sufficiently strong, and any addition to its numbers would only add to the difficulties of its defence by increasing the number of killed and wounded, and exhausting the provisions. Unfortunately, most of the chiefs of the irregular troops wished to quit the place and leave the regular troops in their place, and they took effectual measures to prevent Fabvier's departure by skirmishing with the Turks, and putting them on the alert whenever he made an attempt to pass their lines. It is also asserted with confidence, by persons who had the best means of knowing the truth, and whose honour and sagacity are unimpeachable, that secret orders were transmitted from the executive government at Aegina to Grigiottes, to prevent Fabvier from returning to Methana[1]. This unprincipled conduct of the Greek government and the military chiefs in the Acropolis caused great calamities to Greece, for Fabvier's presence hastened the fall of Athens, both by increasing the sufferings of the garrison, and by his eagerness to quit a fortress where he could gain no honour. After the nomination of Sir Richard Church as commander-in-chief, Fabvier's impatience to quit the Acropolis and resume his separate command at Methana was immoderate ; and Gordon asserts that, had only Greeks been in the Acropolis, it might have held out until the battle of Navarin saved Greece.

Greece fell into the chronic state of political anarchy during the latter part of the year 1826, which continued to influence her history during the remainder of her struggle for independence. The executive body, which retired from Nauplia to Aegina in the month of November, was the legal government ; but its members were numerous, selfish, and incapable, and far more intent on injuring their rivals in the Peloponnesus, who established a hostile executive at Kastri (Hermione), than on injuring the Turks who were besieging

---

[1] This accusation is repeated by Gordon (ii. 400), who was on terms of intimacy with several members of the government.

Athens. Kolokotrones, who was the leader of the faction at Kastri, formed a coalition with his former enemy Konduriottes, and this unprincipled alliance endeavoured to prevent Greece from profiting by the mediation which Great Britain proposed as the most effectual means of saving the inhabitants of many provinces from extermination.

The Treaty of Akerman, concluded between Russia and Turkey on the 6th of October 1826, put an end to the hopes which the Greeks long cherished of seeing Russia ultimately engaged in war with the sultan. But this event rather revived than depressed the Russian party in Greece, whose leading members believed that the emperor would now interfere actively in order to thwart the increasing influence of England. At the same time, the agents of the French Philhellenic committees displayed a malevolent hostility to British policy, and seized every opportunity of encouraging faction, by distributing supplies to the troops of Kolokotrones, who remained idle, and withholding them from those of Karaïskaki, who were carrying on war against the Turks in the field [1].

The active strength both of the army and navy in Greece began to diminish rapidly about this time. The people in general lost all confidence in the talents and the honesty both of their military and political leaders. The bravest and most patriotic chiefs had fallen in battle. Two names, however, still shed a bright light through the mist of selfishness, Kanares and Miaoulis, and these two naval heroes belonged to adverse parties and different nationalities. The Greek navy was unemployed. A small part of the army was in the field against the Turks; the greater part was engaged in collecting the national revenues, or extorting their subsistence from the unfortunate peasantry. The shipowners and sailors, who could no longer find profitable employment by serving against the Turks, engaged in an extensive and organized system of piracy against the ships of every Christian power, which was carried on with a degree of cruelty never exceeded in the annals of crime. The peasantry alone remained true to the cause of the nation, but they could do little more than display their perseverance by patient suffering,

---

[1] Gordon, ii. 356.

and never did a people suffer with greater constancy and fortitude. Many died of hunger rather than submit to the Turks, particularly in the Morea, where they feared lest Ibrahim should transport their families to Egypt, educate their boys as Mohammedans, and sell their girls into Mussulman harems.

The Philhellenic committees of Switzerland, France, and Germany redoubled their activity when the proceeds of the English loans were exhausted. Large supplies of provisions were sent to Greece, and assisted in maintaining the troops who took the field against the Turks, and in preventing many families in different parts of the country from perishing by starvation. The presence of several foreigners prevented the executive government at Aegina from diverting these supplies to serve the ambitious schemes of its members, as shamelessly as Konduriottes' government had disposed of the English loans, or as Kolokotrones' faction at this very time employed such supplies as it could obtain. Colonel Heideck, who acted as the agent of the King of Bavaria; Dr. Goss of Geneva, who represented the Swiss committees and Mr. Eynard; Count Porro, a noble Milanese exile; and Mr. Koering, an experienced German administrator[1], set the Greeks an example of prudence and good conduct by acting always in concord.

Two Philhellenes, General Gordon and Captain Frank Abney Hastings, had also some influence in preventing the executive government at Aegina from completely neglecting the defence of Athens.

General Gordon returned to Greece at the invitation of the government with £15,000, saved from the proceeds of the second loan, which was placed at his absolute disposal. He was intimately acquainted with the military character and resources of both the belligerents. He spoke both Greek

---

[1] This singular man came to Greece with Dr. Goss, who assisted him in escaping from the continent on receiving his word of honour that he was not flying from any fear of criminal law: yet even Dr. Goss never knew his real name. He was of great use to Dr. Goss in organizing the distribution of the stores sent by the various committees, and he displayed a degree of administrative experience, and an acquaintance with governmental business, which could hardly have been acquired by service in an inferior position. To wealth or rank, even to the ordinary comforts of life, he seemed to have resigned all claim. Though of some use to Capodistrias, he was neglected by that statesman, who feared him as a Liberal; and he died of fever during the president's administration.

and Turkish with ease, and could even carry on a correspondence in the Turkish language. His *History of the Greek Revolution* is a work of such accuracy in detail, that it has served as one of the sources from which the principal Greek historian of the Revolution has compiled his narrative of most military operations[1]. Gordon was firm and sagacious, but he did not possess the activity and decision of character necessary to obtain commanding influence in council, or to initiate daring measures in the field.

Captain Hastings was probably the best foreign officer who embarked in the Greek cause. Candour and decision were the prominent features of his character, and he pursued what his conscience told him was the line of his duty with a resolute will, a strong sense of personal honour, and an invariable respect for justice. Though calm and patient in council, he was extremely rapid and bold in action. He brought to Greece the first steam-ship, which was armed with heavy guns for the use of shells and hot shot; and he was the first officer who habitually made use of these engines of war at sea. At this time he had brought his ship, the Karteria, into a high state of discipline.

Mr. Gropius, the Austrian consul at Athens, who then resided at Aegina, was also frequently consulted by individual members of the executive body. His long residence in the East had rendered him well acquainted with the character and views of the Greeks and Turks, but his long absence from Western Europe had prevented him from acquiring any profound political knowledge or any administrative experience.

Mavrocordatos and Tricoupi were generally the medium through which the opinions of the foreigners who have been mentioned were transmitted to the majority of the members of the executive body. Mavrocordatos possessed more administrative capacity than any of his countrymen connected with the government at Aegina; but the errors into which he was led by his personal ambition and his Phanariot education had greatly diminished his influence. Tricoupi was a man of eloquence, but of a commonplace mind, and destitute of the very elements of administrative knowledge.

---

[1] Compare Gordon's *History of the Greek Revolution*, 2 vols. 8vo., 1832, with Tricoupi's Ἱστορία τῆς Ἑλληνικῆς Ἐπαναστάσεως, 4 vols., 1853. Any portion of the military operations of the Turkish armies will afford proof.

These two men served their country well at this time, by conveying to the government an echo of the reproaches which were loudly uttered, both at home and abroad, against its neglect ; and they assisted in persuading it to devote all the resources it could command to new operations for the relief of Athens.

It has been already observed, that the simplest way of raising the siege of Athens was by interrupting Reshid's communications with his magazines in Thessaly. The Greeks could easily bring more men into the field than Reshid, and during the winter months they commanded the sea. An intelligent government, with an able general, might have compelled the army before Athens to have disbanded, or surrendered at discretion, even without a battle ; for with six thousand men on Mount Parnassus, and a few ships in the northern and southern channels of Euboea, no supplies, either of ammunition or provisions, could have reached Reshid's army. The besiegers of Athens might also have been closely blockaded by a line of posts, extending from Megara to Eleutherae, Phyle, Deceleia, and Rhamnus. This plan was rejected, and a number of desultory operations were undertaken, with the hope of obtaining the desired result more speedily.

The first of these ill-judged expeditions was placed under the command of General Gordon. Two thousand three hundred men and fifteen guns were landed on the night of the 5th February 1827, and took possession of the hill of Munychia. Thrasybulus had delivered Athens from the thirty tyrants by occupying this position, and the modern Greeks have a pedantic love for classical imitation[1]. In spite of this advantage, Reshid secured the command of the Piraeus by preventing the Greeks from getting possession of the monastery of St. Spiridion, and thus rendered the permanent occupation of Munychia utterly useless.

While Gordon was engaged in fortifying the desert rock on which he had perched his men, the attention of the Turks was drawn off by another body of Greeks. Colonel Burbaki, a Cephalonian, who had distinguished himself as a cavalry officer in the French service, offered to head a diversion, for

---

[1] Ὁ Θρασύβουλος κατελάβιτο τὴν Μουνυχίαν, λόφον ἔρημον καὶ κάρτερον. Diodorus, xiv. 33.

the purpose of enabling Gordon to complete his defences. Burbaki descended from the hills that bound the plain of Athens to the west, and advanced to Kamatero near Menidhi. He was accompanied by eight hundred irregulars; and Vassos and Panayotaki Notaras, who were each at the head of a thousand men, were ordered to support him, and promised to do so. Burbaki was brave and enthusiastic; Vassos and Notaras selfish, and without military capacity. Burbaki pushed forward rashly into the plain, and before he could take up a defensive position in the olive grove, he was attacked by Reshid Pasha in person at the head of an overwhelming force. Burbaki's men behaved well, and five hundred fell with their gallant leader. The two chiefs, who ought to have supported him with two thousand men, never came into action: they and their followers fled in the most dastardly manner, abandoning all their provisions to the Turks.

After this victory Reshid marched to the Piraeus, hoping to drive Gordon into the sea. On the 11th of February he attacked the hill of Munychia. His troops advanced boldly to the assault, supported by the fire of four long five-inch howitzers. The attack was skilfully conducted. About three thousand men, scattered in loose order round the base of the hill, climbed its sides, covered by the steep declivities which sheltered them from the fire of the Greeks who crowned the summit. Several gallant attempts were made to reach the Greek intrenchments; but as soon as the Turks issued from their cover, they were received with such a fire of musketry and grape that they fled back to some sheltered position. A diversion was made by Captain Hastings, which put an end to the combat. He entered the Piraeus with the Karteria under steam, and opened a fire of grape from his 68-pounders on the Turkish reserves and artillery. The troops fled, one of the enemy's guns was dismounted, and the others only escaped by getting under cover of the monastery. The Turkish artillerymen, however, nothing daunted, contrived to run out one of the howitzers under the protection of an angle of the building, and opened a well-directed fire of five-inch shells on the Karteria. Every boat belonging to the ship was struck, and several shells exploded on board, so that Hastings, unable to remain in the Piraeus without exposing his ship to serious danger, escaped out of the port. His diversion proved completely successful, for Reshid did not renew the attack on Gordon's position.

Reshid had some reason to boast of his success; and in order to give the sultan a correct idea of the difficulties with which he was contending, he sent to Constantinople the 68-lb. shot of the Karteria which had dismounted his gun, and a bag of the white biscuits from Ancona, which were distributed as rations to the Greek troops. At the same time he forwarded to the Porte the head of the gallant Burbaki and the cavalry helmet he wore.

The failure of the double attack on Reshid's front persuaded the Greek government to recommence operations against his rear. General Heideck was appointed to command an enterprise similar to that in which Kolettes had failed in the disgraceful manner previously recounted. But Oropos was selected as the point of attack instead of Talanti[1]. Oropos was the principal magazine for the supplies which the army besieging Athens received by sea. These supplies were conveyed to Negrepont by the northern channel, and sent on to Oropos in small transports. Heideck sailed from the Bay of Phalerum with five hundred men. The naval force, consisting of the Hellas frigate, the steam corvette Karteria, and the brig Nelson, was commanded by Miaoulis. On arriving at Oropos, the Hellas anchored about a mile from the Turkish battery; and Hastings, with the Karteria, steamed to within musket-shot of the Turkish guns, silenced them with a shower of grape, and took possession of two transports laden with flour. One of the carcass shells of the Karteria's 68-pounders set fire to the fascines of the Turkish battery, destroyed the carriage of a gun, and exploded the powder-magazine. The evening was already dark, but Miaoulis urged Heideck to land the troops immediately and storm the enemy's position, or at least endeavour to burn down his magazines, while his attention was distracted by the fire

---

[1] An anecdote proving the folly of the Greek government deserves notice. Ten days before Heideck's expedition sailed, it was announced in the government Gazette that the executive body had resolved to send a body of troops to *surprise* the Turks at Oropos. Yet, after all, the Turks allowed themselves to be surprised. Γενικὴ 'Εφημερὶς τῆς 'Ελλάδος, 23 Feb. (6 March), 1827, p. 122, and MS. journal.

in his battery. Heideck declined to make the attempt on account of the darkness, which the admiral thought favoured his attack. Next day the Greek troops landed in a disorderly manner, nor did Heideck himself put his foot on shore, or visit the Karteria, which remained at anchor close to the enemy's battery. The Turks, however, contrived to remove a gun, which they placed so as to defend their position from any attack on the side where the Greeks had landed. Nothing was done until, a body of cavalry arriving from Reshid's camp, Heideck ordered his men to be re-embarked, and sent them back to the camp at Munychia.

The conduct of Heideck on this occasion fixed a stain on his military reputation which was extremely injurious to his future influence in Greece. It furnished a parallel to the generalship of Kolettes, and encouraged the enemies of military science to express their contempt for the pedantry of tactics, and to proclaim that the maxims and rules of European warfare were not applicable to the war in Greece. It was in vain to point out to the Greeks, immediately after this unfortunate exhibition of military incapacity, that it was by gradually adopting some of the improvements of military science, and establishing some discipline, that the Turks were steadily acquiring the superiority both by sea and land.

Immediately after Heideck's failure, the affairs of Greece assumed a new aspect by the arrival of Sir Richard Church and Lord Cochrane.

The Englishman who hires his military service to a foreign state, violates the law of England, but at this time it was a common practice to seek distinction and high pay wherever it could be gained, though public opinion had ceased to look with much favour on the profession of arms when not sanctioned by natural allegiance. Strong religious sympathies and political convictions were nevertheless admitted as a valid warrant for serving a foreign cause, even although a man's native country might proclaim and endeavour to enforce neutrality. But, in such cases, the most disinterested conduct was necessary to disprove the existence of any mercenary motive, and to warrant a claim to follow the suggestions of individual opinion in opposition to the dictates of national policy. Gordon, Hastings, and Fabvier violated the principles of neutrality in serving against Turkey, but they proved that their motives were pure, by serving Greece as volunteers and not as mercenaries. They were all three indifferent to titular rank, and they refused pecuniary rewards.

When repeated disasters had destroyed the confidence of the Greeks both in themselves and their friends, they, at last, resolved to change their system of warfare. By hiring professional leaders, they expected to obtain a higher degree of warlike skill, than the unbought enthusiasm of Philhellenes had contributed to their cause. They soon learned by experience, that they overrated the power of money when they supposed that it could inspire the efforts of genius. Another motive exerted some influence on their conduct. The disposition which the British government had for some time exhibited in their favour led them to hope that England might be enticed to take Greece under its protection practically if not officially. With these views, the services of mercenary leaders were sought in England, and Lord Cochrane, who had served the South American republics, and Sir Richard Church who had served the despotic King of Naples, were selected to command the navy and army of Greece.

The professional reputation of Lord Cochrane, the naval skill he had displayed, and the daring personal exploits he had performed, both in the service of his own country and of foreign states, pointed him out as the admiral most likely to secure victory to the Greek fleet. His services were therefore secured, and they were purchased at an exorbitant price.

The high character of Colonel Charles Napier, who then governed Cephalonia, induced the Greeks to select him as the soldier best suited to command their army. And, perhaps, the man who was subsequently selected by the Duke of Wellington to command the Indian army at a critical moment, might have succeeded in organizing an efficient army in Greece. But though the demands of Napier were very moderate in a pecuniary point of view, the negotiation failed, because he insisted on some military arrangements as necessary to insure success, and the Greek government was either unwilling or unable to adopt them [1].

---

[1] Napier wrote two pamphlets on Greek affairs, but they were published anonymously—*War in Greece*, with a plan, and *Greece in* 1824, by the author of ' War in Greece.'

The choice then fell on Sir Richard Church, who had recently quitted the Neapolitan service, and who was known to many of the Greek chiefs, when he was major of the first battalion of Greek light infantry, which the British government had formed in the Ionian Islands. He became lieutenant-colonel of a second Greek battalion enrolled shortly before the end of the war with France, and never rose higher in the British service[1]. After the peace in 1815 he entered the Neapolitan service in which he attained the rank of lieutenant-general. His selection to command the Greek army was extremely popular among the military chiefs, who connected his name with the high pay and liberal rations which both officers and men had received while serving in the Anglo-Greek battalion.

The prominent political as well as military position which Sir Richard Church has occupied for many years in Greece, and the influence which his personal views have exercised on the public affairs of the country, render it necessary for the historian to scrutinize his conduct more than once, both as a statesman and a general, during his long career. The physical qualities of military men exert no trifling influence over their acts. Church was of a small, well-made, active frame, and of a healthy constitution. His manner was agreeable and easy, with the polish of great social experience, and the goodness of his disposition was admitted by his enemies, but the strength of his mind was not the quality of which his friends boasted. In Greece he committed the common error of assuming a high position without possessing the means of performing its duties: and it may be questioned whether he possessed the talents necessary for performing the duties well, had it been in his power to perform them at all. As a military man, his career in Greece was a signal failure. His plans of operations never led to any successful result ; and on the only occasion which was afforded him of conducting an enterprise on a considerable scale, they led to the greatest disaster that ever happened to the Greek army. His camps were as disorderly as those of the rudest chieftain, and the

---

[1] His services are thus given in *Hart's Army List* for 1859: Ferrol, 1800; Egyptian campaign, 1801 ;. battle of Maida ; Sicily and Calabria, and wounded at defence of Capri; capture of Ischia, 1809; severely wounded at Santa Maura.

troops under his immediate command looked more like a casual assemblage of armed mountaineers than a body of veteran soldiers.

Shortly after his arrival, Sir Richard Church obtained from a national assembly the empty title of Archistrategos, or Generalissimo; and often, to win over independent chiefs to recognize this verbal rank, he sacrificed both his own personal dignity and the character of the office which he aspired to exercise. He succeeded in attaching several chiefs to his person, but he did so by tolerating abuses by which they profited, and which tended to increase the disorganization of the Greek military system.

As a councillor of state, the career of Church was not more successful than as a general. His name was not connected with any wise measure or useful reform. Even as a statesman he clung to the abuses of the revolutionary system which he had supported as a soldier.

Both Church and the Greeks misunderstood one another. The Greeks expected Church to prove a Wellington, with a military chest well supplied from the British treasury. Church expected the irregulars of Greece to execute his strategy like regiments of guards. Experience might have taught him another lesson. When he led his Greek battalion to storm Santa Maura, his men left him wounded in the breach; and had an English company not carried the place, there he might have lain until the French could take him prisoner. The conduct of the Greek regiments had been often disorderly; they had mutinied at Malta, and behaved ill at Messina. The military chiefs who welcomed him to Greece never intended to allow him to form a regular army, if such had been his desire. They believed that his supposed influence with the British Government would obtain a new loan for Greece, and for them high pay and fresh sources of peculation.

Sir Richard Church arrived at Porto Kheli, near Kastri, on the 9th of March, and was warmly welcomed by Kolokotrones and his faction. After a short stay he proceeded to Aegina, where he found the members of the executive dissatisfied with his having first visited their rivals.

Lord Cochrane (Earl of Dundonald) arrived at Hydra on the 17th March. He had been wandering about the

Mediterranean in a fine English yacht, purchased for him out of the proceeds of the loan in order to accelerate his arrival in Greece, ever since the month of June 1826.

Cochrane was a contrast to Church in appearance, mind, character, and political opinions. He was tall and commanding in person, lively and winning in manner, prompt in counsel, and daring but cool in action. Endowed by nature both with strength of character and military genius, versed in naval science both by study and experience, and acquainted with seamen and their habits and thoughts in every clime and country, nothing but an untimely restlessness of disposition, and a too strongly expressed contempt for mediocrity and conventional rules, prevented his becoming one of Britain's naval heroes. Unfortunately, accident, and his eagerness to gain some desired object, engaged him more than once in enterprises where money rather than honour appeared to be the end he sought.

Cochrane, with the eye of genius, looked into the thoughts of the Greeks with whom he came into close contact, and his mind quickly embraced the facts that marked the true state of the country, and revealed the extent of its resources. To the leading members of the executive body he hinted that the rulers of Greece ought to possess more activity and talent for government than they had displayed. To the factious opposition at Kastri he used stronger language. He recommended them, with bitter irony, to read the first philippic of Demosthenes in their assembly[1]. His opinions and his discourse were soon well known, for they embodied the feelings of every patriot, and echoed the voice of the nation. His influence became suddenly unbounded, and faction for a moment was silenced. All parties agreed to think only of the nation's interests. The executive body removed from Aegina to Poros, and a congress was held at Damala, called the National Assembly of Troezene.

The first meetings of the national assembly of Troezene were tumultuous. Captain Hamilton fortunately arrived at Poros with his frigate the Cambrian. His influence with Mavrocordatos and the executive, the influence of Church with Kolokotrones and the Kastri faction, and the authority

---

[1] Tricoupi (iv. 122) gives a Greek translation of Cochrane's letter.

CAPODISTRIAS ELECTED PRESIDENT.

of Lord Cochrane over all parties, prevented an open rupture. Matters were compromised by the election of Count Capodistrias to be president of Greece for seven years. Lord Cochrane was appointed grand-admiral, and Sir Richard Church generalissimo [1]. As the national assembly could not invest them with ordinary power, it gave them extraordinary titles. As very often happens in political compromises, prospective good government was secured by the resolution to remain for a time without anything more than the semblance of a government. A commission of three persons was appointed to conduct the executive until the arrival of Capodistrias; and three men of no political talent and no party influence, but not behind any of their predecessors in corruption and misgovernment, were selected [2].

The election of Capodistrias was proposed by Kolokotrones and the Russian party, in order to counterbalance the influence which England then exercised in consequence of the enlightened zeal which Captain Hamilton displayed in favour of Greek independence, and the liberal policy supported by the two Cannings [3]. A few men among the political leaders, whose incapacity and selfishness had rendered a free government impracticable, endeavoured to prevent the election of Capodistrias without success. Captain Hamilton observed a perfect neutrality, and would not authorize any opposition by an English party. Gordon's description of the scene on the day of the election is correct and graphic. He says the Anglo-Greeks hung down their heads, and the deputies of Hydra, Spetzas, and Psara walked up the hill to Damala with the air of criminals marching to execution.

It has been said already that the Turkish army before Athens drew the greater part of its supplies from Thessaly. These supplies were shipped at Volo during the winter, and forwarded by sea to Negrepont and Oropos. It was at last decided that an expedition should be sent to destroy the Turkish magazines and transports at Volo, and the command of the expedition was given to Captain Hastings. He

---

[1] 'Αρχιναύαρχος and 'Αρχιστράτηγος.
[2] Gordon gives an able and accurate account of the proceedings at Troezene (ii. 364).
[3] George Canning, Prime Minister of England from March to August, 1827, and Sir Stratford Canning (Lord Stratford de Redcliffe), Ambassador at Constantinople at different times from 1825 to 1858.

sailed from Poros with a small squadron to perform this service[1].

The Gulf of Volo resembles a large lake, and few lakes surpass it in picturesque beauty and historical associations. Mount Pelion rises boldly from the water on its eastern side. The slopes of the mountain are studded with many villages, whose white dwellings, imbedded in luxuriant foliage, reflected the western sun as the Greek squadron sailed up the gulf on the afternoon of the 20th April 1827.

The fort of Volo lies at the northern extremity of the gulf, where a bay, extending from the ruins of Demetrias to those of Pagasae, forms a good port. At the point near Pagasae, on the western side of the bay, the Turks had constructed a battery with five guns. These guns crossed their fire with those of the fort, and commanded the whole anchorage. Eight transports were moored as close to the shore as possible. The Karteria anchored before the fort at half-past four in the afternoon, while the corvette and brig took up their position before the five-gun battery. The Turks were soon driven from their guns, and a few rounds of grape from the Karteria compelled them to abandon the transports, which were immediately taken possession of by the Greeks. Five of these vessels, heavily laden, were towed out of the port; two, not having their sails on board, were burned; and the eighth, which the Turks contrived to run aground within musket-shot of their walls, was destroyed by shells. About nine o'clock a light breeze from the land enabled the Greek squadron to carry off its prizes in triumph.

After carefully examining every creek, Hastings quitted the Gulf of Volo on the 22nd. On entering the northern channel of Euboea he discovered a large brig-of-war and three schooners in a bight near the scala of Trikeri. This brig mounted fourteen long 24-pounders and two mortars. It was made fast head and stern to the rocks, and planks were laid from its deck to the shore. A battery of three guns was constructed close to the bows, and several other batteries were placed in different positions among the surrounding rocks, so that the brig was defended not only by her own broadside and four hundred Albanian marksmen, but also

---

[1] The steamer Karteria, the corvette Themistocles, Captain Raphael, the brig Ares, Captain (Admiral) Kriezes, and the schooners Panaghia and Aspasia.

by twelve guns well placed on shore. Hastings attempted to capture it by boarding during the night. The Greek boats moved silently with muffled oars, but when they had approached nearly within musket-shot, heaps of faggots blazed up at different places, casting long streams of light over the water, while at the same time a heavy fire of round-shot and grape proved the strength and watchfulness of the enemy. Fortunately the Turks opened their fire rather too soon, and Hastings was enabled to regain the Karteria without loss.

On the following day the attack was renewed from a distance in order to destroy the brig with hot shot, for the dispersed positions of the batteries, and the cover which the ground afforded to the Albanian infantry, rendered the grape of the Karteria's guns useless. Seven 68-pound shot were heated in the fires of the engine, brought on deck, and put into the guns with an instrument of the captain's own invention; and as the Karteria steamed round in a large circle about a mile from the shore, her long guns were discharged in succession at intervals of four minutes. When the seven shot were expended, the Karteria steamed out of range of the enemy's fire to await the result. Smoke soon issued from the brig, and a great movement was observed on shore. Hastings then approached the land, and showered grape and shells on the Turks to prevent them from extinguishing the fire. A shell exploding in the brig gave him the satisfaction of seeing her abandoned by her crew. Fire at last burst from her deck, and she burned gradually to the water's edge. Her guns towards the shore went off in succession, and caused no inconsiderable confusion among the Albanians; the shells from her mortars mounted in the air, and then her powder-magazine exploded. The Karteria lost only one man killed, a brave Northumbrian quartermaster, named James Hall, and two wounded.

Experience thus confirmed the soundness of the views which Hastings had urged the Greek government to adopt as early as the year 1823. It was evident that he had practically introduced a revolution in naval warfare. He had also proved that a Greek crew could use the dangerous missiles he employed with perfect security. Sixty-eight pound shot had been heated below, carried on deck, and loaded with great ease, while the ship was moving under the fire of hostile batteries. The Karteria herself had suffered severely in her spars and rigging, and it was necessary for her to return to Poros to refit.

In passing along the eastern coast of Euboea, Hastings discovered that Reshid Pasha did not depend entirely on his magazines in Thessaly for supplying his army before Athens with provisions.

Several vessels were observed at anchor off Kumi, and a number of boats were seen drawn up on the beach. Though the place was occupied by the Turks, it was evidently the centre of a considerable trade. It was necessary to ascertain the nature of this trade. Hastings approached the shore, and a few Turks were observed escaping to the town, which is situated about two miles from the port. The vessels at anchor were found to be laden with grain, shipped by Greek merchants at Syra; and it was ascertained that both Reshid and Omar Pasha of Negrepont had, during the winter, purchased large supplies of provisions, forwarded to Kumi by Greeks. Hastings found a brig under Russian colours and a Psarian schooner just beginning to land their cargoes of wheat. A large magazine was found full of grain, and other magazines were said to be well filled in the neighbouring town. About one-third of the grain on shore was transferred to the prizes taken at Volo. The Russian brig was not molested, but two vessels, fully laden with wheat, were taken to Poros, where they were condemned by the Greek admiralty court. On his return Hastings urged both Lord Cochrane and the Greek government to adopt measures for putting an end to this disgraceful traffic; but the attention of Lord Cochrane was called off to other matters, and some scoundrels who possessed considerable influence with the Greek government, profited by licensing this nefarious traffic.

Military operations were now renewed against the Turkish army engaged in the siege of Athens. Karaïskaki, after his retreat from Distomo, established his force, amounting to three thousand men, at Keratsina, in the plain to the west of the Piraeus. Repeated letters had been transmitted from the Acropolis, written by Fabvier and the Greek chiefs, declaring that the garrison could not hold out much longer[1].

---

[1] Gordon, ii. 387.

Sir Richard Church commenced his career as generalissimo by assembling an army at the Piraeus of more than ten thousand, with which he proposed driving Reshid from his positions [1]. He caused, however, considerable dissatisfaction by hiring a fine armed schooner to serve as a yacht, and establishing his head-quarters in this commodious but most unmilitary habitation [2].

It was decided that the navy should co-operate with the army, so that the whole force of Greece was at last employed to raise the siege of Athens.

Lord Cochrane hoisted his flag in the Hellas, but continued to reside on board his English yacht, not deeming it prudent to remove his treasure, which amounted to £20,000, from under the protection of the British flag. He enrolled a corps of one thousand Hydriots to serve on shore, and placed them under the command of his relation, Lieutenant Urquhart, who was appointed a major in the Greek service. The enrolment of these Hydriots was a very injudicious measure. They were unable to perform the service of armatoli, and they were quite as undisciplined as the most disorderly of the irregulars. When landed at Munychia they excited the contempt of the Romeliot veterans, strutting about with brass blunderbusses or light double-barrelled guns. The army had also reasonable ground for complaint, for these inefficient troops received higher pay than other soldiers.

Lord Cochrane's own landing at the Piraeus was signalized by a brilliant exploit. On the 25th of April, while he was reconnoitring the positions of the two hostile armies, a skirmish ensued. He observed a moment when a daring charge would insure victory to the Greeks, and, cheering on the troops near him, he led them to the attack with nothing but his telescope in his hand. All eyes had been watching his movements, and when he was seen to advance, a shout ran through the Greek army, and a general attack was made

---

[1] Church gives this number in his report on the massacre of the Turks who capitulated in the monastery of St. Spiridion. Lesur, *Annuaire Historique*, 1827.

[2] Gordon blames Church for remaining too much on board this schooner, and not exhibiting himself sufficiently to the troops, and also of being too fond of employing his pen, which was a very useless instrument with armatoli. Gordon himself set the fashion of generals keeping yachts in Greece; but Gordon lived on shore while he commanded at Munychia, and sent his yacht to Salamis. The inaccuracies contained in the published despatches of Sir Richard Church were caused by his isolation on board.

simultaneously on all the positions occupied by the Turks at the Piraeus. The fury of the assault persuaded the Mohammedans that a new enemy had taken the field against them, and they abandoned nine of their small redoubts. Three hundred Albanians threw themselves into the monastery of St. Spiridion; the rest retired to an eminence beyond the head of the port.

The troops in the monastery were without provisions, and only scantily supplied with water. In a short time they must have attempted to cut their way through the Greek army, or surrendered at discretion. Unfortunately, it was determined to bombard the building and carry it by storm. In order to breach the wall of the monastery, the Hellas cannonaded it for several hours with her long 32-pounders. The building looked like a heap of ruins, and the Greek troops made a feeble attempt to carry it by storm, which was easily repulsed by the Albanians, who sprang up from the arched cells in which they had found shelter from the fire of the frigate.

Attempts were made next day to open negotiations with the Albanians, who it was supposed would be now suffering from hunger; but a Greek soldier who carried proposals for a capitulation was put to death, and his head exposed from the wall; at the same time a boat sent from Lord Cochrane's yacht with a flag of truce, was fired on, and an English sailor dangerously wounded. The frigate then renewed her fire with no more effect than on the previous day. The garrison found shelter in a ditch, which was dug during the night behind the ruins of the outer wall, and its courage was increased by observing the trifling loss caused by the tremendous fire of the broadside of a sixty-four gun frigate. The Turks, having now placed four guns[1] on the height to which they had retired on the 25th, opened a plunging fire on the ships in the Piraeus, and by a chance shot cut the main-stay of the Hellas.

There was little community of views between the lord high admiral and the generalissimo. Cochrane objected to granting a capitulation to the Albanians in the monastery, as tending to encourage obstinate resistance in desperate cases,

---

[1] Gordon, ii. 389. My own journal says only three. We both paid particular attention to the effect of the artillery. The hill is named Xypete in Colonel Leake's plan of Athens and its harbours.

and he reproached the Greek chiefs with their cowardice in not storming the building. The irregulars refused to undertake any operation until they gained possession of the monastery. There could be no doubt that a storming party, supported by a couple of howitzers, ought to have carried the place without difficulty. Church determined to make the attempt, and Gordon, who commanded the artillery, was ordered to prepare for the assault on the morning of the 28th of April.

In an evil hour the generalissimo changed his plans. Surrounded by a multitude of counsellors, and destitute of a firm will of his own, he concluded a capitulation with the Albanians, without consulting Lord Cochrane or communicating with General Gordon. Karaïskaki was entrusted with the negotiations. The Albanians were to retire from the monastery with arms and baggage. Several Greek chiefs accompanied them as hostages for their safety. But the generalissimo took no precautions for enforcing order, or preventing an undisciplined rabble of soldiers from crowding round the Mussulmans as they issued from the monastery. He must have been grossly deceived by his agents, for his report to the Greek government states 'that no measures had been neglected to prevent the frightful catastrophe that ensued.' Nothing warranted this assertion but the fact that Karaïskaki, Djavellas, and some other chiefs, accompanied the Albanians as hostages.

As soon as Lord Cochrane was aware that the commander-in-chief of the army had opened negotiations with the Albanians, he ordered Major Urquhart to withdraw the Hydriots from their post near the monastery to the summit of Munychia.

The Albanians had not advanced fifty yards through the dense crowd of armed men who surrounded them as they issued from St. Spiridion's, when a fire was opened on them. Twenty different accounts were given of the origin of the massacre. It was vain for the Mussulmans to think of defending themselves; their only hope of safety was to gain the hill occupied by the Turkish artillery. Few reached it even under the protection of a fire which the Turks opened on the masses of the Greeks. Two hundred and seventy men quitted the monastery of St. Spiridion, and more than two hundred were murdered before they reached the hill. 'The slain were immediately stripped, and the infuriated soldiers fought with each other for the spoil,' as we are told by a conscientious eye-witness of the scene [1].

This crime converted the Greek camp into a scene of anarchy. General Gordon, who had witnessed some of the atrocities which followed the sack of Tripolitza, was so disgusted with the disorder that prevailed, and so dissatisfied on account of the neglect with which he was treated, that he resigned the command of the artillery and quitted Greece. Reshid Pasha, on being informed of the catastrophe, rose up and exclaimed with great solemnity, 'God will not leave this faithlessness unpunished. He will pardon the murdered and inflict some signal punishment on the murderers [2].'

Nothing now prevented the Greeks from pushing on to Athens but the confusion that prevailed in the camp and the want of a daring leader. Some skirmishing ensued, and in

---

[1] Gordon, ii. 391.
[2] The Author was serving as a volunteer on the staff of General Gordon, and accompanied him to join the storming-party on the 28th of April. It had been observed from Gordon's yacht, which was anchored in the Piraeus, that communications passed between the Albanians and the Greeks during the whole morning. The Hydriots were also seen retiring to the summit of Munychia. As Gordon passed in his boat under the stern of Lord Cochrane's yacht, the Author prevailed on him to seek an explanation of what was going on. Cochrane said that he, as admiral, had refused to concur in a capitulation, unless the Albanians laid down their arms, and were transported as prisoners of war on board the fleet. He added, that he feared Church had concluded a capitulation. While this conversation was going on, the Author was watching the proceedings at the monastery with his glass, and, seeing the Albanians issue from the building into the armed mob before the gates, he could not refrain from exclaiming, 'All those men will be murdered!' Lord Cochrane turned to Gordon and said, 'Do you hear what he says?' to which the general replied, in his usual deliberate manner, 'I fear, my Lord, it is too true.' The words were hardly uttered when the massacre commenced.

The Author landed immediately to examine the effect of the frigate's fire on the monastery. He witnessed a strange scene of anarchy and disorder, and while he remained in the building two Greeks were killed by shot from the guns on the hill.

The Hydriots under Major Urquhart mutinied at being deprived of their share of the spoil. Lord Cochrane sent Mr. Masson to pacify them with this message, 'My reason for ordering the Hydriots to muster on Munychia was to remove the forces under my command from participating in a capitulation, unless the Turks surrendered at discretion. My objects were to preserve the honour of the navy unsullied, and at the same time to secure an equal distribution of the prize-money.'

The Author visited the Greek schooner in which Sir Richard Church resided shortly after, and found the staff on board in high dudgeon at what they called the treachery of the Greeks. He did not see the generalissimo. The feeling among the Philhellenes in the camp (and there were many officers of many nations) was amazement at the neglect on the part of the commander-in-chief. *MS. Journal,* 28th April, 1827.

one of these skirmishes, on the 4th of May, Karaïskaki was mortally wounded. His death increased the disorder in the Greek army, for he exercised considerable personal influence over several Romeliot chiefs, and repressed the jealousies of many captains, who were now thrown into direct communication with the generalissimo.

Karaïskaki fell at a moment favourable to his reputation. He had not always acted the patriot, but his recent success in Phocis contrasted with the defeats of Fabvier, Heideck, and Church in a manner so flattering to national vanity, that his name was idolized by the irregular troops. He was one of the bravest and most active of the chiefs whom the war had spared, and his recent conduct on more than one occasion had effaced the memory of his unprincipled proceedings during the early years of the Revolution; indeed, it seemed even to his intimate acquaintances that his mind had expanded as he rose in rank and importance. His military talents were those which a leader of irregular bands is called upon to employ in casual emergencies, not those which qualify a soldier to command an army. He never formed any regular plan of campaign, and he was destitute of the coolness and perseverance which sacrifices a temporary advantage to secure a great end. In personal appearance he was of the middle size, thin, dark-complexioned, and haggard, with a bright expressive animal eye, which, joined to the cast of his countenance, indicated that there was gipsy blood in his veins. His features while in perfect repose, wore an air of suffering, which was usually succeeded by a quick unquiet glance[1].

Sir Richard Church now resolved to change his base of operations from the Piraeus to the cape at the eastern end of the Bay of Phalerum. Why it was supposed that troops who could not advance by a road where olive-trees, vineyards, and ditches afforded them some protection from the enemy's cavalry, should be expected to succeed better in open ground, has never been explained.

On the night of the 5th May the commander-in-chief transported three thousand men, with nine field-pieces, to his new position, but the operation of landing the troops was not completed until it was nearly day-break, and though

---

[1] Compare the characters of Karaïskaki by Gordon (ii. 393) and Tricoupi (iv. 151).

the road lay over open downs, it was then too late to reach the Acropolis before sunrise. Gordon calls the operation 'an insane project,' and says that 'if the plan deserves the severest censure, what shall we say to the pitiful method in which it was executed [1]?'

Early dawn found the Greek troops posted on a low ridge of hills not more than half-way between the place where they had landed and the Acropolis. A strong body of Othoman cavalry was already watching their movements, and a body of infantry, accompanied by a gun, soon took up a position in front of the Greek advanced-guard. The position occupied by the Greeks was far beyond the range of any guns in the Turkish lines, but Sir Richard Church, who had not examined the ground, was under the erroneous impression that his troops had arrived within a short distance of Athens, and counted on some co-operation on the part of the garrison of the Acropolis. Had he seen the position, he could not have allowed his troops to remain on ground so ill chosen for defence against cavalry, with the imperfect works which they had thrown up. The advanced-guard had not completed the redoubt it had commenced, and the main body, with the artillery, was so posted as to be unable to give it any support [2].

Reshid Pasha made his dispositions for a cavalry attack. They were similar to those which had secured him the victory at Petta, at Khaidari, and at Kamatero. He ascertained by his feints that his enemy had not a single gun to command the easy slope of a ravine that led to the crest of the elevation on which the advanced redoubt was placed. Two successive charges of cavalry were repulsed by the regular troops and

---

[1] A Philhellene who arrived from Ambelaki just in time to take part in the action, and who was one of the four who escaped, wrote a few days after:— 'Believing that the object was to reach Athens by a *coup-de-main*, I was much surprised to find that the troops did not quit the sea-side until near morning. Nevertheless, they had some time to fortify themselves before they were attacked. Unfortunately, no disposition had been made, and the troops were dispersed without order.' *Letter of Lieut. Myhrbergh to Gen. Gordon*, dated 9th May, 1827.

[2] The report of Sir Richard Church, printed in Lesur, *Annuaire Historique pour 1827*, App. 127, contains many inaccuracies. The Author not only witnessed the engagement from his tent on the summit of Munychia, but he rode over the ground with Mr. Gropius, the Austrian consul-general in Greece, who had also seen the battle; while the bones of the slain still remained unburied, and the imperfect intrenchments of the Greeks were exactly in the same state as on the morning of the attack. He then compared his notes and recollections with the known facts and the configuration of the ground.

BATTLE OF THE PHALERUM.

the Suliots, who formed the advanced-guard of the Greek force. But this small body of men was left unsupported, while the Turks had collected eight hundred cavalry and four hundred infantry in a ravine, by which they were protected until they charged forward on the summit of the ridge. The third attack of the Turks decided the contest. The cavalry galloped into the imperfect redoubt. A short struggle ensued, and completed Reshid's victory. The main body of the Greeks fled before it was attacked, and abandoned the guns, which remained standing alone for a short interval before the Turkish cavalry took possession of them, and turned them on those by whom they had been deserted. The fugitives endeavoured to reach the beach where they had landed. The Turks followed, cutting them down, until the pursuit was checked by the fire of the ships.

Sir Richard Church and Lord Cochrane both landed too late to obtain a view of the battle. The approach of the Turkish cavalry to their landing-place compelled them to regain their yachts. Reshid Pasha, who directed the attack of the Turkish cavalry in person, was slightly wounded in the hand.

Fifteen hundred Greeks fell in this disastrous battle, and six guns were lost. It was the most complete defeat sustained by the Greeks during the course of the war; it dispersed their last army, and destroyed all confidence in the military skill of their English commander-in-chief, for even the shameful rout of Petta sunk into insignificance when compared with this terrible and irreparable disaster. The Turks took two hundred and forty prisoners, all of whom were beheaded except General Kalergi, who was released on paying a ransom of 5000 dollars[1]. He lived to obtain for his country the inestimable boon of representative institutions by heading the Revolution of 1843, which put an end to Bavarian domination, and placed the independence of Greece on a national foundation.

---

[1] Kalergi's leg was broken, and he was made prisoner by an Albanian bey. Reshid wished his head to be piled up with those of the other prisoners, but his captor insisted on receiving 5000 dollars before he would part with it, as Kalergi had promised him that sum. Fortunately the Turkish military chest was not in a condition to allow the pasha to purchase a single head at so high a price. The money was immediately raised among Kalergi's friends, and was remitted from St. Petersburg as soon as Kalergi's uncle heard of his nephew's misfortune.

The battle of Phalerum caused the army at the Piraeus to melt away. Upwards of three thousand men deserted the camp in three days. The numerous victories of Reshid Pasha were remembered with fear, and Sir Richard Church was so discouraged by the aspect of affairs, that he ordered the garrison of the Acropolis to capitulate[1]. Captain Leblanc, of the French frigate Junon, was requested to mediate for favourable terms, and was furnished with a sketch of the proposed capitulation. This precipitate step on the part of Sir Richard Church drew on him a severe reprimand from the chiefs in the Acropolis, who treated his order with contempt, and rejected Captain Leblanc's offer of mediation with the boast, 'We are Greeks, and are determined to live or die free. If, therefore, Reshid Pasha wants our arms, he may come and take them.' These bold words were not backed by deeds of valour[2].

Church abandoned the position of Munychia on the 27th of May, and the garrison of the Acropolis then laid aside its theatrical heroism. Captain Corner, of the Austrian brig Veneto, renewed the negotiations for a capitulation, and the opportune arrival of the French admiral De Rigny brought them to a speedy termination. The capitulation was signed on the 5th of June. The garrison marched out with arms and baggage. About fifteen hundred persons quitted the place, including four hundred women and children. The Acropolis still contained a supply of grain for several months' consumption, and about two thousand pounds of powder, but water was scarce and bad. There was no fuel for baking bread, and the clothes of the soldiers were in rags.

The surrender of the Acropolis, following so quickly after the bombastic rejection of the first proposals, caused great surprise. The conduct of Fabvier was severely criticised, and the behaviour of the Greek chiefs was contrasted with the heroism of the defenders of Mesolonghi. The sufferings of those who were shut up in the Acropolis were undoubtedly very great, but the winter was past, and had they been

---

[1] Jourdain, *Mémoires Historiques et Militaires sur les Événements de la Grèce depuis 1822 jusqu'au Combat de Navarin.* See also Tricoupi, iv. 160. Not much reliance can be placed either on the accuracy or the judgment of Jourdain, but he prints a few documents.

[2] The proposed articles of capitulation and the reply of the Greek chiefs are printed by Mamouka, ix. 9, 10.

inspired with the devoted patriotism of the men of Mesolonghi, they might have held out until the battle of Navarin.

The conduct of Reshid Pasha on this occasion gained him immortal honour. He showed himself as much superior to Sir Richard Church in counsel, as he had proved himself to be in the field. Every measure that prudence could suggest was adopted to prevent the Turks from sullying the Mohammedan character by any act of cruelty in revenge for the bad faith of the Greeks at the Piraeus. The pasha patrolled the ground in person, at the head of a strong body of cavalry, and saw that his troops who escorted the Greeks to the place of embarkation performed their duty.

The fall of Athens enabled Reshid to complete the conquest of that part of continental Greece which Karaïskaki had occupied; but the Turks did not advance beyond the limits of Romelia, and the Greeks were allowed to remain unmolested in Megara and the Dervenokhoria, which were dependencies of the pashalik of the Morea, and consequently within the jurisdiction of Ibrahim Pasha. Many of the Romeliot chiefs now submitted to the Turks, and were recognized by Reshid as captains of armatoli. In his despatches to the sultan he boasted with some truth that he had terminated the military operations with which he was entrusted, and re-established the sultan's authority in all continental Greece from Mesolonghi to Athens.

The interference of foreigners in the affairs of Greece was generally unfortunate, often injudicious, and sometimes dishonest. Few of the officers who entered the Greek service did anything worthy of their previous reputation. The careers of Normann, Fabvier, Church, and Cochrane were marked by great disasters. Frank Hastings was perhaps the only foreigner in whose character and deeds there were the elements of true glory.

But it was by those who called themselves Philhellenes in England and America that Greece was most injured. Several of the steam-ships, for which the Greek government paid large sums in London, were never sent to Greece. Some of the field-artillery purchased by the Greek deputies was so ill-constructed that the carriages broke down the first time the guns were brought into action. Two frigates were contracted for at New York; and the business of the contractors was so managed that Greece received only one frigate after paying the cost of two.

The manner in which the Greeks wasted the money of the English loans in Greece has been already recorded. It is now necessary to mention how the Greek deputies, and their English and American friends, misappropriated large sums at London and New York. It will be seen that waste and peculation were not monopolies in the hands of Greek statesmen, Albanian shipowners, and captains of armatoli and klephts. English politicians and American merchants had also their share [1].

The grandest job of the English Philhellenes was purchasing the services of Lord Cochrane to command a fleet for the sum of £57,000, and setting apart £150,000 to build the fleet which he was hired to command. Lord Cochrane was engaged to act as a Greek admiral in the autumn of 1825. He went to reside at Brussels while his fleet was building, and arrived in Greece in the month of March 1827, as has been already mentioned, before any of the steam-ships of his expedition. Indeed, the first vessel, which was commenced at London by his orders, did not arrive in Greece until after the battle of Navarin.

The persons principally responsible for this waste of money, and these delays were Mr. Hobhouse, now Lord Broughton; Mr. Edward Ellice; Sir Francis Burdett; Mr. Hume; Sir John Bowring, the secretary of the Greek Committee; and Messrs. Ricardo, the contractors of the second Greek loan. Sir Francis Burdett was floating on the cream of Radicalism, and Lord Broughton was supporting himself above the thin milk of Whiggery by holding on vigorously at the baronet's coat-tails. Both these gentlemen, however, though they were guilty of negligence and folly, kept their hands pure from all money transactions in Greek bonds. The Right Honour-

---

[1] Dr. Howe (*Historical Sketch of the Greek Revolution*, 376) says, 'The shameful waste of a large part of the loan, and the numerous peculations which were committed upon it, have not been fully exposed to the world; but enough has been exposed to show that the London Greek committee shamefully neglected its duty; that some of its members meanly speculated on the miseries of Greece; that others committed, what in men of lesser note would have been called fraud; and it is well known too that Orlando and Luriottes, the Greek deputies, proved themselves fools and knaves.' A pamphlet, however, was published defending the Greek deputies, written by an Italian lawyer, Count Palma, who was afterwards a judge in Greece. *Summary Account of the Steamboats for Lord Cochrane's Expedition*, London, 1826.

able Edward Ellice was a contractor for the first Greek loan, but was not a bear, at least of Greek stock. In a letter to the *Times* he made a plain statement of his position, and owned candidly that he had been guilty of 'extreme indiscretion in mixing himself up with the Greek deputies and their affairs.' What he said was no doubt perfectly true; but we must not overlook that it was not said until Greek affairs had ceased to discount the political drafts of the Whigs, and a less friendly witness might perhaps have used a stronger phrase than 'extreme indiscretion.' The conduct of Mr. Hume and Sir John Bowring was more reprehensible, and their names were deeply imbedded in the financial pastry which Cobbett called 'the Greek pie,' and which was served with the rich sauce of his savoury tongue in the celebrated *Weekly Register*[1]. Where there was both just blame and much calumny, it is difficult and not very important to apportion the exact amount of censure which the conduct of each individual merited. The act which was most injurious to Greece, and for the folly of which no apology can be found, was entrusting the construction of all the engines for Lord Cochrane's steamers to an engineer (Mr. Galloway), who failed to construct one in proper time. He contracted to send Captain Hastings' steamer, the Perseverance (Karteria), to sea in August 1825. Her engines were not ready until May 1826[2].

When the Greeks were reduced to despair by the successes of Ibrahim Pasha, the government ordered the deputies in London to purchase two frigates of moderate size. With the folly which characterized all their proceedings, they sent a French cavalry officer to build frigates in America. The cavalry officer fell into the hands of speculators. The Greek deputies neglected to perform their duty. The president of the Greek Committee in New York, and a mercantile house also boasting of Philhellenic views, undertook the construction of two leviathan frigates[3]. The sum of £150,000 was expended before any inquiry was made. It was then found that the frigates were only half finished. The American

---

[1] *Cobbett's Weekly Register*, vol. lx. Nos. 7, 8, and 10, Nov. and Dec. 1826.
[2] Compare Gordon, ii. 275.
[3] Gordon (ii. 275) says, 'On the western side of the Atlantic the Greeks were yet more infamously used by some of their pretended friends than on the eastern.'

Philhellenes who had contracted to build them became immediately bankrupts, and the Greek government, having expended the loans, would have never received anything for the money spent in America, had some real Philhellenes not stepped forward and induced the government of the United States to purchase one of the ships. The other was completed with the money obtained by this sale, and a magnificent frigate, named the Hellas, mounting sixty-four 32-pounders, arrived in Greece at the end of the year 1826, having cost about £100,000.

Shortly after the defeat of Sir Richard Church at the Phalerum, Lord Cochrane assembled the Greek fleet at Poros. His first naval review revealed the discouraging fact, that the disorganization of the navy was as complete as that of the army of which he had just witnessed the total overthrow. The ships of Hydra and Spetzas were anchored in the port; but before their Albanian crews would get their vessels under weigh, they sent a deputation to the grand-admiral asking for the payment of a month's wages in advance. They enforced their demand by reminding Lord Cochrane, with seamanlike frankness, that he had received funds on board his yacht for the express purpose of paying the fleet. His lordship replied, that he had already expended so much of the money entrusted to him in the abortive attempt to raise the siege of Athens, that he could only now offer the sailors a fortnight's wages in advance. This proposal was considered to be a violation of the seaman's charter in the Albanian islands, and it was indignantly rejected by the patriotic sailors. In vain the grand-admiral urged the duty they owed to their country. No seaman could trust his country for a fortnight's wages. Without waiting for orders, the crews of the ships ready for sea weighed anchor and returned to Hydra and Spetzas, from whence some of them sailed on privateering and piratical cruises. This dispersal of the Greek fleet was a spectacle as impressive as it was humiliating. The afternoon was calm, the sun was descending to the mountains of Argolis, and the shadows of the rocks of Methana already darkened the water, when brig after brig passed in succession under the stern of the Hellas, from whose lofty mast the flag of the High Admiral of Greece floated, unconscious of the disgraceful stain it was as she[1] receiving, and at whose table sat the noble admiral steadily watching the scene[1].

The whole of Greece was now laid waste, and the sufferings of the agricultural population were so terrible that any correct description, even by an eye-witness, would be suspected of exaggeration. In many districts hundreds died of absolute starvation, and thousands of the diseases caused by insufficient nourishment. The islands of the Archipelago, which escaped the ravages both of friends and foes, did not supply grain in sufficient quantity for their own consumption. Poverty prevented the people from obtaining supplies of provisions under several flags.

During this period of destitution, which commenced towards the end of 1825, and continued until the harvest of 1826, the greater part of the Greeks who bore arms against the Turks were fed by provisions supplied by the Greek committees in Switzerland, France, and Germany. The judicious arrangements adopted by Mr. Eynard at Geneva and Paris, and the zeal of Dr. Gosse, General Heideck, and Mr. Koening in Greece, caused the limited resources at their disposal to render more real service to the troops than the whole proceeds of the English loans.

While the continental committees were supporting the war, the Greek committees in the United States directed their attention to the relief of the peaceful population. The amount of provisions and clothing sent from America was very great. Cargo after cargo arrived at Poros and fortunately there was then in Greece an American Philhellene capable, from his knowledge of the people, and from his energy, honour, and humanity, of making the distribution with promptitude and equity. Dr. Howe requires no praise from the feeble pen of the writer of this History, but his early efforts in favour of the cause of liberty and humanity in Greece deserve to be remembered, even though their greatness be eclipsed by his more mature labours at home. He found able coadjutors in several of his countrymen, who were guided by his counsels[2]. Thousands of Greek families, and many members of the clergy and of the legislature, were relieved from severe

---

[1] The Author was also in that cabin at the time.
[2] Mr. x Colonel Miller, Dr. Russ, and Mr. Stuyvesant.

privations by the food and clothing sent across the Atlantic. Indeed, it may be said without exaggeration that these supplies prevented a large part of the population from perishing before the battle of Navarin.

In the summer of the year 1827 Greece was utterly exhausted, and the interference of the European powers could alone prevent the extermination of the population, unless it was averted by submission to the sultan.

www.ingramcontent.com/pod-product-compliance
Lightning Source LLC
Chambersburg PA
CBHW021232300426
44111CB00007B/515